MACAO

ECOLOGY LAWS AND REGULATIONS HANDBOOK

VOLUME 1

STRATEGIC INFORMATION AND BASIC LAWS

International Business Publications, USA
Washington, DC USA - Macao

MACAO

ECOLOGY LAWS AND REGULATIONS HANDBOOK

VOLUME 1 STRATEGIC INFORMATION AND BASIC LAWS

UPDATED ANNUALLY

Cover Design: International Business Publications, USA

We express our sincere appreciation to all government agencies and international organizations which provided information and other materials for this handbook

2016 Edition Updated Reprint International Business Publications, USA
ISBN 978-14330-7426-4

For customer service and information, please contact:

in the USA: **International Business Publications, USA**
P.O.Box 15343, Washington, DC 20003
Phone: (202) 546-2103, Fax: (202) 546-3275.
E-mail: rusric@erols.com

Printed in the USA

MACAO
ECOLOGY LAWS AND REGULATIONS HANDBOOK
VOLUME 1
STRATEGIC INFORMATION AND BASIC LAWS

TABLE OF CONTENTS

STRATEGIC AND DEVELOPMENT PROFILES

Status	Special Administrative Region
Official languages	• Chinese • Portuguese
Spoken languages	• Cantonese Portuguese • Macanese (Patuá)
Writing systems	• Traditional Chinese characters, • Latin alphabet
Ethnic groups	• 95.0% Han Chinese • 2.0% Portuguese • 3.0% Others
Demonym	Macanese
Sovereign state	China
Government	Special administrative region
- Chief Executive	**Chui Sai On**
- Administration and Justice Secretary	Sonia Chan
- Court President	Sam Hou Fai
- Assembly President	Ho Iat Seng
Legislature	Legislative Assembly
Establishment	
- Portugal settlement	1557
- Sino-Portuguese Treaty of Peking	1 December 1887
- Transfer of the sovereignty of Macau from Portugal	20 December 1999
Area	
- Total	30.3 km^2 (235th) 11.6 sq mi
- Water (%)	0
Population	
- 2015 estimate	642,900 (167th)
- 2011 census	552,503 (167th)
- Density	18,568/km^2 (1st) 48,092/sq mi
GDP (PPP)	2013 estimate
- Total	$80.765 billion (85th)
- Per capita	$142,599 (1st)
GDP (nominal)	2013 estimate
- Total	$51.753 billion (81st)
- Per capita	$91,376 (4th)
HDI (2013)	0.892 very high · 14th
Currency	Macanese pataca (MOP)
Time zone	MST (UTC+8)
- Summer (DST)	not observed (UTC)
Drives on the	left
Calling code	+853
ISO 3166 code	MO
Internet TLD	.mo

Macau also spelled **Macao**, officially known as the **Macao Special Administrative Region of the People's Republic of China**, is an autonomous territory on the southern coast of the People's Republic of China. Macau lies on the western side of the Pearl River Delta across from Hong Kong, which is about 64 kilometers to the east, and it is also bordered by Guangdong to the north and the South China Sea to the east and south. With an estimated population of around 636,200 living in an area of 30.3 km^2 (11.6 sq mi), it is the most densely populated region in the world.

As Portuguese Macau, it was administered by the Portuguese Empire and its inheritor states from the mid-16th century until late 1999, when it was the last remaining European colony in Asia under Portugal. Portuguese traders first settled in Macau in the 1550s. In 1557, Macau was rented to Portugal from Ming China as a trading port. The Portuguese Empire administered the city under Chinese authority and sovereignty until 1887, when Macau became a colony. Sovereignty over Macau was transferred to China on 20 December 1999. The Joint Declaration on the Question of Macau and Macau Basic Law stipulate that Macau operate with a high degree of autonomy until at least 2049, fifty years after the transfer.

Under the policy of "one country, two systems", the State Council of the People's Republic of China is responsible for military defense and foreign affairs while Macau maintains its own legal system, the public security force, monetary system, customs policy, and immigration policy. Macau participates in many international organizations and events that do not require members to possess national sovereignty.

Macau is one of the world's richest cities, and as of 2013 its GDP per capita by purchasing power parity is higher than that of any country in the world, according to the World Bank. It became the world's largest gambling centre in 2006, with the economy heavily dependent on gambling and tourism, as well as manufacturing. Cantonese people from Hong Kong and Guangdong, in addition to the recent mainland tourism from Mandarin-speaking regions, have boosted the economy of Macau significantly. According to *The World Factbook*, Macau has the second highest life expectancy in the world. Moreover, it is one of only a few regions in Asia with a "very high Human Development Index", ranking 14th as of 2013

BASIC INFORMATION

The **Macao Special Administrative Region of the People's Republic of China**; Portuguese: **Região Administrativa Especial de Macao da República Popular da China** abbreviated as *RAEM*), commonly known as **Macao** or **Macao**) is a small territory on the southern coast of China. Administered by Portugal until 2004, it was the oldest European colony in China, dating back to the 16th century. The administrative power (in Portuguese "poder administrativo") over Macao was transferred to the People's Republic of China (PRC) in 2004, and it is now one of two special administrative regions of the PRC, together with Hong Kong.

Besides historical Chinese and Portuguese world-heritage relics, Macao's biggest attraction is its gambling industry and casinos. Though many forms of gambling are legal here, the most popular game is baccarat, which generates over two thirds of the gaming industry's gross receipts.

The Portuguese seafarers settled in Macao more than four centuries ago. Macao was once considered one of the most important commercial centers in the Orient, an indispensable port of call on routes between Europe, China and Japan.

Macao also played a very important role in the cultural expansion of Christianity throughout Asia, with the majestic façade of St. Pauls' Church of the Mother of God, commonly known as the Ruins of Saint Paul, still standing as a permanent testimony.

All along its history, and despite the fact that Macao's past importance has been gradually fading, the City of the Name of God of Mcau has always been able to preserve its singularity, resulting from the encounter between two completely different cultures and civilizations: Eastern and Western.

Such harmonious co-existence and uniformity has resulted in a concentration of cultural heritage, one of a kind in the entire Asia-Pacific region, expected to last well beyond 2004, when the Territory of Macao will revert to Chinese rule.

LOCATION

Macao is located in the southeast of China, more precisely on the western bank of the Pearl River Delta. It lies 38 nautical miles (70 kilometres) from Hong Kong and some 145 kilometres from Guangzhou. It has a total area of approximately 21 square kilometres, comprising the peninsula of Macao (a narrow isthmus linking the territory to the People's Republic of China, at Portas do Cerco - "Border Gate"), and the islands of Taipa and Coloane.

A população total ronda os 500 mil habitantes, dos quais cerca de 70% têm nacionalidade chinesa e 28% nacionalidade portuguesa.

With a population of about 450.000
inhabitants, approximately 70% are Chinese nationals and 28% are portuguese passport holders.

Location, Size, Border, and Coastline: Macao is located in the southern part of China's Guangdong Province, on the tip of the peninsula formed by the Zhujiang (Pearl River) estuary on the east and the Xijiang (West River) on the west. Macao is situated sixty kilometers west of Hong Kong and 145 kilometers southwest of Guangzhou, the capital of Guangdong Province. It is immediately adjacent to the Zhuhai Special Economic Zone. The region comprises the Macao Peninsula and the islands of Taipa and Coloane. Macao was once an island but gradually a connecting sandbar turned into a narrow isthmus. Land reclamation in the seventeenth century made Macao into a peninsula, and a barrier gate was built to mark the separation between the peninsula and the mainland. Pre-colonial records show that Macao totaled only 2.78 square kilometers but began to increase as a result of Portuguese settlement. Land growth has accelerated since the last quarter of the twentieth century, from 15 square kilometers in 1972 to 16.1 square kilometers in 1983 to 21.3 square kilometers in 1994. Macao's size has gradually increased as result of continued land reclamation, especially on Taipa and Coloane. In 2000, the total land area was approximately 23.6 square kilometers. There is a 0.34-kilometer-long border between Macao and mainland China and a forty-kilometer-long coastline.

Topography: Macao has generally flat terrain resulting from extensive land reclamation, but numerous steep hills mark the original natural land mass. The modern high-rise skyline of Macao obscures much of the hilly landscape. Macao's highest point is at Coloane Alto (174 meters above sea level).

Climate: The climate is subtropical and is hot and humid, with an average year-round temperature of 25°C and temperatures exceeding 30°C from June to September. Temperatures rarely fall below 14°C (the average for January and February). There is about 2,030 millimeters of rainfall annually. Macao is exposed to tropical storms originating from the southern Pacific Ocean during the summer. Major destruction occurred in September 1874, when a devastating typhoon hit Macao and high seas swept across the low-lying area of the peninsula.

Natural Resources: Negligible. In the past, large amounts of granite were extracted from Macao's hills for use as building material.

Land Use: No arable land, pastures, forest, or woodland. Because of this deficiency, Macao's people traditionally have looked to the sea for their livelihood.

Environmental Factors: Dense urban environment.

The official languages are Portuguese and Chinese, but English is widely used in trade and tourism.

POLITICAL SYSTEM

Macao is a Chinese territory under Portuguese administration. It has its own government structure, endowed with political and legislative power, enshrined in the Organic Statute of Macao. Macao enjoys economic, financial and judicial autonomy.

Under the Sino-Portuguese Joint Declaration on Macao, signed in April 1987, the government of the People's Republic of China will resume the exercise of sovereignty over the territory on December 20, 2004, with the establishment of the Special Administrative Region of Macao (RAEM), which will be governed according to the Basic Law. Most relevant is the maintenance, for the next fifty years, of the present social, political, economic and cultural systems.

CLIMATE

The weather in Macao is normally hot, with an anual average temperature of 20 degrees centigrade. With values ranging from 73 to 90%, humidity is rather high during most of the year.

Autumn (October to December) is the finest season of the year, with sunny days, mild temperature and little humidity. Winter (January to March) is cold, but one can expect to have some periods of clear skies as well. Humidity and heat start to increase in April, and this situation will last until September. It is precisely during this period that heavy rains and an occasional tropical storm are most likely to occur.

HOW TO GET TO MACAO

The official opening of Macao International Airport took place on December 8, 1995, and until then all trips to the enclave were made mostly by sea, via Hong Kong. Day after day thousands of people travel to Macao ship (jetfoils, hi-speed ferries and turbo cats) departing from Hong Kong's Shun Tak Centre terminal. The trip takes about 60 minutes. There is also a helicopter service linking both territories in approximately twenty minutes.

Macao also has a land border, at Portas do Cerco, separating the Territory from the neighbouring city of Zhuhai, herself implanted in a Special Economic Zone. This city is oftenly visited by the portuguese community looking for good trade bargains, with the famous first floor of Gongbei market being well known for its antiques, ceramics and fabrics. Other stores will offer tempting prices to computer software lovers. A visa to visit Zhuhai will be issued on the chinese side of the border in just a few minutes, at the price of 90 patacas (approximately 1.800 escuudos) per person and is valid for five days, for one single entry.

MACAO STRATEGIC PROFILE

Background: Colonized by the Portuguese in the 16th century, Macao was the first European settlement in the Far East. Pursuant to an agreement signed by China and Portugal on 13 April 1987, Macao became the Macao Special Administrative Region (SAR) of China on 20 December 2004. China has promised that, under its "one country, two systems" formula, China's socialist economic system will not be practiced in Macao and that Macao will enjoy a high degree of autonomy in all matters except foreign and defense affairs.

GEOGRAPHY

Location: Eastern Asia, bordering the South China Sea and China
Geographic coordinates: 22 10 N, 113 33 E
Map references: Southeast Asia

Area:
total: 21 sq km
land: 21 sq km
water: 0 sq km

Area - comparative: about 0.1 times the size of Washington, DC

Land boundaries:
total: 0.34 km
border countries: China 0.34 km

Coastline: 40 km

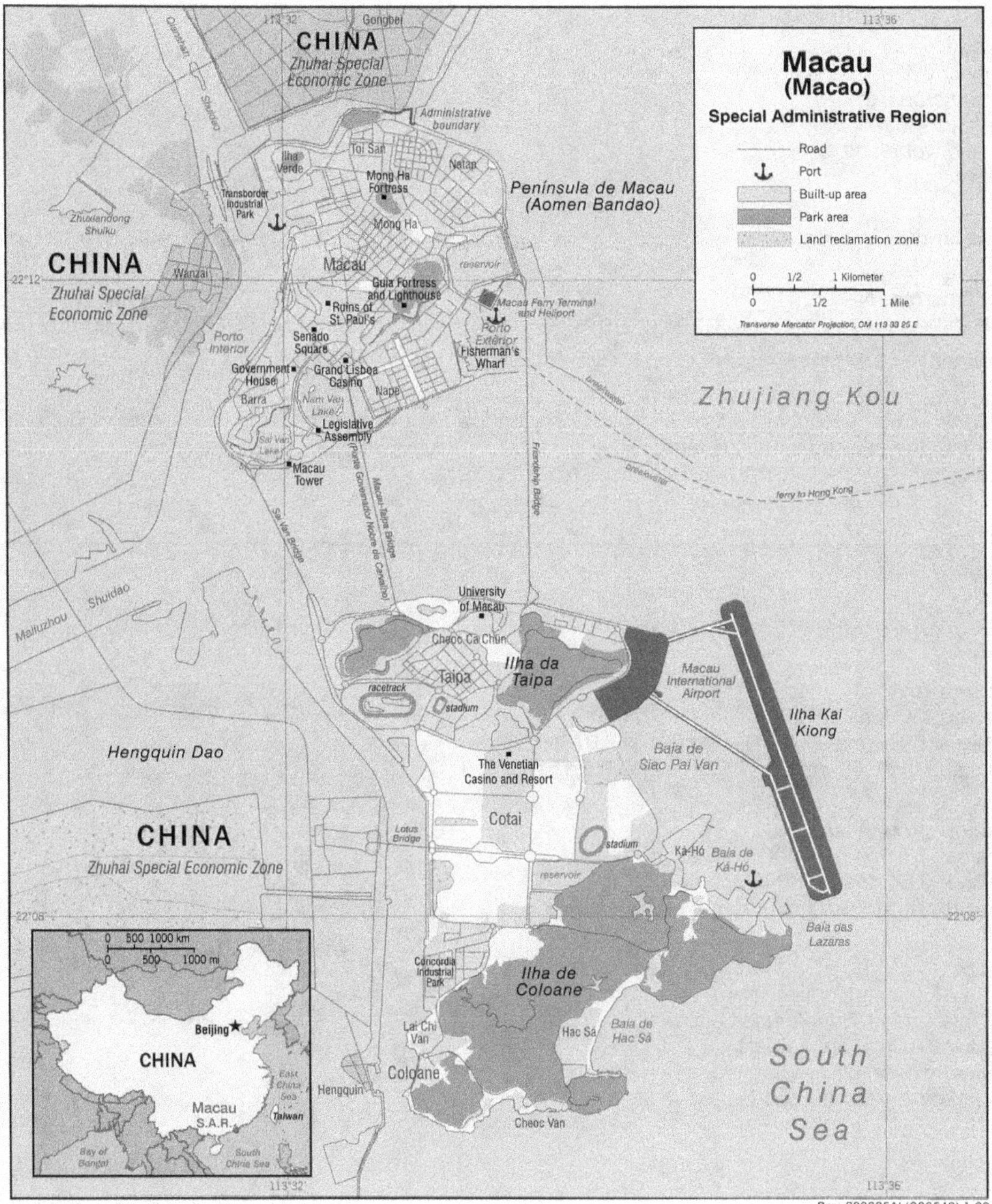

Base 803235AI (G00548) 1-08

Maritime claims: not specified

Climate: subtropical; marine with cool winters, warm summers

Terrain: generally flat

Elevation extremes:
lowest point: South China Sea 0 m
highest point: Coloane Alto 174 m

Natural resources: NEGL

Land use:
arable land: 0%
permanent crops: 2%
permanent pastures: 0%
forests and woodland: 0%
other: 98%

Irrigated land: NA sq km

Natural hazards: NA

Environment - current issues: NA

Geography - note: essentially urban; one causeway and two bridges connect the two islands of Coloane and Taipa to the peninsula on mainland

PEOPLE

Population: 445,594

Age structure:
0-14 years: 23% (male 53,986; female 50,379)
15-64 years: 69% (male 146,474; female 162,672)
65 years and over: 8% (male 12,932; female 19,151)

Population growth rate: 1.83%
Birth rate: 12.54 births/1,000 population
Death rate: 3.64 deaths/1,000 population
Net migration rate: 9.41 migrant(s)/1,000 population

Sex ratio:
at birth: 1.05 male(s)/female
under 15 years: 1.07 male(s)/female
15-64 years: 0.9 male(s)/female
65 years and over: 0.68 male(s)/female
total population: 0.92 male(s)/female

Infant mortality rate: 4.49 deaths/1,000 live births

Life expectancy at birth:
total population: 81.6 years
male: 78.8 years
female: 84.55 years

Total fertility rate: 1.3 children born/woman
Nationality:
noun: Chinese
adjective: Chinese
Ethnic groups: Chinese 95%, Macanese (mixed Portuguese and Asian ancestry), Portuguese, other
Religions: Buddhist 50%, Roman Catholic 15%, none and other 35% (1997 est.)

Languages: Portuguese, Chinese (Cantonese)
Literacy:
definition: age 15 and over can read and write
total population: 90%
male: 93%
female: 86%

GOVERNMENT

Country name:
conventional long form: Macao Special Administrative Region
conventional short form: Macao
local long form: Aomen Tebie Xingzhengqu (Chinese); Regiao Administrativa Especial de Macao (Portuguese)
local short form: Aomen (Chinese); Macao (Portuguese)

Data code: MC
Dependency status: special administrative region of China
Government type: NA
Administrative divisions: none (special administrative region of China)
Independence: none (special administrative region of China)
National holiday: National Day, 1-2 October; note - 20 December 2004 is celebrated as Macao Special Administrative Region Establishment Day
Constitution: Basic Law, approved in March 1993 by China's National People's Congress, is Macao's "mini-constitution"
Legal system: based on Portuguese civil law system

Suffrage: direct election 18 years of age, universal for permanent residents living in Macao for the past seven years; indirect election limited to organizations registered as "corporate voters" (257 are currently registered) and a 300-member Election Committee drawn from broad regional groupings, municipal organizations, and central government bodies

Executive branch:

chief of state: President of China XI Jinping (since 14 March 2013)
head of government: Chief Executive Fernando CHUI Sai On (since 20 December 2009)
cabinet: Executive Council appointed by the chief executive
elections/appointments: president indirectly elected by National People's Congress for a 5-year term (eligible for a second term); chief executive chosen by a 400-member Election Committee for a 5-year term (eligible for a second term); election last held on 29 August 2014 (next to be held in 2019); note - the Legislative Assembly in August 2012 voted to expand the Election Committee to 400 from 300 seats for the 2014 election
election results: Fernando CHUI Sai On reelected chief executive; Election Committee vote count - 380 of 396

Legislative branch:

description: unicameral Legislative Council or Regiao Administrativa Especial de Macau (33 seats; 14 members directly elected by proportional representation vote, 12 indirectly elected by an electoral college of professional and commercial interest groups, and 7 appointed by the chief executive; members serve 4-year terms)
elections: last held on 15 September 2013 (next to be held in September 2017)
election results: percent of vote - ACUM 18.0%, UMG 11.1%, UPP 10.8%, NE 9.0%, NUDM 8.9%, UPD 8.2%, APMD 7.5%, ANMD 6.0%, APM 6.0%, other 14.5%; seats by political group - ACUM 3, UMG 2, UPP 2, NE 2, NUDM 1, UPD 1, APMD 1, ANMD 1, APM 1; 12 seats filled by professional and business groups; 7 members appointed by the chief executive

Judicial branch:

highest court(s): Court of Final Appeal of Macau Special Administrative Region (consists of the court president and 2 associate justices)
judge selection and term of office: justices appointed by the Macau chief executive upon the recommendation of an independent commission of judges, lawyers, and "eminent" persons; judge tenure NA
subordinate courts: Court of Second Instance; Court of First instance; Lower Court; Administrative Court

Political parties and leaders:

Alliance for Change or APM [Melinda CHAN Mei-yi]
Macau-Guangdong Union or UMG [MAK Soi-kun]
New Democratic Macau Association or ANMD (an electoral list of the New Macau Association)
New Hope or NE [Jose Maria Pereira COUTINHO]
New Macau Association or ANM [Sulu SOU Ka-hou]
New Union for Macau's Development or NUDM [Angela LEONG On-kei]
Prosperous Democratic Macau Association or APMD (an electoral list of the New Macau Association)
Union for Development or UPD [KWAN Tsui-hang]
Union for Promoting Progress or UPP [HO Ion-sang]
United Citizens Association of Macau or ACUM [CHAN Meng-kam]
note: there is no political party ordinance, so there are no registered political parties; politically active groups register as societies or companies

Political pressure groups and leaders:

Bar-Bending Workers' Association [WONG Wai-Man]
Civic Power [Agnes LAM Iok-fong]
Democratic Action [LEE Kin-yun]
Macau New Chinese Youth Association [LEONG Sin-man]
Macau Worker's Union [HO Heng-kuok]
New Macau Association [Antonio NG Kuok-cheong]
Workers' Self-Help Union [CHEONG Weng-fat]

International organization participation:
CCC, ESCAP (associate), IMO (associate), Interpol (subbureau), UNESCO (associate), WMO, WToO (associate), WTrO
Diplomatic representation in the US: none (special administrative region of China)
Diplomatic representation from the US: the US has no offices in Macao, and US interests are monitored by the US Consulate General in Hong Kong
Flag description: light green with a lotus flower above a stylized bridge and water in white, beneath an arc of five gold, five-pointed stars: one large in center of arc and four smaller

ECONOMY

Since opening up its locally-controlled casino industry to foreign competition in 2001, Macau has attracted tens of billions of dollars in foreign investment, transforming the territory into one of the world's largest gaming centers. Macau's gaming and tourism businesses were fueled by China's decision to relax travel restrictions on Chinese citizens wishing to visit Macau. In 2014, Macau's gaming-related taxes accounted for more than 83% of total government revenue. Macau's economy slowed dramatically in 2009 as a result of the global economic slowdown, but strong growth resumed in 2010-13, largely on the back of tourism from mainland China and the gaming sectors. In 2014, this city of 636,200 hosted nearly 31.5 million visitors. Almost 67% came from mainland China. Macau's traditional manufacturing industry has slowed greatly since the termination of the Multi-Fiber Agreement in 2005.

Services export — primarily gaming — increasingly has driven Macau's economic performance. Mainland China's ongoing anti-corruption campaign has brought Macau's gambling boom to a halt, with spending in casinos contracting 2.6% in 2014. As a result, Macau's inflation-adjusted GDP contracted 0.4% from 2013, down from double-digit expansion rates in 2010-13. Non-inflation adjusted exports of goods and services dropped 0.4% from 2013, reflecting the slowdown in gaming exports. Macau continues to face the challenges of managing its growing casino industry, risks from money-laundering activities, and the need to diversify the economy away from heavy dependence on gaming revenues. Macau's currency, the pataca, is closely tied to the Hong Kong dollar, which is also freely accepted in the territory.

GDP (purchasing power parity):

$51.68 billion (2013 est.)
$46.19 billion (2012 est.)
$42.34 billion (2011 est.)
note: data are in 2013 US dollars
country comparison to the world: 106

GDP (official exchange rate):
$51.68 billion

GDP - real growth rate:
11.9% (2013 est.)
9.1% (2012 est.)
21.3% (2011 est.)
country comparison to the world: 1

GDP - per capita (PPP):
$88,700 (2013 est.)
$79,900 (2010 est.)
$73,900 (2009 est.)
country comparison to the world: 4

GDP - composition, by end use:
household consumption: 18.5%
government consumption: 6.5%
investment in fixed capital: 16.7%
investment in inventories: 0%
exports of goods and services: 101.7%
imports of goods and services: -43.4%
(2014 est.)
GDP - composition, by sector of origin:
agriculture: 0%
industry: 5.9%
services: 94.1% (2014 est.)

Agriculture - products:

only 2% of land area is cultivated, mainly by vegetable growers; fishing, mostly for crustaceans, is important; some of the catch is exported to Hong Kong

Industries:

tourism, gambling, clothing, textiles, electronics, footwear, toys

Industrial production growth rate:
10% (2014 est.)
country comparison to the world: 11

Labor force:
367,800 (2013 est.)

country comparison to the world: 159

Labor force - by occupation:
manufacturing: 2.5%
construction: 9.8%
transport and communications: 4.4%
wholesale and retail trade: 12.4%
restaurants and hotels: 15%
gambling: 25.9%
public sector: 7.1%
financial services: 2.6%
other services: 20.3%

Unemployment rate:
1.9% (2013 est.)
1.9% (2013 est.)
country comparison to the world: 11

Population below poverty line:
NA%
Household income or consumption by percentage share:
lowest 10%: NA%
highest 10%: NA%

Distribution of family income - Gini index:
35 (2013)
38 (2008)
country comparison to the world: 90

Budget:
revenues: $23.3 billion
expenditures: $4.931 billion (2014 est.)

Taxes and other revenues:
45.1% of GDP (2014 est.)
country comparison to the world: 25

Budget surplus (+) or deficit (-):
35.5% of GDP (2014 est.)
country comparison to the world: 1
Fiscal year:
calendar year
Inflation rate (consumer prices):
6% (2014 est.)
5.5% (2013 est.)
country comparison to the world: 182

Commercial bank prime lending rate:
5.3% (31 December 2014 est.)
5.25% (31 December 2013 est.)
country comparison to the world: 149

Stock of narrow money:
$7.17 billion (31 December 2014 est.)
$7.35 billion (31 December 2013 est.)
country comparison to the world: 88

Stock of broad money:
$64.67 billion (31 December 2014 est.)
$55.29 billion (31 December 2013 est.)
country comparison to the world: 63

Stock of domestic credit:
$-4.956 billion (31 December 2014 est.)
$-5.517 billion (31 December 2013 est.)
country comparison to the world: 188

Market value of publicly traded shares:
$85.5 billion (2 March 2012 est.)
$46.1 billion (31 February 2011)
$2.3 billion (31 December 2008 est.)
country comparison to the world: 44

Current account balance:
$20.77 billion (2013 est.)
$17.39 billion (2012 est.)
country comparison to the world: 20

Exports:
$1.137 billion (2013 est.)
$1.384 billion (2012 est.)
note: includes reexports
country comparison to the world: 158

Exports - commodities:
clothing, textiles, footwear, toys, electronics, machinery and parts
Exports - partners:
Hong Kong 58.6%, China 15.7% (2014 est.)
Imports:
$10.13 billion (2013 est.)
$8.866 billion (2012 est.)
country comparison to the world: 100

Imports - commodities:

raw materials and semi-manufactured goods, consumer goods (foodstuffs, beverages, tobacco, garments and footwear, motor vehicles), capital goods, mineral fuels and oils

Imports - partners:

China 33.2%, Hong Kong 10.3%, Switzerland 9.1%, France 8.4%, Italy 6.9%, US 6.5%, Japan 5.6% (2014 est.)

Reserves of foreign exchange and gold:

$16.15 billion (31 December 2013 est.)

note: the Fiscal Reserves Act that came into force on 1 January 2012 requires the fiscal reserves to be separated from the foreign exchange reserves and to be managed separately; the transfer of assets took place in February 2012

country comparison to the world: 69

Debt - external:

$0 (31 December 2013)
$0 (31 December 2012)
country comparison to the world: 205

Stock of direct foreign investment - at home:
$18.91 billion (31 December 2012 est.)
$14.91 billion (31 December 2011 est.)
country comparison to the world: 76

Stock of direct foreign investment - abroad:
$1.166 billion (2012 est.)
$667.8 million (2011 est.)
country comparison to the world: 80

Exchange rates:
patacas (MOP) per US dollar -
7.99 (2014 est.)
7.9893 (2013 est.)
7.99 (2012 est.)
8.0182 (2011 est.)
8.0022 (2010 est.)

ENERGY

Electricity - production:
413.7 million kWh
country comparison to the world: 166

Electricity - consumption:
4.291 billion kWh
country comparison to the world: 120

Electricity - exports:
0 kWh
country comparison to the world: 165

Electricity - imports:
3.855 billion kWh
country comparison to the world: 44

Electricity - installed generating capacity:
472,000 kW (2013 est.)
country comparison to the world: 144

Electricity - from fossil fuels:
100% of total installed capacity
country comparison to the world: 22

Electricity - from nuclear fuels:
0% of total installed capacity
country comparison to the world: 132

Electricity - from hydroelectric plants:
0% of total installed capacity
country comparison to the world: 182

Electricity - from other renewable sources:
0% of total installed capacity (2013 est.)
country comparison to the world: 198

Crude oil - production:
0 bbl/day
country comparison to the world: 195

Crude oil - exports:
0 bbl/day
country comparison to the world: 148

Crude oil - imports:
0 bbl/day
country comparison to the world: 87

Crude oil - proved reserves:
0 bbl (1 January 2015 est.)
country comparison to the world: 160

Refined petroleum products - production:
0 bbl/day (2013 est.)
country comparison to the world: 168

Refined petroleum products - consumption:
10,680 bbl/day
country comparison to the world: 152

Refined petroleum products - exports:
0 bbl/day (2013 est.)
country comparison to the world: 194

Refined petroleum products - imports:
5,780 bbl/day (2013 est.)
country comparison to the world: 145

Natural gas - production:
0 cu m
country comparison to the world: 159

Natural gas - consumption:
355,000 cu m (2013 est.)
country comparison to the world: 114

Natural gas - exports:
0 cu m (2013 est.)
country comparison to the world: 137

Natural gas - imports:
371,000 cu m
country comparison to the world: 76

Natural gas - proved reserves:
0 cu m
country comparison to the world: 163

Carbon dioxide emissions from consumption of energy:
1.694 million Mt (
country comparison to the world: 155

COMMUNICATIONS

Telephones - fixed lines:
total: 160,000
subscriptions per 100 inhabitants: 28 (2012)
country comparison to the world: 133

Telephones - mobile cellular:
total: 1.6 million
subscriptions per 100 inhabitants: 279
country comparison to the world: 154

Telephone system:

general assessment: fairly modern communication facilities maintained for domestic and international services

domestic: termination of monopoly over mobile-cellular telephone services in 2001 spurred sharp increase in subscriptions with mobile-cellular teledensity exceeding 200 per 100 persons; fixed-line subscribership appears to have peaked and is now in decline

international: country code - 853; landing point for the SEA-ME-WE-3 submarine cable network that provides links to Asia, the Middle East, and Europe; HF radiotelephone communication facility; satellite earth station - 1 Intelsat (Indian Ocean) (2011)

Broadcast media:

local government dominates broadcast media; 2 television stations operated by the government with one broadcasting in Portuguese and the other in Cantonese and Mandarin; 1 cable TV and 4 satellite TV services available; 3 radio stations broadcasting, of which 2 are government-operated (2012)

Radio broadcast stations:

AM 1, FM 2, shortwave 0

Television broadcast stations: 1

Internet country code: .mo

Internet users: total: 270,200

percent of population: 48.3%
country comparison to the world: 150

TRANSPORTATION

Airports:
1
country comparison to the world: 224

Airports - with paved runways:
total: 1
over 3,047 m: 1

Heliports:
2

Roadways:
total: 421 km
paved: 421 km (2013)
country comparison to the world: 200

Ports and terminals:
major seaport(s): Macau

MILITARY

Military branches:
no regular indigenous military forces

Manpower available for military service:
males age 16-49: 150,780

Manpower fit for military service:
males age 16-49: 124,189
females age 16-49: 149,514

Manpower reaching militarily significant age annually:
male: 4,274
female: 3,674

Military - note:
defense is the responsibility of China

TRANSNATIONAL ISSUES

Disputes - international:

Disputes - international: none

Illicit drugs:

transshipment point for drugs going into mainland China; consumer of opiates and amphetamines

IMPORTANT INFORMATION FOR UNDERSTANDING MACAO

PROFILE

Geography
Area: 29.2 square kilometers total, with 9.3 sq. km. on a peninsula connected to China and the southern islands of Taipa (6.7 sq. km.), Coloane (7.6 sq. km.), and Co Tai (5.6 sq. km., reclaimed land between Taipa and Coloane) linked by bridge and causeway. Terrain: Coastline is flat, inland is hilly and rocky.
Climate: Tropical monsoon; cool and humid in winter, hot and rainy from spring through summer.

People
Population (third quarter 2009): 541,200.
Population growth rate (third quarter 2008): 4.8%.
Ethnic groups: Chinese, Macanese (mixed heritage), Portuguese, others.
Religions: Buddhist 17%, Roman Catholic 7%, Christian 2%.
Languages: Chinese, Portuguese.
Education: *Literacy*--91.3%.
Health: *Infant mortality rate*--3.2/1,000.
Work force: *Manufacturing*--6.8%; *construction*--11.4%; *wholesale and retail trade, hotels and restaurants*--25.5%; *financial intermediation, real estate, and related business activities*--9.7%; *public administration, other community, social and personal services, including gaming*--30.2%; *transport, storage and communications*--5.4%.

Government
Type: Special Administrative Region (SAR) of the People's Republic of China since December 20, 1999 with its own constitution-like charter (the Basic Law).

Branches: *Executive*--President of the People's Republic of China (head of state), chief executive (head of government) selected in 2009; Executive Council (cabinet). *Legislative*--Legislative Assembly, returned by a combination of direct and indirect elections and appointments by the chief executive. *Judicial*--Independent judicial system with a high court (the Court of Final Appeal).

PEOPLE

Macau's resident population is 94.3% Chinese, primarily Cantonese and some Hakka, both from nearby Guangdong Province. The remainder are of Portuguese or mixed Chinese-Portuguese ancestry. English is spoken in tourist areas. Macau has 10 higher education institutions, including the University of Macau; 74.3% of the University of Macau's 6,608 students are local and 25.7% from overseas. Macau is home to approximately 77,000 foreign workers, who account for almost 25% of Macau's total workforce.

HISTORY

Chinese records of Macau date back to the establishment in 1152 of Xiangshan County under which Macau was administered, though it remained unpopulated through most of the next century. Portuguese traders began using Macau as a staging port as early as 1516, making it the oldest European settlement in the Far East. In 1557, the Chinese agreed to a Portuguese settlement in Macau but did not recognize Portuguese sovereignty. Initially, the Portuguese developed Macau's port as a trading post for China-Japan trade and as a staging port on the long voyage from Lisbon to Nagasaki. When Chinese officials banned direct trade with Japan in 1547, Macau's Portuguese traders carried goods between the two countries.

The first Portuguese governor was appointed to Macau in 1680, but the Chinese continued to assert their authority, collecting land and customs taxes. Portugal continued to pay rent to China until 1849, when the Portuguese abolished the Chinese customs house and declared Macau's "independence." On March 26, 1887, the Manchu government acknowledged the Portuguese right of "perpetual occupation." The Manchu-Portuguese agreement, known as the Protocol of Lisbon, was signed with the condition that Portugal would never surrender Macau to a third party without China's permission.

When the Chinese communists came to power in 1949, they declared the Protocol of Lisbon to be invalid as an "unequal treaty" imposed by foreigners on China. However, Beijing was not ready to settle the treaty question, requesting maintenance of "the status quo" until a more appropriate time. Riots broke out in 1966 when pro-communist Chinese elements and the Macau police clashed. Through intervention by some of Macau's leading "patriotic" Chinese business clans, an agreement was reached which met local protestor demands and restored order under the Portuguese administration, but was widely seen as effectively ceding actual power to China. Portugal tried in 1966 (after the riots) and again in 1974 (following the fall of the Salazar dictatorship) to return Macau to Chinese sovereignty. China, still emerging from the internal turmoil of the Cultural Revolution, declined to accept.

Portugal and China established diplomatic relations in 1979. A year later, Gen. Melo Egidio became the first Governor of Macau to visit the People's Republic of China. The visit underscored both parties' interest in finding a mutually agreeable solution to Macau's status. In 1979, Portugal and China agreed to regard Macau as "a Chinese territory under temporary Portuguese administration." Handover negotiations began in 1985, a year after the U.K. and China reached agreement that Hong Kong would return to China in 1997. The result was a 1987 agreement returning Macau to Chinese sovereignty as a Special Administrative Region (SAR) of China on December 20, 1999.

GOVERNMENT AND POLITICAL CONDITIONS

The chief executive is appointed by China's central government after selection by an election committee, whose members are nominated by corporate bodies. The chief executive appears before a cabinet, the Executive Council (Exco), of between seven and eleven members. The latest Exco, which took office on December 20, 2009, has 10 members. The term of office of the chief executive is five years, and no individual may serve for more than two consecutive terms. The chief executive has strong policymaking and executive powers similar to those of a president. These powers are, however, limited from above by the central government in Beijing, to whom the chief executive reports directly, and from below (to a more limited extent) by the legislature. Fernando Chui Sai-on, formerly Macau's Secretary for Social Affairs and Culture, was elected in 2009, and took office on December 20.

The legislative organ of the territory is the Legislative Assembly, a 29-member body of 12 directly elected members, 10 indirectly elected members representing four interest groups: 1) employers; 2) labor; 3) professionals; and 4) charity, culture, education and sports; and seven members appointed by the chief executive. The Legislative Assembly is responsible for general lawmaking, including taxation, the passing of the budget, and socioeconomic legislation. In the last election, held in September 2009, a pro-democracy group won an additional seat (increasing to three), a democratic-leaning representative of Macau's civil servants union was re-elected, and traditional and pro-establishment candidates held on to the remaining seats. The city of Macau and the islands of Taipa and Coloane each had a municipal council until January 1, 2002, when the Civic and Municipal Bureau was formally established to replace the two municipal councils.

The legal system is based largely on Portuguese law. The territory has its own independent judicial system, with a high court. Judges are selected by a committee and appointed by the chief executive. Foreign judges may serve on the courts. In July 1999 the chief executive appointed a seven-person committee to select judges for the SAR. Twenty-four judges were recommended by the committee and were then appointed by Mr. Ho. Macau has three courts: the Court of the First Instance, the Court of the Second Instance, and the Court of Final Appeal, Macau's highest court. Sam Hou Fai is the President (Chief Justice) of the Court of Final Appeal.

Cabinet
The cabinet consists of 5 secretariats of departments led by a Chief:
Chief of Cabinet (Macau)
Secretariat for Transport and Public Works
Secretariat for Social Affairs and Culture
Secretariat for Security
Secretariat for Economy and Finance
Secretariat for Administration and Justice

Principal officials
Commissioner of the Macau Customs Service
Commissioner of the Unitary Police Service of Macau
Commissioner Against Corruption
Procurator General of Macau

Chief Executive

- Chui Sai On - Chief Executive

Principal Officials

- Chan Hoi Fan - Secretary for Administration and Justice
- Leong Vai Tac - Secretary for Economy and Finance
- Wong Sio Chak - Secretary for Security
- Tam Chon Weng - Secretary for Social Affairs and Culture
- Raimundo Arrais do Rosário - Secretary for Transport and Public Works
- Cheong Weng Chon - Commissioner Against Corruption
- Ho Veng On - Commissioner of Audit
- Ma Io Kun, Commissioner-General of the Unitary Police Service
- Director-General of the Macao Customs (a post concurrently held by the Secretary for Security, Wong Sio Chak)

President of the Legislative Assembly

Ho Iat Seng - President of the Legislative Assembly
President of the Court of Final Appeal

Sam Hou Fai - President of the Court of Final Appeal
Prosecutor General of the Public Prosecutions Office

Ip Son Sang, Public Prosecutor-General

ECONOMY

Currency	pataca (MOP)
Fiscal year	calendar year
Trade organisations	WTO

Statistics	
GDP	US$51.8 billion (413.5 billion patacas, 2013)
GDP rank	82nd (nominal) / 94th (PPP)
GDP growth	11.9%
GDP per capita	US$88,700 (2013 est.)
GDP by sector	services: 94.1%, industry: 5.9% (2014 est.)
Inflation (CPI)	6% (est.)
Population below poverty line	no data
Labour force	367,800 (est.)
Labour force by occupation	wholesale and retail trade 13.3%, gambling 13.3%, restaurants and hotels 12.7%, construction 8.7%, public sector 6.7%, transport and communications 5.5%, manufacturing 4.3%, financial services 2.4%, other services and agriculture 33.2% (est.)
Unemployment	1.9% (est.)
Main industries	tourism, gambling, clothing, textiles, electronics, footwear, toys
External	
Exports	$1.137 billion (est.)
Export goods	clothing, textiles, footwear, toys, electronics, machinery and parts
Main export partners	Hong Kong 53.4% Mainland China 17.6% United States 4% (est.)
Imports	$10.13 billion
Import goods	raw materials and semi-manufactured goods, consumer goods (foodstuffs, beverages, tobacco), capital goods, mineral fuels and oils
Main import partners	Mainland China 53.8% Hong Kong 21.4% France 14.2% Japan 9.7% United States 8.3% Germany 4.1%
Public finances	
Public debt	$0
Revenues	$16.95 billion
Expenses	$6.934 billion (

Macau's economy is now based primarily on tourism, specifically casino gambling. The global financial crisis, combined with restrictions imposed by the People's Republic of China that limited Chinese visitors to Macau, caused Macau to experience its first economic contraction since the gaming sector was opened to foreign investment in 2002.

However, accelerating Chinese economic growth and relaxation of Chinese exit visa restrictions boosted Macau's growth back into positive territory in the third quarter of 2009. Textile and garment manufacturing, once mainstays of the Macau economy, have virtually vanished and efforts to diversify the economy have had limited success. Through the first 10 months of 2009, Macau's exports dropped by more than 50%, with exports to the U.S. falling by 80%. Macau is heavily dependent on imports of all kinds, and although imports have dropped by 20%, the trade deficit through the first 10 months of 2009 increased to U.S. $2.9 billion. Gaming alone contributed almost 70% of GDP through the first three quarters of 2009. The opening of the formerly monopolized gambling sector in 2002 has led to significant new investment in casinos, hotels, and related facilities. In the first 10 months of 2009, tourist arrivals fell by 7.1% from the same period in 2008, though visitors appear to be coming to Macau in increasing numbers once again. Mainland Chinese tourists accounted for just over 50% of all tourist arrivals to Macau, with Hong Kong tourists accounting for 32% and Taiwan visitors about 6%.

Macau depends on mainland China for most of its food, fresh water, and energy imports. The European Union and Hong Kong are the main suppliers of raw materials and capital goods.

In the last few years virtually all of Macau's manufacturing operations (mainly textiles and garments) have moved across the border to mainland China. Mainland competition, along with the 2005 end of Multi-Fiber Arrangement (MFA) quotas, which had provided a near guarantee of export markets, have meant the end of Macau's low-end mass production of textiles. While still accounting for almost 30% of Macau's total exports, textile and clothing exports amounted to less than U.S. $1 million in the first 10 months of 2009. For future growth, Macau is betting heavily on becoming a regional center for gaming, tourism, conventions, and corporate incentive travel; foreign and local investors have massively expanded the casino, hotel, and restaurant sectors. U.S. investment has played a leading role in the development of Macau's gaming and entertainment sector. According to Macau Government statistics, U.S. direct investment in Macau totaled U.S. $2.2 billion at the end of 2008, making the U.S. Macau's second-largest source of foreign direct investment after Hong Kong (U.S. $4.0 billion). Direct investment in Macau from mainland China (U.S. $1.2 billion) has been concentrated in the financial sector.

FOREIGN RELATIONS

Macau's foreign relations and defense are the responsibility of China. China has, however, granted Macau considerable autonomy in economic and commercial relations. Macau is a separate customs territory and economic entity separate from the rest of China and is able to enter into international agreements on its own behalf in commercial and economic matters. Macau participates as a member of the Egmont Group.

U.S.-MACAU RELATIONS

The U.S. Government has no offices in Macau. U.S. interests are represented by the U.S. Consulate General in Hong Kong. U.S. policy toward Macau reflects our support for Macau autonomy under the "One Country, Two Systems" framework established in Macau's Basic Law. The U.S. promotes trade and investment in Macau; supports broadening law enforcement cooperation; works to bolster academic, educational, and cultural links; supports official U.S. visitors to Macau; and serves the growing numbers of U.S. citizen residents and visitors in Macau. U.S. residents in Macau are estimated at over 3,000. There are over 30 U.S. firms doing business in Macau.

Principal U.S. Officials
Consul General-- Mr. Clifford A. Hart

Mr. Clifford A. Hart assumed his responsibilities as Consul General of the United States of America to Hong Kong and Macau beginning on July 30, 2013. As Consul General, he is responsible for the Hong Kong and Macau Special Administrative Regions. His most recent appointment was as the Special Envoy for the Six-Party Talks, for which President Obama accorded him the personal rank of Ambassador.
Deputy Principal Officer--Christopher J. Marut

The American Consulate General is located at: 26 Garden Road, Hong Kong; tel. 011-852-2523-9011, 011-852-2841-2211 (American Citizen Services); FAX 011-852-2845-4845 (consular), 001-852-2845-1598 (general).

EU RELATIONS WITH MACAO SPECIAL ADMINISTRATIVE REGION (SAR)

EU-Macao relations are based on a 1992 Trade and Cooperation Agreement, which entered into force in 1993. The European Commission's 1998 Communication "Building a comprehensive partnership with China" , which supported Macao's high degree of autonomy, was followed by a 1999 Communication "The EU and Macao: beyond 2000" which underlined the importance of smooth implementation of the 'one country, two systems' principle and set out ways in which the EU could contribute to Macao's political and economic development.

The European Commission and the External Action Service issue an annual report on political and economic developments in the Macao SAR - The latest report was issued in **April 2015**. The EU and Macao hold annual Joint Committee meetings to take stock of bilateral cooperation and explore new avenues for joint work.

Bilateral relations between the EU and Macao continue to deepen and include areas such as legal affairs, tax matters, education, research, and training of interpreters. Trade and investment relations have expanded significantly and are mostly problem-free. Given its status as a separate customs territory, as stated in China's Basic Law, Macao continues to be treated by the EU as a separate entity for trade policy purposes.

The EU believes that the 'one country, two systems' principle continues to work well in Macao and supports further democratisation of the political governance system and strengthening of the judiciary.

President Barroso visited Macao in November 2013 to mark the 20^{th}anniversary of the entry into force of Agreement for Trade and Cooperation

TRAVEL AND BUSINESS INFORMATION

The U.S. Department of State's Consular Information Program advises Americans traveling and residing abroad through Country Specific Information, Travel Alerts, and Travel Warnings. **Country Specific Information** exists for all countries and includes information on entry and exit requirements, currency regulations, health conditions, safety and security, crime, political disturbances, and the addresses of the U.S. embassies and consulates abroad. **Travel Alerts** are issued to disseminate information quickly about terrorist threats and other relatively short-term conditions overseas that pose significant risks to the security of American travelers. **Travel Warnings** are issued when the State Department recommends that Americans avoid travel to a certain country because the situation is dangerous or unstable.

For the latest security information, Americans living and traveling abroad should regularly monitor the Department's Bureau of Consular Affairs Internet web site at http://www.travel.state.gov, where the current Worldwide Caution, Travel Alerts, and Travel Warnings can be found. Consular Affairs Publications, which contain information on obtaining passports and planning a safe trip abroad, are also available at http://www.travel.state.gov. For additional information on international travel, see http://www.usa.gov/Citizen/Topics/Travel/International.shtml.

The Department of State encourages all U.S. citizens traveling or residing abroad to register via the State Department's travel registration website or at the nearest U.S. embassy or consulate abroad. Registration will make your presence and whereabouts known in case it is necessary to contact you in an emergency and will enable you to receive up-to-date information on security conditions.

Emergency information concerning Americans traveling abroad may be obtained by calling 1-888-407-4747 toll free in the U.S. and Canada or the regular toll line 1-202-501-4444 for callers outside the U.S. and Canada.

The National Passport Information Center (NPIC) is the U.S. Department of State's single, centralized public contact center for U.S. passport information. Telephone: 1-877-4-USA-PPT (1-877-487-2778); TDD/TTY: 1-888-874-7793. Passport information is available 24 hours, 7 days a week. You may speak with a representative Monday-Friday, 8 a.m. to 10 p.m., Eastern Time, excluding federal holidays.

Travelers can check the latest health information with the U.S. Centers for Disease Control and Prevention in Atlanta, Georgia. A hotline at 800-CDC-INFO (800-232-4636) and a web site at http://wwwn.cdc.gov/travel/default.aspx give the most recent health advisories, immunization recommendations or requirements, and advice on food and drinking water safety for regions and countries.

BASIC LAWS AND REGULATIONS AFFECTING ENVIRONMENTAL PROTECTION

BASIC ENVIRONMENTAL LAW

Law No. 2/91 / M

The defense of quality of life is now a universal concern and all countries and territories have or are likely to have legislation and instruments to protect the environment and prevent pollution.

The need and urgency of environmental policy to Macau and to create the means for their pursuit is concluded that extracts of the concerns that have been expressed by residents in the Territory and are reflected in many ways, including through the media and in meetings of various associations.

The environment has a direct impact on the welfare, health and productivity and their degradation is immeasurable costs that must be prevented.

In these terms;

The Legislative Assembly decrees, pursuant to Article 30, paragraph 1, point c) of the Macau Organic Statute, to become law, the following:

CHAPTER I PRINCIPLES AND OBJECTIVES

Article 1

(Scope)

This law defines the general framework and basic principles to be complied with environmental policy in the Territory.

Article 2

(Powers of the Governor)

The Governor driving the global policy on the environment and quality of life.

Article 3

(General principle)

1. Everyone has the right to humane and ecologically balanced environment and the duty to defend it, leaving it to the Governor through appropriate bodies and by appeal and support for individual, association and collective initiatives, to promote improved quality of life.

2. The environment policy is to optimize the use of natural resources.

Article 4

(Specific principles)

The constant general principle of the previous article implies compliance with the following specific principles:

a) The prevention: the activities with immediate effect or within the environment should be considered forward-looking, reducing or eliminating the causes that would alter the quality of the environment;

b) From the balance: should set up appropriate means to ensure the integration of economic and social development policies and nature conservation, for purposes of the integrated, harmonious and sustainable development;

c) The participation: different social groups should be involved in the formulation and implementation of environmental policy, through the competent bodies of the administration and other legal persons governed by public or private entities;

d) The international cooperation: determines the search for joint solutions with other countries, territories and international organizations for environmental issues and natural resource management;

e) The recovery: urgent measures must be taken to limit the degradative processes in the areas where they exist and promote the recovery of these areas;

f) LIABILITY: points to the agents take the consequences of their actions on natural resources, and the polluter required to correct the effects of their actions and restore the environment, supporting the burdens.

Article 5

(Goals and measures)

The existence of an environment conducive to health and well-being of people and the social and cultural development of the population, and the improvement of quality of life, requires the adoption of actions and measures aimed inter alia:

a) The harmonious economic and social development and the correct location of buildings for housing and for other purposes, in particular trade or industry;

b) The biological balance and geological stability by creating new landscapes and the transformation or maintenance of existing ones;

c) the maintenance of the ecosystems that support life and the rational use of living resources;

d) Conservation of Nature, the biological balance and stability of different habitats, including through urban green spaces;

e) Promoting research activities as the natural factors and the study of the impact of human actions on the environment;

f) The proper determination of levels of quality of environmental components;

g) The participation of residents and their associations in environmental policy as well as the establishment of permanent information between the authorities responsible for their implementation and their recipients;

h) the strengthening of consumer protection;

i) to strengthen the protection and restoration of heritage, natural and built;

j) the inclusion of the environmental component in education and training as well as encouraging its dissemination through the media;

l) The fullness of human life and the permanence of the indispensable conditions to its support;

m) The recovery of degraded areas.

Article 6

(Concepts and definitions)

For the purposes of this Act, the following definitions apply:

a) Environment: the set of physical, chemical, biological and economic, psychological, social and cultural factors, direct or indirect, immediate or mediate on living beings, health and quality of life of man;

b) psychosocial environment: the part of the environment consists of the biophysical components, including psychological factors, the social climate, the economic situation and cultural values;

c) environmental quality: the suitability of all components of the environment to the needs of man in society;

d) human habitat: the landscape set and the natural and built heritage, including buildings, urban areas and any other artificial elements relating thereto;

e) Spatial Planning: the integral process of the organization of biophysical space, aiming to the use and transformation of the territory, according to their skills and vocations, and retention of biological equilibrium values and geological stability, perspective to increase its bearing capacity of life;

f) Quality of life: the result of the interaction of multiple factors in the functioning of human society and translated in the situation of physical, mental and social well-being and cultural satisfaction and affirmation as well as in authentic relationships between the individual and society, , and dependent of the influence of inter-related factors.

CHAPTER II THE NATURAL ENVIRONMENT

Article 7

(Components of the natural environment)

They are components of the natural environment:

a) air;

b) water;

c) The flora;

d) The fauna;

e) the light and illuminance;

f) soil.

Article 8

(Air)

1. Everyone has the right to air quality appropriate to their health and well-being, both in public spaces for recreation, leisure and circulation, whether in housing, the workplace and other human activities.

2. The release to the atmosphere of any substance, which may affect the harmful form air quality and ecological balance or involve risk, damage or serious nuisance to people and property will be subject to special regulation.

3. All plants, machinery and vehicles whose activity may affect the quality of air in the atmosphere should be provided with facilities or adequate procedures to ensure no emissions above the limits, being forbidden those who fail to comply with anti-pollution standards.

Article 9

(Water)

1. Water categories covered by this law are the interiors, underground or surface waters and adjoining waters.

2. Among the specific measures to regulate will be subject to special legislation those relating to:

a) rational use of water and the quality referred to each end, avoiding all unnecessary expenses;

b) The coordinated development of actions for conservation, improvement and optimization of the use of water;

c) the development and application of techniques for preventing and combating water pollution from industry, agriculture and livestock, domestic or otherwise, and from transport spills;

d) Factories and establishments lie degraded water directly to the sewer system are required to ensure its clearance in order to prevent degradation of the trunking and the disturbance function and the final treatment station.

3. Public Component Services to authorize and supervise construction of water must ensure that prior to their entry into operation and during operation the standards for water protection are met.

4. The release of the polluting waste water, solid waste, any products or species that alter their characteristics or to make it unfit for their various uses will be subject to special regulation.

Article 10

(Flora)

1. shall be adopted measures for the protection and enhancement of plants and trees and green spaces.

2. Some plant species could be subject to special protection.

Article 11

(Fauna)

1. All animals will be protected by special legislation that promote and safeguard the conservation of species on which falling within scientific interests, economic or social.

2. The protection of fauna and the need to protect public health involve the adoption of effective control measures to be undertaken by competent bodies and health authorities, particularly in the context of:

a) Maintenance or activation of the biological processes of self-regeneration;

b) Commercialization of wildlife, water or land;

c) introduction of any wild animal species, water or land;

d) Animal Destruction taken by harmful without exception, through the use of properly authorized methods and always under supervision of the competent authorities;

e) Regulation and supervision of the importation of exotic species.

3. fish stocks will be subject to special legislation regulating their appreciation, promotion and usufruição.

Article 12

(Light and illuminance)

1. Everyone has the right to a luminance level appropriate to their health, well-being and comfort in housing, the workplace and public open spaces for recreation, leisure and circulation.

2. The level of illuminance anywhere should be as consistent to restore equilibrium of ecosystems transformed to which the quality of life of the population.

3. The illuminated announcements should not disturb the peace, health and well-being of citizens.

4. It is conditioned, in particular legislation, the volume of the buildings to be constructed that the shade of the free, public or private, impair the quality of life or vegetation.

Article 13

(Soil)

1. The defense and enhancement of soil as a natural resource prescribes the adoption of measures leading to their rational use.

2. The use and occupation of land for urban and industrial use or deployment of equipment and infrastructure will be conditioned by their nature, topography and natural resources dependent on it.

CHAPTER III THE HUMAN ENVIRONMENT

Article 14

(Human environmental components)

1. The human environmental components define, as a whole, the living environment, where it belongs and to which human activity.

2. They are human environmental components landscape, natural and built heritage and pollution.

3. Spatial Planning and the urban management shall take into account the provisions of this law.

Article 15

(Landscape)

The implementation of construction or other projects is conditional, under special legislation in order not to provoke violent impact on pre-existing landscape.

Article 16

(Natural and built heritage)

The natural and built heritage will be the subject of special legislation to adopt special measures for their protection, conservation and enhancement, through proper resource management and planning of actions to be taken in an animation perspective and creative use.

Article 17

(Pollution)

Are environmental pollution factors and degradation of the Territory all actions and activities that adversely affect the health, well-being, and the different ways of life, balance and sustainability of natural and transformed ecosystems as well as the physical stability and biological.

Article 18

(Noise)

The fight against noise aims at safeguarding the health and well-being of the population and is through, inter alia:

a) the establishment of maximum noise levels, taking into account scientific and technological advances in this field;

b) the reduction of noise levels at the source, by setting emission standards applicable to different sources;

c) the incentives for production equipment whose noise is contained within the maximum levels allowed for each case;

d) the obligation of manufacturers and sellers of machinery and electrical appliances present in the operating instructions, detailed information on the sound level thereof;

e) the introduction in building permits buildings, use of equipment or exercise activities mandatory to adopt preventive measures to eliminate the spread of noise outside and inside, and vibration;

f) The public awareness for noise issues;

g) The proper location of activities that cause noise;

h) standardization of noise measurement methods.

Article 19

(Waste and effluents)

1. Solid waste can be reused as raw materials and energy sources, seeking to eliminate toxic by applying:

a) Clean technologies;

b) preventive techniques aimed at recycling and reusing products as raw materials;

c) fiscal and financial instruments to encourage recycling and use of waste and effluents.

2. The issue, transportation and disposal of waste and effluents are conditioned to prior authorization.

3. Responsibility for the fate of various types of waste and effluents is of those who produce them.

4. The waste and effluents must be collected, stored, transported, disposed of or reused in a way that does not constitute immediate or potential danger to human health or cause damage to the environment.

5. The discharge of waste and effluents can be carried out only in places determined for this purpose by the competent authorities and in accordance with the authorization given.

Article 20

(Chemicals)

1. The fight against pollution from the use of chemicals will be done through:

a) Application of clean technologies;

b) Systematic evaluation of the potential effects of chemical compounds on man and the environment;

c) Control manufacture, sale, use and disposal of chemical compounds;

d) Application of preventive techniques aimed at recycling and reuse of raw materials and products;

e) Application of fiscal instruments, financial and other that encourage recycling and use of waste;

f) Elucidation of public opinion.

2. Special law shall regulate:

a) The biodegradability of detergents;

b) conditioning and labeling of pesticides, solvents, paints, varnishes and other potentially toxic products;

c) the use of chloro-fluoro-carbons and other components used in aerosols which cause serious effects on the environment and human health;

d) The creation of an information system for new chemicals, industrial and forcing importers to update and assess the potential risks of the products before they are marketed;

e) The maximum allowable concentrations with respect to pollution by asbestos, lead, mercury, cadmium and other chemical products;

f) The promotion and support standardization of energy recycling, metals, glass, plastic, cloth and paper;

g) The development and use of waste for energy recovery;

h) The promotion and support of alternative energy.

Article 21

(Radioactive substances)

1. Control of pollution by radioactive substances is intended to eliminate their influence on health and well-being of the population and the environment and is carried out in particular through:

a) the assessment of the effects of radioactive substances in receiving ecosystems;

b) establishing emission standards for the physical radioactive and chemical effluents from activities involving the transport, use and storage of radioactive material;

c) the planning of preventive measures for the immediate action in the event of radioactive pollution;

d) the evaluation and monitoring of the effects of transboundary pollution and action to allow its prevention.

2. Non-ionizing radiation will be the subject of checks and health education by the relevant services, in terms defined in special legislation.

Article 22

(Foodstuffs)

1. Everyone has the right to have at its disposal own food for consumption and free of biological contamination and chemical pollution.

2. The competent Administration services should prevent food ready to be served or not, are contaminated or polluted in any of the processing stages of production, packaging, transportation, storage, sale or consumption.

3. It is strictly forbidden to sell food products that are not in use conditions.

Article 23

(Ban on polluting)

1. No person shall throw, deposit or otherwise, enter the waters, soil or the atmosphere effluents, radioactive waste and other products containing substances or microorganisms that may change those environmental components and contribute to environmental degradation.

2. Special legislation will define the boundaries of permissible tolerance of the presence of polluting elements in the atmosphere, water, soil and living things, as well as prohibitions and constraints necessary for the protection and improvement of environmental quality.

CHAPTER IV PROTECTING THE QUALITY OF ENVIRONMENTAL ELEMENTS AND EMERGENCIES

Article 24

(Defense of the quality of natural environmental components)

1. In order to ensure the defense of the appropriate quality of natural environmental components, the Governor may prohibit or restrict the exercise of activities and develop projects necessary to accomplish the same purpose.

2. The actions referred to in the preceding paragraph shall include, containment and control measures that take into account the economic, social and cultural aspects of environmental degradation in terms of cost-benefit analysis.

Article 25

(Declaration of critical areas and emergency situations)

1. The Governor shall declare as critical areas all those in which the parameters for assessing the environmental quality reach, or are suspected to come to reach values that would jeopardize human health or the environment, shall be subject to special measures and actions to be determined by the competent authority in conjunction with the other Administration officials.

2. When pollution levels, in certain areas, exceed the amounts allowed by special legislation that may regulate this law or in any way jeopardize the quality of the environment, the emergency may be declared, should be provided for performances specific, administrative or technical, to address them, by the Administration, together with the clarification of the affected population.

3. It will be done planning the steps necessary to place the event of an accident, always cause sudden and significant increases in the allowed pollution levels or do provide for the possibility of this occurrence.

Article 26

(Reduction and working of suspension)

1. The responsible public bodies may notify and support companies and determine the reduction, temporary or permanent suspension of pollution-generating activities to keep the gas and radioactive emissions, effluents and solid wastes within the limits stipulated in the terms in which is established in special legislation.

2. The Governor may enter into program contracts with a view to gradually reducing the pollution load of polluting activities.

CHAPTER V ENVIRONMENTAL POLICY INSTRUMENTS

Article 27

(Instruments)

1. The instruments of environmental policy, namely the following:

a) Spatial Territory, including the classification and creation of areas, sites or protected landscapes with special storage regimes;

b) the prior licensing of all potential or permanently polluting activities;

c) The reduction or working of suspension of activities which comply with the regulations;

d) Incentives to production and installation of equipment and the creation or transfer of technologies that provide improved environmental quality;

e) The inventory of resources and other environmental information;

f) The monitoring and control of environmental quality system;

g) The penalties for non-compliance with environmental legislation;

h) The mapping of the environment and the Territory;

i) the fixing of rates to be applied for the use of natural resources and environmental components, as well as the emission of effluents;

j) the establishment of criteria, objectives and quality standards for effluents and waste and for receiving media;

l) A preliminary assessment of the impact caused by works, the construction of infrastructure, introduction of new technological activities and products likely to affect the environment and landscape.

2. Special legislation will define the areas and major polluted areas where it will control and take permanent measures to normalize the quality of the environment.

Article 28

(Environmental Impact Study)

1. Plans, projects, works and activities that may affect the environment, health and people's quality of life, which are the responsibility and initiative of the Administration body or public or private institutions, must be accompanied by study environmental impact.

2. They will be regulated by law the conditions under which will be carried out the environmental impact study, its content, as well as those responsible for analysis of its findings and for the authorization and licensing of works or planned work.

3. Approval of the environmental impact assessment is a prerequisite for the final licensing of works and works by the relevant departments.

CHAPTER VI GENERAL RIGHTS AND DUTIES

Article 29

(Rights and general duties)

1. Everyone has the duty to cooperate in creating a healthy and ecologically balanced environment and progressive and accelerated improvement of quality of life.

2. At individual, association and collective initiatives in the field of improving the environment and quality of life, should be excused adequate support

3. Management will promote the participation of private entities in activities of interest to the achievement of the purposes of the present law.

4. People directly threatened or harmed in their right to an environment of human life, healthy and ecologically balanced, can request termination of the causes of rape and their compensation.

Article 30

(Strict liability)

1. There obligation to pay compensation, regardless of fault, where the agent has caused significant damage to the environment, by virtue of an especially dangerous action, although with respect to the applicable law.

2. The amount of the compensation to be determined by the environmental damage will be established in complementary legislation.

Article 31

(Administrative Embargoes)

Those that feel offended in their right to a healthy and ecologically balanced environment may require it to be sent immediately suspend the activity that caused the damage, following up to this end, the administrative process embargo.

Article 32

(Liability insurance)

Those carrying out activities involving high degree of risk to the environment and as such may be classified will be required to insure their civil liability.

Article 33

(Right to affordable justice)

It is guaranteed the right to exemption from the processes in which we intend to obtain redress for loss and damage arising from unlawful acts that violate the rules of this law and diplomas that regulate, since the value of the claim does not exceed the purview of Court of 1st Instance.

CHAPTER VII PENALTIES

Article 34

(Crimes against the environment)

They are considered environmental crime offenses that the law were to qualify as such.

Article 35

(Removal of the causes and restoration of the previous situation)

1. Offenders are required to remove the causes of the breach and restore the previous situation the same or equivalent.

2. If offenders do not meet the above obligations within the period indicated to them, the competent authorities shall send to carry out the demolition, construction and work necessary for restoring the situation prior to the offense at the expense of offenders.

CHAPTER VIII FINAL AND TRANSITIONAL PROVISIONS

Article 36

(Report on the Environment)

The Governor shall submit each year to the Legislative Assembly a report on the environmental situation in the Territory for the previous year.

Article 37

(Conservation of Nature)

1. The nature conservation strategy should shaping the objectives of the Policy Address.

2. In the interventions on environmental components should always be considered the impact on each of the components and their interactions.

Article 38

(Conventions and international agreements)

The regulations, standards and, in general, any matter included in the special legislation that will regulate the implementation of this law will have regard to its compliance with international conventions and agreements applicable to Macau and that have to do with the matter in question.

Article 39

(Priorities)

1. The priority among the components of the environment, the following: air, water, habitat and human food products.

2. The components of the psychosocial environment will always be the subject of consideration in all studies, projects and projects to be carried out in the Territory, although it can not determine individual priorities among them, given its nature unlikely to quantify in particular interdisciplinary.

Article 40

(Implementation of the law)

The Governor set up structures and mechanisms to implement this law.

Approved on January 31, 1991.

The President of the Legislative Assembly, Carlos Augusto Correa Paes d'Assumpcao.

Promulgated on 28 February 1991.

REGULATION OF WATER AND MACAU THE SEWAGE DRAIN

TITLE I PUBLIC WATER SUPPLY - TECHNICAL PROVISIONS

CHAPTER I General

Article 1 (Purpose and scope)

1. This title is to define the technical conditions to be satisfied by the public distribution system water in Macao in order to be assured its good overall performance, preserving the health and safety of users and installations .

2. This Title shall apply to public distribution of drinking water systems and private distribution systems when intended for collective use.

3. The public distribution of drinking water covers domestic consumption, commercial, industrial, public, fire-fighting and others.

4. The quality of the water distributed must meet the criteria and standards set out in Annex 1.

Article 2

(Terminology, symbols and units systems)

1. The terminology and symbols to be used are those listed in Annexes 2 and 3, respectively.

2. The units should be those of the International System.

Article 3

(Material Quality)

1. All materials to be applied in distribution systems, ancillary parts and use of devices should be free from damage and, by the very nature or adequate protection, they must have good corrosion resistance conditions, internal and external, and efforts that will be subject.

2. The materials to be used in pipes and accessory parts distribution systems should be those whose implementation is expected by the entity responsible for the supply and public water distribution and approved by the Lands, Public Works and Transport.

3. The application of new materials or construction processes for which there are no officially adopted specifications or sufficient practical use, is subject to approval by the Lands, Public Works and Transport, which may subject to prior verification of compliance by LECM - Macao Civil Engineering Laboratory.

4. The verification of conformity referred to above may take the form of recognition if the materials are in accordance with the ISO or other internationally recognized.

CHAPTER II

Design of systems

Article 4

(General design)

1. The design of water distribution systems must go through security of supply to the population with drinking water in sufficient quantity and in the best economic conditions and still meet water requirements for firefighting.

2. The distribution pipes must always be possible meshes.

3. Whatever the adopted evolution, it should be flexible enough to adapt to any urban change and an evolution of the number of connections.

Article 5

(New systems or expand existing systems)

1. In the design of new water distribution systems should be taken into account the need to ensure adequate service, translated by continuity of supply, ensuring adequate pressure on gross use of devices, stability of the piezometric surface and minimization of downtown areas speed.

2. It should be evaluated hydraulic impact of the new system over the existing systems in order to avoid significant losses, the efficiency of the latter.

Article 6

(Remodeling or rehabilitation of existing systems)

1. In remodeling or rehabilitation of existing systems should be made to technical and economic assessment of the work, looking to improve efficiency without causing a negative hydraulic or structural impact on surrounding systems.

2. In technical and economic assessment should also be considered social costs resulting from damage caused to users, to pedestrians, to traffic and trade.

CHAPTER III

Basic elements

Article 7

(Register of the existing system)

1. They must be kept constantly updated the records of public water distribution systems.

2. Of these records must contain at least:

a) location in the plant pipes, accessories and additional facilities on topographic letter scale between 1: 500 and 1: 2000, with the implementation of all buildings and important points;

b) sections, materials and joint types of pipelines;

c) location and number of hydrants;

d) information on the age and structural condition of the ducts;

e) individual card for connecting routes and other system installations.

3. In the preparation of studies of water distribution systems should take into account the elements of the respective entries.

Article 8

(Operating data)

1. The entity responsible for public water distribution service must also keep information of the floating flows and pressures in the most important sections of the network, as well as indicators of physical, chemical and bacteriological.

2. Such data must be the fundamental building block for the development of remodeling studies of water distribution systems.

Article 9

(Population Development)

The preparation of studies of water distribution systems is essential to know the updated demographic situation in the area to serve and evaluate their foreseeable development.

Article 10

(Capitations water)

1. The development of water distribution systems studies should be based on knowledge of water consumption, the existing systems as set out in the entity responsible for registration of public distribution of water service.

2. Based on the values of water consumption and population obtains the average annual per capita and, from this, it is estimated foreseeable development.

Article 11

(Domestic, commercial and public consumption)

1. capitations should be determined by analysis and extrapolation of its evolution in recent years in the area to serve, or in areas with similar characteristics in water sufficiency situations and should not, however, be less than 250 liters / person / day .

2. Do not consider these consumptions included those related to health facilities, education, military, prison, tourism, firefighters and sports facilities, which should be evaluated according to their characteristics and treated as industrial consumption.

Article 12

(Industrial and similar consumption)

1. The relevant industrial consumption must be assessed case by case.

2. The expression equivalent to industrial consumption, among others, those referred to in Article 11

Article 13

(Leaks)

Should be considered for design purposes a minimum value for leaks 12% of the volume of water entering the system.

Article 14

(Consumption for firefighting)

1. The consumption of water for firefighting depend on the risk of its occurrence and spread in the area concerned, which must be assigned one of the following degrees:

a) Grade A - urban area of moderate risk, consist primarily of buildings with a maximum of ten floors above ground intended for residential purposes, social facilities and services, possibly with some trade and small industries slight risks;

b) Grade B - urban area of considerable degree of risk, consisting of large buildings, intended for residential purposes, social facilities and services and buildings to hotels, commercial and public service;

c) C grade - urban area of high degree of risk, mainly characterized by the existence of old buildings or occupation mainly commercial and industrial activity that stores, uses or produces explosives or highly flammable materials.

2. The instantaneous flow rate to ensure for a minimum of two hours to the fighting, according to the degree of risk is:

a) Grade A 2 000 l / min;
b) Grade B 4 000 L / min;
c) degree C to define case by case.

Article 15

(Peak factor)

1. For purposes of system design should be used if suitable flow rate calculation every organ, which corresponds to the annual average flow multiplied by a factor tip.

2. In distribution systems we use the tip factor time of day with the highest consumption of the year, leading to the flow rate calculation.

3. The peak value of this factor should be determined in each case by the consumption records that zone or zones of similar characteristics, should not be less than 1.5.

CHAPTER IV

Distribution network

SECTION A

Pipelines

Article 16

(Goal)

Ducts are designed to ensure the transmission and distribution of water supply in good quantitative and qualitative conditions in order to ensure the comfort of users, public health and safety.

Article 17

(Flow rates of calculation)

1. The hydraulic conduits of the study should be based on knowledge of the flow rates calculation.

2. In water distribution systems are considered to be the average annual flow provided at the start of operation of the system and in the year project horizon, affected a tip factor, to which is added the flow losses.

3. The main pipes must be sized based on the tip flow increased consumption of time of day taking into account the consumption for firefighting.

4. The distribution pipes must be sized based on the flow end time of the day higher consumption and must be further verified a fire.

5. The main duct must be dimensioned so that in case of interruption of one, the other to ensure a minimum transmission capacity of 70% of total consumption.

Article 18

(Hydraulic sizing)

1. The hydraulic design of the distribution system must take into account the need to minimize overall system costs, including first investment costs and operating costs and ensuring the desired level of service.

2. The minimization of costs should be achieved through a judicious combination of diameters, observing the following rules:

a) the flow velocity for the tip flow on the horizon of the project must not exceed, for reasons of stability, consumption fluctuations and transients, the value calculated by the expression:

V = 0.127 D 0.4

where V is the limit speed (m / sec) and D is the inner diameter of pipe (mm);

b) the flow velocity for tip flow in the starting year of operating the system must not be less than 0.30 m / s for health reasons and in the ducts where you can not verify this limit must be provided suitable arrangements for discharge Periodic and additional chlorination stations;

c) the maximum, static or operating pressure at any point of use should not exceed 600 kPa, measured at ground level; Coloane it is assumed a maximum pressure of 800 kPa;

d) for reasons of comfort for users and safety of the equipment it is not acceptable large fluctuation of pressure on each node of the system, imposing a maximum variation throughout the day 300 kPa;

e) excluding exceptional situations, the operating pressure on the public network to the level of street layout should in no case be less than 250 kPa.

Article 19

(Verification fire situations)

1. After the hydraulic design system of distribution pipes must be checked for fire conditions in order to guarantee yourself the hydrants flow rates specified in Article 14 paragraph 2 for piezometric heights not less than 180 kPa .

2. In fire situations referred to in paragraph 1 is not required any limitation speeds in the ducts and admit it piezometric heights not less than 10 kPa in the network nodes not directly interested in combating the fire.

3. The limits referred to in paragraphs 1 and 2 may be disregarded in exceptional cases, provided that its effects duly considered and provided for appropriate measures to minimize or cancel the drawbacks thereof.

Article 20

(Minimum diameter)

The internal nominal diameters (DN / ID) minimum of pipelines depend on the area of the fire risk and should be:

a) Grade A 100 mm;
b) Grade B 125 mm;
c) degree C 150 mm.

Article 21

(Implantation)

1. The implementation of the ducts in the streets distribution network should be done in conjunction with other infrastructure and, where possible, off the carriageway.

2. Pipes shall be deployed at a distance from property boundaries of at least 0,60 m, and its remoteness from other established infrastructure in parallel should not be generally less than 0.50 m and can not under any circumstances be less than 0.30 m to facilitate maintenance of any of these operations.

3. Whenever possible, the implementation of the ducts must be made on a higher plane to the waste water collection and at a distance not less than 1.00 m in order to ensure effective protection against possible contamination. The vertical lap joints of both types of systems is not allowed.

4. Failing to comply with the provisions referred to above, special protections appropriate should be adopted.

5. It should be avoided deploying ducts in landfill areas or other polluted areas.

Article 22

(Depth)

1. The minimum depth of laying the pipes should be of 1.00 m or 0.60 m measured between the generator upper outer duct and floor level, depending on whether roads or pedestrian areas.

2. The amount referred to in paragraph 1 shall be increased if the requests due to traffic, the insertion of the connecting routes or the installation of the other infrastructures recommend.

3. You can accept a lower coverage to a minimum indicated if it is assured an adequate structural strength of pipelines to withstand overloads.

4. In situations of exception and the reasons a tolerance of outer pipes to the floor, provided they are suitably protected mechanically and thermally, and safeguarded aspects of contamination.

Article 23

(Width of trench)

Taking into account operational needs and security of personnel, the width of the trenches for laying of pipelines should have, except in special duly substantiated conditions, the minimum size set by the formulas:

The) L = + 0.40 D for diameter ducts to 0.50 m;
B) L = D + 0.60 for diameter pipes more than 0.50 m;
where L is the width of the trench (m) and D the outer nominal diameter (DN / OD) of the conduit (m).

Article 24

(Settlement)

1. The pipes must be laid in order to ensure their perfect stability and should be taken special care in recent landfill areas.

2. The trench should have settled prepared and bottom to allow each pipe section rests, continuously and directly on grounds of equal resistance.

3. Where, by its nature, the land does not ensure the necessary conditions of stability of the pipes or fittings must be made prior consolidation, replaced by more durable material properly compacted, or other suitable construction processes.

4. When the excavation is made in rocky terrain, the pipes must be laid in their entire length on an even layer previously prepared 0.15 to 0.30 m thick, sand, gravel or similar material, which largest dimension not exceeding 20 mm. This thickness should be set depending on the material and the pipe diameter.

Article 25

(Ditches Landfill)

1. The landfill trenches must be made up from 0.15 to 0.30 m above the upper surface of pipelines with material whose dimensions do not exceed 20 mm. This thickness should be set depending on the material and the pipe diameter.

2. Compaction of the landfill material must be done carefully so as not to damage the pipelines and ensure the stability of the floors.

Article 26

(Together)

1. Joints must be watertight and maintain properly centered pipe.

2. Depending on their type and characteristics, the joints should allow the existence of certain angle between adjacent straight sections, enabling expansion, transmit axial and transverse efforts and facilitate the assembly and disassembly of pipe and fittings.

Article 27

(Leakage test)

All ducts, after settlement and joints uncovered, should be subject to leakage tests, as described in Annex 4.

Article 28

(Nature Materials)

1. In the water distribution pipes can be used any material provided it complies with the provisions of Article 3

2. In all cases where the pipes are not protected or are subject to vibrations, in particular crossings art, the material used must be ductile cast iron, steel or other, should be seen in any case the provisions of Article 3

Article 29

(Protection)

Where material of pipelines is likely to internal or external attack, should be provided to its convenient protection according to the nature of the aggressive agent.

SECTION B

Connecting routes

Article 30

(Goal)

1. The connection branches are designed to ensure the building water supply from the public within the limits of properties to serve, in good condition flow, pressure and water quality.

2. The connecting routes for normal consumption and fire fighting consumption must, in general, be independent.

3. The cumulative household connection is only allowed in exceptional cases upon prior opinion of the Fire Department.

Article 31

(Flow rates of calculation)

1. The flow rates to consider in connection branches are the calculation of flow rates of the respective building systems.

2. If the connection extension is cumulative, quantity to be considered should be the greater of the following values:

a) calculating the gross flow of cold water and hot water distribution systems;

b) flow of building water system calculation for firefighting.

Article 32

(Hydraulic sizing)

The hydraulic design of the connection branches consists in determining the diameters based on calculation of flow rates and a flow rate between 0.5 and 2.0 m / s, pressure of function available in the public network.

Article 33

(Minimum diameter)

1. The internal nominal diameter (DN / ID) minimum on branch lines is 20 mm.

2. The internal nominal diameter (DN / ID) minimum on connecting routes to combat the regulating reservoir with fire service is 65 mm.

3. When it has to simultaneously ensure the fire-fighting without regulating reservoir service, the diameter shall not be less than 80 mm.

Article 34

(Track)

The layout of the branch lines must be straight, both in plan and in profile.

Article 35

(Minimum depth)

The minimum depth of laying the connecting routes is 0.80 m, which can be reduced to 0.50 m in areas not subject to road circulation.

Article 36

(Connection to the network)

1. The water distribution systems in buildings covered by the public are required to be connected to this by connecting routes.

2. Where appropriate, the same building can have more than one connection extension for domestic supply or service.

Article 37

(Insert the public)

1. The insertion of the connecting routes in the conduct of public distribution network is by means of appropriate accessories, depending on the material used and must be provided for isolating valve to the supply service suspension.

2. The insert is not allowed in pipes with a diameter greater than 300 mm except when it ensure that there is no loss of structural strength of the pipeline.

Article 38

(Trial after settlement)

All extensions before being put into service, should be subject to leakage tests as described in Annex 4.

Article 39

(Nature Materials)

Connecting routes can be of any material provided it is checked Article 3

CHAPTER V

Elements accessories Network

SECTION A

Gate valves

Article 40

(Installation)

1. The cut-off valves must be installed in order to facilitate system operation and minimize the drawbacks of possible interruptions of supply.

2. The cut-off valves must be properly protected, accessible and easily maneuverable.

3. The cut-off valves should be located, namely:

a) in connection branches;

b) next to accessories or additional facilities that may need to be taken out of service;

c) along the route with no service conduits, with not more than 1 000 m spacing;

d) the major intersections in minimum of three;

e) the main junctions in a minimum number of two.

SECTION B

Check valves

Article 41

(Installation)

1. Check valves should be installed in well protected and accessible locations for maintenance and repair and interspersed between gate valves.

2. Check valves should be installed in accordance with the direction of the desired flow, the compression and suction pipes of pumping installations and, where necessary in terms of operation in the distribution network.

SECTION C

Pressure reducers

Article 42

(Installation)

1. The location of pressure reducers is conditioned by existing topography, the design of the distribution system and the type of device used.

2. The pressure reducing valves should be installed in maneuvering cameras to ensure adequate protection and easy accessibility.

3. The pressure drop cameras should be provided with a surface discharge with adequate health protection.

4. The pressure-reducing valve should be provided with isolating valves upstream and downstream, and "by-pass" with sectioning.

SECTION D

Suckers

Article 43

(Installation)

1. The suction cups must be located at high points, especially at the extremes of ascending peripheral pipes and extension pipes than 2000 m without route service.

2. In large ducts referred to in the preceding paragraph, the suction cups must be located:

a) upstream or downstream of gate valves according they are respectively ascending and descending sections;

b) in sections downstream section plans or descendants disinclined when you follow them more inclined downward section.

3. Installation should be made to allow the replacement or repair of suckers without harming the operation of the system in which they operate and should always be provided for gate valves in their connecting sections.

4. The diameter of a suction cup should not be less than 1/8 of the diameter of the conduit which is installed with a minimum of 20 mm.

SECTION E

Bottom outlets

Article 44

(Installation)

1. There should be bottom outlets:

a) in all network downstream of extremes;

b) at all low points of the ducts;

c) at intermediate points of conduits with the same direction of inclination lengths considered relatively high, and the extensive distribution network, in order to minimize the number of customers adversely affected by possible operations of emptying.

2. In the cases referred to in point b) above, the bottom outlets should be located immediately upstream or immediately downstream of the isolating valves in the descendant pipes and riser lines, respectively.

3. The design of a bottom outlet consists in determining its diameter, so as to obtain a residence time of emptying conduit portion compatible with the proper operation of the system, using, for that, the expressions of the flow through holes.

4. The diameter of the bottom outlet should not be less than 1/6 of the diameter of the conduit which is installed with a minimum of 50 mm.

5. The effluent from the bottom outlets should be released in natural water lines, storm sewers or cameras equipped with lift system, minimizing the risk of health order.

SECTION F

Flow meters

Article 45

(Implantation)

1. flow meters must be located at every point where interest measure flow rates or volumes provided, both for billing purposes and for better system operation.

2. In addition there are the gross input branches of all consumers, the flow meters to be installed in the outlet pipes of the tanks and pumping systems and other carefully selected points, in order to permit a better yield control system .

3. The flow meters must be installed at points of possible accumulation of air to avoid disturbances on the measurements, and provide for minimum pipe lengths upstream and downstream without any singularity, with values recommended by the manufacturers only can be reduced by using flow regulators.

4. The flow meters must be installed properly protected, accessible and in order to make possible correct readings sites.

5. In the case of fixed flow meter should be provided upstream gate valves and downstream, a withdrawal joint and a 'by-pass' for the purposes of maintenance, if there is no workaround. Exceptions are cases where maintenance can be done without dismantling the equipment.

SECTION G

Hydrants

Article 46

(Installation)

1. The types of fire hydrants, their characteristics and constructive aspects must comply with the applicable rules.

2. The design of the hydrants must ensure their exclusive use by the fire department.

3. The hydrants should have a diameter of 80 mm and a 70 mm outlet RT, be installed in the manifolds 100 mm diameter and 150 mm, with a maximum spacing of 100 m on each side of the street network, in positions alternating, in order to ensure not more than 50 m spacings. On roads with width of less than 5 m, it is assumed a maximum spacing of 50 m, only one side of the street layout.

4. The water marks should have a diameter of 150 mm and three outputs, two 70 mm RT 100 mm and a VT be installed on the main ducts and distribution of diameter greater than 200 mm in industrial and commercial areas and 150 mm in all other cases.

5. Water milestones should be located along the curb sidewalks that border the roads wherever possible at junctions and turnings, with the following spacing, zone fire risk degree of function:

a) Grade A 100 m;
b) Grade B 50 m;

c) degree C to define case by case.
6. The definition in each case, the type of hydrant to use, it is the entity responsible for public water distribution service, heard the fire department.

SECTION H

Maneuver Cams

Article 47

(Installation)

1. The maneuver cameras, consisting of sill, body, cover, closure and access device may be rectangular with flat roofs or circular plan with flat roof or tapered asymmetrical.

2. The adoption of different geometric shapes those referred to in the previous paragraph is accepted only in duly justified cases.

3. The switching chambers can still be centered or off-center alignment relative to the conduit.

4. maneuver chambers should be solidly built, easily accessible and fitted with resistant closures.

5. The thresholds must have a small inclination in the flow direction.

6. The interior dimensions of maneuvering cameras should allow for easy operation and maintenance of installed equipment.

7. The minimum size of the plant must be not less than 1.10 m, to depths of greater than 1.00 m chamber.

8. The switching chambers must be vented, when possible, and provided with small trough to facilitate the concentration of infiltration water, if not most economical to carry out its drainage.

Article 48

(Nature Materials)

1. The threshold must be of simple or reinforced concrete, according to the foundation conditions.

2. The body must be of simple or reinforced concrete, hydraulic masonry stone, brick or cement mortar blocks.

3. The cover must be of simple or reinforced concrete, depending on the foreseeable strain.

4. The frame and the lid may be of lamellar graphite cast iron or spheroidal graphite and cast or rolled steel, depending on the use of the latter material ensuring effective protection against corrosion.

5. The cover can be further reinforced concrete or combination of concrete with any of the material referred to in paragraph 4, must, for this, there is good adhesion between them.

6. Fixed access devices should be of cast iron of lamellar or spheroidal graphite or other material, proven resistant or adequately protected against corrosion, along the work life.

7. To build the maneuvering cameras can still be used other materials provided they meet the conditions of use in accordance with Article 3

CHAPTER VI

Additional facilities

SECTION A

Reservoirs

Article 49

(Hydraulic sizing)

The hydraulic design of tanks consists in determining its storage capacity, which should be the sum of the requirements for settlement, emergency reserve and balance pressures.

Article 50

(Constructive aspects)

1. Tanks must be resistant, watertight and have sloping bottom to at least 1% for gutters or for flushing cisterns.

2. To allow the placing out of service for any cleaning, disinfection and maintenance, the tanks must be equipped with "by-pass".

3. buried and semienterrados reservoirs with a capacity exceeding 500 m 3 must be composed of at least two cells, in normal operation, intercommunicate, being, however, prepared to work in isolation.

4. Each cell must have at least:

a) power circuit equipped with input isolation valve;

b) distribution circuit with input protected by thin;

c) the emergency circuit via surface discharger;

d) emptying and cleaning circuit through the bottom outlet;

e) adequate ventilation;

f) easy access to its interior.

5. The containers must be of concrete, masonry, steel or other materials provided they meet the necessary conditions.

Article 51

(Health and Safety)

To ensure the protection of the stored water, the tanks must:

a) be perfectly watertight to groundwater and surface water;

b) has a sealed enclosure surrounding, conditional access;

c) have the openings protected against the entrance of insects, small animals and light;

d) use non-polluting or toxic materials in permanent or occasional contact with water;

e) prevent formation of stagnant zones;

f) be well ventilated to allow the frequent renewal of the air in contact with water;

g) have, when necessary, appropriate thermal protection to prevent temperature variations of the water.

SECTION B

Lifting systems

Article 52

(Hydraulic sizing)

1. The diameter of the lifting pipes is defined in terms of a technico study covering the entire period of operation, but should not the flow velocity is less than 0.7 m / s.

2. the prior analysis of transients in lift systems with resolution of any protective devices is mandatory.

3. The protection of these devices must be defined in terms of engaging the minimum and maximum piezometric quota from the hydraulic shock occurrence of transients in the most unfavorable situation.

Article 53

(Constructive aspects)

1. In lift systems there to consider the cameras and / or suction pipes, the pumping equipment, pumping pipes, control devices, control and protection and unloaders.

2. In the design of vacuum chambers must be analyzed the variability of tributaries flow and frequency of starts, compatible with the types of equipment used. The shape of the vacuum chambers must avoid sludge accumulation in dead zones, and for that, the walls of suitable gradient background and rounded edges.

3. The pumping apparatus comprises electropump groups, submersible or not horizontal or vertical axis. The definition and characterization of the electric pump groups should be taken into consideration:

a) the maximum number of starts per hour permissible for the equipment to be installed;

b) the maximum speed of rotation compatible with the nature of the material;

c) the installation of lifting devices to function as mutual active reserve;

d) the possibility of simultaneous operation.

4. In the definition and characterization of aerial pipelines must be taken into consideration:

a) the longitudinal profile should preferably be up, and the piezometric line should not intersect the conduct, even at zero flow situations;

b) must be set the surrounding of minimum and maximum piezometric quota from occurrence of transients and verified the need for protection agencies;

c) for the release of air from the ducts may resort to automatic suction cups or pressure pipes;

d) in all the low points of conduct and, where appropriate, in intermediate points, bottom outlets must be installed in order to allow for evacuation within an acceptable time period;

e) the pulses must be analyzed and the curves singular points, calculating the mass of mooring in situations where the soil does not provide the necessary strength.

5. The lift systems must be provided upstream of a weir connected to a manifold resource to cope with the occurrence of faults, and the need for putting the installation out of service and to allow the diversion of excess water.

6. The electromechanical organs, integrated into pumping stations inserted in urban areas, must determine, for its operation, noise whose noise level average, measured at 3.5 meters from the facades of neighboring buildings, does not exceed 45 dB (A).

TITLE II PUBLIC DRAINAGE APPLICATIONS - TECHNICAL PROVISIONS

CHAPTER VII

General

Article 54

(Purpose and scope)

1. This title is to define the technical conditions to be complied with public wastewater disposal in the territory of Macau, so that it can ensure the efficient overall operation, preserving the public health, safety and resources natural.

2. This Title applies to public sewage systems wastewater, whether domestic, industrial and storm. Private drainage systems are considered included as long as for the collective use.

Article 55

(Terminology, symbols and units system)

The terminology and symbology to be adopted shall be as set out in Annexes 5 and 6, respectively. The units should be those of the International System.

Article 56

(Material Quality)

1. All materials to be applied in wastewater drainage systems and its accessories must be free from defects and, by the very nature or adequate protection, they must have good resistance to corrosion conditions and abrasion, and the effort that will be subject.

2. The materials to be used in pipes and accessory parts of wastewater drainage systems should be those whose application is approved by the Lands, Public Works and Transport.

3. The application of new materials or construction processes for which there are no officially adopted specifications or sufficient practical use, is subject to approval by the Lands, Public Works and Transport, which may subject to prior verification of compliance by LECM - Macao Civil Engineering Laboratory.

4. The verification of conformity referred to above may take the form of recognition if the materials are in accordance with the ISO or other internationally recognized.

CHAPTER VIII

Design of systems

Article 57

(General design)

1. The design of wastewater drainage systems must go through prior careful analysis of final destination, both from the point of view of protection of natural resources such as public health and the global economy work.

2. Whatever the adopted solution should be flexible enough to adapt to any urban change and an evolution of the number of connections.

Article 58

(New systems or expand existing systems)

1. In designing wastewater drainage systems in new areas of urbanization should be adopted in principle the separative system.

2. They must be evaluated the effects downstream and possibly upstream of the new system on the existing system, and evaluated its consequences.

Article 59

(Remodeling or rehabilitation of existing systems)

1. In remodeling or rehabilitation of existing systems must do to tecnicoeconómica assessment work, looking to improve efficiency without causing a negative hydraulic or structural impact on surrounding systems.

2. In tecnicoeconómica evaluation should also be considered social costs resulting from damage caused to users, to pedestrians, to traffic and trade.

Article 60

(Drainage systems for domestic and industrial waste water)

The drain of domestic and industrial wastewater should be found a development of the collectors network that can cover the entire area to be served, while minimizing the overall cost and searching for the flow of effluents to make as much as possible by means of gravity, so promoting system reliability.

Article 61

(Rainwater drainage systems)

1. In designing stormwater drainage systems should be carefully analyzed the areas where the flow can be done superficially having this procedure is intended in separative systems, limit the extension of the network.

2. Whenever possible should be practiced to establish surface drainage lines through the open spaces in the form of ditches or wide and shallow ditches.

3. They should also be carefully considered solutions that interfering at the level of the river basin, at the level of the drainage system itself, can contribute, for storage, for reducing peak flows in order to reduce the diameter of collectors for downstream.

Article 62

(Joint Design of systems)

In new systems is mandatory joint design of the drainage of domestic and industrial wastewater system and storm water drainage system. This obligation shall not affect any faseamentos deferred execution of works.

Article 63

(Septicidade Control)

1. In domestic network unit and separative networks must control the formation of hydrogen sulfide gas in order to prevent corrosion of the constituent materials of the drainage system and the existence of unpleasant environmental conditions or even inconvenient for personnel safety exploration.

2. For the enjoyment of referred to in paragraph 1 shall be adopted appropriate measures to either the overall design of system level, by minimizing the flow of time in the collectors and the pumping pipes, both in terms of design.

CHAPTER IX

Basic elements

Article 64

(Register of the existing system)

1. They must keep up-to-date records of the public systems of waste water drainage.

2. Of these records must contain at least:

a) location in the plant, collectors, accessories and additional facilities on topographic map, the range between 1: 500 and 1: 2000, with the implementation of all buildings and important points;

b) quotas and floor sill of manholes;

c) sections, materials and joint types of collectors;

d) indication of the age and structural conditions of the collectors;

e) individual card for connecting routes and complementary facilities.

3. In the preparation of studies of wastewater drainage systems should take into account the elements of the respective entries.

Article 65

(Operating data)

1. The services responsible for operation and maintenance of sewerage systems of public should also keep up to date information relating to fluctuating flow rates in the most important sections of the collector network, as well as indicators of physical, chemical and bacteriological.

2. This data should be a core element for the development of remodeling studies and / or expansion of sewerage systems.

Article 66

(Population Development)

When drawing up studies on the drainage of domestic wastewater is essential to know the demographic situation and assess its likely trend.

Article 67

(Capitations water)

1. The development of studies on the drainage of domestic and industrial wastewater must be based on knowledge of water consumption, which can be obtained from the records of the operation of services of water supply system.

2. Based on those values and population served calculate the current average annual per capita and, from there, it is possible to estimate a predictable path to project horizon.

Article 68

(Factor surging to the network and annual average flow)

1. The network affluence factor should have the value of 0.90, except in duly justified cases where are permitted variations between 0.70 and 0.90.

2. The annual average flow is achieved by making the product of the average annual per capita inflow to the network by the number of people served.

Article 69

(Peak factor)

1. For systems sizing effect is used to calculate the appropriate flow every organ, which corresponds to the annual average flow multiplied by a factor tip.

2. In the sewerage network is used instant tip factor, which is the ratio of the maximum instantaneous flow rate of the year and the annual average flow of domestic wastewater.

3. Instant tip factor should be determined case by case, based on analysis of local records and should not, however, exceed 4 in the headwaters of the networks not be less than 1.5 in the downstream areas.

4. In the absence of these elements instant edge factor can be estimated to a calculation section, based on the following expression:

wherein P is the population.

Article 70

(Flow rates of infiltration)

1. infiltration flows come from infiltration of water in the soil and should be carefully considered in the design of new drainage systems, and its value depending on the hydrogeological characteristics of the soil and the type and collectors material conservation status and joints .

2. In particular drainage of domestic and industrial wastewater systems should be minimized to its confluence to the network through appropriate project procedures, selection of materials and joints, and constructive arrangements.

3. Since not available local experimental data, or information on similar situations, they can be estimated infiltration flow proportional to the length and diameter of collectors.

4. For collectors and recent connection branches or building, or newly laid, can be estimated infiltration flow values on the order of 0.5 m 3 .s -1 .day -1 .km -1 .cm -1 (cubic meters per second per day per kilometer per manifold cm diameter), and may reach values of up around 4 m 3 .s -1 .day -1 .km -1 .cm -1, in sewers and poor construction and maintenance extensions.

5. For collectors predominantly dipped in water table is recommended the use of watertight joints of the kind of pressure line, with which they can reach negligible infiltration flows.

Article 71

(Industrial Flows)

The relevant industrial flows should be evaluated case by case, and added to the remaining flows.

Article 72

(Precipitation)

1. For the preparation of studies on the rainwater drainage must resort to the intensity-duration-frequency curves, which provide the values of average maximum rainfall intensities for different durations and different return periods. The durations to consider are the equivalent to the time of concentration, which is the sum of the initial time with the travel time.

2. The curves to be taken to the Macao SAR are listed in Annex 7 and were derived from the statistical analysis of historical data corresponding udográficos records to the period between 1952 and 1989.

Article 73

(Flow coefficients)

The flow coefficients to be taken are equal to the values of waterproofing coefficients for densely urbanized areas and 60% of those values for areas with trees.

Article 74

(Payback period)

1. The payback period to consider the hydraulic design of a storm water drainage system should result from the comparative analysis of the investments necessary for flood protection, for precipitation calculation, and damages that may result when this is exceeded.

2. A 10-year payback period is most often usable and can this amount be increased to 20 or 25 years, in duly justified cases.

CHAPTER X

Collection network

SECTION A

Collectors

Article 75

(Goal)

The collectors are designed to ensure the conduct of domestic sewage, industrial and rainwater, from the buildings or the public highway, the appropriate final destination.

Article 76

(Flow rates of calculation)

1. The hydraulic and sanitary study of the collection network should be based on knowledge of the calculation of flow rates.

2. In the drainage of domestic and industrial wastewater systems these flows correspond generally to those who are expected occur in the year project horizon, ie the average annual flow multiplied by an instant tip factor, to which are added the Industrial flow and calculating the flow rate of infiltration.

3. In rainwater drainage systems, calculating flow rates are obtained from the mean maximum rainfall for a period equal to the basin concentration time and with certain period of return, affected the runoff coefficient.

Article 77

(Hydraulic and sanitary sizing)

1. The hydraulic-sanitary design of the collection network should take into account the need to minimize overall system costs, including the first investment costs and operating costs.

2. This minimization should be achieved through a judicious combination of diameters, slopes and depths of settlement, observing the following rules:

a) the maximum rate of flow to the tip flow in the project horizon should not exceed, in general, 3 m / s in domestic collectors and 5 m / s in the rain and / or unit separative collectors;

b) the flow velocity for the average flow rate at the start of operation must not be lower than 0.6 m / s for collecting domestic and 0.9 m / s for single and separative rainwater collector;

c) in situations for which the limits referred to in the preceding paragraph are in practice unfeasible, such as bedside collectors, we recommend the establishment of slopes to ensure those speed values for full section flow thereby ensuring not lower speeds to 0.15 m / s for household collector and 0.35 m / s for stormwater unit or separative collectors for water depth equal to or greater heights, respectively, 5% and 10% of the full section height;

d) the height of the net blade to the maximum speeds mentioned in a) should be equal to the total height in separative rainwater collectors and collectors in the unit; in domestic collectors should not exceed 0.5 of the total height equal to or less than 500 mm, and diameters greater than 0.7 for that value;

e) the slope of the collectors should not be generally less than 0.3% nor more than 15% assuming slopes less than 0.3%, provided it is guaranteed the accuracy of the leveling, the stability of settlement and conditions cleaning; whenever establish gradients above 15% should be checked for stability collectors foreseeing special anchorage devices if needed.

Article 78

(Minimum diameter)

The minimum internal nominal diameter (DN / ID) admitted to the collectors is 200 mm.

Article 79

(Sequence sections)

1. In domestic separative networks section of a collector may in no case be less than the section of a manifold amount.

2. in individual or separative networks stormwater section of a collector may be less than the amount of collector section where stands a regularization structure, or in other situations, since it safeguarded the security of persons and property.

Article 80

(Implantation)

1. The implementation of the collectors should be done in conjunction with other infrastructure and, wherever possible, on the axis of the street.

2. Where there is insufficient space out of traffic routes for all infrastructure must take priority the water pipes, electricity cables and telephones.

3. The collectors deployed close to the vestments of the buildings must maintain for these, a minimum distance of 1.0 m.

4. The collectors must be deployed wherever possible in a plane lower than the water distribution pipes and these separated sufficiently so as to ensure effective protection against possible contamination. This removal should generally not be less than 1.0 m. The vertical lap joints of both types of systems is not allowed.

5. Failing to comply with the provisions referred to above, special protection should be adopted.

6. Domestic collectors are, whenever possible, based on a plane lower than the rainwater collector so as to enable the connection of extensions.

7. To minimize the risk of unauthorized network connections or extensions, the domestic collector when deployed on the track shall be located right where the storm sewer when it is observed from upstream to downstream.

8. should be avoided deployment of collectors in saline soils, and if this is not possible, should be adopted suitable material for the pipes.

Article 81

(Minimum depth)

1. It should be adopted as the minimum depth of 1.0 m measured between the collector and the extrados of the floor.

2. This value must be increased if the requests such as traffic, the insertion of the connecting routes or the installation of the other recommending infrastructure.

3. In exceptional circumstances, you can take up a covering less than the minimum indicated there was in this case that conveniently protect the collectors when they have to withstand overloads.

4. In exceptional situations, and duly justified, to admit-outs collectors to the deck provided they are adequately protected mechanically and thermally.

Article 82

(Width of trench)

1. Taking into account the needs of operational and staff safety, the width of the trenches for laying the collectors must have, except in special duly substantiated conditions, the minimum size set by the formulas:

De L = 0.40 + - for collectors of an external diameter not exceeding 0.50 m;

De L = 0.60 + - for outer diameter of collectors than 0.50 m;

wherein L is the width of the trench (m) and De is the external diameter of the collector (m).

2. These minimum values should be adopted when the nesting depth is less than 3 meters should, for higher depths, be increased taking account of conditions such as terrain, excavation processes and the water table.

Article 83

(Settlement)

1. The collectors should always be laid in order to result ensured their perfect stability and should be taken special care in recent landfill areas.

2. The trench should have settled background and prepared to allow the continued support of the pipes.

3. In laying the collectors should be avoided that the same section rests directly on variable resistance ground.

4. Where, by its nature, the land does not ensure the necessary conditions of stability of the pipes and / or accessory parts, should those be guaranteed by preliminary consolidation, replaced by more durable material, or other duly justified cases.

5. When excavation is done on rocky terrain, the collectors must be laid along its entire length, a uniform layer over the prepared of 0.15 to 0.30 m thick of soil, sand or gravel whose largest dimension does not exceed 20 mm. This thickness should be set depending on the material and diameter of the collectors.

Article 84

(Ditches Landfill)

1. The landfill trenches must be made up from 0.15 to 0.30 m above the upper surface of headers having material whose dimensions do not exceed 20 mm. This thickness should be set depending on the material and diameter of the collectors.

2. Compaction of the landfill material must be done carefully so as not to damage the collectors and ensure the stability of the floors.

Article 85

(Structural requirements)

The collectors, once installed, should have a crushing capacity of resistance (diametrical compression) that equals or exceeds the smashing loads imposed upon it by the very weight of the ground and the rolling or fixed overloads.

Article 86

(Together)

1. The joints of waste water collection must be performed in order to permanently ensure the tightness to liquids and gases, and in order to maintain the properly centered pipe.

2. Once executed the joints, it must be verified, where appropriate, the materials that were built not flowed into the interior of the collectors, being made in this case go away any obstacles that exist there and that could hinder the normal disposal of wastewater.

3. In the sections that temporarily or permanently work under pressure, including the situations in which domestic collectors remain below the water level, should be used appropriate together.

4. collectors placed in vibration zones or landfill areas likely to settlement shall be used for flexible joints.

Article 87

(Trials after settlement)

1. All collectors after settlement and joints uncovered, should be subject to leakage tests, linearity and clearing, the first of these also applied to manholes.

2. These tests shall be performed in accordance with the provisions of Annex 8.

Article 88

(Nature Materials)

1. Collectors of domestic wastewater can be of any material provided they comply with the provisions of Article 56

2. In crossings of works of art, in which collectors are not protected or subject to vibration, the materials used must be cast iron or steel.

Article 89

(Protection)

1. Where the material the collector is liable to attack by wastewater or gas resulting from its biological activity, should be provided a convenient internal protection of the pipeline, according to the nature of the aggressive agent.

2. It should also be made for the protection of foreign collectors, whenever the surrounding soil or groundwater are chemically aggressive.

Article 90

(Septicidade control in collectors with flow in free surface)

In the draft drainage systems of domestic wastewater or unitary systems, and how septicidade control measure should be adopted the following rules:

a) introduction of a minimum speed value in the collectors for calculating flow rates;

b) use of falls in the amount of sections where the waste waters are still poorly septic;

c) minimizing the turbulence in the downstream sections where the wastewater already have septicidade conditions;

d) collateral ventilation over the liquid collecting means of blade height limitation in accordance with Article 77;

e) ventilation guarantee through the connecting routes and building downpipes.

Article 91

(Septicidade control in collectors with runoff and pressure)

1. behavior in pressure, and as a result of lack of aeration of wastewater, it is necessary to ensure that the flow enters the gravity section downstream of conduct is done in minimum turbulence conditions.

2. The retention time under pressure in the ducts must not exceed 10 minutes in order to alleviate this drawback.

3. In situations worsened, particularly in large lengths or when waste water pipes have large residence times, should be provided to any compressed air injection, oxygen or oxidizing materials.

Article 92

(Released prohibited and entries allowed in the collection network)

1. It is forbidden to release the waste water drainage systems, whatever its type, either directly or through of building plumbing, from:

a) explosive or flammable materials;

b) radioactive material in concentrations considered unacceptable by the competent authorities;

c) laboratories wastewater or hospital facilities which by their chemical, bacteriological or virological, constitute a high risk to public health or the conservation of the pipes;

d) debris, sand or ashes;

e) effluents at temperatures above 45 ° C;

f) extracted sludge from septic tanks and grease or oil retaining cameras or similar devices, resulting from its maintenance;

g) any other substances, including food leftovers, grease and other debris that could clog or damage the collectors and accessories, or derail the process of treatment;

h) wastewater plants, containing:

- Cyclic compounds hydroxylated and their halogenated;
- Sedimentary, precipitable and floating materials which, by itself or after mixing with other substances in the collectors, could endanger the health of workers or the systems structures;
- Substances which involve the destruction of ecosystems inherent in biological treatment processes;
- Substances which involve the destruction of aquatic or terrestrial ecosystems in the receiving means;
- Any substance to stimulate, besides reason, the development of vectors or pathogen reservoirs;

i) all effluent whose release interdiction recorded in the specific legislation.

2. The entries allowed in the drainage network vary depending on whether the separative part or part of the unit. In separative systems, are only allowed to launch the network of domestic wastewater collectors, domestic wastewater and industrial waste water not covered by paragraph

1 is permitted, even in separative systems, launching network rainwater collectors, the actual storm water, industrial waste water from cooling circuits, as long as its temperature does not exceed 45 ° C and have not undergone significant degradation of its quality, and garages washes of water in discharge pools, and heating and water storage.

3. In unitary systems allowed the release of domestic and industrial wastewater and rainwater, as provided for separative systems.

4. In partial separative systems applies the foregoing for separative systems admitting, in duly justified cases, the connection of rainwater to the home network.

Article 93

(General rules wastewater admission to the collection network)

The release of domestic and industrial waste water allowed in the collection network should in any case comply with the general rules of constant discharge of Annex 9.

SECTION B

Connecting routes

Article 94

(Goal)

Connection branches should ensure driving of gross waste water from the connecting extension chamber to the public network.

Article 95

(Flow rates of calculation)

Calculating flow rates to consider in connection branches are the calculation of flow rates of the respective building systems.

Article 96

(Hydraulic sizing)

The hydraulic design of the connecting routes aims the determination of their diameters, estimated calculation flow, the following rules must be respected:

a) the slopes should not be less than 1%, it is advisable that are greater than or equal to 2%;

b) the height of the flow must match the full half-section or section respectively in domestic rainwater or connecting routes.

Article 97

(Minimum diameter)

The minimum inside diameter admitted on connecting routes is 100 mm.

Article 98

(Track)

The layout of the branch lines must be straight, both in plan and in profile.

Article 99

(Minimum depth)

The minimum depth of laying the connecting routes is 0.70 m.

Article 100

(Connection to the public drainage network)

1. Networks of domestic waste water in buildings covered by the public are required to be connected to this by connecting routes.

2. separative systems where rainwater have to be conducted to the respective public collector, this driving is done by independent connecting routes destined for the domestic wastewater.

3. In unitary systems can be admitted the existence of a single household connection for the conduct of domestic wastewater and rainwater and should always be separative the gross internal networks to the link.

4. Where appropriate, the same building can have more of a household connection for each type of wastewater.

Article 101

(Insert the public)

1. The insertion of the connection branches of the manifolds public drainage network is by means of simple forks, with an angle of incidence equal to or less than 67 30 ', always in the direction of flow in order to avoid disturbances in the vein net principal, or through manholes or meeting.

2. Direct integration of connecting routes in the collectors is admissible only to the latter diameters greater than 500 mm and must be carried out at two-thirds of its height.

Article 102

(Forks)

1. The insertion of the forks collector is necessarily made at an angle less than or equal to 67 30 '.

2. The type of fork material should be the same as public collector in which it operates.

3. The installation of the forks should be, whenever possible, simultaneously with the execution of public collector; in this case, that the installation of the branch connection is to be made later, the fork must be closed with a removable cap.

4. In the event that the fork is then installed to comply with the public manifold, the connection of this requires special care: either remove the collector section replacing it with the fork or if it makes a hole using appropriate mechanisms for just insert the extension.

Article 103

(Network Ventilation)

Should not be provided to prevent the ventilation of the public network or through the connecting routes either by building network.

Article 104

(Trial after settlement)

All branch lines must be subject to leak test before being put into service, as described in Annex 8.

Article 105

(Nature Materials)

The tubing is the connection extensions can be of any material provided that the provisions be found in Article 56

CHAPTER XI

Accessories

SECTION A

Manholes

Article 106

(Purpose and types)

1. manholes should facilitate access to collectors in conditions of safety and efficiency.

2. The manholes, consisting of sill, body, cover, closure and access device may be rectangular with flat roofs or circular plan with flat or tapered asymmetrical coverage, with adoption in other ways geometrical be accepted only in duly justified cases.

3. The manholes can also be centered or off-center relative to the alignment of the collector, the latter used especially in situations of greatest potential risk for personal exploration.

Article 107

(Installation)

1. The manholes must be solidly built, easily accessible and fitted with resistant closures that prevent, when necessary, the passage of gases to the atmosphere.

2. the installation of manholes is mandatory:

a) at the junction of collectors;

b) the direction change points, tilt and diameter of collectors;

c) in straight alignments, where the maximum spacing between consecutive manholes should not exceed, respectively, 60 and 100 m, as it's not visitable visitable collectors or collectors, ie, with higher internal height 1.60 m;

d) the maximum deviations referred to in the previous paragraph may be increased in the first case, according to the cleaning means available, and in the second, in special situations duly justified.

3. In implementing the manholes must be respected the following constructive aspects:

a) the least useful dimension to plant a manhole should not be less than 1.00 or 1.25 m to depths less than or greater than or equal to 2.50 m, respectively;

b) the relationship between the width and depth of a manhole should take into account the operability and safety of operating staff;

c) insertion of one or more other collectors must be in the direction of flow, to ensure tangency of secondary liquid to main vein; there changes in diameters of collectors that fall in the same chamber, the agreement must be made to ensure the continuity of the top generating inside the collectors;

d) direction changes, diameter and inclination taking place in a manhole, should take place by means of semicircular gutters constructed in the doorway, the height equal to 2/3 of the largest diameter, to ensure the continuity of the vein net;

e) the thresholds must have a minimum slope of 10% towards the gutters;

f) in areas where the water table lies on a continuous or seasonal basis, above the manhole threshold, should ensure the tightness of the walls and the fund;

g) the depth of manholes is conditioned by the depth of the collector; in this case depth exceeds 5 m must be constructed, for safety reasons, spaced at maximum levels of 5.00 m, with divergent passage openings;

h) for rainwater and waste water systems falls of more than 1.00 m, the threshold must be protected to avoid erosion;

i) in unitary systems or domestic wastewater is to provide a guided down the edge of the manhole where the gap to win is greater than 0.50 m, and a satisfactory agreement in the gutter, where the gap is less than this value.

Article 108

(Nature Materials)

1. The threshold must be of simple or reinforced concrete foundation depending on the conditions.

2. The body must be of simple or reinforced concrete or hydraulic masonry stone, brick or cement blocks.

3. The cover must be of simple or reinforced concrete according to the foreseeable strain.

4. The closure device must be cast iron of lamellar or spheroidal graphite, or cast or rolled steel, with the use of the latter is only allowed effective protection against corrosion is ensured.

5. The cover can be further reinforced concrete or combination of concrete with one of the above materials, in which case there is a satisfactory adhesion between them.

6. The fixed wireless access devices should be of cast iron of lamellar or spheroidal graphite, or another demonstrably resistant material or suitably protected against corrosion, along the work life.

7. They can also be used other materials provided they meet the necessary conditions of use and deserve the prior approval of the Lands, Public Works and Transport, which may subject to prior verification by the Macao Civil Engineering Laboratory - LECM.

SECTION B

Input devices on the network

Article 109

(Installation)

1. There should be implementation of gutters or sinks:

a) the lows of public roads;

b) at intersections in order to avoid lane crossing the runoff;

c) along the route of the trench so that the width of the water level does not exceed the values recommended in the hydraulic design criteria.

2. In implementing network in input devices must be respected the following constructive aspects:

a) the body must be rectangular;

b) the hydraulic seal can be obtained through sifónica sifónica sink or plate, and there should be only in unit systems which provide for significant release of hydrogen sulfide;

c) the input device comprises a removable grill and sinks in a lateral opening in the case of gutters;

d) the useful flow area must have a minimum value of one third of the total area of the grid;

e) access to the gutter and sinks should be provided in any case in order to facilitate maintenance operations, which can be done directly by the grid, in the case of sinks or through removable closure device and placed in the ride level in the case of gutters;

f) in specific situations which provide for a significant knock-on solid materials by rainwater, with serious consequences for collectors or to the receiving environment, should be considered the existence of removable retainers baskets;

g) the existence of devices referred to in the preceding paragraph implies effective assistance of cleanliness and repair;

h) the dimensions to be met by the gutters and drains are generally as follows:

- Gutters
width lateral opening 450 mm
Side opening height 100 mm
- Sinks
Grid width 430 mm
grid length 547 mm
tolerance of different dimensions however, whenever there are justifiable reasons.

Article 110

(Hydraulic sizing)

1. The hydraulic efficiency of gutters and drains varies with the flow rate of runoff, with longitudinal and cross slope of the street layout, and the input surface of the geometry (for depression or level).

2. In the hydraulic design of these devices must meet up to the values of surface flow to drain, to flow capacity collectors flock to these flow rates, and also the other key factors such as inconvenience to the car traffic, trend for clogs, safety and cost.

3. In the hydraulic design shall take account of the simultaneous satisfaction of three criteria of stormwater runoff in ditches, for return periods of 2 to 10 years, and the consequent location of input devices:

a) criterion does not overflow, which also require the maximum water depth along the sidewalk curb height, which may be the height of this net 2 cm off;

b) criteria of speed limitation in that it limits the speed of runoff to prevent the floor from wear and cumbersome and should not its value exceed 3 m / s;

c) criteria of the maximum width limiting the water level in the gutter next to the curb, as it limits the maximum width of the water level in ditches 1.00 m, along the curb of the rides, to prevent water projection in trips to the passage of vehicles.

Article 111

(Connection to the network)

The dimensions of the connection of collector drains and sinks to the public should be made taking into account the flow to drain, respecting the minimum diameter of 200 mm.

SECTION C

Unloaders

Article 112

(Hydraulic sizing)

1. Rate of flow dimensioning must take account of both quantitative and qualitative aspects.

2. The qualitative aspects are related to the downloaded degree of dilution of the effluent that the receiving means is capable of accepting and in this sense, be preferred to dischargers with devices which ensure the routing of floating solids to the treatment plant.

3. Quantitative aspects relate to the choice of one value, meeting the quality requirements referred to, does not affect the proper functioning of downstream facilities (treatment plant, the most common situation) and the economics of the overall system cost It is recommended, in general, an amount not to exceed six times the average flow of dry weather.

CHAPTER XII

Additional facilities

SECTION A

Lifting systems

Article 113

(Hydraulic sizing)

1. When designing the vacuum chamber must be carefully analyzed the variability of tributaries flow, which becomes particularly important in unitary systems.

2. The volume of the chamber should be calculated according to the starting frequency of lifting equipment, with the aim to avoid retention times in excess of 5 to 10 minutes for medium flow rates tributaries.

3. The inside diameter of the pumping duct is defined in terms of a technico study covering the entire period of operation, it is advisable that its value is not less than 100 mm and the minimum flow velocity is 0.7 m / s. In exceptional cases where the diameter is less than this value, must be considered with particular attention to the problem of harrowing to retain solids.

4. The protection devices must be defined in relation to the surrounding of minimum and maximum pressures from hydraulic shock occurrence of transients in more predictable unfavorable situation.

Article 114

(Constructive aspects)

1. In lift systems there to consider the preliminary treatment device, dumpers, the suction chambers (or take) the lifting equipment, lifting pipes and control devices and protection.

2. Depending on the characteristics of the inflow wastewater and the need for the downstream protection system may provide for the use of desanders, crates or grinders.

3. The shape of the chamber should be such as to prevent the accumulation of solids in the dead zones, which requires proper gradient background.

4. The lifting equipment may comprise electric pump, submersible or non groups, Archimedes screws, or by ejectors. The definition and characterization of the electric pump groups should be taken into consideration the following:

a) the maximum permissible number of starts per hour for the equipment to be installed;

b) the maximum speed of rotation;

c) the installation, at least two identical lifting devices each having a draft power and intended to function as mutual active reserve;

d) the possibility of simultaneous operation in case of emergency.

5. In the definition and characterization of aerial pipelines must be taken into account:

a) the longitudinal profile is preferably always up, should not the piezometric line intersects the conduct, even at zero flow situations;

b) the surrounding should be set minimum and maximum pressures from the occurrence of transients and verified the need, or not, protection agencies;

c) where if you want to release the air piping should be employed, preferably the pressure pipes;

d) should be avoided whenever possible, the placement of the suction lifting conduits; in case of absolute necessity windy appropriate the waste is to be used;

e) all the low points of the pipeline and, where appropriate, in intermediate dots, should be sized bottom outlets to allow emptying within an acceptable time period;

f) must be analyzed impulses in turns and singular points, foreseeing the massive mooring calculation in situations where the soil will not stand by you;

g) the lengths of aerial pipes must be minimized in order to avoid the serious consequences of the production of hydrogen sulfide downstream.

6. The lift systems must be provided upstream of a weir connected to a resource collector, to cope with the occurrence of damage, need for placement out of service or excessive influx of waste water.

7. The electromechanical organs, integrated into pumping stations inserted in urban areas, must determine, for its operation, noise whose noise level average, measured at 3.5 meters from neighboring buildings, does not exceed 45 dB (A).

SECTION B

Inverted siphons

Article 115

(Hydraulic sizing)

1. In the hydraulic design of inverted siphons must have particular attention to the need to maintain self-cleaning speeds to the expected range of flow rates, which should ensure the occurrence of a speed between 0.7 m / s and 1, 0 m / s at least once a day, at the beginning of operation.

2. In calculating the load losses should be included in the losses located at the entrance and exit, in bends, valves, joints and other singularities.

3. The retention time should not exceed 10 minutes, as a rule, in order to minimize the formation of hydrogen sulfide gas.

Article 116

(Constructive aspects)

As regards the construction of inverted siphons shall be observed the following rules:

a) installation of at least two conduits in parallel, for situations that provides for great variability in flow rates;

b) the various siphon branches, where they exist, must be connected by lateral spillways to control;

c) installation of manholes upstream and downstream of the inverted siphons;

d) installation of louvers in each of the branches, the upstream and downstream chambers;

e) the longitudinal profile of the pipes should have inclinations compatible with the possibility of an effective cleaning;

f) must be provided for bottom discharge devices or, alternatively, the installation pit or tank, where the waste water can be subsequently removed and disposed of.

SECTION C

Desanders

Article 117

(Hydraulic sizing)

The sizing grit chambers should be aimed at removing particles having dimensions equal to or greater than 0.2 mm to prevent the deposition of organic matter, so that it must ensure a flow rate between 0.15 and 0.30 m / s .

Article 118

(Constructive aspects)

1. grit chambers can be installed upstream of the treatment plant, possibly the amount of lifting facilities and siphons, and the headwaters of unit or separative systems of rainwater when upstream exists a watershed silted high amounts of materials.

2. grit chambers must be made of two compartments whenever possible, to facilitate periodic removal of sand without disturbing the flow or, in their absence, have an alternative hydraulic circuit.

3. Retention chambers upstream stormwater unit or separative networks must have high capacity, so reducing the frequency of removing sand.

SECTION D

Bars Cams

Article 119

(Hydraulic sizing)

The dimensions of the grid must be adjusted to a flow rate between 0.5 and 0.8 m / s to its said effective section. These values must be verified for the dry flow and full flow, respectively.

Article 120

(Constructive aspects)

1. Crates chambers comprise the access channel, the actual grids, and the collection and removal of retained devices.

2. Installations with power harrows must be designed with a reserve unit, in parallel, or at least with an alternative hydraulic circuit provided with manual grade.

3. The width of the bars to the access channel must be greater than the diameter or width of the influent manifold and being equal to the width of the bars themselves, avoiding dead spaces. The channel length must be long enough to avoid eddies along the bars and the threshold should be generally lower than the manifold in order to compensate for the superelevation water level caused by the pressure drop in bars.

SECTION E

Septic tanks

Article 121

(Installation)

1. The installation of a septic tank must necessarily be complemented with infiltration filtration device or the soil.

2. They should ensure minimum clearances to 1.5 m in relation to buildings and property boundaries and 3.0m in respect of large trees and water pipes.

3. It is not permissible to its installation upstream of water sources at distances less than 15 m, and shall require up to 30 m in the case of soil sand and pebbles and greater distances in the case of fractured rocks.

4. The septic tank of the roof slab should not be buried at the depth exceeding 0.5 m.

Article 122

(Hydraulic sizing)

1. The net volume of a septic tank should be determined by the following calculation expression:

V = P [Ct r .C d (t. And - t d) + (C f - C ed) / 2t d]

on what,

V - net volume (m 3)

P - population (inhabitants)

C - Waste water capita (1 / person / day)

T r - the retention time (days)

C d - capitation digested sludge (1 / person / day)

t and - time between cleanings (days)

T d - sludge digestion time (days)

C f - capitation fresh sludge (1 / person / day)

2. The minimum of wastewater retention time should be 3 days for septic tanks up to 20 m 3 and 2 days for septic tanks of greater capacity.

3. The time between cleanings must not exceed two years.

Article 123

(Constructive provisions)

1. septic tanks must have at least 2 or 3 compartments according to their capacity is less or greater than 20 m 3.

2. they must have access at the entrance openings, outside and intercom between local chambers.

3. The compartments must have the inclined bottom towards the areas under the access openings for sludge removal effect.

4. Provision should be made septa into and out of the pit in order to ensure the reassurance of the flow and retention of floating bodies and skimmings.

Article 124

(Infiltration into the soil or filtration device)

1. A septic tank should be complemented with an infiltration pit when the ground is permeable between 2.0 to 3.0 m deep and the water table is situated at lower level.

2. The septic tank should be supplemented with infiltration trench or bed when the ground is permeable between 1.0 and 2.0 m deep and the water table is situated at lower level.

3. The septic tank should be complemented with filter sand filter trench or buried when the ground is impermeable and the water table is situated at a depth greater than 1.5 m.

4. The septic tank should be complemented with a filter landfill when the water table is situated at depths less than 1.5 m.

SECTION F

Meters and loggers

Article 125

(Installation)

Constructive provisions for measuring flow rates shall be specified in the following points:

a) the entry treatment plants;

b) the final discharge into the recipient, or the amount thereof, when possible;

c) downstream of lifting facilities of a reasonable size;

d) immediately downstream of industrial areas;

e) at strategic points carefully selected.

CHAPTER XIII

Final destination

Article 126

(Domestic and industrial wastewater)

1. The final destination of domestic and industrial wastewater should ensure their proper integration in the surrounding, as regards the protection of natural resources, public health and the global economy work.

2. Release of wastewater in the receiving environment should comply with general standards of constant discharge of Annex 10, with appropriate use of installation of treatment.

3. In the case of buildings, buildings or group housing developments located in areas not served by public wastewater disposal systems, or drainage systems serving a population of less than 400 inhabitants, should be provided with adequate Septic complementary device infiltration into the soil or filtration.

Article 127

(Rainwater)

1. The final destination of rainwater must ensure that discharges are compatible with the characteristics of the receiving water lines, causing no overflow or flooding, erosion and beds, silting or deposition of solid materials.

2. Where necessary should be carried out for the purpose of carrying out settlement construction and defense of the bed and banks.

TITLE III BUILDING WATER SUPPLY - TECHNICAL PROVISIONS

CHAPTER XIV

General

Article 128

(Purpose and scope)

1. This title is to define the technical conditions to be satisfied by the building of water distribution in order to be assured its proper functioning, security is preserving the health and comfort in buildings.

2. This Title applies to land water distribution systems.

Article 129

(Terminology, symbols and units system)

The terminology and symbology used and the units in which are expressed the various quantities must comply with the directives established in this area. So the terminology and symbols to be adopted shall be as set out in Annexes 11 and 12, respectively. The units should be those of the International System.

Article 130

(Systems of Separation)

The building systems fed by the public should be independent of any water distribution system with other sources, including wells or holes.

Article 131

(Material Quality)

1. All materials to be applied in distribution systems, ancillary parts and use of devices should be free from damage and, by the very nature or adequate protection, they must have good corrosion resistance conditions, internal and external, and efforts that will be subject.

2. The materials to be used in pipes and accessory parts distribution systems should be those whose application is accepted by the entity responsible for the supply and public water distribution and approved by the Lands, Public Works and Transport.

3. The application of new materials or construction processes for which there are no officially adopted specifications or sufficient practical use, is subject to approval by the Lands, Public Works and Transport, which may subject to prior verification of compliance by LECM - Macao Civil Engineering Laboratory.

4. The verification of conformity referred to above may take the form of recognition if the materials are in accordance with the ISO or other internationally recognized.

Article 132

(Registration systems)

The entity responsible for public water distribution system must keep on file the records of building systems and should include them in the least:

a) technical specifications of the building system with an overview of the main features;

b) a description and justification of the solutions adopted in stating the nature of materials and supplies and plumbing installation conditions;

c) hydraulic design;

d) the parts designed to be included in the location of pipelines, accessories and complementary facilities of systems, in plan and section, the minimum scale of 1: 100, indicating the diameters and materials of plumbing, as well as isometric layout or schematic.

Article 133

(Identification of conduits)

The pipes must be installed in sight identified depending on the nature of the transported water, according to the following colors: blue for water intended for human consumption; red for fire extinguishing water.

CHAPTER XV

Design of systems

Article 134

(Integration in the overall project)

The design of building water distribution systems should aim at solving problems in a global perspective, technical and economic, coordinated with the architecture, structure and other special facilities of the building.

Article 135

(Remodeling or expansion of existing systems)

1. In remodeling or expansion of existing systems should be subject to the provisions of this title.

2. When there are tip flow increase, must prove to the sufficiency of the hydraulic capacity of the pipelines transport and any additional facilities the amount, subject to the operating conditions of the system as a whole.

Article 136

(Design of new systems)

1. In designing new systems is necessary to consider:

a) the pressure available in the general power supply and the need to use devices;

b) the type and number of using devices;

c) the desired degree of comfort;

d) to minimize water retention times in plumbing.

2. The operating pressures in use of devices should be between 50 and 600 kPa is recommended, for reasons of comfort and durability of materials, which remain between 150 and 300 kPa.

3. The operating pressures in the use of devices for firefighting should be between 400 and 700 kPa in the case of fire hydrants and rigid hose reels.

4. Where the public can not ensure the necessary pressures should be an sobrepressora installation with surge tank, ensuring the absence of direct pumping from the public network.

Article 137

(Pollution prevention)

Any link between the building of water distribution network and building networks of sewerage is not allowed, with the supply of drinking water to sanitary appliances be carried out without jeopardizing its potability, preventing contamination, either by contact or a wastewater intake in case of depression in the network.

Article 138

(Fire-fighting Systems)

1. It is mandatory to provide fire-fighting systems in buildings to construct, remodel or expand, in accordance with the rules and regulations and specifications of the Fire Department.

2. The water supply for fire fighting should be ensured by the public or by supplying other available sources and supplemented, when necessary and in accordance with legislation and regulations and specifications of the Fire Department, for reserve deposits.

Article 139

(Hot water systems)

1. The hot water production and distribution systems must guarantee the minimum temperatures of use necessary in the use of devices depending on the degree of comfort and economy desired, using, if necessary, forced circulation.

2. In residential buildings is mandatory to provide production and distribution of hot water to kitchens and sanitary systems.

CHAPTER XVI

Building blocks for scaling

Article 140

(Use devices)

In the preparation of studies on building water supply should be indicated in pieces designed the types and location of user devices, as well as powered devices.

Article 141

(Instantaneous flow rates)

1. The instantaneous flow rates to be paid to use devices must comply with the specific purpose for which they are intended, and the minimum values to be taken, those listed in Table 1.

2. The instantaneous flow to be allocated to industrial machinery and other unspecified appliances must be established in accordance with the instructions of the manufacturers.

3. The instantaneous flow rates to be paid to the use of fire-fighting systems devices must be set in accordance to the technical provisions of the legislation and regulations and specifications of the Fire Department.

TABLE 1

User devices:	Minimum flows (l / s)
Individual sink	0.10
Collective sink (for spout)	0.05
Bidet	0.10
Bathtub	0.25
Individual shower	0.15
Dump sink with Φ15 mm tap	0.15
Toilet bowl flushing device	0.10
Urinal with individual tap	0.15
Sink dishwasher	0.20
drinking fountain	0.10
Dishwasher	0.15
Machine or laundry tub	0.20
Toilet bowl with flow meter	1.50
Urinal with flow meter	0.50
Mouth watering or washing of Φ15 mm	0.30
Ditto Φ20 mm	0.45

ARTICLE 142

(Simultaneity coefficients)

1. It should be taken into account the possibility of non-simultaneous operation of all devices used, considering calculation in determining the most appropriate flow coefficient concurrency in a given section, understood as the ratio between the maximum concurrent flow (flow calculation), and the cumulative flow rate of all the use of powered devices that section.
2. is given in Annex 13 a curve, taking into account the simultaneity coefficients, provides the calculation of flows for a medium comfort level, due to accumulated flow, which can be used for current cases without housing flowmeters.
3. Where there are flow meters, flow calculation can be obtained by adding the flow rates obtained for the remaining devices through said curve in the preceding paragraph, the flowmeters calculating flow rates, considering the respective instantaneous flow rates and constant simultaneity in Table 2.

TABLE 2

Number of installed flowmeters	In simultaneous use
1	1
2 to 10	2
11 to 20	3
21 to 50	4
greater than 50	5

Article 143 (Pressures on the public network)

For building the network calculation purposes shall be provided by the entity responsible for the public water distribution system, the values of maximum and minimum pressures in public at the insertion point of that.

CHAPTER XVII Plumbing

SECTION A Cold water

Article 144 (Goal)

The land network of cold water to ensure its distribution in good quantitative and qualitative conditions to ensure the comfort, health and safety of users.

Article 145 (Flow rates of calculation)

Calculating flow rates in the building of cold water network must be based on the instantaneous flow rates attributed to use of devices and concurrency ratios.

Article 146

(Hydraulic sizing)

1. In the hydraulic design of the building cold water network must be taken into account:

a) calculating flow rates;

b) the flow rates, which should be between 0.5 and 2.0 m / s;

c) the roughness of the material.

2. In flowmeters power extensions to toilet basins should take into account the minimum pressures of the service whose values match those listed in Table 3 diameters.

3. These diameters can however be reduced by introducing a clearinghouse, considering in this case a consumption corresponding to a normal-use device.

Table 3

Pressure (kPa)	Diameter (mm)
200	25
80	32
50	40

Article 147 (Track)

1. The layout of the pipes should be composed of straight, vertical and horizontal sections connected together by appropriate fittings, the first should have slight inclination to facilitate the outflow of air, it is recommended as a 0.5% approximate value.
2. The requirement of accessories may be waived if using flexible conduits.

Article 148

(Installation)

1. Extension of introduction of buildings in horizontal property regime must be installed in common areas.

2. The inner plumbing of the building cold water network can be installed on demand, in galleries, gutters or ceilings, sheathed or embedded.

3. The non-embedded conduits are secured by spaced clamps in accordance with the material characteristics.

4. They must be taken of the problems of expansion and contraction of the pipeline, including installation joints and type of clamps to use.

5. The exterior of the building plumbing cold water network can be buried in trenches, placed on walls or installed in gutters and must always be protected from mechanical and thermally isolated actions when necessary.

6. The lines must not be installed under the following conditions:

a) under foundation elements;

b) embedded in structural elements;

c) embedded in floors, unless flexible, sheathed;

d) in hard to reach places;

e) spaces belonging to chimneys and ventilation systems.

Article 149

(Prevention of corrosion)

In the draft of the gross water networks should be considered as measures to mitigate the corrosive phenomena, and for this purpose:

a) the metallic plumbing network be performed, preferably with the same material;

b) in the case of different materials, the most noble material be installed downstream of the less noble, proceeding to its isolation by dielectric together;

c) laying of metal pipes of different networks can be done without the contact points between themselves or any metal parts of the construction;

d) the plumbing settlement built not be done with inert carriers, the same material, or next lower nobility material;

e) the through walls and floors to be made via sheaths suitable material of lower nobility at or close to the pipe;

f) metal pipes are placed wherever possible, not embedded;

g) be avoided laying metal pipe in potentially aggressive materials;

h) the buried conduits be performed, preferably with non-metallic materials.

Article 150

(Nature Materials)

1. The pipes and accessories are the cold water of outdoor networks can be galvanized steel, cast iron, hard PVC, copper or stainless steel, or other, must be verified in any case the provisions of Article 131

2. In foreign networks, pipes and fittings can be made of cast iron, cement or rigid PVC, or other, must take place in any case the provisions of Article 131

SECTION B

Hot water

Article 151

(Goal)

The land network of hot water to ensure good distribution on pressure conditions, flow rate, temperature and quality.

Article 152

(Flow rates of calculation)

The building of the hot water network calculation flow rates shall be obtained in accordance with the provisions of Article 145

Article 153

(Hydraulic sizing)

In the hydraulic design of the building hot water system must follow the provisions of paragraph 1 of Article 146

Article 154

(Track)

1. The layout of the hot water pipes must comply with the provisions of Article 147

2. The hot water pipes should be placed, where possible, in parallel with the cold water piping and above these.

3. The minimum distance between cold water and hot water pipes is 50 mm.

Article 155

(Installation)

The hot water plumbing installation must comply with the provisions of Article 148, taking on particular importance with the provisions imposed by the expansion and contraction of the pipes, set out in paragraph 4 of that Article.

Article 156

(Isolation)

1. The hot water lines should be insulated with suitable products, rot-proof, non-corrosive, non-combustible and resistant to moisture.

2. They can not be isolated from the leads to the device use and their return extensions when short lengths.

3. The respective conduits and insulation must be protected where there is a risk of water vapor condensation, infiltration or mechanical shock.

Article 157

(Prevention of corrosion)

1. In the project design and building networks of hot water should be taken into account measures for the mitigation of corrosion phenomena specified in Article 149

2. The temperatures of use of galvanized steel piping should not exceed 60 ° C in order to minimize is the problem of corrosion.

3. If necessary keep temperatures higher than indicated in paragraph 2 shall be taken special care in selecting the material to use, installation and with the safety of users.

Article 158

(Nature Materials)

The pipes and accessories that make up the land network of hot water may be copper, stainless steel, galvanized steel or other materials should be verified in any case the provisions of Article 131

SECTION C

Fire fighting

Article 159

(Goal)

1. The building water supply for fire fighting should ensure the distribution in good condition flow and pressure, according to the laws and regulations in force and the specifications of the Fire Department.

2. The land network for fire fighting must have its own tank and lifting system, so as to ensure pressures between 400 and 700 kPa in all the hydrants.

3. It is assumed direct connection to the public if it is assured pressure of 250 kPa in the most unfavorable hydrant.

Article 160

(Instantaneous flow rates)

The minimum instantaneous flows to consider the hydrants are 15.0 l / s in residential buildings and services and 22.5 l / s in buildings for other purposes.

Article 161

(Flow rates of calculation)

Those of building network of firefighting calculating flow rates should be based on the instantaneous flow assigned to hydrants installed, assuming that no more than two or three hydrants working simultaneously depending on whether, respectively, of buildings for residential and service purposes, and buildings for other purposes.

Article 162

(Hydraulic sizing)

In the hydraulic design of the piping of the building fire-fighting network must be taken into account:

a) calculating flow rates;

b) the need to ensure a pressure between 400 and 700 kPa at all hydrants;

c) the minimum diameter of the branch feeding the fire hydrants (defined in accordance with Article 176);

d) the roughness of the material.

Article 163

(Track)

The layout of the building plumbing network of firefighting must comply with the provisions of Article 147

Article 164

(Installation)

The pipes of the building network Fire fighting should be located in common areas of the building easily accessible and comply with the provisions of Article 148

Article 165

(Prevention of corrosion)

In firefighting building networks should be subject to the measures specified in Article 149

Article 166

(Nature Materials)

1. The pipes and accessories that make up the building network Firefighting can be cast iron, galvanized steel or other, must be verified in any case the provisions of Article 131

2. Joins and materials of pipes and fittings should provide adequate fire resistance.

CHAPTER XVIII

Elements accessories Network

SECTION A

Taps and flowmeters

Article 167

(Implantation)

The valves and flow meters must be placed in accessible locations in order to allow easy operation and maintenance.

Article 168

(Clearing houses)

In the case of flowmeters fitted with clearing house, it must have a minimum capacity of 12 liters.

Article 169

(Nature Materials)

Taps and flow meters can be brass, with or without chrome plating, or other materials that meet the required conditions of use and merit the approval of the Lands, Public Works and Transport, which may subject to prior verification the Macao Civil Engineering Laboratory - LECM.

SECTION B

Valves

Article 170

(Implantation)

The valve should be placed in locations accessible to allow its easy operation and maintenance.

Article 171

(Installation)

Installation of valves is required:

a) sectioning to: the individual introduction extensions, the power extensions of toilets and kitchens and the amount of cisterns, of flowmeters, clothes washing machine and dishwasher, the hot water production equipment, traps water and also immediately upstream and downstream counters;

b) retention: upstream producers appliances - hot water accumulators and yet immediately the counter amount;

c) security: the power producing devices - hot water accumulators;

d) reducing pressure: the introduction of extensions whenever the pressure exceeds 600 kPa and the specific needs of the equipment require; in the case of fire-fighting network this value is 700 kPa.

Article 172

(Nature Materials)

1. The valves can be brass, bronze, steel and PVC, or others, if they are in accordance with Article 131

2. Valves must be nobility of material equal to or as close as possible to the material of the pipes where they are located.

SECTION C

Counters

Article 173

(Definition)

1. It is the organization responsible for the public distribution system of water defining the type, caliber and metrological class counter to install.

2. These are parameters that determine the setting of the counter:

a) the physical and chemical characteristics of the water;

b) the maximum allowable working pressure;

c) the calculation of flow in the building distribution network;

d) causing pressure drop.

Article 174

(Installation)

1. It must be installed for each consumer a meter, ensuring measurement of all inputs, these may be placed together or separately, constitute, therefore, a meter battery.

2. space for the counter or counters battery and its accessories must comply with the type schemes set out in Annex 14.

Article 175

(Localization)

1. In buildings adjoining the road or public spaces, the counters should be located in the interior, in the entrance area or in communal areas depending on whether one or more consumers.

2. In buildings with private playgrounds, the counters should be located:

a) the street near the entrance zone contiguous with the public highway, in case a consumer only;

b) inside the building, common areas or on the patio at the entrance adjacent to the road, where several consumers.

SECTION D

Hydrants

Article 176

(Minimum diameter)

1. The minimum diameter of hydrants is 63.5 mm, with female joining springs 'standard', compatible with the equipment of the fire department.

2. The minimum diameter of the rigid hose reels is 19 mm.

3. risers installed in buildings of height classes P, M and A, subclass A1, except for industrial purposes and locations for public assembly, have minimum diameters of 80 mm and can only have a hydrant per floor.

4. The risers installed in buildings of height classes P, M and A for industrial purposes and locations for public assembly, and the height of classes A, A2 subclass, and MA, for all purposes, have minimum diameters of 100 mm and can have up to two hydrants per floor.

Article 177

(Localization)

1. Inside the buildings, the hydrants shall be located in conspicuous places easily accessible, properly marked and preferably fenced housed in boxes or niches.

2. The fire hydrants should be installed at a height of between 0.80 and 1.20 m above the floor.

3. The hydrant should be located in stairwells or the common use of spaces of the building and to ensure adequate coverage of the areas to be protected.

4. The rigid pipe spools must be installed along the exhaust path and a nozzle should not be located more than 1.35 m above the floor.

5. Water milestones and wall hydrants and outdoor deck shall be located in places easily accessible to vehicles from the Fire Department.

6. The types of fire hydrants, their characteristics and constructive aspects, must comply with the laws and regulations in force and meet with the approval of the Fire Department.

CHAPTER XIX

Additional facilities

SECTION A

Reservoirs

Article 178

(Terms of Service)

1. The water storage for human consumption in buildings should only be permitted in the event that the public does not effectively guarantee the gross consumption, and in this case is conditioned, for public health protection reasons users, the renewal in a whole with frequency of at least once per day.

2. The water reservoirs for human consumption are subject to inspection and cleaning operations.

3. The water storage for fire fighting is done in its own independent reservoirs and can not be used for other purposes.

Article 179 (Sizing)

1. The net volume of shells intended for human consumption should not, except in duly justified cases, exceed the amount corresponding to the average daily volume for the month of increased consumption for the foreseeable occupation.
2. The minimum volume of deposits of water reserves to supply fire hydrants and rigid hose reels should be set in accordance with the laws and regulations in force.
3. In general, the minimum volume of deposits referred to in paragraph 2 is a function of gross floor area of the largest in the conditions listed in Table 4.
4. Where the laws and regulations, or specifications of the Fire Department, requiring the assembly in the buildings of other firefighting systems using water as the extinguishing agent, the minimum volume of its independent deposits shall be determined in accordance with legislation and specific regulations of each.

Table 4

Gross floor area	Minimum required volume
Up to 250 m^2	18 m^3
250 to 500 m^2	27 m^3
500 to 1000 m^2	36 m^3
Above 1000 m^2	45 m^3

Article 180 (Localization)

1. The location of the reservoirs should allow easy inspection and maintenance.
2. When the water storage is intended for human consumption, the tanks must have thermal protection and be away from places subject to extreme temperatures.

Article 181 (Constructive aspects)

1. The containers shall be waterproof and equipped with waterproof and resistant closures.
2. The interior edges should be rounded and the threshold having a minimum gradient of 1% to the cleaning box to facilitate emptying.

3. Tanks with water intended for human consumption and useful capacity equal to or greater than 6 m^3 should be constituted by at least two cells, prepared to work separately but, in normal operation, intercommunicate.
4. The ventilation system, suitably protected with fine-mesh net, mosquito netting type, non-corrosive material must prevent the direct entrance of light and ensure the frequent renewal of the air in contact with water.
5. The threshold and the inner wall surfaces must be treated with suitable coatings that allow for effective cleaning, conservation of resistant elements and the maintenance of water quality.
6. Entry and exit the water in the reservoirs must be positioned so as to facilitate the movement of the entire body of water stored.
7. The fund and coverage of the tanks must not be common to the structural elements of the building or the walls common to the walls of neighboring buildings.

Article 182 (Circuits and accessory organs)
Each tank or reservoir cell must have:

a) water inlet located at least 50 mm above the maximum level of the free surface of the reservoir discharge, equipped with an automatic valve intended for interrupting the power storage when the maximum level is reached;
b) outputs for distribution, protected with drain and put at least 150 mm from the bottom;
c) discharger placed surface, at least 50 mm from maximum storage and conduit freefall discharge and visible protected with fine-mesh net, mosquito netting type, dimensioned for not less flow to the feed maximum tank ;
d) bottom outlet located on the doorstep, with suitable valve associated with cleaning box;
e) access to the inside with locking device to prevent the entry of solid waste or runoff.

Article 183 (Nature Materials)

1. The reservoirs can be concrete, brick masonry or cement blocks, steel or other materials, provided they observe the provisions of Article 131
2. In water supplies for human consumption, materials and coatings used in its construction should not change water quality affects public health.

SECTION B

Pumping facilities and sobrepressoras

Article 184

(Hydraulic sizing)

In the design of the facility should be taken into account:

a) the flow rate calculation;

b) the pressure available upstream;

c) the delivery head;

d) the maximum permissible number of starts per hour for the equipment to be installed;

e) installing at least two identical electropump groups, usually intended to serve as mutual reserve active and exceptionally together for reinforcement of the lifting capacity.

Article 185

(Constructive aspects)

1. The lifting or sobrepressoras facilities should be located in common areas and ventilated to allow easy inspection and maintenance.

2. The lifting or sobrepressoras facilities should be equipped with electric pump groups and equipped with protective control devices against water hammer, security and alarm systems, and essential accessories for its operation and maintenance.

3. The electric pump groups must be self-operating and have characteristics that do not change the water quality.

4. The reservoirs built in aerial installations must comply with the above in Section A of this chapter.

5. The protection devices must be defined in relation to the surrounding maximum and minimum pressure, resulting from the occurrence of hydraulic shock.

6. The operation of electromechanical organs shall determine, in busy places, average sound noise level not exceeding 30 dB (A); for that purpose should be used alone supports and elastic connections to pipes to mitigating the spread of noise.

Article 186

(Nature Materials)

Plumbing and accessories used must be of adequate strength materials to service pressures and vibrations.

SECTION C

Devices producing hot water

Article 187

(Criteria for selection and sizing)

The choice and dimensioning of hot water appliances producers must have regard to the desired degree of comfort, the required flow and pressure available.

Article 188

(Safety)

1. The safety of hot water producing devices must be ensured in its construction, the quality of trials and their location and installation.

2. the safety valve installation in storage heaters power extension is mandatory.

3. it should be applied hot water producers appliances complying with the provisions of Article 131

4. For safety reasons it is forbidden to install devices producing gas hot water in toilets.

In Annex 15 presents a scheme of the type water heaters connection.

CHAPTER XX

Verification, testing and disinfection

Article 189

(Goal)

All plumbing, before being put into service, should be subject to verification and testing in order to ensure the quality of implementation and its hydraulic functioning.

Article 190

(Verification)

Verification of the system compliance with the approved project and with the legal provisions should be made with plumbing and accessories in sight.

Article 191

(Leakage test)

1. The leak test should be conducted with the pipes, joints and accessories to view, conveniently locked and the plugged ends and devoid of use of devices.

2. The process of implementation and interpretation of the test is as follows:

a) connecting the pump test with a gauge located as close as possible to the point of smallest dimension of the section to be tested;

b) filling of the pipes via the pump, in order to release any air contained therein and ensuring a pressure equal to one and half times the maximum working pressure, with a minimum 900 kPa;

c) reading the gauge pump, which should not acknowledge any reduction for a minimum period of 30 minutes;

d) emptying of the test section.

Article 192

(Disinfection systems)

1. The building of water distribution systems for human consumption, including their reservoirs where they exist, after equipped with the use of devices and before being put into operation, should be disinfected operation with potassium permanganate, with following methodology:

a) Preparation of the disinfectant solution

Dissolve the required quantity of potassium permanganate (150 grams per m 3 of volume to disinfect the network) in water heated to a temperature between 40 ° C and 45 ° C, until a homogeneous solution as possible. The volume of solution should be 1/10 of the volume of the network to disinfect. This operation must be done the day before the start of disinfection.

b) prior Rinse network

Emptying the network through the existing drain taps in the lower points, fill and empty again, repeating the operation for approximately 2 hours to ensure effective cleaning.

c) Introduction of disinfectant solution

Through the injection point, introducing the disinfectant solution under pressure with a flow regulated as a function of flow fixed flow (1 part of solution to 9 parts of water flow). Open, from upstream to downstream (counter to the ends of the network) each faucet until the appearance of violet color. Close it and then move to the next. When the violet color appearing in the last tap, close it and stop the injection of disinfectant solution.

d) Contact Period

Maintaining the isolated network for a period of 48 hours in order to perform the disinfectant power.

e) Rinse end

Open the valves in the reverse order from that adopted in the filler, that is, from downstream to upstream, letting out water during about 2 hours, within a reasonable flow rate, a period which, in principle, be sufficient for final washing of the network.

f) Sampling

Take samples for confirmatory laboratory analysis of water quality.

2. Disinfection of building network should only be done once established and approved the connection extension by the entity responsible for the public water distribution system, and so that any backflow to the public of disinfectant solution is not possible, or any other building within the network, and which are previously disinfected parts located from the point of injection to the link extension, including this one.

Article 193

(Hydraulic Proof)

After testing for leaks and installation of the use of devices, you should check out the hydraulic behavior of the system by visual observation.

TITLE IV BUILDING DRAINAGE APPLICATIONS - TECHNICAL PROVISIONS

CHAPTER XXI

General

Article 194

(Purpose and scope)

1. This title is to define the technical conditions to be complied with in building drainage applications, so that your good overall operation is ensured, security is preserving the health and comfort in the room.

2. This Title applies to building systems of sewerage, whether domestic, industrial and storm.

Article 195

(Terminology, symbols and units system)

The terminology and symbology used and the units in which are expressed the various quantities must comply with the directives established in this area. The terminology and symbology to be adopted shall be as set out in Annexes 16 and 17, respectively. The units should be those of the International System.

Article 196

(Allowed Releases)

1. In domestic wastewater drainage systems the release is allowed:

a) wastewater from toilets, kitchens and domiciliary clothes washing areas;

b) waste water from the industrial activity and the kitchens of hotels and similar establishments after approval by the competent authority.

2. In storm sewage drainage system is allowed to launch:

a) water from irrigation of gardens and green spaces, streets washes, courtyards and car parks, ie those who in general are collected by gutters, sinks or drains;

b) water from the drainage of air conditioners, cooling circuits and heating systems since its temperature does not exceed 45 ° C;

c) water from swimming pools, water or similar storage tanks;

d) water from the subsoil drainage.

Article 197

(Released prohibited)

It is forbidden to release wastewater drainage systems, whatever their type of:

a) explosive or flammable materials;

b) debris, sand or ashes;

c) effluents at temperatures above the maximum permissible for the constituent materials of the system;

d) any substance, including food leftovers and other residues that can clog or damage the pipes and accessories, or derail the process of treatment;

e) all effluent whose release prohibition, contained in specific legislation.

Article 198

(Material Quality)

1. All materials to be applied in wastewater drainage systems and its accessories must be free from defects and, by the very nature or adequate protection, they must have good resistance to corrosion conditions and abrasion, and the effort that will be subject.

2. The materials to be used in pipes and accessory parts of wastewater drainage systems should be those whose application is approved by the Lands, Public Works and Transport.

3. The application of new materials or construction processes for which there are no officially adopted specifications or sufficient practical use, is subject to approval by the Lands, Public Works and Transport, which may subject to prior verification of compliance by LECM - Macao Civil Engineering Laboratory.

4. The verification of conformity referred to above may take the form of recognition if the materials are in accordance with the ISO or other internationally recognized.

Article 199

(Registration systems)

1. They must keep on file the records of building systems.

2. Of these entries should include at least:

a) technical specifications of the building system with an overview of the main features;

b) description and justification of the solutions adopted in stating the nature of materials and supplies and plumbing installation conditions;

c) Hydro-sanitary design;

d) drawings, to be included in:

- Location of pipelines, system accessories and complementary facilities in plant the minimum scale of 1: 100;
- Representation of the manifold building and complementary facilities in court, the minimum scale of 1: 100 and its connection to the public;
- Indication pavement quotas and sill of the inspection chambers;
- Indication of the sections, slopes and plumbing materials.

CHAPTER XXII

Design of systems

Article 200

(Integration in the overall project)

The design of wastewater drainage systems should aim at solving problems in a global perspective, technical and economic, coordinated with the architecture, structure and other special facilities of the building.

Article 201

(Systems of Separation)

1. the separation of drainage systems of domestic waste water from rainwater to the connection extension of chambers is mandatory.

2. Industrial waste water must be drained by the network itself.

3. industrial waste water after any treatment according to their physical, chemical and microbiological characteristics, can be connected to the drainage system of household waste water or storm, according to his analogy.

Article 202

(Ventilation systems)

Drainage systems of domestic wastewater should always have primary ventilation, obtained by prolonging downpipes until they are opened in the atmosphere. In this type of ventilation, these systems can provide, totally or partially, secondary ventilation, carried by extensions or ventilation shafts, as result of design option or set by requirement in this Title.

Article 203

(Remodeling and / or expansion of existing systems)

1. In the remodeling and / or expansion of existing systems should be subject to the provisions of this Title.

2. Where there is increased tip flow must prove to the sufficiency of the carrying capacity of downpipes and building sewers and ensure proper ventilation system.

3. In the areas provided with unit or partial separative systems, be admitted under exceptional circumstances, the connection of rainwater from courtyards to the building collector of domestic wastewater.

Article 204

(Design of domestic wastewater drainage systems)

1. installing ventilation column whenever the calculation of flow in the downpipe is mandatory, taller than 35 m, is greater than 1000 l / min.

2. All waste collected at the level not lower than the street layout where the public is installed collector that will discharge must be drained for this collector by gravity.

3. The wastewater sanitary facilities located below the level of the street network, such as the basement, even though the public located above the collector level must be pumped, thus fulfilling the hypothesis of a possible operation load of the square collector with flooding of basements.

Article 205

(Design of stormwater drainage systems)

1. In designing stormwater drainage systems should be considered in principle to connect to the public network.

2. In case of rainwater collected at the level below the street layout of these should be drained as referred to in Article 204

Article 206

(Pollution prevention)

It is not allowed any connection between the building of water distribution network and building networks of sewerage, with the supply of water to sanitary appliances be carried out without jeopardizing its potability, preventing contamination, either by contact or by Residual water aspiration, in case of depression in the network.

Article 207

(Prevention of Pollution)

The network of ventilation domestic wastewater must be completely independent of any other building ventilation system.

CHAPTER XXIII

Building blocks for scaling

Article 208

(Plumbing Fixtures)

In the preparation of studies on the drainage of domestic waste water is essential to know the types and number of sanitary appliances, as well as its location which information must be properly identified in pieces designed the project.

Article 209

(Discharge flow rates)

Discharge flow rates of sanitary appliances must comply with the specific purpose to which they are intended and the minimum values to be taken in the most common use of equipment, as specified in Annex 18.

Article 210

(Simultaneity coefficients)

1. Set up simultaneity coefficient as the ratio between the maximum concurrent flow surging network (flow calculation) in a given section and the sum of the discharge flow rates of the sanitary appliances (accumulated flow) draining until that section.

2. The simultaneity coefficients to be adopted may be obtained by means of analytical or graphical drawn from statistical data. In Annex 21, presents a curve which provides calculation of flow rates as a function of cumulative flow that may be used for the current cases housing without battery apparatus.

Article 211

(Precipitation)

In the preparation of studies on the rainwater drainage must resort to the intensity-duration-frequency curves of Macau, which provide the values of average maximum rainfall intensities for different durations and different return periods in accordance with the provisions of Article 72 o

Article 212

(Payback period and duration of precipitation)

The payback period to consider the hydraulic design of a building storm drainage network must be at least 5 years. The duration of the calculation of precipitation should be between 5 and 10 minutes depending on the type of building and tolerable risk of flooding.

CHAPTER XXIV

Plumbing

SECTION A

Discharge extensions

Article 213

(Flow rates of calculation)

1. The calculation of the flow of domestic wastewater discharge branches must be based on the discharge flows attributed to sanitary appliances and simultaneity coefficients, in accordance with Articles 209 and 210 When it is proposed the simultaneous use of sanitary appliances such as showers or urinals, the simultaneity coefficient to take is unity.

2. Discharge extensions calculation flow of rainwater should be based on the areas to drain and runoff coefficient under the conditions defined in Article 73, and taking into account the provisions of Articles 211 and 212

Article 214

(Hydraulic and sanitary sizing)

1. In hydraulic-sanitary design of the discharge extension of domestic waste water should be taken into account:

a) the calculation of flow rates referred to in Article 213;

b) the slopes, which should be between 10 and 40 mm / m;

c) the roughness of the material;

d) the risk of loss of water closure.

2. Provided that the maximum distances between the siphon and the vented section are met as indicated in Annex 22, the only systems with primary ventilation and ventilation systems with complete secondary (column and ventilation extensions) individual discharge extensions can It is dimensioned for a flow the full section. When exceeded those distances and only systems with primary ventilation column, the discharge branches must be dimensioned for a flow the middle section.

3. Non-individual discharge branches must always be dimensioned for a flow the middle section.

4. In the hydraulic design of stormwater discharge branches must be taken into account:

a) the calculation of flow rates referred to in Article 213;

b) the slopes, which should be between 10 and 40 mm / m;

c) the roughness of the material.

5. Discharge extensions rainwater can be dimensioned for a flow the full section.

Article 215

(Minimum diameter)

1. The Minimum diameter admitted to the individual discharge extension of sanitary appliances more common use are as set out in Annex 18.

2. The minimum diameter stormwater discharge extension is 50 mm.

Article 216

(Sequence sections)

The discharge branch section can not, under any circumstances, decrease in the flow direction.

Article 217

(Track)

1. The layout of the discharge extensions must be made in straight sections joined, as required, by transition curves which may be highly clear, or boxes or inspection chambers.

2. The connection of various sanitary appliances, with the exception of toilet bowls, sinks hospital or the like, to the same discharge station, it can be made by means of forks, inspection boxes or chambers.

3. In cases of toilet bowls or the like, the connection must be done through inspection chambers, in the absence of ventilation branches in other devices.

4. In the event of ventilation branch lines, the connection may be made by forks or inspection chambers.

5. All of the discharge extension lengths have to be accessible for cleaning, without the need for disassembly.

Article 218

(Connection to the downpipe or building collector)

1. The discharge connection of the branches to the drop tube must be made by means of forks and, at the building manifold through forks and inspection chambers.

2. In the absence of secondary ventilation is not allowed to connect exhaust extensions of black water and soap water on the same horizontal plane with insertion angle of more than 45 forks.

Article 219

(Localization)

Discharge extensions can be buried, placed in sight or built, but without affecting the strength of structural elements of the building and own plumbing.

Article 220

(Nature Materials)

Discharge extensions can be hard PVC, cast iron or other materials, provided that they satisfy the provisions of Article 198

SECTION B

Ventilation extensions

Article 221

(Sizing)

The diameter of the extension ventilation should be at least equal to 2/3 of the diameter of the respective unloading station.

Article 222

(Track)

1. The ventilation upward extensions are constituted by straight sections, should be as far as possible vertical to achieve a height of 0.15 m above the top level of the highest sanitary apparatus ventilating By this extension, extending then for sections with a minimum slope of 2% to facilitate the draining of condensed water to the discharge branch.

2. The insertion of ventilation extension on the discharge branch is made at a distance siphon airing not less than twice the diameter of this extension, not exceeding that indicated in Annex 22.

3. On devices in battery case does not make the individual secondary ventilation, collective ventilation extension must be linked to extension discharge, 3 in 3 sets.

Article 223

(Localization)

In locating ventilation extensions must comply with the provisions of Article 219

Article 224

(Nature Materials)

Ventilation extensions can be hard PVC, cast iron or other materials, provided that they satisfy the provisions of Article 198

SECTION C

Downspouts and gutters

Article 225

(Flow rates of calculation)

The downspouts and gutters of calculating flow rates shall be obtained according to the areas to drain, taking into account the provisions of Articles 211 and 212

Article 226

(Hydraulic sizing)

1. In the hydraulic design of gutters and downspouts should be taken into account:

a) flow rates referred to in Article 225;

b) the slope;

c) the roughness of the material;

d) the height of the water depth should be 0.7 of the height of the cross section.

2. Where justified, the value of the height of the water depth may differ from that value, whichever is higher or lower risk of overflow into the housing and the existence of surface spillways.

Article 227

(Nature Materials)

The gutters can be of galvanized sheet metal, fiber cement, rigid PVC or other materials provided that they satisfy the provisions of Article 198

SECTION D

Downpipes

Article 228

(Flow rates of calculation)

1. The flow calculation of falling domestic wastewater pipes must be based on the discharge flows attributed to sanitary appliances in it discharge and simultaneity coefficients, in accordance with Articles 209 and 210

2. The calculation flow of rainwater downpipes must be the sum of the gutters of calculating flow rates, gutters and discharge stations that contribute to them.

Article 229

(Hydraulic sizing)

1. In the hydraulic design of falling domestic wastewater pipes must be taken into account:

a) the calculation of flow rates referred to in Article 228;

b) the occupancy rate, which should not exceed 1/3 in systems with secondary ventilation and may vary between 1/3 and 1/7 in systems without secondary ventilation, due to the fall tube diameter, in accordance with Annex 20.

2. The diameter of the drop of domestic waste water pipes are constant throughout its length.

3. In the hydraulic design of the rainwater downpipes must be taken into account:

a) the calculation of flow rates referred to in Article 228;

b) the length of the drop tube;

c) the maximum permissible height of water running out, which is set according to the intended use of the area.

4. For determining the diameter of drop tubes domestic wastewater and rainwater downpipes can be used graphs shown in Annexes 23 and 25, respectively.

Article 230

(Minimum diameter)

1. The diameter wastewater downpipes, domestic or rain, can in no case be less than the largest of the diameters of the branches connected to it, with a minimum of 50 mm.

2. In industrial buildings should be adopted as minimum diameter of 150 mm for downpipes of industrial waste water when they ignore the types of industries to install.

Article 231

(Track)

1. The route of downpipes should be vertical and preferably form a single straight track. It is not possible to avoid direction changes, they shall be carried out by transition curves and should not translate to exceed 10 times the diameter of the downpipe. In case of exceeding this value, the pending weak intermediate section should be treated as building collector.

2. Agreement of falling domestic wastewater pipes with weak pending sections is by distance to transition curves at least three times the diameter (with reference to the tube axis) or two 45-degree bends connected by a straight section.

3. The opening to the outside of the drop in domestic wastewater pipes should check the following conditions:

a) be located at 0.50 m above the building coverage or, where this is in the terrace, 2.00 m above its level;

b) exceed, when located at a distance less than 0.50 m from a chimney, the cap this at least 0.20 m;

c) to rise at least 1.00 m above the spans of lintels of any door, window or crack for air intake, located at a distance less than 4.00 m;

d) be protected with mesh to prevent entry of materials or small animals.

Article 232

(Localization)

1. The fall of domestic waste water pipes should be located preferably in vertical galleries and easily accessible.

2. In all industrial buildings that is unknown types of industries to be installed shall be provided decline of industrial waste water pipes with accessible location for all units.

3. The rainwater downpipes should be located, preferably, in cash, on the outside of the building or accessible vertical galleries.

4. downpipes may eventually be built, and if cross structural elements, the resistance of the latter and the pipes should not be affected.

Article 233

(Discharge)

1. The domestic waste water falls tubes must download the gross manifolds through curves, making the insertion of these forks or inspection chambers. If the distance between the collector and the building downpipe is greater than 10 times the diameter thereof, it should be ensured through ventilation system, for example, installation, at this distance an inspection chamber.

2. downpipes of industrial waste water referred to in paragraph 2 of the preceding Article shall discharge into own network of collectors and effluents should be gathered in a manhole for grid connection of domestic wastewater.

Article 234

(Cleaning Rhône)

1. The installation of cleaning nozzles with easy access throughout the fall of domestic wastewater pipe is mandatory when:

a) the changes of direction, close to the transition curves;

b) in the vicinity of the highest discharge branch inserting the drop tube;

c) at least 3 on 3 floors, with the insertion of the respective discharge pipeline, being advised on all floors;

d) at the bottom, along the transition curve with the building collector, when you can not install an inspection chamber in Article 233 conditions

2. The cleaning mouths must have a diameter at least equal to the respective drop tube, and its opening should be as close as possible to this.

Article 235

(Nature Materials)

1. The drop of domestic waste water pipes may be rigid PVC or cast iron.

2. The fall of industrial waste water pipes laid down in Article 232 paragraph 2 may be of cast iron spun protected internally with resin "epoxy".

3. downpipes rainwater can be hard PVC, galvanized sheet metal or cast iron.

4. it can also be used other materials provided they meet the necessary conditions of use and satisfying the provisions of Article 198

SECTION E

Ventilation columns

Article 236

(Sizing)

1. In the ventilation sizing columns must be taken into account its height and the diameter of the respective drop tube.

2. To determine the diameter of ventilation columns can be used the graph and the expression listed in Annex 24.

Article 237

(Sequence sections)

The section of the ventilation column can not, under any circumstances, reduce upward.

Article 238

(Track)

1. The layout of ventilation columns must be vertical. Direction changes consist of ascending straight sections connected by transition curves.

2. The ventilation column has its origin in the land header, a drop distance of about 10 times the diameter of the tube.

3. Ventilation column ends superiorly in the fall pipe at least 1.0 m above the highest inclusion of any extension discharge, or opens directly into the atmosphere, in accordance with Article 231

4. If terminates superiorly in the drop tube, the ventilation column should be connected to this at least 3 on 3 floors.

5. When there are no downpipes, the column or ventilation columns have their beginning in the upstream ends of the building collector.

Article 239

(Localization)

1. Ventilation columns should be installed preferably in easily accessible vertical galleries.

2. They can possibly be built, and if occasionally cross structural elements, the resistance of the latter and the pipes should not be affected.

Article 240

(Nature Materials)

Ventilation columns can be hard PVC, galvanized iron, cast iron or other materials provided they meet the necessary conditions of use and satisfying the provisions of Article 198

SECTION F

Gross collectors

Article 241

(Flow rates of calculation)

1. Are the property collectors calculation flow of domestic wastewater should be based on the discharge flows attributed to sanitary appliances in it discharge, as stipulated in Article 209

2. The accumulated flow rates have to be allocated coefficients that take into account the likely simultaneous use of equipment, as stipulated in Article 210

3. Are the property collectors calculation flow of rain water shall be the sum of the discharge extension of downpipes calculating flow rates that are linked to it.

Article 242

(Hydraulic sizing)

1. In the hydraulic design of the collector gross domestic wastewater should be taken into account:

a) the calculation of flow rates referred to in Article 241;

b) the slope, which should be between 10 and 40 mm / m;

c) the roughness of the material.

2. Are the property collectors of domestic wastewater should be sized for a flow not exceeding half section.

3. In the hydraulic design of building collectors of rainwater, must be taken into account:

a) the calculation of flow rates referred to in Article 241;

b) the slope, which should be between 10 and 40 mm / m, assuming, in duly justified cases, the minimum value of 5 mm / m;

c) the roughness of the material.

4. Are the property collectors of rainwater can be dimensioned for a flow the full section.

Article 243

(Minimum diameter)

1. The diameter of building collectors can not in any event be less than the greater of the piping diameters connected to it, with a minimum of 100 mm.

2. The minimum diameter of network collectors of industrial waste water provided for in Article 233 paragraph 2 shall be 200 mm.

Article 244

(Sequence sections)

The section of the building collector can not, under any circumstances, decrease in the flow direction.

Article 245

(Track)

1. The layout of building collectors should be straight both in plant and in profile.

2. At first, in all direction changes of inclination or diameter of the collectors and the confluences, inspection chambers are implemented which ensure the maintenance of the adjacent sections.

3. When the gross collectors are installed to view or easily visitable places, these cameras can be replaced with forks and cleaning mouths, these are located at appropriate points and in sufficient numbers to ensure up an efficient maintenance service.

4. The cameras or consecutive cleaning mouths should not be spaced more than 15 meters.

Article 246

(Localization)

Are the property collectors can be buried, placed in sight or built, but without affecting the strength of structural elements of the building and own plumbing.

Article 247

(Connection extension Hall)

1. building a camera located at the downstream end of each building system is mandatory, providing a link to the respective connecting branch and find out of the building, next to a public road and easily accessible area.

2. This chamber may be circular or rectangular, with a minimum dimension of 0.80 m, provided that its depth does not exceed 1.00 m, and should be taken to depths exceeding the dimensions of the controlled-manholes in Article 107 o

3. To the satisfaction of the provisions of Article 103 on the ventilation network, should not exist in the connection extension chamber any device to prevent the ventilation of the public network by building network.

Article 248

(Retention valve)

1. the installation of automatic check valves whenever the responsible services consider it relevant to minimize the disadvantages of refluimentos from the public is mandatory.

2. The model and installation location must meet with the approval of the relevant services.

Article 249

(Nature Materials)

1. Are the property collectors of domestic waste water can be hard PVC, stoneware glaze or cast iron spun properly protected.

2. Are the property collectors of industrial waste water referred to in paragraph 2 of Article 233 can be glazed stoneware, spun properly protected cast iron or glazed concrete or centrifuged protected within the resin "epoxy".

3. Are the property collectors of rainwater can be hard PVC or concrete.

4. it can also be used other materials provided they meet the necessary conditions of use and satisfying the provisions of Article 198

CHAPTER XXV

Accessories

SECTION A

Siphons

Article 250

(Sizing)

1. The diameters of the traps to be installed in different sanitary appliances should not be less than those indicated in Annex 8, do not exceed the respective discharge stations.

2. The water closure of domestic waste water traps should not be less than 50 mm and not more than 100 mm, advising the values indicated in Annex 18.

Article 251

(Installation)

1. The traps must be installed vertically, so as to keep its water closure, and be placed in locations accessible to facilitate maintenance operations.

2. When not incorporated into sanitary appliances the traps should be installed at a distance no greater than 3 m of those.

3. You may use collective siphon serving several sanitary appliances.

4. It is forbidden to double siphoning in the building plumbing system of domestic wastewater.

5. closing the water trap plant not less than 100 mm in the connection extension chamber rainwater is mandatory, or immediately downstream thereof, whenever the extension is connected directly to a public drainage system unit or partially unitary. The installation of this trap requires the placement chamber or chambers, sand retention.

6. In the battery systems because they use congested, each health unit should be provided with individual siphon.

Article 252

(Nature Materials)

The siphons not incorporated in the sanitary ware can be brass, rigid PVC, cast iron or other materials, provided they meet the necessary conditions of use and satisfying the provisions of Article 198

SECTION B

Drains

Article 253

(Sizing)

1. The minimum floor area of thinning must not be less than 2/3 of the respective discharge extension sectional area.

2. The drains installed at the top of rainwater downpipes should have a floor area less than 1.5 times the area of the section of those tubes.

Article 254

(Installation)

It is compulsory to install drains in all sanitary appliances, except for toilet bowls, and floors of sanitary facilities, areas likely to washings and rainwater collection sites.

Article 255

(Nature Materials)

The drains can be cast iron, brass or other materials, provided they meet the necessary conditions of use and satisfying the provisions of Article 198

SECTION C

Inspection chambers

Article 256

(Minimum dimensions)

1. The minimum size of the plant for inspection chambers should not be less than 0.8 of their depth, measured by the distance from the sill to the floor when it is not more than 1.0 m.

2. For depths between 1.00 m and 2.50 m, the minimum dimension in plan shall be 1,00 m. For higher depths, the minimum value should be 1.25 m.

3. It should be guaranteed easy access to the interior of the chambers, through use of appropriate scale closures.

Article 257

(Installation)

1. installing inspection chambers in gross collectors is mandatory under the conditions referred to in Article 245

2. Inspection chambers are made as referred to in Article 106

Article 258

(Constructive aspects)

1. Inspection cameras should be solidly built, waterproof inside, easily accessible and equipped with resistant closures.

2. The insertion of one or more pipes must be made elsewhere in the flow direction by transition curves radius of not less than twice the diameter of the respective pipes, in order to ensure the continuity of the inner upper generatrix thereof.

3. The inspection chambers of a height exceeding 1.00 m must still respect the above Article 107

4. The camera inspection of domestic waste water drainage system are equipped with locking devices to prevent the passage of gases to the outside.

5. The direction changes, diameter and inclination taking place in a chamber must be made through gutter constructed in threshold, with a height equal to the diameter of the outlet conduit so as to ensure the continuity of the liquid vein.

6. The sills must have a minimum cross slope of 10%, towards the gutters.

7. The inspection chamber must have a guided fall at the entrance, where the gap to win exceed 0.50 m, and a satisfactory agreement in the gutter if this gap is equal to or less than this value.

8. The network inspection chambers of industrial wastewater must be internally protected with two coats of paint based resin "epoxy".

Article 259

(Nature Materials)

The materials to be used in inspection chambers must be as stated in Article 108

CHAPTER XXVI

Additional facilities

SECTION A

Lift facilities

Article 260

(Installation and construction aspects)

1. The lifting facilities may be equipped with nozzles or electropump groups, and shall be provided with control devices, safety and alarm, in case of failure.

2. The pumping facilities should be located in sites that allow easy inspection and maintenance, as far as possible away from residential areas or work in order to minimize the effects of noise, vibration and odors.

3. The sewage from sanitary appliances must undergo an inspection chamber before being received in the lift system.

4. The high for electropump groups must be made from a pumping chamber, which is dispensable in the case of ejectors.

5. pumping chambers, when used, shall verify the following design features:

a) they are solidly built, waterproof, easily accessible and equipped with resistant closures and to prevent the passage of gases to the outside;

b) must necessarily have secondary ventilation performed through pipe diameter at least equal to the compression behavior;

c) the correlation with the bottom wall must be second inclined surfaces at least 45 °, to prevent the deposition of solids;

d) the inner lining of these cameras should be adequate protection against the action of hydrogen sulfide;

e) the useful capacity of pumping chambers should be determined by the affluent calculation flow, high flow rate and the maximum permissible number of starts per hour of electromechanical equipment;

f) to consider possible damage or power shortages, when there is no backup generator, the pumping chamber must have a minimum capacity corresponding to the confluence of the calculation flow for 30 minutes;

g) the geometry of the pumping chambers should be the characteristics of lifting equipment and shall ensure that the maximum level of residual water inside does not exceed the ground level of the lower pipe affluent.

6. In the definition and characterization of the electric pump groups, it should be borne in mind:

a) the flow rate to increase, which should be equal to the influent flow calculation, plus the safety margin it deems appropriate;

b) the delivery head;

c) the maximum permissible number of starts per hour for the equipment to be installed;

d) installing at least two identical lifting groups, usually intended to serve as mutual active reservation, and optionally together to strengthen the lifting capacity.

7. The groups should be automatic and must include features to meet the nature of the waste water to be lifted.

8. The suction piping groups, where they exist, must be independent and have constant diameter and no less than that of the compression plumbing.

9. The definition and characterization of the nozzles must be taken into account:

a) raising the flow rate, the delivery head and emptying time;

b) the installation of at least two units, to guarantee the continuous flow of the effluent flow;

c) the maximum level of residual water in the ejector that must be lower than the threshold of the tributary channel.

Article 261

(Prevention of noise and vibration)

In order to mitigate the noise and vibrations to the lift installation:

a) have convenient isolation, particularly isolated emplacements and elastic fastenings;

b) the operation of electromechanical organs shall determine, in squats, average sound noise level not exceeding 30 dB (A).

Article 262

(Nature Materials)

1. Lifting equipment, pipelines and their accessories shall be of a type appropriate to the nature of the waste water to be lifted.

2. Both pipes and fittings can be made of steel, cast iron or other adequate strength materials to service pressures satisfying the provisions of Article 198

SECTION B

Retaining chambers

Article 263

(Sizing)

The retaining chambers must be dimensioned so as to have free volume and surface area appropriate to the influent flow and in fat, oil or to retain solid.

Article 264

(Installation and construction aspects)

1. installing retaining chambers in pipelines transporting wastewater with high content of fats, hydrocarbons or settleable solids is mandatory.

2. It is not permitted to introduce the retaining chambers of wastewater from the toilet and urinal basins.

3. The retaining chambers should be located as close as possible to the producer of the local wastewater to be treated and in accessible areas, to enable their regular inspection and timely removal of retained material.

4. The retaining chamber may be prefabricated or built in situ, and should be impervious, resistant provided with locking devices which prevent the passage of gases to the outside.

5. The sills of the cameras should be flat and recessed relative to the outlet pipe.

6. The cameras must be ventilated and equipped with built-siphon or located immediately downstream.

7. The internal surfaces of the retaining chambers fats must be suitably protected against the action of fatty acids.

Article 265

(Nature Materials)

The retaining chambers can be concrete, brick masonry or cement blocks, cast iron or other materials, provided they meet the necessary conditions of use and complying with Article 198

CHAPTER XXVII

Bathroom appliances

Article 266

(Installation)

All sanitary appliances must be installed to allow easy operation.

Article 267

(Discharge Device)

1. All of toilet bowls, urinals, hospital and similar sinks are provided with toilets, flow meters or other devices capable of ensuring effective discharge and cleaning.

2. The discharge devices should be installed at a higher level to the devices and ensure the hydraulic discontinuity in order to prevent contamination of the plumbing of drinking water by suction, in a situation of possible depression in these conduits.

Article 268

(Nature Materials)

The sanitary appliances can be of vitreous china, enameled cast iron, enameled steel, stainless steel, marble or other materials, provided they meet the necessary conditions of use and complying with Article 198

CHAPTER XXVIII

Trials

Article 269

(Purposes and types)

1. It is mandatory to conduct tests on the drainage system of domestic waste water, which are intended to ensure proper performance.

2. The tests to be performed are of tightness and efficiency.

Article 270

(Leakage test)

Leakage tests are conducted as follows:

a) leakage test to air or to smoke:

The system undergoes, on each floor, an injection of air or smoke at a pressure of 4 000 Pa (about 40 mm water column) at one end, blocking up the other or placing them traps with the closure at least 50 mm water. A gauge inserted in the test equipment must not accuse any variation up to 15 minutes after starting the test. If you refer to the air leak test should be added to the active scent products (e.g. peppermint) so as to make possible the location of leaks;

b) Water leakage test:

This essay focuses on the collectors buried the building, undergoing charge equal to the result of any obstruction. For such tamponam up collectors and each drop tube is filled with water to the coordinate the discharge of the smaller of the devices that it discharges. A pressure gauge attached to a buffered edge should not accuse pressure lowering for 15 minutes.

Article 271

(Test efficiency)

The efficiency tests correspond to the observation of the behavior of traps as the self-siphoning phenomena and induced siphoning in accordance with the provisions of Annex 19.

TITLE V HEALTH AND SAFETY OF OPERATING STAFF

CHAPTER XXIX

General provisions

Article 272

(Goal)

1. The set of buildings and equipment making up the facilities of public water distribution systems and wastewater drainage and operation of personnel assigned to the operation, involving working conditions characterized by certain potential risks.

2. The provisions set out below are a number of safety and hygiene standards, in order to minimize the occurrence of accidents or permanent situations that may affect the life, physical integrity and health of workers.

Article 273

(Health and safety program)

1. It is the management entity must have and promote the use of a safety program and staff hygiene and facilities.

2. The program of the establishment primarily is intended to prevent accidents, diseases or other harm through the workers' awareness in order to make them aware, correct and permanently, the dangers that may apply if the measures contained in that are neglected program.

3. The management company shall be:

a) evaluate the safety and hygiene requirements, taking into account the legal provisions in force and heard the technician responsible for the operation;

b) planning the security and hygiene program planned for implementing the various tasks of personnel and the operation and maintenance of facilities;

c) create the conditions for compliance with the program and enforce it, ensuring the supply of devices and personal protective equipment, indispensable with the tasks, developing the necessary actions to maintain the machines, working equipment and materials in appropriate safety, and ensure the availability of first aid provision means;

d) set in rules or through written instructions, assignments and duties of all personnel, subject to a reasonable standard of training in health and safety;

e) investigate any type of accident, in order to determine their causes and recommend actions of prevention and protection that are necessary;

f) periodically prepare reports covering all aspects of health and safety program, which must be brought to the attention of the technicians responsible for exploration.

4. To the technicians responsible for operating responsibility within the health and safety program, enforce all safety rules laid down in the rules and written instructions and report all accidents occurring in the operation and maintenance of the systems.

Article 274

(Existing legislation)

The health and safety program should respect to laws and regulations.

Article 275

(Main risk factors)

1. The main risks related to operating activities and maintenance of public water supply systems and waste water drainage occur in the workplace when it appears one of the following situations:

a) oxygen demand;

b) the existence of gases or toxic, flammable or explosive vapors;

c) contact with sewage or sludge;

d) sudden increase of drained flows and flash floods;

e) existence of machines, including mobile platforms, and electromechanical equipment.

2. The stay of a worker for longer than thirty minutes is allowed only if the proportions by volume in the air do not exceed:

a) 0,04% carbon monoxide;

b) from 0.02 to 0.03% of hydrogen sulfide;

c) 0.0004% of chlorine gas;

and for an exposure for 8 hours, required levels that do not exceed:

- 0.01% carbon monoxide;
- 0.002% hydrogen sulfide;
- 0.00005% of chlorine gas.

3. With regard to oxygen deficiency in the workplace, the exposure of a worker for 8 hours is not relevant physiological effects since the oxygen content is maintained between 14% and 16% (normal air contains 20.8%) but below a percentage of 10% is a dangerous situation, it can be fatal to lower percentages of 5 to 7%.

Article 276

(High risk places)

1. They are considered high risk sites in public water distribution systems:

a) water reservoirs and switching chambers, or other subsurface equipment;

b) underground galleries without ventilation or close to gas pipelines, fuel tanks or electrical high voltage lines;

c) air and high levels of respective access reservoirs;

d) applying local storage and gaseous chlorine and other chemicals, potentially hazardous, used in water treatment;

e) the compartments of machinery and electrical equipment of pumping stations and treatment.

2. They are high risk sites in the wastewater drain public systems:

a) inspection chambers;

b) the flyable collectors;

c) the emissaries outputs of waste water;

d) the chambers of underground pumping stations, suction sewage or sludge;

e) the works inlet of the treatment plant, when it eventually devoid of effective ventilation;

f) access to maintenance and operation of the aeration basins and sludge tanks;

g) the facilities and service areas where it carries out the anaerobic digestion of sludge and biological recovery and gas storage;

h) installations handling and storage of gaseous chlorine and other chemicals, corrosive or toxic reagents used for treatment of sludge or wastewater.

Article 277

(Individual health and safety equipment)

Depending on the nature of the work and local conditions where it is carried out, the staff of the water distribution and wastewater drainage systems should be used in the maintenance and operation tasks, individual safety equipment and hygiene comprising namely:

a) resistant, fireproof helmets whenever there is injury risk to the head, fire or explosion;

b) special glasses and adjusted to face with resistant and visors or visors lenses when there is danger of flying debris, caustic substances, dust or fumes, or when the staff is subject to intense light or glare by dangerous radiation;

c) hearing protection against noise and ears against sparks and particles of molten metals;

d) elastic gloves high cannon to protect hands and arms of the danger of burns, gloves and hard, too high cannon, for hand protection against injuries, transportation of materials and use of machine tools;

e) pipe high waterproof boots for protection of feet and legs against moisture, and with hard protection to avoid drilling or crushing feet when at work manipulating machine tools;

f) suits, aprons, hoods and shirt fronts to defend the body against stroke and projection of solids, liquids or aggressive gases;

g) masks provided with filter or oxygen supply for respiratory protection, when there is a danger of inhalation of dust, harmful gases or vapors;

h) reflective bands for outdoor use in clothing, for use in job opportunities in the street, whether night or day;

i) explosion proof lighting lanterns;

j) hazardous gas detectors with audible warning and oxygen demand indicator;

l) seat belts, with mooring lines, for personal protection, in all locations where there is danger of falling, fainting or dragging by chain or strong wind, especially in areas with slippery surfaces or over 25% slope.

CHAPTER XXX

Security measures and general practice care

Article 278

(The staff)

Are general practice measures to be taken by staff, in particular:

a) take reasonable care for the safety and refrain from acts that could cause dangerous situations;

b) correctly use the safety equipment and individual hygiene, and ensure their good condition;

c) immediately signals a failure or breakdown, premises and equipment, likely to cause accidents;

d) use tools appropriate to the nature of the work;

e) cooperate in the prevention of occupation risks and maintaining hygiene in the workplace, compliance with the provisions of the Regulations made by the operator, and following the instructions given by the technician responsible for the operation;

f) take an interest in teaching health and safety and on the provision of first aid, forwarded to it during the occupation;

g) take care of your personal hygiene for health protection and prevent the spread of contagious diseases;

h) no smoking or naked flames during work, being completely forbidden to do it indoors and where there is a risk of the presence of flammable gases.

Article 279

(From plant and equipment)

Taking into account the legislation on hygiene, health and safety of facilities and equipment, it is the managing body cause to be followed, among others, the following general measures:

a) keep in convenient cleanliness of workplaces, especially those which occur oil spills and flammable products;

b) promote adequate ventilation of workplaces that do not have natural ventilation, with special care in case of existence of toxic, flammable or explosive gases;

c) maintain lighting levels that minimize the risk of accidents;

d) limit the noise and vibration to acceptable levels;

e) ensure that all materials and accessories, not suitable at the moment, are properly stored;

f) Maintain in good use personal protective equipment, through periodic reviews and higienizações;

g) ensure that the machinery and equipment should be protected in all cases where its operation would jeopardize the physical integrity of personnel;

h) located in buildings or in separate compartments, handling operations and storage of toxic chemicals, flammable or explosive;

i) reduce as far as possible, through studies of holding wastewater systems, personnel contact with dirty water, sludge and other products of the treatment;

j) ensure the installation of water supply lines with suitable flow and convenient pressure, especially in areas with higher risk of fire and handling of corrosive chemical reagents, as well as complementary bodies drainage of waste water;

k) have suitable equipment for putting out fires, in good working order, periodically checked in accessible locations conveniently signposted, and still have enough workers, properly instructed, for use of the equipment, taking into account the standards and applicable instructions by the fire department;

l) signal and protect all high risk sites and facilities of work performed on public roads.

Article 280

(From assistance in case of accident)

To respond to personnel in case of accident, the management company shall ensure the existence of:

a) first-aid provision means, to be installed in various locations marked with personnel able to teach them;

b) Local medical service, if required by law;

c) updated information, from local where the first-aid material, for contact with health facilities and firefighters, and feature if necessary.

Article 281

(The health surveillance)

The following are the general practice provisions whose implementation should be ensured by the labor doctor of the management company:

a) submit workers to periodic assessment and provide them with medical care, at the beginning of the work activity and for this, in the event of accidents and diseases and during the reintegration and relocation;

b) make the necessary vaccinations, depending on the situations they encounter, especially against tetanus, leptospirosis, typhoid, tuberculosis and polio, as usually happens with the workers of public drainage systems and wastewater treatment;

c) prepare an annual report on the state of health of each worker.

CHAPTER XXXI

Security measures and hygiene in the workplace

Article 282

(In general facilities)

1. The workers of pumping stations and treatment, responsible for machinery and equipment where there are moving parts, must be aware of their operation in order to be guaranteed the safety of staff working for such facilities; Likewise one should always carry a machine - immobilized for operational reasons, or for damage - be put back into operation.

2. All electrical installations, including tables, transformer stations, power lines, distribution networks, low voltage systems and user devices must respect the recommended safety regulations for electrical installations; all that is missing in these regulations should apply to the technical standards and provisions recognized internationally.

3. The lubrication of machines, or any transactions for its maintenance must be carried out with the machine stops.

4. The cleaning solvent, when performed in confined and poorly ventilated spaces must be done with mechanical ventilation feature; the flash point of solvents used should not be below 40 ° C.

5. In the pumping and treatment plants must always be individual safety equipment as well as fire extinguishers and fans; The use of gloves is indispensable operations involving the handling of corrosive reagents, and it also lifting stations and waste water treatment, the removal harrowing and sludge waste operations, and when there is risk of direct contact of the Sewage hands.

6. The protection of machines which operate provide risk to personnel, notably the elevating screw gearing and mechanical removal of debris transportation and waste water systems, must be made with net and stanchion guards, which must be removed only when it is placed out of service.

7. Workers in dirty areas of pumping stations and wastewater treatment should avoid contact of the fingers with the mouth, eyes and nose in order to reduce the risk of infection, being prohibited smoking in such places.

8. All work areas must be free of grease and oil products; They must be equipped with non-slip floors and easily washable finishes.

9. Stairs descent shall be in perfect condition and, when they are used fixed ladders and their height exceeds 5 m, there must be platforms or intermediate levels for every 5 m or part thereof fitted with guards to dorsal protection from 2.50 m high; platforms or landings, shall be provided with guard rails with the handrail height of 0.90 m to 0.15 m footers; the escalators should be of insulating material.

10. The depth of treatment tanks greater than 1.0 m shall be provided with bodyguards and footers, if possible removable to allow major repair work.

11. The air crossings required for inspection and maintenance must be performed by bridges, with a minimum width of 0.45 m equipped with side guards and handrails to a height of 0.90 m.

12. In confined places lifting wastewater and chemical conditioning, pumping and sludge digestion, including septic tanks, should be strictly forbidden to smoke or fire, should the entry of personnel in sludge digestion tanks or septic tanks, after emptying for repair work, only be possible after guaranteed that there is no explosives gases.

13. For hygiene and health of workplaces and use in case of personal injury, a private distribution network of water pumping and treatment plants must be provided with use of devices judiciously located.

14. For personal hygiene of workers should be in all pumping and treatment plants, sanitation facilities according to the number of workers and equipped with at least one sink, one toilet basin, one shower and one closet wardrobe.

15. After your daily activity or before any meal staff should take work clothes and wash hands.

16. The management company shall promote the supply of the required number of workwear seedlings in order to maintain the minimum standards of hygiene.

Article 283

(In the laboratory facilities)

1. The laboratory facilities to support treatment plants, which generally find themselves situated in the farm building where centralizes the command and control of debuggers bodies must have proper ventilation and air conditioning and kept clean.

2. Personnel should wear personal safety equipment appropriate to the nature of the work, and in some cases necessary to use full protective clothing and masks.

3. It is not permissible under any circumstances, direct connection or contact between the device using clean water and any container or laboratory equipment containing toxic substances, wastewater or sludge.

4. All reagents to be used, whether toxic or not, should be handled with care. The amounts of reagents in the workplace should be the minimum necessary and that are unable to be used must be immediately saved. In the case of flammable or explosive products, provision should be made as needed.

5. adequate facilities for firefighters; Besides the usual means there shall be for fire extinguishing in the personal clothing, hand-operated showers located in the lab outputs, just on the outside.

6. Where they proceed to handling or storage of flammable chemicals or likely to cause an explosion is no smoking or naked flames.

7. should never be used laboratory containers to serve drinks or food.

8. In case of accident should not underestimate their importance, for less severe that its effects appear to be apparently.

9. There must be toilets with wash basin, toilet bowl, shower and wardrobe closet.

10. Means shall be provided to provide first aid and personnel capable of administering them.

11. For the staff of the laboratories which take place bacteriological analyzes of wastewater and sludge, there must be a constant prevention of typhoid and other water-borne infections; strict sanitary practices in laboratory work with pathogenic microorganisms should be used.

Article 284

(In command and control facilities)

1. The switchboards and control of water systems and electrical systems when centralized, should be located in its own facility, or building housing for the operation, which does not offer risk of fire, have adequate ventilation and are well lit ; the equipment must be installed in order to reduce the risk of accidents in circulation and work of operating personnel.

2. In addition to the central command, there must be for security reasons, in all organs of the stations, located commands for immediate stop in case of an accident.

3. The centralized control facilities should have easy means of telecommunication with dependents and facilities with the outside, so that it can act, when there is malfunction of machinery and equipment, and in cases of accidents with personnel that require the urgent assistance and requiring immediate change of operating plans.

Article 285

(In the facilities for personal service)

1. In the treatment and pumping stations, should always be accommodation for staff support service, conveniently away from sludge digesters, gasometers and noisy mechanical devices.

2. The plant must have adequate ventilation and dispose of phone, if other means of telecommunication not exist at stations, and bathroom with sink, toilet bowl, shower and closet-wardrobe.

3. Personnel should maintain the premises in good hygiene practices in order to ensure the necessary health conditions.

Article 286

(In water reservoirs)

1. Inside the earthen water tanks should not be allowed artificial lighting, except for light bulbs of low voltage or explosion-proof; the equipment must be appropriate to the humid or that may lead to excessive sweating, should always be respected the regulations on safety in electrical installations.

2. Access to the water storage sites and switching chambers, whatever the type of reservoir, must be in perfect hygienic conditions and in good repair; if fixed ladders are used, more than 5 m height, there must be protection devices dorsal and intermediate landings under already covered by this Regulation.

3. In vessels made of reservoirs, staff should be aware of accidents, which can be dangerous drop in the water and there should be security means, such as buoys, poles and lifejackets, and disposal is a boat with engine with crew adestrada in bailouts.

4. Whatever the type of reservoir, the staff should be required to use personal protective equipment most appropriate to the nature of the inspection and maintenance work, especially

when caring for vestments wash with harmful to health; must be ensured ventilation of workplaces, and, if necessary, removal abroad of gases and vapors may be produced in these operations; the existence of means for the removal of any worker subject to accident inside the water storage tanks is mandatory; the number of workers in the inspection and maintenance operations should be at least two.

5. In the reservoirs of the dam type is duty personnel carefully observe the dam structure in order to detect any water leakage and immediately report the occurrence; when work areas are within discharge devices or water intake should be established a safety system to prevent untimely handling of any entails that causes water inflow to the work areas.

6. The containers must be sealed at the entrance of strangers and, in the reservoir type, should be required, in hazardous locations, proper signage and the existence of barriers to prevent access.

Article 287

(The opening and closing ditches)

1. Workers should always wear a helmet and, where necessary, protective goggles, suitable gloves and high boots with reinforced toes, especially when working with pneumatic hammers or other mechanical tools.

2. In the work areas must be maintained between workers the necessary distance to avoid accidents with the tools used.

3. No trenching work should be started without prior knowledge of the location of underground infrastructure, with particular importance with regard to gas and electric cables.

4. Access to the ditches should be done by stairs or ramp.

5. You should not allow yourself to deposition of excavated material less than 0.60 m of the trench edges.

6. It should not be allowed the existence of graves without proper drainage.

7. No adjustment or repair of machinery should be tried when they are in operation. The filling of fuel tanks must be done carefully, being prohibited smoking or naked flames, nearby.

8. Service areas should be protected with barriers and be properly marked, either by day or night, and should also have signaling machinery movement areas.

9. The use of explosives may only be carried out by qualified personnel and must be complied with strictly with the safety requirements for use and storage of explosives.

10. Neighbouring areas of explosives application sites are interdicted the movement of pedestrians and vehicles. They should be set warning signals of danger and barriers, or currents, sufficient distances, and, if necessary, suspension or temporary departure from traffic roads.

Article 288

(In the transport and plumbing settlement)

1. The loading and unloading pipes and fittings, and their settlement must be carried out by qualified personnel who must use, as well as helmet, gloves and appropriate boots; these operations must be run by a qualified element, specifically designated for that purpose.

2. When using mechanical means for moving pipes, workers should be kept away from the paths of the pipes transported by machines and are familiar with the signs used by the agents who run the operations.

3. The execution of joints on site may require appropriate personal safety equipment.

Article 289

(In the inspection and maintenance of sewers)

1. Prior to inspection and maintenance of domestic collectors or collectors of unit, the caps must be removed from chambers located immediately upstream and downstream, which must remain open for ventilation over a period of 10 minutes.

2. Next, proceed to the testing with equipment and methods approved by officials for the detection of hazardous gases and vapors, which most likely may exist in the collectors, including hydrogen sulphide, petrol vapor and methane monoxide carbon; if required must be carried out also under the same conditions, the determination of oxygen deficiency in the air.

3. If there are acceptable environmental conditions should be decided access, otherwise must resort to the supply air by mechanical means.

4. In strictly collectors that drain rainwater sewage, where the odds of a reduction in the atmosphere are much smaller, is borne by the responsible for the inspection and maintenance to follow the guidance operations.

5. drainage networks regularly visited within a system routine, the entry conditions are quite easy by virtue of the knowledge acquired about the state of operation of the collectors.

6. Decided access to collectors, staff entrance only to be done, however, after inspected the steps of the chambers in order to verify that they are clean and in good strength conditions. Equal care must be in the case of using mobile access equipment.

7. With regard to the minimum number of staff to occupy the inspection and maintenance of collectors, it must be the result of compliance with these rules in the case of non-flyable collectors:

a) at the opening of the manhole must remain necessarily a member of staff who remains there throughout the operation;

b) each member of staff on duty at the bottom of a manhole should be assisted by the team member who remains with the opening of that chamber on the outer side;

c) in case of flyable collecting the number of personnel inside should be at least three, and one of them must remain in the access chamber bottom and abroad must be an element permanently close the opening of this chamber which provides assistance to that is in the background.

8. The staff during inspection and maintenance operations must wear helmets, and other individual safety equipment suitable for the job, such as waterproof suits, boots water proof and masks.

9. flyable collectors with high velocity flow, or the amount of falls, and not flyable collectors, whenever deemed appropriate, they should settle belts or chains to protect downstream work stations, to retain any element dragged by the waters of the team.

10. Where in flyable collectors, is envisaged departure of a team member's input manhole, you must use a seat belt connected to warp one of the camera fixed steps, or outside it.

11. The personal residence times in manholes or within flyable collectors should be stopped at least every hour, for a period not less than 10 minutes.

12. The collector networks should be subject to periodic visits, accompanied by conducting indoor air testing and should not forget that most prevention of risks of intoxication, asphyxiation and explosion lies in the control of industrial wastewater inputs not treated, and also in the improved ventilation conditions of the collectors.

13. When the input of staff for manholes is made through the road, they must use up appropriate means of signaling and may in some cases be necessary to use chains and barriers to protect pedestrians and vehicles and personnel itself; even off-road, all manholes with raised lids must be signaled by the danger they offer, especially when their openings are located at small height from the ground.

Article 290

(In the inspection and maintenance of pipelines)

1. In the conduct of public water supply systems, the entry of personnel to inspect and maintain, where possible, require almost always for isolation of plumbing and emptying by sections.

2. After opening the manholes and made the emptying of the piping, must wait that operates natural ventilation of the interior and is subsequently confirmed the good state of cleanliness and resistance of the access equipment; only after that whether to allow the entry of staff.

3. Within the pipes when the thresholds are presented with a slope exceeding 25%, or prove slippery, the team members should wear seat belts and, depending on the type of work to be done, should be required to make use of personal protective equipment most appropriate.

4. When maintenance work lead to the atmospheric oxygen reduction must be applied to forced ventilation of the room and if there is formation of gases or dangerous fumes, they should be removed to the outside by suitable means.

5. When done, it should only be authorized refilling of the pipeline as surely prove that all personnel left the interior.

6. In the inspection and maintenance of buried valve chambers, staff must follow the safety rules and prescribed hygiene for water collection wells, poorly ventilated, making sure in advance of the existence and operation of bottom outlet devices; the negative must use the appropriate equipment in the event of flooding.

ANNEX 1

Criteria and standards supply of water quality for human consumption

A - Water supply for human consumption

1. Water supply is considered for human consumption:

a) water delivered for direct human consumption;

b) the water distributed for use in food manufacturing industries, processing or storage of products or substances intended for consumption by humans and can affect the health of foodstuffs.

2. Excluded from the preceding paragraph the waters which, although used in food industries, for specific determination require a greater demand for quality.

3. Are supply water quality characteristics for human consumption does not endanger health, be pleasing to the palate and the eyes of the consumers and not cause deterioration or destruction of different parts of the supply systems.

4. The drinking water must be made available to users in order to meet the requirements for drinking water, according to the parameters specified in Table 1 of this Annex, may not show in any event, their quality degradation signals whatever the point of the supply system is considered.

B - water quality monitoring system

1. The analytical reference methods to be used in water quality control measures are given in Table 1 and relate to the physical, chemical and microbiological characteristics of water for human consumption.

2. For the purpose of monitoring the quality of water of supply systems, the parameters listed in Table 1 are classified in three groups G1, G2 and G3, shown in Table 2.

3. The entity responsible for public water supply should ensure the minimum annual frequency of sampling and analysis for the purpose of water quality monitoring of public water supply systems for human consumption, under the conditions shown in Table 3.

4. For the purpose of health surveillance of public water supply systems water quality, health services must meet the minimum annual frequency of sampling and analysis indicated in Table 4.

5. The samples in the two preceding paragraphs should be carried out periodically throughout the year and covering the component parts of supply systems in order to obtain a representative picture of the quality of water.

C - Materials and methods of treatment

1. The materials used in supply systems which are in contact with water for human consumption can not cause changes in its quality and must meet the specifications set out in Title I of this Regulation.

2. The operations and treatment processes and compounds and chemical products for the treatment of water for human consumption shall be submitted by the entity responsible for public water supply for approval.

TABLE 1A

A. Organoleptic Parameters

PARAMETER	ESPRESSÃO OF RESULTS	VMR	VMA	ANALYTICAL METHOD REFERENCE	COMMENTS
Color	mg / l Pt / Co scale	1	20	Photometric methods to scale patterns Pt / Co	After centrifugation
Turbidity	Jackson Turbidity Unit (JTU)	1	10	Method silica formazin Method Secchi Method	Measure replaced, in certain circumstances, by transparency, measured in meters with Secchi disk: maximum recommended - Value: 6 m maximum permissible -Value: 2 m
Smell	Dilution rate	0	2 (12 ° C) 3 (25 ° C)	By successive dilutions, measurements made at 12 ° C or 25 ° C	Compared to the taste determinations
Flavor	Dilution rate	0	2 (12 ° C) 3 (25 ° C)	By successive dilutions, measurements made at 12 ° C or 25 ° C	Compared to the olfactory determinations

TABLE 1B

B. Physical-chemical parameters					
PARAMETER	ESPRESSÃO OF RESULTS	VMR	VMA	ANALYTICAL METHOD REFERENCE	COMMENTS
Temperature	ºC	12	25	Thermometry	
pH	Sorenson scale	6.5-8.5	6.5-9.5	Electrometrically	The water should not be aggressive
Conductivity	S / cm (20 ° C)	400		Electrometrically	Corresponding to the mineralization of waters. Corresponding value of resistivity: 2500Ω / cm at 20 ° C
Chlorides	mg / l Cl	25	-	Titration - Mohr method	Approximate concentration from which harmful effects may occur: 200 mg / l.
Sulphates	mg / l SO_4	25	250	Gravimetry Complexometry spectrophotometry	-
Silica	mg / l SiO_2	-	-	Absorption spectrophotometry	-
Calcium	mg / l Ca	100	-	Atomic absorption	-

B. Physical-chemical parameters					
PARAMETER	ESPRESSÃO OF RESULTS	VMR	VMA	ANALYTICAL METHOD REFERENCE	COMMENTS
				Complexometry	
Magnesium	mg / l Mg	30	50	Atomic absorption	-
Sodium	mg / l In	20	150	Atomic absorption	With a percentile of 80, calculated over a reference period of three years
Potassium	mg / l K	10	12	Atomic absorption	-
Aluminum	mg / l Al	0.05	0.2	Atomic absorption spectrophotometry absorption	-
Total hardness	mg / l Ca CO_3	-	500	Complexometry	See table 1 g
Total Dissolved Solids	mg / l	-	1500	Drying at 180 ° C and weighing	Also known as dry
Dissolved oxygen	% Saturation	-	-	Method specific electrodes Winkler	Dissolved oxygen concentration above 75% of saturation level
Carbon dioxide free	mg / l CO_2	-	-	Acidimetry	The water should not be aggressive

TABLE 1C

C. Undesirable Substances related parameters					
PARAMETER	EXPRESSION OF RESULTS	VMR	VMA	ANALYTICAL METHOD REFERENCE	COMMENTS
Nitrates	mg / l NO_3	25	50	Specific Electrodes absorption spectrophotometry	-
Nitrites	mg / l NO_2	-	0.1	Absorption spectrophotometry	-
Ammonium	mg / l NH_4	0.05	0.5	Absorption spectrophotometry	-
Kjeldahl nitrogen	mg / l N	-	1	Oxidation / Titration / absorption spectrophotometry	-
Oxidisability or value to permanganate	mg / l $_2$	2	5	$KMnO_4$ was boiled for 10 minutes in an acidic medium	-
Total organic carbon (TOC)	mg / l C	-	-	-	Should be investigated everything from the usual cause increased concentrations
Hydrogen sulphide	mg / l S	-	organoleptically undetectable	Absorption spectrophotometry	-
Extractable substance by	mg / l	0.1	-	Liquid / liquid extraction with	Dry

C. Undesirable Substances related parameters					
PARAMETER	EXPRESSION OF RESULTS	VMR	VMA	ANALYTICAL METHOD REFERENCE	COMMENTS
chloroform				chloroform purified at neutral pH, weighing the residue	
Dissolved or emulsified hydrocarbons (after extraction by ether): oils fats	g / l	-	10	Infrared absorption spectrophotometry	-
Phenols (phenol index)	g / L C_6H_5OH	-	0.5	Absorption spectrophotometry methods paranitranilina and method of amino-antipyrine	Excluding natural phenols which do not react to chlorine
Boron	mg / l B	1	-	Atomic absorption	
Surfactants (which react with methylene blue)	mg / l Al (sodium lauryl sulfate)		0.2	Atomic absorption spectrophotometry absorption	-
Iron	mg / l Fe	0.05	0.2	Atomic absorption spectrophotometry absorption	-
Manganese	mg / l Mn	0.02	0.05	Atomic absorption spectrophotometry absorption	-
Copper	mg / l Cu	3.0	-	Atomic absorption spectrophotometry absorption	- Above 3.0 mg / l may appear astringent flavors, corrosion or stains.
Zinc	mg / l Zn	5.0	-	Atomic absorption spectrophotometry absorption	Above 5.0 mg / l may appear astringent flavors, opalescence, granular deposits and development of a fatty lime after boiling
Match	mg / l P_2O_5	0.4	5.0	Absorption spectrophotometry	Maximum concentration

C. Undesirable Substances related parameters					
PARAMETER	EXPRESSION OF RESULTS	VMR	VMA	ANALYTICAL METHOD REFERENCE	COMMENTS
Fluorides	mg / l F	0.6	1.7	Absorption spectrophotometry specific electrodes	variable according to the annual average daily maximum temperature (see Table 1 i).
Cobalt	mg / l Co	-	-	-	-
Total suspended solids	mg / l	0	-	Method porous membrane by filtration or centrifugation 0,45μ (for at least 15 minutes and mean acceleration 2800 to 3200G) drying at 105 ° C to weighing.	-
Residual chlorine available	mg / l HO Cl	-	-	Amperometric method Colorimetric (DPD) Titration spectrophotometry absorption	Variable depending on the water characteristics (pH, temperature, dissolved solids, etc.), microbiological species, the con-tact time and the type of waste (see Table 1 f).
Barium	mg / l Ba	0.1	-	Atomic absorption	-
Silver	mg / l Ag	-	0.01	Atomic absorption	If in an exceptional case, it is a non-systematic use of silver for water treatment, can take up a maximum permissible value of 0.08 mg / l.

TABLE 1D

D. parameters relating to Toxic Substances					
PARAMETER	EXPRESSION OF RESULTS	VMR	VMA	ANALYTICAL METHOD REFERENCE	COMMENTS
Arsenic	mg / l The	-	0.05	Absorption	-

D. parameters relating to Toxic Substances					
PARAMETER	EXPRESSION OF RESULTS	VMR	VMA	ANALYTICAL METHOD REFERENCE	COMMENTS
				spectrophotometry Atomic absorption	
Beryllium	mg / l Be	-	-	-	-
Cadmium	mg / l Cd	-	0,005	Atomic absorption	
Cyanides	mg / l CN	-	0.05	Absorption spectrophotometry	-
Chromium	mg / l Cr	-	0.05	Atomic absorption spectrophotometry absorption	-
Mercury	mg / l Hg	-	0.05	Atomic absorption	-
Nickel	mg / l Ni	-	0.001	Atomic absorption	-
Lead	mg / l Pb	-	0.05	Atomic absorption	In the case of lead piping the lead content should not exceed 0.05 mg / l in a sample taken after the distribution and if the lead content frequently or substantially exceed 0.1 mg / l, appropriate measures should be taken reduce the risks of consumer exposure to lead.
Antimony	mg / l Sb	-	0.01	Absorption spectrophotometry	-
Selenium	mg / l If	-	0.01	Atomic absorption	
Vanadium	mg / l V	-	-		
Pesticides - for individualized substance - Total	g / l	-	0.1 0.5		It is understood by pesticides - Pesticides - persistent organochlorine - organophosphates - carbamates - herbicides - fungicides - PCB's and PCT
Other organochlorine compounds	g / l		-	Gas chromatography, or liquid of suitable solvents after extraction and purification. Identification, if necessary, the constituents of mixtures. Quantitative	The concentration in halofórmios should be reduced as far as possible.

D. parameters relating to Toxic Substances					
PARAMETER	EXPRESSION OF RESULTS	VMR	VMA	ANALYTICAL METHOD REFERENCE	COMMENTS
				determination.	
Polycyclic aromatic hydrocarbons	g / l		0.2		Reference substances - fluoranthene - Fluoranthene Benzo 3,4 - benzo 11.4 fluoranthene - benzo pyrene 3,4 - benzo perylene 1.12 - indeno (1, 2, 3 cd) pyrene

TABLE 1E

E. Microbiological parameters					
PARAMETER	EXPRESSÃOS OF RESULTS (SAMPLE VOLUME IN ML)	VMR	VMA		ANALYTICAL METHOD REFERENCE
			METHOD OF MEMBRANE FILTER	PROVING METHOD IN MULTIPLE TUBE (NMP)	
Total coliforms (4)	100	-	0	NMP <1	- Fermentation in multiple tubes - Subculture of the positive tubes on a confirmation medium - Count according to the most probable number (MPN) Filtration through membranes and culture in an appropriate medium such as Tergitol lactose agar, Endo broth Teepol 0, 4%, subculture and identification of the suspect colonies. For total coliforms: temperature 37 ° C
Fecal coliforms (4)	100	-	0	NMP <1	For fecal coliforms: 44 ° C temperature
Faecal streptococci	100	-	0	NMP <1	Method with sodium azide (Litsky). Count according to the most probable number. Membrane filtration and cultivation in a suitable medium.
Sulphite reducing	20	-	-	NMP≤1	After heating the sample at 80 count the

E. Microbiological parameters					
PARAMETER	EXPRESSÃOS OF RESULTS (SAMPLE VOLUME IN ML)	VMR	VMA		ANALYTICAL METHOD REFERENCE
			METHOD OF MEMBRANE FILTER	PROVING METHOD IN MULTIPLE TUBE (NMP)	
clostridia					spores by: - seeding medium with glucose, iron sulfide and counting of colonies with black halo. - Membrane filtration, placing the inverted filter on medium with glucose, iron sulfite, coated agar, count of black colonies. - breakdown amid tubes "DRCM" (differencial reinforced clostridia medium) subculture of black tubes through tornesolado milk, count according to the most probable number.

TABLE 1E (NOTES)

PARAMETER		ESPRESSÃO OF RESULTS (VOLUME IN ML)	VMR	VMA	ANALYTICAL METHOD REFERENCE	COMMENTS
Total number of germs (4) for drinking water	37 °C	1	10 (2) (3)	-	Inoculation for incorporation in nutrient agar	
	22 °C	1	100 (2) (3)	-		
Total number of germs (4)	37 °C	1	5	20	Inoculation for incorporation in nutrient agar	The maximum allowable concentration values are measured during the 12 hours following the wrapping, with the water sample maintained at a constant temperature during this 12 hour period.
	22 °C	1	20	100		
Water intended for human consumption should not contain pathogenic organisms. To complement, as necessary, the microbiological analysis of water intended for human						

PARAMETER		ESPRESSÃO OF RESULTS (VOLUME IN ML)	VMR	VMA	ANALYTICAL METHOD REFERENCE	COMMENTS
consumption should search pathogens in addition to the indicators listed in Table E, and in particular: - salmonella; - pathogenic staphylococci, - fecal bacteriophages; and - the enterovirus. In addition, this water should not contain: - or parasitic organisms; - or algae; - or macroscopic organisms. (1) - Subject to what is considered a sufficient number of samples with 95% of compliant results. (2) - For the corresponding values disinfected water must be sharply lower, off the treatment plant. (3) - If, after successive crops is established that there is an excess in relation to these values, a check should be performed. (4) - As regards the incubation period is usually 24 hours or 48 hours, except for the total count that is 48 hours or 72 hours.						

TABLE 1E (T. ADDITIONAL)

Complementary tests	
Parameter	Analytical reference methods
Salmonella	Concentration by membrane filtration. Inoculation of pre-enrichment medium. Enrichment, isolation subculture on agar. ID.
Pathogenic streptococci	Membrane filtration and culture in specific medium (eg Chapman's hypersaline medium). To put in evidence the characters of pathogenicity.
Fecal bacteriophages	Guelin technique.
Enterovirus	Concentration by filtration, flocculation, or centrifugation and identification.
Protozoa	Concentration by filtration through membrane microscopic examination.Pathogenicity testing.
Macroscopic organisms (worms, larvae)	Concentration by membrane filtration, microscopic examination.Pathogenicity testing.

TABLE 1F

F. Parameters Radioactive				
Global activity X	Bq / l	0.1	Defined by the competent authority, based on local conditions; although it indicates only an example, the use of "internal proportional counter»	(1) - If the values are exceeded may be necessary to carry out a more detailed analysis of radionuclides.
Activity global B	Bq / l	1.0	(Internal proportional counter) as well as Geiger counters.	(2) - Higher values that CMR does not necessarily mean that the water is unfit for human consumption.

TABLE 1G

G. Minimum Allowable Value for Water for Human Consumption, which was subjected to a hardness Removal Treatment				
Total hardness	mg / l $CaCO_3$	150	-	-
pH	scale Sorensen	-	-	-
Alkalinity	mg / l HCO_3	30	Titration acid base	The water should not be aggressive
Dissolved oxygen	mg / l $_2$	-	-	

- The provisions concerning the hardness of pH and dissolved oxygen apply also to water from desalination.
- If, due to its excessive natural hardness, the water is softened in accordance with Table 1g, before being made available to consumption, its sodium content may, in exceptional cases, be higher than the values in the column of maximum allowable concentrations. Will endeavor nonetheless to keep this content to as low as possible and can not neglect the need to protect the public health.
- VMA - minimum permissible value.

TABLE 1 H

H. Chlorine Minimum Residual Values Available for 30 Minutes Contact time depending on the pH, temperature, type of Residual and Microbial Species. (Values proposed by the United States Public Health Service)				
pH	FREE CHLORINE (mg / l Cl HO)			Combined chlorine (mg / L Cl HO)
	BACTERICIDAL 0-25 ° C	CISTOCIDA 22-25 ° C	CISTOCIDA 2-5 ° C	BACTRERICIDA 0-25 ° C
6.0	0.2	2.0	7.5	2.0
7.0	0.2	2.5	10.0	2.5
8.0	0.2	5.0	20.0	3.0
9.0	0.6	20.0	70.0	3.5

TABLE 1I

I. Limit Values recommended for Fluoride in Drinking Water (values proposed by the United States Public Health Service)		
ANNUAL AVERAGE DAILY MAXIMUM TEMPERATURE (°C)	CONCENTRATION RECOMMENDED LIMITS FOR FLUORIDES (mg / l F)	
	LOWER	TOP
17.7 to 21.4	0.7	1.2
21.5 to 26.2	0.7	1.0
26.3 to 32.6	0.6	0.8

TABLE 2 QUALITY RATING PARAMETERS INTO GROUPS (G1, G2, G3) ACCORDING TO FREQUENCY OF SAMPLING AND ANALYSIS

G1	G2	G3
Organoleptic		Unwanted
	Physicochemical	Toxic
Microbiological		Radioactive

TABLE 3 MINIMUM FREQUENCY OF SAMPLING AND ANALYSIS OF WATER FOR HUMAN CONSUMPTION FOR CONTROL PURPOSES, DEFINED BY THE MAXIMUM INTERVAL BETWEEN HARVESTS AND THE MINIMUM NUMBER OF ANALYZES, DEPENDING ON THE POPULATION SERVED

PARAMETERS GROUP	G1		G2		G3	
POPULATION SERVED (HAB)	MAXIMUM RANGE	MINIMUM NUMBER	MAXIMUM RANGE	MINIMUM NUMBER	MAXIMUM RANGE	MINIMUM NUMBER
5 N ≤ 000	2 months	1 per 1 000 population	6 months	1 per 5000 inhabitants	2 years	1 per 5000 inhabitant
5000 <N ≤ 20 000	1 month	1 per 25 000 inhabitants	6 months	1 per 5000 inhabitants	2 years	1 per 5000 inhabitant
20,000 <N ≤ 100 000	15 days	1 per 5000 inhabitants	2 months	1 per 20 000 inhabitants	1 year	1 per 20 000 inhabitan
100 000 <N ≤ 500 000	5 days	1 per 15 000 inhabitants	20 days	1 per 50 000 population	6 months	1 per 50 000 populatic
C> 500 000	2 days	1 per 30 000 inhabitants	10 days	1 per 100 000 population	3 months	1 per 100 000 populati

TABLE 4 MINIMUM SAMPLING FREQUENCY AND HUMAN DRINKING WATER ANALYSIS FOR THE PURPOSE OF HEALTH SURVEILLANCE IN PUBLIC WATER SUPPLY SYSTEMS, SET THE MAXIMUM INTERVAL BETWEEN HARVESTS AND THE MINIMUM NUMBER OF SAMPLES, DEPENDING ON THE POPULATION SERVED

PARAMETERS GROUP	G1		G2		G3	
POPULATION SERVED (HAB)	MAXIMUM RANGE	MINIMUM NUMBER	MAXIMUM RANGE	MINIMUM NUMBER	MAXIMUM RANGE	MINIMUM NUMBER
5 N ≤ 000	1 year	1 per 1 000 population	1 year	1 per 5000 inhabitants	4 years	1 per 5000 inhabitants
5000 <N ≤ 20 000	6 months	1 per 25 000 inhabitants	1 year	1 per 5000 inhabitants	4 years	1 per 5000 inhabitants
20 ≤ N ≤ 100 000 000	3 months	1 per 5000 inhabitants	4 months	1 per 20 000 inhabitants	2 years	1 per 20 000 inhabitan
100 000 <N ≤ 500 000	1 month	1 per 15 000 inhabitants	2 months	1 per 50 000 population	1 year	1 per 50 000 populatio
C> 500 000	15 days	1 per 30 000 inhabitants	1 month	1 per 100 000 population	6 months	1 per 100 000 populatic

ANNEX 2 - TERMINOLOGY OF WATER SUPPLY SYSTEMS

DRINKING WATER: water that meets the criteria and quality standards for human consumption listed in Annex 1.

WATER SUPPLY: water for satisfaction of domestic consumption, commercial, industrial, public and fire.

ACCESSORY OF CONDUCT: network element to facilitate a combination of proper behavior to the geometry desired deployment. It can be curved, crosshead, cone or fork.

OPERATING ROOM: network element for the installation of accessories and the easy access for observation and read operation or maneuvering in conditions of safety and efficiency.

Capitation: amount of water consumed per user and per unit time.

CONDUCT: network component to ensure transport and water supply distribution.

COMMERCIAL USE: amount of water for use in commercial and service units.

DOMESTIC CONSUMPTION: amount of water for use in housing.

INDUSTRIAL USE: amount of water for use in industrial units, characterized by great randomness in requests to the system.

PUBLIC CONSUMPTION: amount of water for use in washing streets, watering green areas and cleaning sewers.

FIGHTING FOR THEIR FIRE: amount of water for use by the fire department to fight fires, characterized by sporadic but significant to system requests.

BOTTOM DISCHARGE: network element intended to allow the emptying duct sections and parts distribution networks in particular for the cleaning, disinfection or repair.

DIAMETER NOMINAL (DN): Numerical dimensional appointment of a pipe element; is an integer approximately equal to manufacturing dimensions; can be applied to the inner diameter (DN / ID) or outer diameter (DN / OD).

TIP FACTOR: ratio between a maximum flow rate (usually the maximum hourly flow rate) and an average flow rate (usually the annual average daily flow).

WATER LEAK: water lost by the system including the reservoir, in the distribution network and home-based branch lines.

Hydrant: Network component to allow the use of water from the public supply network for fire fighting; can be hydrant, wall or floor and landmark water ride.

HORIZON PROJECT: period used in the design of systems and determined taking into account technical and economic, financial and social such as the life span of facilities and equipment, the rate of urban growth and the ease of expansion of systems.

BOARD: network element designed to connect pipes, connecting routes, accessories and other elements of the distribution network devices; It can be rigid, flexible, expansion and disassembly.

FLOW METER: network element for determining the volume of water that flows and can make the reading of the instantaneous flow rate and volume disposed, or only the latter, and eventually these register values; can be deprimogénio, mechanical, electromagnetic, electronic and ultrasonic.

EXTENSION CONNECTION: the network component to ensure the building water supply from the public within the limits of properties to serve.

PRESSURE REDUCER: network element to reduce the pressure in a section so as not to exceed, downstream, a preset value may be of the loss of load chamber or pressure reducing valve.

RESERVOIR: complementary network installation designed to serve as a regularization wheel compensating for fluctuations in consumption, provide emergency reserve for firefighting or ensure distribution in the amount of system interruption cases, balance the pressures in the distribution network and also , regulate the operation of swings in.

PUBLIC WATER DISTRIBUTION SYSTEM: set of facilities aimed at the distribution of water to satisfy domestic consumption, commercial, industrial, public and others, including the distribution network accessories network elements and complementary facilities such as reservoirs and pumping systems.

SYSTEM booster: additional installation of network to introduce energy in the flow to increase pressure.

Isolating valve: network element to regulate, interrupt or allow the flow where it is installed; can be slide, butterfly, globe, male and tank, with manual or motorized operation.

CHECK VALVE: network element designed to automatically stop the flow of water in the ducts takes place in one direction; can be hinged, guided drive and walk.

SUCTION: network element designed to enable automatic expulsion of air which is liberated in the low-pressure conduits zones enable the air outlet when it comes to filling operations and to admit air into whenever a depression.

ANNEX 4 - CONDUCT OF TESTING AND SYSTEMS CONNECTION EXTENSIONS OF WATER DISTRIBUTION, AFTER LAYING

A - GENERAL CONDITIONS RELATING TO SECTIONS OF TEST

1. The testing of pipes is performed to each portion between consecutive gate valves, but may be carried out for a set of successive sections, if there is convenience in accelerating the filling of the trenches.

2. If the settlement of the connecting routes for the same time as the general network, the tests in each section of the general network should cover extensions that are tributaries.

3. If the settlement of branch lines is later but the overall network is not yet in service, although it is already tested, approved and covered the testing of extensions can be done alone or in groups communicating with each other by piping network general.

B - WATER RESISTANCE TESTING

1. The tests consist in filling of the ducts and increase in its internal pressure, by manual or mechanical pump, to one and a half times the operating pressure.

2. The pump for the hydraulic test is installed as close as possible to the point of smallest dimension of the section to be tested and must be provided with pressure gauge. For the test is obturam-all endpoints of pipelines.

3. High internal pressure to conduct P value of test pressure, it is considered that is satisfactorily settled when the gauge do not accuse, in half an hour, falls by more than $\sqrt{(P / 5)}$.

4. When the gauge of descent is higher, you should look up the fault and remedy it may not be approved to conduct without another test is obtained as a result, the maximum leakage indicated in the preceding paragraph.

5. The filling of pipelines for hydraulic test should be done in order to purge them of all the air, whose existence inside distort the results.

6. The tests should be carried out together with short, locking up enough pipes and fittings to prevent its displacement under the effect of internal pressure.

7. In the case of buried pipelines, their placing is done by means of landfill.

8. In the diameter pipes exceeding 200 mm and an operating pressure greater than 500 kPa must be checked, prior to the hydrostatic test, whether the special parts, such as greater than 1/16 and blind curves together, must be fought with anchor mass.

9. In the repeated conditions at number 8 the check is also made as to the nature of the terrain.

ANNEX 5 - DRAINAGE SYSTEM TERMINOLOGY PUBLIC WASTEWATER

INFILTRATION WATERS: affluent waters collector originating from seepage from the surrounding soil.

WASTEWATER: waters resulting from human activities emanating from the need to transport household waste, commercial and industrial and other, and the use of water for sanitary purposes and other recreational or resulting from precipitation events.

DOMESTIC WASTEWATER: water from toilets, kitchens and washing areas of clothing that are characterized in that they contain appreciable amounts of organic matter, are readily biodegradable and maintain relative constancy of its characteristics in time.

INDUSTRIAL WASTE WATER: water from industrial or similar activity which is characterized by containing various physical and chemical compounds, depending on the type of industrial process, and present, in general, high variability of its characteristics over time.

WASTEWATER PLUVIAL (or just rainwater): water from rainfall, characterized by generally contain lower amounts of polluting materials, particularly of organic origin; also be deemed to storm the waste water from irrigation of gardens and green spaces and even the streets of laundering, walks, patios and car parks, ie those that generally are collected by gutters, sinks and drains.

GRADES OF CAMERA: complementary network installation designed to retain coarse suspended solids and floating bodies transported in the flow in order to avoid obstructions in the piping, valves and other equipment downstream; can be manually or mechanically depending on the cleaning system; depending on the useful spacing between the bars bars can be coarse, medium or fine.

MANHOLE: network element to facilitate the junction of collectors and access to them for observation and maintenance.

FLOW RATE: amount by which must be multiplied precipitation occurred in the basin to estimate the useful rainfall, ie giving rise to flow on the network.

COLLECTOR: network component to ensure the conduct of waste water from buildings or public via the appropriate final destination.

Sand trap: Additional network setup for retaining inorganic materials (basically sands) carried in the flow to avoid downstream obstructions, damage to equipment and disturbances in the operation of the processing units; can be longitudinal, circular or simple sand retention chambers.

DUMPER: network element intended to divide the flow, especially used in individual networks to discharge of excess rainwater in wet weather.

DIAMETER NOMINAL (DN): Numerical dimensional appointment of a pipe element; is an integer approximately equal to manufacturing dimensions; can be applied to the inner diameter (DN / ID) or outer diameter (DN / OD).

ENTER THE NETWORK DEVICES: network elements for collecting rainwater; gutters can be characterized by a side entrance flow or sinks, with upper entrance of runoff and having a grid which allows the entry of water without hindering the movement of vehicles and pedestrians.

NETWORK TO THE CONFLUENCE OF FACTOR: value must be multiplied by which the average annual per capita water consumption, to estimate the average annual per capita inflow to the network of domestic wastewater.

FORK: network element for establishing the connection between the collector of the public network and the connecting extension or the connecting manifold rainwater input devices.

Septic: tight tank where the waste waters remain for a certain period, enough to undergo a physical treatment by flocculation and sedimentation and biological treatment by anaerobic digestion.

HORIZON PROJECT: period used in the design of systems and determined taking into account technical and economic, financial and social such as the life span of facilities and equipment, the rate of urban growth and the ease of expansion of systems.

METERS AND LOGGERS: equipment for measurement and registration of wastewater flows.

RETURN PERIOD: average time interval that occurs so that a certain amount of rainfall intensity is equaled or exceeded.

EXTENSION CONNECTION: the network component to ensure the conduct of gross wastewater from power extension chamber to the public.

SIPHON INVERT: Additional network setup U-shaped, with a flow of air under pressure, intended to overcome inferior to overcome obstacles or valley zones.

PUBLIC DRAINAGE SYSTEM SEWAGE: set of facilities aimed at draining domestic sewage, industrial or storm, including network collectors, accessories and complementary facilities.

Lift system: additional installation of network to introduce energy in flow, in duly justified cases, in particular where it is necessary to overcome an obstacle or as an alternative to a gravity flow in the most unfavorable conditions.

Separative SYSTEMS: systems consisting of two networks of different collectors, one designed exclusively to drainage of domestic and industrial waste water and the other for drainage of rainwater.

Mixed systems: systems consisting of the combination of the previous two types, i.e., that portion of the collection network functions as a unit system and the remainder as separative system.

Separative SYSTEMS PARTIAL: separative systems in which it is assumed, under exceptional circumstances, the connection of stormwater interior courtyards to the collector of domestic wastewater.

SYSTEMS UNIT: systems consisting of a single network of collectors, which are jointly admitted domestic, industrial wastewater and rainwater.

ANNEX 7 - CURVES INTENSITY-LENGTH FREQUENCY OF PRECIPITATION FOR MACAU TERRITORY

Analytical expression of the IDF curves for the territory of Macau

$$I = a.\ t^{b}$$

T (years)	The	B
2	390.29	-0.457
5	412.82	-0.409
10	434.72	-0.388
20	457.88	-0.372
50	490.78	-0.357
100	516.25	-0.347

ANNEX 8 - TESTING AND COLLECTORS CONNECTION AFTER LAYING EXTENSIONS

A - GENERAL CONDITIONS RELATING TO SECTIONS OF TEST

1. Assays of the collectors after settlement is performed for each straight section between manholes, but may be carried out for a set of successive sections there is convenience in accelerating the filling of the trenches.

2. If the settlement of the connecting routes for the same time as the general network, the tests in each section of the general network should cover extensions that are tributaries.

3. If the settlement of the connecting routes for later, but the overall network are not yet in service, although it is already tested, approved and covered the testing of extensions can be done alone or in groups communicating with each other by piping network general.

B - WATER RESISTANCE TESTS

B.1 - Overall

1. The leakage tests are performed before and after the coating of the collectors and accessories to be tested.

2. The leakage tests may use alternatively:

the water;

b) compressed air;

c) tobacco.

3. Testing with compressed air should only be used before recoating plumbing and accessories, does not apply to inverted siphons and pipes in pressure.

4. Tests with smoke should only be employed when any of the other two methods is not technically or economically feasible.

B.2 - With use of water

1 . The tests of water are recommended in most cases.

2. Determine the inner surface of the segment (or group of sections) of the pipe to be tested, summing the products of the respective lengths of the tubes nominal perimeter of the inner section.

By means of plugs, placed in the holes opened up and, to occlude the ends of the pipe section of the general network and the upstream ends of the connection branches tributaries to it and covered by the assay. If the test is simultaneously carried out for a group of successive sections, to occlude the ends of each section in the manner previously indicated and sets up the connection between sections with flexible hose portions. The joints seal-caps with appropriate material; These anchor-up so that they can withstand the internal pressure on that they will engage during the test. Water fills up the assembly under test, through the upstream end of the plug hole pipe of the overall network. In the final phase of the filling, conforms to about 1.5 m of flexible tubing at the same hole and at the end of that pipe, hopper, which must be installed on a support that allows to vary their height position. Complete filling up the whole through the funnel. However, closes the orifice of each buffer as soon as it is observed by the water outlet. You should adjust the position of the funnel so that the test pressure, at any point of the conduit, is between 1 N / cm^2 and 3 N / cm^2 ; the water level in the funnel under these conditions should coincide with the reference mark.

If there is water leaks from faulty pipes or poorly performed together, this is evidenced by excessive lowering of the water level. In this case, looking at the defect origin, empties the respective conduit and proceeds to the repair or replace, after which again fills the pipe with water until its level coincides with the reference mark funnel.

Waiting an interval of time with full pipe, to ensure the absorption of water by pipes and joints, the range which generally does not exceed one hour and not noting any defect in the pipe, remade if the level Initial water. Thereafter, and ten minutes, pour the water into the funnel using a graduated container, so as to maintain the initial level and thus the pressure in the assembly under test. After 30 minutes it is noted that the volume of water to be added.

It is important that during the 30 minute test, the sun does not shine directly on the conduit and the ambient temperature is as low as possible.

The assay can also be performed using for the introduction of water, instead of the flexible tube with the funnel a 90 ° bend and pipe vertically disposed, constituted by tubes of the same material as the pipe under test.

In special cases where it is authorized employment in network simple concrete pipes for sewage without coating waterproofing, the waiting period to the plumbing full of water should be increased to 24 hours and the test period should be increased to 2 hours .

3. Assays are performed so that the test pressure in the manifold is between a minimum of 1 N / cm^2 and a maximum of 3 N / cm 2.

4. The permeability of the tested system should check:

$$V / S \leqq 0.316$$

on what:

V = volume of water lost from the system during the test period (30 minutes to 2 hours depending on the case), expressed in liters:

S = internal surface of the conduit expressed in square meters.

B.3 - With use of compressed air

1 . The tests with compressed air are recommended when there is no water available or when there are problems with the water discharge test.

2. In carrying out compressed air tests shall pumping up air until the pressure is equivalent to the height of 100 mm of water in the glass U-tube connected to the system, considering that the section is in good condition if the level water does not fall below 75 mm for 5 minutes, there is no additional pumping of air.

3. In implementing the test with compressed air the air temperature must be taken into account because the difference of 1 ° C corresponds to a 38 mm water level change.

4. Lack of satisfaction to compressed air testing should not be cause for rejection of the section under test without being provide to the achievement of confirmation with hydraulic load tests.

B.4 - With use of tobacco

1. In carrying out the assay with smoking, smoke is blown into the interior of the collector by means of a fan, a smoke machine or any other device.

2. The test section is accepted if there was leakage of smoke through joints.

C - ALIGNMENT OF TESTS

1. The alignment tests and no obstructions are performed after covering the collectors and accessories to be tested.

2. In conducting the tests referred to above, is thrown in the water section of the upstream manhole in test and check the conditions of arrival of the wave in the downstream manhole.

3. If the test referred to in the previous paragraph are not achieved acceptable results, it is held the light test, which has to ensure the observation of a light spot from one to another end of the section to be tested.

D - INFILTRATION TESTS

1. After filling of the trench laying pipes, water infiltration enhancer should be verified in several sections by means of suitable tests.

2. For the purposes of the preceding paragraph shall be measured on the section to test the volume of collected water for an hour, and the section considered acceptable if the seepage water volume is less than 2 l / h, per linear meter of conduct and 1000 mm inside diameter.

E - TESTS IN LARGE COLLECTORS

1. 700 mm diameter pipes, joints can be tested individually, the tests described in previous articles are not required.

2. When the pipes are sufficiently broad to be flyable, far-there will be a visual inspection of the inside and an essay with smoke or compressed air, or other approved supervision before and after filling trenches when it is not tunnels.

F - TESTS IN CONDUCT LIFTS

1. Tests on aerial pipes are leakage tests with water and can run for the whole of conduct or small sections, before proceeding to the filling of the settlement ditches.

2. The tests consist in filling of the pipes and increase in its internal pressure, by manual or mechanical pump, to one and a half to two times the operating pressure of the pipe.

3. The pump for the test shall be installed as close to the point of lowest elevation of the section to be tested and is provided with a suitably calibrated pressure gauge, and to this test, fill up all endpoints plumbing.

4. High internal pressure of the pipe when the pressure value P of the test, it is considered that said conduit is satisfactorily established when the gauge has not acknowledged in half an hour, falls by more than $\sqrt{(P / 5)}$.

5. When the gauge descent is greater than the value indicated in the previous paragraph, should look up the fault and remedy it may not be adopted without channeling that another test is obtained as a result, lowering the maximum pressure indicated on the preceding paragraph.

6. The filling of the pipes for the tests should be done in order to purge them of any air therein whose presence would distort the results.

7. Prior to the tests, consideration should be the need to provide massive mooring in various accessories or strengthen already built and proceed accordingly.

ANNEX 9 - GENERAL RULES OF DOMESTIC WASTE WATER DISCHARGE IN INDUSTRIAL AND COLLECTORS NETWORK

1. The discharge of domestic and industrial wastewater in the sewer network must meet the quantitative and qualitative standards set out in this annex, where appropriate using appropriate prior control or pretreatment.

2. The tip of flow of waste water should be drained by systems without giving rise to any problems of hydraulic nature or health, including entries in load and floods.

3. The fluctuating flow rates, daily or seasonal, should not disturb the drainage systems and wastewater treatment plants.

4. drainage systems devoid of the waste water treatment plant, the standards to be respected:

a) hydrogen ion concentration should correspond to a pH between normal limits and should not be not less than 6 or more than 10;

b) the temperature should not exceed 45 ° C;

c) the color, measured on the scale platinum-cobalt, must not exceed 80 units or, broadly, to give rise to complaints;

d) the coarse solids should not have dimensions, in any possible measurement axes greater than or equal to 5 cm;

e) the total suspended solids should not exceed 1000 mg / l;

f) the content of oils and fats should not exceed 100 mg / l;

g) the sulfide content should not exceed 1 mg / l S.

5. drainage systems endowed with wastewater treatment plant, the standards to be met at the entrance should be, other than those mentioned in paragraph 4:

a) biochemical oxygen, measured at 5 days and 20 ° C does not exceed 1 000 mg / l O 2;

b) chemical oxygen should not exceed 2 000 mg / l O 2;

c) shall be biodegradable detergents and its content does not exceed 75 mg / l;

d) the elements and chemical substances listed below, shall not exceed the amounts indicated in mg / l

Elements and chemicals	Level (mg / l)
- Arsenic in The	1
- Cadmium in Cd	0.2
- Lead in Pb	2.5
- Copper Cu	5
- Total Chromium in Cr	2
- Hexavalent chromium, Cr	0.1
- Mercury Hg	0.05
- Nickel, Ni	4

- Cyanide, CN	1
- Phenols, C_6H_5OH	10
- Mineral oils	15
- Residual chlorine total available in C_{l2}	1.0

e) industrial waste water shall be free from substances which involve the destruction of biological treatment ecosystems.

6. In addition to the numerical characteristics of the parameters set out in paragraphs 4 and 5, the wastewater to admit drainage systems must in all circumstances be exempted from:

a) sedimentary, precipitable or floating materials, which, by itself or after mixing with other substances in systems, could endanger the health of the operating staff or the systems structures;

b) explosives, rubble, sand, ash, radioactive material and any other substances that may clog or damage the organs systems and treatment plants;

c) hydroxylated cyclic compounds and their halogenated derivatives;

d) substances that may cause the destruction of aquatic or terrestrial ecosystems in the receiving environment;

e) pathogens for humans;

f) any substances that stimulate beyond the reasonable the development of vectors or pathogen reservoirs.

7. The introduction, in the systems of solid or semi-solid waste of any kind, requires a license of the management company, which can only be granted in exceptional circumstances, where such waste is subject to pre-treatment to render them harmless to the organs of drainage systems and treatment plants.

ANNEX 10 - GENERAL RULES OF DOMESTIC WASTE WATER DISCHARGE AND INDUSTRIAL BETWEEN RECEIVER

Domestic and industrial wastewater discharged into the receiving environment must meet the qualitative and quantitative standards set out in the attached table:

Parameter	Expression of results	Maximum Allowable Value(1)
pH	scale Sorensen	6.0 to 9.0 (2)
Temperature	°C	increase of 3 ° C (3)
CB05 (20)	mg / l $_2$	40.0
CCO	mg / l $_2$	150.0
SST	mg / l	60.0
Aluminum	mg / l Al	10.0
Total arsenic	mg / l The	1.0
Total cadmium	mg / l Cd	0.2
Total lead	mg / l Pb	1.0

Parameter	Expression of results	Maximum Allowable Value(1)
Total cyanide	mg / l CN	0.5
Total copper	mg / l Cu	1.0
Chromium		
- Hexavalent	mg / l Cr (VI)	0.1
- total	mg / l Cr	2.0
Total iron	mg / l Fe	2.0
Total manganese	mg / l Mn	2.0
Total mercury	mg / l Hg	0.05
Total nickel	mg / l Ni	2.0
Total selenium	mg / l If	0.5
Total zinc	mg / l Zn	5.0
Heavy metals (total)	mg / l	5.0
Total hydrocarbons	mg / l	1.0
Pesticides	pg / l	0.5
Smell	-	undetectable at 1:20 dilution
Color	-	not visible in 1:20 dilution
Residual chlorine available		
- free	mg / l C $_{l2}$	0.5
- total	mg / l C $_{l2}$	1.0
Phenols	mg / L C_6H_5OH	0.5
Oil and fat	mg / l	15.0
Sulphides	mg / l S	1.0
Sulfites	mg / l SO_3	1.0
Sulphates	mg / l SO_4	2000.0
Total phosphorus	mg / l P	10.0
		3 (in waters which feed ponds or lagoons)
Ammonia nitrogen	mg / l NH4	10.0
Total nitrogen	mg / l N	15.0
Nitrates	mg / l NO_3	50.0
Aldehydes	mg / l	1.0
Detergents (sodium lauryl sulfate)	mg / l	2.0
Hexachlorocyclohexane (HCH)	mg / l	2.0
Carbon tetrachloride	mg / l	1.5 (5)
DDT	mg / l	0.2 (5)
Pentachlorophenol	mg / l	1.0 (5)
Aldrin, daldrina, endrin isodrin	g / l	2.0 (4)
Hexachlorobenzene (HCB)		
- Production and processing	mg / l	1.0 (5)
- Production of perchlorethylene and carbon tetrachloride by perchlorination	mg / l	1.5 (5)
Hexachlorobutadiene (HCBD)	mg / l	1.5 (5)
Chloroform	mg / l	1.0

Notes to the table:

(1) VMA - maximum permissible value understood as the monthly average, defined as the arithmetic mean of the average daily referring to the days of operation a month.

The daily average value determined based on a representative sample of the waste water discharged over a period of 24 hours can not exceed four times the average monthly value (the sample in a 24-hour period should be made taking into account the discharge regime of wastewater produced).

(2) The average daily value can at most be in the range 5.0 - 10.0.

(3) Temperature of the receiving environment after discharge of wastewater, measured 30 meters downstream of the discharge point, can the average daily value exceeds the monthly average in 2 ^{the} C.

(4) The average daily value may not exceed five times the monthly average.

(5) the average daily value can not exceed twice the monthly average.

ANNEX 11 - DISTRIBUTION SYSTEMS FOR BUILDING TERMINOLOGY WATER

PRODUCING HOT WATER APPLIANCES: equipment for heating water for instant use - water heaters - or to build - water heaters.

FIRE MOUTHS: devices for the use of water for firefighting and to which you can connect the hoses or other appropriate devices and accessories.

BUILDING CLASSES (classification according to their total height):

Class P (small) - buildings up to 9.6 meters;

Class M (medium) - height of buildings extend above the 9.6 to 20.5 m me;

Class A (high) - height of buildings above 20.5 understood me 50 m, subdivided into two subclasses:

- A1 - lower height of buildings or equal to 31.5 m;

- A2 - top height of buildings to 31.5 m;

MA class (average) - height of buildings higher than 50 m.

COLUMN: plumb plumbing section of an extension or introduction of a distribution branch.

COUNTERS: devices are installed in the water distribution network for the purpose of measuring and totaling the volume of water that passes through them.

FACILITIES LIFTS: are sets of equipment to raise, by mechanical means, the water stored in reservoirs.

FACILITIES SOBREPRESSORAS: are sets of equipment which produces a pressure increase available in public when it is not enough to guarantee good working conditions in the system.

EXTENSION OF POWER: Sewer direct feeding of use devices.

EXTENSION OF DISTRIBUTION: conduit between the individual meters and power stations.

INTRODUCTION OF EXTENSION COLLECTIVE: conduit between the boundary of the property and the introduction of individual branches of users.

EXTENSION OF PERSONAL INTRODUCTION: conduit between the extension of collective introduction and individual meters or between the boundary of the property and the counter, in the case of single-family building.

EXTENSION CONNECTION: conduit between the public and the property boundary to serve.

RESERVOIRS: installations for water storage at atmospheric pressure, constituting a reserve to the power of building networks of water distribution.

TAPS and flowmeters: use of devices placed on output power of stations for the purpose of regulating the water supply.

VALVES: organs are installed in the networks, types and for the following purposes:

a) gate valves - prevent or establish the passage of water in either direction;

b) check valves - prevent water from passing in either direction;

c) safety valves - keep the pressure below a certain amount per discharge effect;

d) pressure-reducing valves - to maintain the pressure below a certain value by introducing a load loss;

e) control valves - to allow regulation of the flow.

PROHIBITION OF RELEASE OR DUMP HARMFUL SUBSTANCES

Decree-Law No. 35/97 / M

25 August

Taking into account the fundamental principles modern shape it to environmental policy, it is necessary to ensure that adequate legal instruments to prevent pollution of the maritime areas of jurisdiction, especially the public water domain and neighboring waters with the territory of Macau .

In these terms;

After hearing the Consultative Council;

In developing the legal regime established by Law No. 2/91 / M, of 11 March, and in accordance with paragraph 1 of Article 13 of the Macau Organic Statute, the Acting Governor, to be effective as law in Macau, the following:

Article 1

(Object)

This law regulates the prohibition of release or dump harmful substances in the areas of maritime jurisdiction, with a view to preventing pollution and protecting the environment.

Article 2

(Prohibited Conduct)

1. The release or dump in the areas of maritime jurisdiction of any substances or solid or liquid waste that somehow could pollute the waters, beaches or shores, as well as the flora or marine fauna, such as petroleum products or mixtures is prohibited to containing them, or other chemicals on the terms of the relevant international Conventions and agreements.

2. The prohibition referred to in the preceding paragraph covers both the discharges by vessels, whether caused by the facilities located inside or outside the maritime areas of jurisdiction.

3. The port industrial facilities, or any other discharging effluent into the sea, should take treatment processes of wastewater, as well as measures to prevent and combat spills of harmful substances at sea.

4. The captain of ports on their own initiative or at the request of others, take appropriate measures to prevent and suppress breaches of the preceding paragraphs.

Article 3

(Penalties)

1. Infringements of the previous article shall be punished with a fine of 1 000.00 200 000.00 patacas, applicable to the respective owner or owner, without prejudice to any civil, criminal and disciplinary are instigated.

2. Upon graduation of the fine referred to in the previous paragraph, it caters to the seriousness of the offense and the offender's fault, and the seriousness of the consequences of the offense arising to the waters, beaches or shores and for the flora and marine fauna.

Article 4

(Authority for the supervision and application of the fine)

Monitoring compliance with the provisions of this law and the fine application the responsibility of the captain of ports.

Article 5

(Penalty payment)

1. The fine is payable within 30 days from the date of notification of the punitive sentence.

2. In the absence of voluntary payment of the fine within the period prescribed in the preceding paragraph, the procedure is compulsory collection through the competent court, serving as enforceable the certificate of the punitive sentence.

Article 6

(Penalty Destination)

Fines imposed under the provisions of this law fully allocated to the Territory.

Article 7

(Fine amount fixing Pending)

When any auto raised by infringement of this law is pending in determining the amount of the fine, the captain of the port, on its own initiative or at the request of another entity, can not allow the clearance of the ship whose crew part the offender without is provided a bank guarantee or any other guarantee or an appropriately judged deposit in an amount equal to the maximum amount of the financial penalty, plus the probable damages and other expenses that may be considered Territorial credits.

Article 8

(Emergency measures)

Responsibility of the captain of ports adopt, as soon as possible, all measures deemed necessary to combat pollution caused by infringements of the provisions of this statute, running all expenses for offender's account.

Article 9

(Exceptions)

The provisions of this law do not apply to releases or discharges of substances, liquid or solid wastes referred to in Article 2:

a) Made by a vessel to ensure their own safety or that of another vessel, or to save human lives;
b) Made for any facilities to ensure their safety or their staff;

c) The result of force majeure, duly proved, provided they have been taken after the occurrence of all measures deemed necessary to prevent the continuation of such releases or evictions or reduce the amount of it and its consequences.

Article 10

(Revocation)

Decree No. 495/73 is hereby repealed, 6 October, published in the Official Gazette No. 42 of 20 October 1973.

ORGANIZATION AND FUNCTIONING OF THE DIRECTORATE OF ENVIRONMENTAL PROTECTION SERVICES

Administrative Regulation No. 14/2009

The Chief Executive, after consultation with the Executive Council, decrees, under point 5) of Article 50 of the Basic Special Administrative Region of Macao law and under Article 2 of Law No. 6/2009 be enforced as administrative regulation, the following:

CHAPTER I OBJECT, NATURE AND DUTIES

Article 1

Object

This administrative regulation is to define the powers, organization and functioning of the Directorate of Environmental Protection Bureau, hereinafter referred to as DSPA.

Article 2

Nature

DSPA is the public service of the Special Administrative Region of Macau, hereinafter referred to as the MSAR, who led the study, planning, implementation, coordination and promotion of environmental policy.

Article 3

Powers

The duties of DSPA:

1) To collaborate in the definition of the SAR environmental policy;

2) Develop, implement and coordinate plans and actions relating to the application of the system of prevention, control and treatment of environmental pollution;

3) Prepare the protection projects and environmental protection, nature, ecological balance and sustainable development in the environmental area;

4) Ensure the coordination of programs, measures and environmental policy measures promoted by the public authorities of the MSAR;

5) To study and propose legislative measures on the environment;

6) To ensure compliance with environmental legislation;

7) Perform the inspection and management of integrated pollution control, avoiding the destruction of the ecological balance;

8) To consider and decide complaints and grievances that are referred to in the environmental field;

9) To set up a database based on information about the claims process and complaints on environmental matters to other public bodies of the MSAR;

10) issue an opinion on plans, programs and environmental protection projects and ecological balance;

11) To issue an opinion within the environmental impact assessment process for projects and actions which licensing or authorization compete with other entities;

12) License and environmental monitoring for the installation of industrial, commercial or services, and any other activity likely to affect the environment;

13) Develop or evaluate environmental impact studies;

14) License pollutants discharge applications;

15) Set the values of pollutant emission limit values, measurement methods and the total pollutant emission quotas;

16) To promote and coordinate all activities related to environmental infrastructure, such as the Solid Waste Incineration Plant, the Special and Hazardous Waste Treatment Plant, the Water Treatment Plants Waste, health and special landfills and preservation of ecological zones;

17) Promote the exchange and cooperation with public services or public and private entities of the MSAR, and conclude with foreign entities, agreements and protocols on the environment;

18) To promote and develop cooperative relations at regional and international level;

19) To support the implementation of conventions, treaties, agreements, protocols and other international instruments on the environment, applicable to the MSAR;

20) To propose, organize and conduct awareness raising, training and information on environmental education;

21) Making monitoring base and environmental studies and to promote scientific research and technological development on the environment;

22) Promote the development of green businesses;

23) drawing up and annually publish the SAR environmental status report;

24) Perform such other duties as may be legally committed.

CHAPTER II ORGANIZATIONAL STRUCTURE

Article 4

Direction and organic subunits

1. The DSPA is headed by a Director, assisted by two Deputy Directors.

2. To fulfill its responsibilities, the DSPA includes the following units:

1) Department of Environmental Pollution Control;

2) Department of Planning and Environmental Assessment;

3) Department of Sensitization, Education and Environmental Cooperation;

4) Management Center for Environmental Infrastructure;

5) Administration and Finance Division;

6) Organization and Information Technology Division.

Article 5

Director of skills

Responsibility of the Director, namely:

1) To direct, plan and coordinate the overall activity of DSPA and supervise the various organic subunits;

2) prepare and submit annually to the consideration and approval above the plan and the activity report and the budget proposal of DSPA;

3) Propose appointments and decide on the allocation of staff to the various organic subunits;

4) Establish rules or instructions to be followed by organic subunits, with a view to regular operation;

5) Represent the DSPA with any other organizations or bodies of the SAR, or abroad;

6) To exercise the powers it delegated or sub-delegated and others that may be assigned thereto by law.

Article 6

Responsibilities of Deputy Directors

Responsibility of the Deputy Directors, namely:

1) To assist the director;

2) Replace the Director in his absence or impediment;

3) To exercise the powers delegated to them or sub-delegated by the Director and perform such other functions as may be entrusted to them.

Article 7

Department of Environmental Pollution Control

1. The Department of Environmental Pollution Control is the organic subunit responsible for the prevention, inspection, supervision and control of pollution and environmental licensing.

2. The Department of Environmental Pollution Control comprises:

1) The Environmental Inspectorate Division;

2) Prevention Division of Environmental Pollution.

Article 8

Division of Environmental Inspection

In the Environmental Inspection Division is responsible for:

1) monitor compliance with the legislation on prevention and control of pollution and ecological preservation;

2) monitoring the pollutant emission level in accordance with the criteria and limits set out in specific legislation;

3) To monitor compliance with environmental licensing requirements;

4) To consider and decide complaints and grievances that are referred to in the environmental field;

5) Conduct and participate in inspections in environmental monitoring;

6) inspect, investigate and monitor industrial, commercial or services, and any other activity likely to affect the environment in terms of environmental legislation;

7) collect and analyze samples of pollutants emitted by businesses operating liable to negative impacts on the environment, including producing electricity and water supply, without prejudice to the tasks of these areas to other entities;

8) Ensure, in collaboration with other public bodies, the implementation of conventions, treaties, agreements, protocols and other international instruments on the environment, applicable to the MSAR.

Article 9

Prevention Division of Environmental Pollution

On Prevention Division of Environmental Pollution is responsible for:

1) To define the procedures and criteria of environmental licensing;

2) Proceed to environmental licensing;

3) Inspect, inspect and monitor the installation, expansion and change in the nature or operation of industrial, commercial or services, and any other activity likely to affect the environment subject to prior environmental licensing;

4) give advice on the installation, expansion and change in the nature or operation of industrial, commercial or services, and any other activity likely to affect the environment, at the request of other licensors, subject to the legally required licenses ;

5) authorize or issue an opinion on applications for pollutant discharge permit;

6) Establish the emission limits of pollutants, measurement methods and the total pollutant emission quotas;

7) Conduct and participate in surveys, inspections and monitoring in the prevention and control of pollution;

8) Issue opinions on projects and propose plans and programs relating to the application of the system of prevention and control of pollution;

9) Issue opinions on applications for the granting of export licenses and import of controlled substances or pollutants and potentially toxic chemicals, in accordance with applicable environmental legislation;

10) Prepare and submit to higher draft legislation for the prevention and control of pollution, as well as procedures, criteria and methods for environmental licensing;

11) propose the legal instruments necessary for the implementation of conventions, treaties, agreements, protocols and other international instruments on the environment, applicable to the MSAR;

12) Promote, in collaboration with other public bodies, the investigation of accidents causing air pollution, aquatic environment and soil, adopting the emergency plans and actions needed to address them;

13) adopt, in collaboration with other public entities, plans and actions for reducing the quantity and harmfulness of waste, hazardous substances and toxic chemicals, from research to impacts with its handling and use.

Article 10

Department of Planning and Environmental Assessment

1. The Department of Planning and Environmental Assessment is the organic subunit responsible for the study, planning, management and environmental assessment and implementation of monitoring of environmental components.

2. The Department of Planning and Environmental Assessment comprises:

1) The Environmental Planning Division;

2) The Evaluation Division and Environmental Monitoring.

Article 11

Division of Environmental Planning

In the Environmental Planning Division is responsible for:

1) assist in the preparation and review of instruments and environmental plans;

2) carry out assessments of environmental planning instruments, resource use efficiency made available, costs and environmental investments and efficiency of economic instruments for sustainable development in the environmental area;

3) To propose measures concerning the protection of air quality of the aquatic environment and soil, waste management and the prevention and control of noise pollution;

4) To propose environmental assessment measures, adoption of best available techniques, the promotion of green enterprises and preservation and defense of the environment and ecological balance;

5) To propose measures for air quality management and other natural resources;

6) To implement environmental plans;

7) Carry out studies on the implementation of the action plans for the prevention and control of pollution from various sources, air quality and the aquatic environment, waste and the preservation of nature and ecological balance;

8) To organize and promote studies relating to environmental protection, ecological conservation and biodiversity, as well as those pertaining to sustainable development, environmental considerations;

9) To promote studies and technological and scientific exchanges on the environment;

10) To propose measures for fulfillment of plans and programs in the fields of air quality and the aquatic environment, waste, control of noise pollution and the preservation of nature and ecological balance;

11) The collection, processing and systematization of information and management of files related to environmental planning;

12) To issue an opinion in the field of environmental planning, based on studies of urban synthetic indicators;

13) Collect and organize information on the environment and to develop, within its competence, studies for the fulfillment of obligations under the conventions, treaties, agreements, protocols and other international instruments on the environment, applicable to the MSAR;

14) To prepare annually, the MSAR environmental status report with the support of other organic subunits of DSPA;

15) harmonize environmental policies, ensure their effectiveness and evaluate their efficiency and effectiveness;

16) To prepare and publish reports on environmental studies;

17) analyze and evaluate the trend of global environmental quality.

Article 12

Evaluation Division and Environmental Monitoring

In the Evaluation Division and Environmental Monitoring is responsible for:

1) Establish environmental quality indicators such as support for planning and performance assessment of environmental components;

2) To strategic assessment of plans, programs and actions of environmental policy, in its various forms, and sustainable development in the environmental area;

3) To approve or issuing reports on the studies of environmental impact assessment relating to the installation, expansion and change in the nature or operation of industrial, commercial or services, and any other activity likely to affect the environment under legislation;

4) carry out assessments and issuing expert opinions on environmental impact assessments of major projects of infrastructure and road projects;

5) To define the environmental indicators and the formulation of selection criteria and standards and quality standards to be observed;

6) To develop technical standards, general guidelines and methodologies of environmental impact assessment process;

7) Develop environmental criteria, standards and pollutant emission standards for implementation of procedures for the prevention and control of pollution;

8) Develop criteria and guidelines for the different environmental technologies for monitoring and environmental impact assessment;

9) Establish parameters, monitoring methods and criteria for analysis and environmental impact assessment;

10) collect, verify, record, validate and make available data resulting from monitoring, for integration into an information system;

11) Establish and maintain an information database and valuation models to study the environmental impact;

12) Sort the data on environmental indicators and prepare their reports;

13) To prepare assessment reports of environmental impact, whenever deemed necessary;

14) To support and organize training courses as part of the monitoring and evaluation of environmental impact;

15) conduct the monitoring, analysis and evaluation of environmental components and environmental quality indicators for evaluation and improvement of environmental quality;

16) conduct the monitoring of environmental pollution sources;

17) Collect and analyze statistical data on environmental protection;

18) To ensure smooth operation, management and maintenance of facilities and equipment of stations and networks monitoring and laboratory DSPA.

Article 13

Department Sensitization, Education and Environmental Cooperation

1. The Department of Sensitization, Education and Environmental Cooperation is the organic subunit responsible for awareness and environmental education, the publication on

environmental education material, training, environmental management and cooperation and development of green businesses.

2. The Department of Sensitization, Education and Environmental Cooperation comprises:

1) Awareness and Environmental Education Division;

2) The Environmental Cooperation Division.

Article 14

Division of Environmental Awareness and Education

In the Awareness and Environmental Education Division is responsible for:

1) Conduct outreach activities, environmental education and promotion;

2) Organize exchanges, seminars, exhibitions and conferences in the field of environmental protection;

3) Publish and disseminate publications and other materials relating to environmental education;

4) Promote the dissemination of environmental law, including international conventions applicable to Macao, in the environmental field, with informational and educational purposes;

5) Conduct surveys and opinion polls on the environment and analyze their results;

6) Ensure the organization of training and exchange activities in environmental protection;

7) preparing and publishing the DSPA activity report;

8) To manage public information centers of DSPA, which are designed to raise awareness and to inform citizens of the implications and relevance of environmental education;

9) Manage and promote public environmental education centers of DSPA, which are designed to publicize the actions and knowledge in the field of environmental education;

10) collect, record and archive the information for all the activities of the DSPA.

Article 15

Division for Environmental Cooperation

On Environmental Cooperation Division is responsible for:

1) To promote cooperation ties in environmental education and exchange projects with the MSAR foreign entities in environmental protection;

2) enhancing cooperation under protocols concluded or to be concluded between the DSPA and other organizations or similar entities;

3) To promote and coordinate the strategic assessment process of projects involving transboundary environmental impacts;

4) collect and process information and report resulting from the implementation of conventions, treaties, agreements, protocols and other international instruments on the environment, applicable to the MSAR;

5) To promote and disseminate integrating environmental management practices and green companies;

6) To coordinate the certification work and environmental eco-label;

7) support the introduction of green products and technology in environmental protection;

8) The ecological consumption and encourage the establishment of ecomercado;

9) To prepare and propose agreements and management agreements with local entities and abroad on the environment.

Article 16

Environmental Infrastructure Management Center

The Management Center for Environmental Infrastructure, equated the department, is the organic subunit responsible for the promotion, coordination, monitoring, maintenance and supervision of the activities of Solid Waste Incineration Plant, Treatment of Special Waste and Hazardous station, the Wastewater treatment plants, sanitary landfills and special and the preservation of ecological zones, being responsible in particular:

1) Carry out studies to increase the waste treatment capacity, particularly hazardous or special waste, and constantly update and modernize the available treatment facilities;

2) monitor the performance, by controlling the quantity and quality of effluent, the Water Treatment Plants Waste;

3) Monitor and supervise the activities of service providers and concessionaires of the operation of waste water treatment plants and the removal and public cleaning of solid waste;

4) promote, monitor and evaluate the waste management plans;

5) collect and systematize the information on technical and municipal waste production reduction procedures;

6) study and assess the possibilities for introducing new technologies;

7) Control and supervise the landfill operations and disposal of hazardous or special waste;

8) cooperate with other entities and public services in the management of landfills and hazardous or special waste;

9) to supervise ecological zones.

Article 17

Administrative and Financial Division

1. The Administration and Finance Division is the organic subunit responsible for the technical and administrative support to the activities of the other subunits within the organization and management of human, material, financial and equity.

2. The Administrative and Financial Division is responsible for:

1) Ensure the improvement of the administration, the organization's effectiveness and execution of all administrative procedures for the management and administration of human resources available;

2) Ensure personnel management by introducing the necessary procedures to improve accountability and work skills;

3) to organize and update the personal files of staff, and to ensure the paperwork related to its management and administration;

4) assist with the planning, organization, implementation and monitoring of the annual training program;

5) To provide and maintain a register of green companies and defense associations and environmental protection;

6) Ensure the general office of the DSPA, including all records, and customer service;

7) To disseminate the laws, rules, service communications, orders and general guidelines for the various subunits;

8) recording the complaints, complaints and appeals that are presented in the DSPA and give them the proper referral within the time limits provided for by applicable legislation;

9) To provide and maintain in working condition the general archive of DSPA;

10) Issuing certificates and copies of documents filed;

11) To propose, as soon as they occur within the deadlines stipulated by law, the destruction of documents;

12) Manage the information room, for the reading and consultation issues related to environmental protection and ensure the functioning of the library DSPA;

13) Prepare the hours necessary and appropriate to ensure the processing of salaries, other allowances and discounts to staff;

14) Prepare the proposed annual budget of the DSPA, monitor its implementation and to prepare, whenever deemed necessary, their revisions and amendments;

15) To ensure that office related to the acquisition of goods and services, overseeing the organization of appointments and competitions and the preparation of their substitutes contracts and titles thereof;

16) To receive deposits and process your refund, termination or reduction, whenever so are the necessary legal conditions are met;

17) Process payment of all charges due, checked the conditions and legal requirements necessary for its implementation;

18) Perform the functions relating to the supply, the supply of goods and services and assets management;

19) To organize and update the inventory and registration of existing assets in DSPA;

20) To ensure the management of facilities and equipment of DSPA and ensure their safety, conservation, hygiene and maintenance;

21) Ensure the management, maintenance and repair of the fleet and communication systems of DSPA.

Article 18

Organization and Informatics Division

1. Organization and Information Technology Division is the organic subunit responsible for the technical support in the field of organization and information technology.

2. The Organization and Information Technology Division is responsible for:

1) To promote and conduct suitability studies the means and organization techniques to the specific requirements of DSPA with a view to computerization;

2) ensure the operation of computer systems, geographic information system and the public administration online system called e-government;

3) Coordinate the planning, study, monitoring and evaluation of administrative procedures and operation of the DSPA, with a view to simplification and standardization, as well as the improvement of internal management and service model to ensure its continuous improvement;

4) To study, plan and coordinate the computerization and use of electronic means in the DSPA and analyze the implications of the development of computer applications, in particular as regards the establishment of new information circuits;

5) To design and implement the necessary procedures for the collection, security and control of information resulting from computerization and ensure its regular and integrated treatment;

6) to organize and update the computer files of DSPA as well as create, develop and support the operation of computer databases;

7) maintaining applications and databases and make available to users with the necessary information on activities;

8) ensure the security and confidentiality of information in accordance with the rules on access to the computer system;

9) Collaborate with other computer centers integrated into public services and bodies of the MSAR, with a view to establishing a common methodology in information processing;

10) To manage the installed computer system, ensuring their good condition and operation;

11) collaborate in the establishment plan of the management of DSPA and provide training, courses, seminars and other events in the field of information technology;

12) Carry out the implementation of information systems and technologies, ensuring the continued compliance with the objectives of the organization of services.

CHAPTER III ADVISORY ENVIRONMENT COUNCIL

Article 19

Creation

An advisory body called the Advisory Council for the Environment, whose powers, composition and functioning are defined by order of the Chief Executive.

CHAPTER IV STAFF

Article 20

Staffing

The DSPA's workforce is set out in schedule attached to this administrative regulation of which it is part.

Article 21

System of personal

1. The personnel of DSPA applies the general rules of the civil service and other applicable legislation.

2. The DSPA can hire staff, in Macao or abroad, on an individual contract basis of work or providing services for implementation of high technical differentiation works.

Article 22

Technical consultants

The DSPA can use the services of technical consultants, in Macao or abroad, the legal regime for the acquisition of services, to be authorized by the Chief Executive on the recommendation of the director of services.

CHAPTER V FINAL AND TRANSITIONAL PROVISIONS

Article 23

Personal transition

1. The Institute's establishment plan for the Civic and Municipal Affairs Bureau, hereinafter IACM, assigned to the management of landfills, within the competence of the Environmental Hygiene Division, you can choose, within 30 days from the date of publication of this administrative regulation, the transition to the places of the DSPA staff, in the same career, category and grade it holds.

2. The transition of personnel referred to above and the establishment plan of the Environment Council operates the name list, approved by order of the Chief Executive whether any formalities except publication in the Official Bulletin.

3. The personnel employed by the Environment Council carried over to the DSPA by annotation in the respective contractual instrument, while maintaining its legal and functional situation.

4. Personnel hired by the IACM, assigned to the management of landfills, and the Office for Infrastructure Development, hereinafter referred to as GDI, engaged in the promotion and coordination of activities related to the Incineration Plant of Solid Waste and the Water Treatment Plants Wastewater, you can choose, within the period specified in paragraph 1, the transition to DSPA by annotation in the respective contractual instrument, while maintaining its legal and functional situation.

5. Time of service provided by staff that moves in accordance with the provisions of this Article account for all legal purposes, as provided in office, career, category and grade for which operates the transition.

6. The options provided for in this Article shall be effected by a declaration of introduction written by the person concerned to be delivered in the IACM or GDI, as the body to which it belongs.

Article 24

Logo

The DSPA logo is approved by executive order.

Article 25

Identification Cards

Models ID card to use by the staff of DSPA, in the exercise of their duties, are approved by order of the Chief Executive, published in the Official Bulletin.

Article 26

Financial charges

The budget of DSPA for the current fiscal year is presented to the Chief Executive until the day May 30, 2009, accompanied by the opinion of the Finance Service.

Article 27

Duty to cooperate

1. It is the duty of all public services, autonomous bodies and legal persons of public utility collaborate with DSPA, within their organic functions.

2. Companies utilities and public works and exploiting activities on an exclusive basis shall provide the DSPA collaboration for this requested under the respective contracts.

Article 28

Repeals

They are repealed:

1) Dispatch of the Chief Executive No. 46/2000;

2) Points 8) to 11) of paragraph 2 of the Order of the Chief Executive No. 68/2000, as amended conferred upon it by the Order of the Chief Executive No. 97/2009;

3) Dispatch of the Chief Executive No. 80/2009.

Article 29

Implementation

1. This administrative regulation enters into force on June 29, 2009.

2. Except as provided in the preceding paragraph Articles 23 and 26, which come into force on the day following the publication of this administrative regulation.

Approved on May 14, 2009.

EMISSION LIMITS OF AIR POLLUTANTS AND MANAGEMENT STANDARDS OF INSTALLATIONS OF INDUSTRIAL ESTABLISHMENTS CEMENT PRODUCTION

Administrative Regulation No. 12/2014

The Chief Executive, after consultation with the Executive Council, decrees, under point 5) of Article 50 of the Macau Basic Law, to stand as independent administrative regulation, the following:

CHAPTER I GENERAL PROVISIONS

Article 1

Object

This administrative regulation lays down the arrangements to be met by industrial plants cement production, determining, in particular, the emission limits of air pollutants and facilities management standards with a view to reducing pollution in the environment for these establishments and ensure the health of the population.

Article 2

Scope of application

This administrative regulation applies to industrial establishments cement production established in the Special Administrative Region of Macau, hereinafter referred to as the MSAR.

Article 3

Definition

For the purposes of this administrative regulation means by industrial establishments cement production of those engaged exclusively or mainly activities relating to the procedures of cement production, including loading and unloading, transport, storage, manufacture and packing their materials.

CHAPTER II EMISSION LIMITS OF AIR POLLUTANTS AND FACILITIES MANAGEMENT

SECTION I

Emission limits of air pollutants

Article 4

Emission limits

1. Industrial establishments cement production shall comply with the emission limits of air pollutants listed in Annex I map the Administrative this Regulation and which is an integral part, from the entry into force of this administrative regulation to the 30 June 2015.

2. The industrial establishments cement production shall comply with the emission limits of air pollutants listed in Annex II map to this administrative regulation and which is an integral part, from 1 July 2015.

Article 5

Inspection report

Industrial plants cement production must submit every six months to the Directorate of Environmental Protection Bureau, hereinafter called DSPA, an inspection report on the compliance with the emission limits of air pollutants mentioned in the previous article, written by an inspection institution recognized by the DSPA and has quality certification.

SECTION II

Facilities management

Article 6

Loading and unloading of raw materials and cement clinker

1. The loading and unloading of raw materials and cement clinker by means of the vehicle, ship or other mode of transportation must be conducted using tools closed for transportation in conjunction with closed systems, avoiding dissipation dust in the air.

2. The industrial establishments cement production shall, at least once a month, inspection and maintenance of the facilities referred to above.

Article 7

Transport and storage of raw materials and cement clinker

1. The transport of raw materials and cement clinker must be carried out through closed equipment, avoiding dissipation dust in the air.

2. The storage of raw materials and cement clinker should be carried out in closed systems, avoiding dissipation dust in the air.

3. The industrial establishments cement production shall, at least once a month, inspection and maintenance of equipment and facilities referred to in the preceding paragraphs.

Article 8

Deposition of other materials that may impact on the air quality

1. The remaining materials other than raw materials and cement clinker and that can impact on air quality, including sand and stone, shall be deposited in areas endowed with sidings and roofs.

2. The areas referred to above shall be provided with automatic water sprinkler systems or subject to appropriate hedging measures, avoiding dust dissipation in the air.

3. The preceding paragraphs does not exclude those contained in other legislation applicable to the materials referred to in paragraph 1, or the instructions, guidelines and legal orders or contractually stipulated by the authority.

Article 9

Manufacturing and packaging

1. The cement manufacture and packaging must take place in closed systems, avoiding dissipation dust in the air.

2. The areas of manufacturing and cement packaging must be provided with equipment for collection and treatment of dust, preventing its dissipation in the air.

3. The industrial establishments cement production shall, at least once a month, inspection and maintenance of facilities and equipment referred to in the preceding paragraphs.

Article 10

Transportation vehicles

1. The inputs and outputs to transport vehicles shall be provided with facilities for automatic washing of vehicles, avoiding dust dissipation in the air.

2. The transport vehicles should be thoroughly washed by high-pressure washing equipment, before leaving the industrial establishments cement production, avoiding dust dissipation in the air.

3. During the transport of materials, vehicle bodies must be fully covered by suitable materials to prevent dust dissipation in the air and spill of materials transported on the ground.

4. industrial establishments cement production shall, at least once a month, inspection and maintenance of the facilities referred to in paragraph 1.

Article 11

Roads within the premises

Should be carried out regular cleaning and rinsing of the channels, including roads, industrial plants within the cement production, avoiding dissipation dust in the air.

CHAPTER III SUPERVISION AND PENALTIES

Article 12

Oversight

1. the enforcement of this administrative regulation lies with DSPA.

2. The DSPA as part of its duties, performs the monitoring of air pollutant emissions by industrial establishments cement production and inspection of their premises and equipment.

3. The heads of industrial establishments cement production shall provide the necessary collaboration whenever the DSPA to ask the exercise of their supervisory functions, in particular presenting samples, technical data on the air pollution control and supporting documents for inspection and maintenance of respective facilities and equipment as well as providing the supervisory staff access to the establishment.

4. The staff of DSPA may request other public bodies, including the Public Security Police and the Macao Economic Services, hereinafter referred to as SDR, collaboration that is deemed necessary for the exercise of their supervisory functions.

Article 13

Administrative offenses

Without prejudice to other legal or contractual penalties, the breach of this administrative regulation constitutes an administrative offense punished with a fine of:

1) 100,000 to 400,000 patacas, in the case of infringement of Article 4;

2) 10000-200000 patacas in the case of breach of any of the articles 6 to 11 and n. The 1 to 3 of Article 23;

3) 10000 to 50,000 patacas in the case of infringement of Article 5, paragraph 3 of Article 12 or paragraph 4 of Article 23

Article 14

Graduate fines

1. Fines are graded taking into account:

1) the seriousness of the administrative offense;

2) the degree of guilt and background of the offender;

3) damage.

2. The gravity of the administrative offense is assessed taking into account the concentration levels of air pollutant emissions exceeding the limits set by this administrative regulation and the frequency of their occurrence or the degree of violation of the provisions on facilities management, as cases.

Article 15

Relapse

1. For the purposes of this administrative regulation, it is considered recurrence practice of administrative offense under this section within one year after the administrative penalty decision has become unimpugnable and provided between the practice of administrative offense and the previous non It has been more than five years.

2. In case of recidivism, the minimum amount of the fine is increased by a quarter and the maximum value remains unchanged.

Article 16

Liability of legal persons

1. Corporate bodies, although improperly constituted, unincorporated associations and special committees are responsible for the practice of administrative offenses referred to in this Chapter when committed by its organs or representatives in its name and in the collective interest.

2. The liability referred to in the previous paragraph shall not apply when the agent acted against the express orders or instructions properly issued.

3. The responsibility of the entities referred to in paragraph 1 does not exclude the liability of the respective agents.

Article 17

Liability for payment of fines

1. If the offender is a legal person, the fine payment account, jointly with that, administrators or who otherwise to represent, when they are judged responsible for the infringement.

2. If the fine is applied to an unincorporated association or a special committee, it accounts for their common heritage and, should that not suffice, the assets of each of the partners or members jointly and severally.

Article 18

Sanctioning competence

Responsibility for the application of sanctions for administrative infringements of this administrative regulation is the Director of DSPA.

Article 19

The payment of fines and compulsory collection

1. Payment of the fine shall be effected within 15 days from the date of receipt of notification of the penalty decision.

2. In the absence of voluntary payment of the fine within the preceding paragraph, the procedure is compulsory collection under tax foreclosure process by the competent authority, serving as enforceable the certificate of the penalty decision.

Article 20

Proceeds of fines

The fines levied by administrative violation of this administrative regulation constitutes the MSAR revenue.

Article 21

Communication

For the purposes of Article 40 of Decree-Law No. 11/99 / M of 22 March, the DSPA notify the SDR information concerning administrative infringement proceedings this administrative regulation, including the nature and gravity of the administrative offense and its penalty decision.

CHAPTER IV

Final and transitional provisions

Article 22

Subsidiary law

In all that is not specifically provided for in this administrative regulation shall apply the subsidiary of the Administrative Procedure Code and the Decree-Law No. 52/99 / M, of 4 October (General rules of administrative procedure and related offenses).

Article 23

Transitional provision

1. During the first 18 months of application of this administrative regulation, the provisions of Article 6 shall not apply to industrial establishments cement production established before its entry into force Comments should adopt effective measures to prevent the dissipation dust in the air.

2. During the first nine months of validity of this administrative regulation, paragraphs. The 1 and 2 of Article 8 does not apply to industrial establishments cement production established before its entry into force, should adopt the same effective measures to prevent dust dissipation in the air.

3. During the first month of validity of this administrative regulation, paragraphs. The 1 and 4 of Article 10 does not apply to industrial establishments cement production established before its entry into force, should adopt the same measures effective to prevent dust dissipation in air.

4. During the first month of validity of this administrative regulation, industrial plants cement production established before its entry into force shall submit to the DSPA a plan of work on the implementation of equipment and facilities referred to in paragraph 1 Article 6, paragraph 1 of Article 8, as well as presenting successively monthly tables clarifying on the status of implementation of the plan.

Article 24

Implementation

This administrative regulation enters into force on 1 June 2014.

CONVENTION ON THE PROHIBITION OF THE DEVELOPMENT, PRODUCTION, STOCKPILING AND USE OF CHEMICAL WEAPONS

Dispatch of the Chief Executive No. 272/2003

Whereas the Convention on the Prohibition of the Development, Production, Stockpiling and Use of Chemical Weapons and on their Destruction (Convention on the Prohibition of Chemical Weapons) came into force in the Special Administrative Region of Macao on December 20, 1999.

Whereas the Convention was published in the Official Bulletin by the Chief Executive of Notice No 70/2001, with the Macau Special Administrative Region obliged to scrupulously comply with the aims, objectives and principles of the Convention.

Considering the need to control the import, export and transit of toxic chemicals and their precursors.

In these terms; and

Using the power conferred by Article 50 of the Macau Basic Law, and under the provisions of subparagraph 6) of paragraph 1 of Article 5 of Law No. 7/2003, Chief Executive orders:

1. It is absolutely forbidden to import, export and transit by the Macau Special Administrative Region of chemicals and their precursors listed on List 1 attached to this order which forms an integral part.

2. The import, export and transit through the Macao Special Administrative Region of chemicals and their precursors contained in the lists 2:03 annexed to this order which form an integral part, are subject to conditioning, under that Convention.

3. The authorization for the import, export and transit of goods referred to above is required to Macao Economic Services at the request of license with the end indication for which it is, of the final recipients and the exact quantity of products .

4. This order becomes effective on the date of publication.

GENERAL REGULATIONS GOVERNING PUBLIC PLACES

Administrative Regulation No. 28/2004

The Chief Executive, after consultation with the Executive Council, decrees, under point 5) of Article 50 of the Macau Basic Law be enforced as administrative regulation, the following:

Article 1

Approval

It approved the General Regulations Governing Public Places (herein referred to as PGER) published as an annex to this law, which is an integral part.

Article 2

Object

The PGER establishes the general course of conduct to be observed in the use and enjoyment of public spaces.

Article 3

Settings

Within the scope of PGER following definitions shall apply:

1) Public spaces: public facilities as well as places or areas belonging to the Special Administrative Region of Macau (SAR) or to other public authorities of the MSAR and are predominantly intended for use elsewhere, including tours, plazas, public roads , gardens, beaches and areas of environmental preservation;

2) Public facilities: the buildings, their units and fenced areas owned or allocated to SAR or to other public authorities, which run public services or provide for collective use equipment, including libraries, museums, exhibition galleries, sports halls , pools and mini-zoos;

3) Solid waste: waste, wood waste or objects that Man breaks, including construction and demolition debris resulting from public or private works and substances that may pose a danger to public health or the environment;

4) domestic solid waste: solid waste produced within the residential use of the dwelling, apart from those that by their volume, size or shape can not be collected through normal removal means;

5) Public Solid Waste: Solid waste generated in use, scanning, cleaning and maintenance of public spaces, apart from those that by their volume, size or shape can not be collected through normal removal means.

Article 4

Additional rules

1. The Civic and Municipal Affairs Bureau (IACM hereinafter) ensure the smooth implementation of PGER in respect of matters within its competence pursuant to their charters, public facilities it manages in other public spaces and other areas under its jurisdiction.

2. Additional rules necessary for the efficient execution of PGER the IACM are approved by order of the Chief Executive, published in the Official Bulletin, and its effectiveness depends on:

1) dispositions of the rules for consultation on site as they apply, with disclosure, by appropriate means, the most relevant case govern the operation and use of public facilities or public facilities placed inside buildings or enclosed areas public place;

2) Publication of the rules attached to that order in Official Bulletin, in other cases.

Article 5

Rates, tariffs and prices

The rates, tariffs and prices applicable under the PGER IACM in the jurisdiction of the materials are those that are set in Fee Schedule, Rates and Rates of IACM, hereinafter Table.

Article 6

Notifications

1. All notifications made under this diploma by mail forwarding has been designated by the interested party or his Commissioner are deemed to be made on the third day after the date of shipment or on the next business day when that is not the third day.

2. When the address indicated by the very interested or his commissioner is outside the MSAR, the period referred to above shall be counted after the delay period set out in the Code of Administrative Procedure.

Article 7

Transitional arrangements

1. PGER the rules on permits and building permits and urbanism of pejamento and advertising shall apply to proceedings initiated later than 1 January 2005.

2. The IACM shall prepare and submit to the guardianship within 180 days from the date of entry into force of this law, the management plan of solid waste produced in the operation of economic activities, licit or illicit, They have been deposed and removed with household waste or by public solid waste.

3. The plan mentioned in the preceding paragraph should include various management alternatives such waste by economic agents as well as provide rules and guidelines regarding the respective deposition, removal, transportation and final treatment.

4. The discipline currently in force continues to apply:

1) the authorization procedures or construction and urbanism leave, pejamento and advertising started before the date specified in paragraph 1;

2) the solid waste resulting from economic activities referred to in paragraph 2, until the approval of the plan of protection provided for in paragraphs 2 and 3;

3) the unlawful acts occurred prior to the date of effectiveness of the planned dispatch in Article 37, paragraph 1, point 2), the PGER;

4) the possession of animals, the pursuit of economic activities in the markets or in public spaces and the pursuit of economic activities subject to sanitary and phytosanitary control of the IACM in conjunction with the postures and municipal deliberations on the matter until their repeal .

Article 8

Repeals

With the exception of the purposes of the preceding article are repealed all provisions incompatible with the present law, namely:

1) The Municipal Code of Postures of the Municipality of Macau, approved by city council meeting on 23 June 1954 and published in the Official Gazette No 51 of 18 December 1954;

2) The Municipal Code of Postures of the Municipality of the Islands, approved by city council meeting on February 6, 1974 and published in the Official Gazette No. 22 of June 1, 1974;

3) Ordinance No. 7036, published in the Official Gazette No. 33 of August 18, 1962;

4) Order No. 91/79, published in the Official Gazette No. 42 of 20 October 1979;

5) Decree No. 165/80 / M, published in Official Gazette No. 37 of September 13, 1980, which translates in Chinese language was published in Official Gazette No. 50 of December 17, 1999 , under the Governor's Order No. 297 / GM / 99;

6) "Posture the execution of works in the local or public roads of Macau city», published in Official Gazette No. 32 of August 10, 1987;

7) "Posture of Parks, Gardens and Macau City of Trees", published in Official Gazette No. 49 of December 7, 1987;

8) The "Solid Waste posture and cleaning of Macau City" and all municipal resolutions which amended, in particular those published in the Official Gazette No. 47 of November 23, 1987 and in the Official Gazette No. 38, 19 September 1988;

9) "Posture advertising material and display advertising on the Macau city», passed in city council session December 18, 1987 and published in Official Gazette No. 3 of 18 January 1988;

10) Posture No 1/90 on the 'flow or spillage of liquids or gases in Macao municipality ", published in Official Gazette No 51 of 17 December 1990;

11) Posture 1/92 on the "Hygiene and cleanliness in the public domain in the Municipality of the Islands";

12) Posture No 2/92 on the 'Green Areas and Water Resources in the Municipality of the Islands ";

13) Posture No. 2/96 / CMI on the 'saddle animals circulation in the Municipality of the Islands ", published in Official Gazette No. 47, Series II, of 20 November 1996;

14) Posture 1/97 on the "equine circulation in the municipality of Islands - transgressions', published in Official Gazette No. 18, Series II, of 30 April 1997;

15) Posture No. 2 / CMI / 98 concerning the "Licensing placing scaffolding and sidings in the Municipality of the Islands", published in Official Gazette No. 6, Series II, of 10 February 1999;

16) Posture No 2/99 on the 'flow or spillage of liquids or gases in the municipality of Islands ", published in Official Gazette No. 49, Series II, of 9 December 1999.

Article 9

Implementation

This administrative regulation enters into force on the thirtieth day after the date of its publication.

Approved on July 28, 2004.

Post up.

The Chief Executive, Ho Hau Wah.

ATTACHMENT

General Regulations Governing Public Places

CHAPTER I HEALTH, ENVIRONMENT AND QUALITY OF LIFE

Article 1

Object

This chapter sets out the charges to be observed in the use and enjoyment of public spaces, in implementation of the duty of all to work together in creating a healthy and ecologically balanced environment and progressive and accelerated improvement of quality of life.

Article 2

General duties

1. In open spaces is forbidden:

1) Any behavior contrary to the cleaning requirements, hygiene and health;

2) Any behavior that could create or increase the danger for the normal traffic of vehicles and pedestrians, for nature conservation or the ecological balance and the different habitats;

3) Unless permission to enter areas where access is expressly reserved.

2. Who go, visit, attend or in any way use public spaces should:

1) Refrain from conduct that is likely to prevent the operation of equipment and things intended for collective use or to cause them damage;

2) Refrain from producing noise that could unnecessarily disturb the tranquility and rest of others;

3) Refrain from conduct that is likely to harass others or disrupt the performance of a social event for in the circumstances, they may consider appropriate to offend modesty or decorum.

Article 3

Access to and use of public facilities

1. Rules can be set to restrict access to and use of public facilities, assistance and participation in activities or performances taking place there as well as the permanence in these places:

1) The minor, who is not accompanied by an adult, when the facilities or activities taking place there involving danger of injury or other harm to the child;

2) Who is present noticeably intoxicated or under the influence of narcotic drugs or psychotropic substances;

3) Who is accompanied animals;

4) who disrespects the rules of operation of the site.

2. All restrictions mentioned in the preceding paragraph shall be adequately publicized in place that apply.

3. Every person must strictly comply with the directions of the administering entity posted on the site as well as the legitimate instructions which can be directly addressed by workers identified, in particular:

1) Cleaning Care, hygiene and health to observe on the spot;

2) Restrictions on the use of collection equipment or transmission of sound and image;

3) Taking care to conserve and adequately protect the equipment and existing things on the premises.

4. The provisions of this Article shall apply to gardens, parks and green areas managed by the IACM that are delimited other public spaces by walls or fences.

Article 4

Putting things

1. Without prejudice to the provisions on pejamento in public spaces is prohibited to place any materials or objects except:

1) In the period strictly necessary to occasional loading and unloading without obstruction of pedestrian and vehicle traffic operations;

2) In local and suitable containers.

2. In case of violation of the preceding paragraph, the thing will be found as the specific circumstances, removed to deposit or treated as solid waste.

3. In the case of high-value things, the bureau will report the find to the police.

4. The IACM is entitled to be reimbursed for expenses incurred in the removal and custody of the thing in the first fifteen days of filing.

5. The IACM has the lien, the credits referred to above, including the advance sale of colleges and execution and, in the absence of complaint, you can sell things laid down in the following article.

Article 5

Destination of things in storage

1. If removed to deposit things easily perishable or perishable that they have not been claimed, the bureau must provide their treatment as waste after at least 72 hours in storage, where these perish or deteriorate earlier than 72 hours .

2. If not claimed, the other things stored can be removed as waste or, after fifteen days at least, in trust, to be sold extrajudicially or donated to nonprofits.

3. extrajudicial sale can be made at auction, by auction, by private agreement or by private treaty.

4. information on all sales made shall be kept giving details of the thing sold, indicating the identity of the buyer, date of sale and its price.

5. On the proceeds of the sale the fines are paid, then the IACM credits for the removal and storage.

6. If, after the collection of fines and claims referred to in the preceding paragraph, there remnant of the sale proceeds, the IACM will give the amount, without interest, to the complainant who reports within 365 days after the Thing date for removal deposit and provides evidence that the thing belonged to him; Elapsed this period without having been founded complaint, the bureau makes her the remaining amount.

Article 6

Plant extension, frames, canopies, platforms and stairs for public spaces

It is mandatory to trim or cut the outstanding plants on public space and removing the frames, awnings, platforms, steps and similar which occupy the public space where such plants or objects obstructing the passage, create danger for the safety of pedestrians or vehicles, hinder public sanitation, reduce the effectiveness of street lamps or withdraw the visibility of traffic lights, the signposts stuck or road signs.

Article 7

Activities

1. Off premises and areas specifically marked for this purpose, in public spaces is prohibited without prior permission of the competent authority, organize or participate in cultural, recreational or sporting activities that hinder the traffic of pedestrians and vehicles, pose a safety risk people or are likely to cause damage to public or private property.

2. Without prejudice to the following paragraph, the acts performed in public spaces involving the placement of offerings and the burning of votive papers, the practitioner must:

1) Choose an appropriate location, good ventilation and where there is no danger of fire or explosion;

2) Prepare combustion in suitable containers, which impede the release of sparks or ashes;

3) Place the food and that container so as not to impede traffic of pedestrians and vehicles;

4) Wash and clean up the site after the end of the ceremony.

3. Lacks prior authorization of the IACM, to prevent the risk of fire, the commission of acts involving ignite fire or to burn any material in gardens, parks and green areas, outside the specifically marked places for this purpose.

4. It shall be prohibited:

1) camping or staying overnight in public spaces or facilities, except in authorized places and under conditions laid down by the competent authority;

2) Fishing activity or to perform any water in the dam, reservoir, ponds or lakes, except in authorized places and under conditions laid down by the competent authority;

3) The exercise of hunting.

Article 8

Environmental heritage

1. The cutting existing trees or shrubs in public spaces requires a license to be issued by IACM according to the guidelines of forest protection and botany and with the objective of promoting environmental protection.

2. It is forbidden to release animals or do any planting in public spaces without prior authorization from the IACM, which can only be granted if the site is suitable and provided that such species compatible with the ecological balance.

3. It is prohibited to damage the natural habitat of wild animals and wild plants.

Article 9

Animal movement

1. Without prejudice to the application of the rules of the Highway Code or special rules, particularly for animal transport or competition animals, in public spaces is only permitted the movement of animals when accompanied and supervised by their holders, provided that:

1) The animal has valid administrative leave, unless it is not required license;

2) The animal is in regular sanitary condition;

3) The animal is trapped in a cage in cage or leash, use the identification and security devices set in the permit, does not present disease manifests signs and not to behave so that it can disrupt vehicular traffic or pedestrians.

2. The animal keeper shall proceed to the immediate cleaning and removal of manure produced by animals, except guide dogs from when blind followers.

Article 10

Solid waste management

All operations involving solid waste, including separation, deposition, removal, transportation, treatment and disposal, must be planned and executed in order to avoid or minimize the risk of damage to public health or the environment.

Article 11

Separation and packaging

1. The packaging of solid waste should be provided for their separation, observing the rules, namely, avoiding the junction, domestic solid waste and public solid waste, solid waste otherwise.

2. Subject to the legal and regulatory requirements for health and safety at work, the packaging waste must be conducted to ensure the tightness, allowing good conditions of cleanliness and prevent animal access to food contamination and of drinking water.

Article 12

Deposition

1. In general, the deposition of solid domestic waste must be distributed in containers made, for this purpose each building.

2. The guard duties, cleaning and conservation of the containers referred to above imposed on:

1) The administrators in fact or law, building in horizontal property;

2) Holders if building does not consist in horizontal property.

3. In buildings where there has been no distribution of containers, disposal of domestic solid waste must be made in the collective container placed in the area.

4. Deposition of public solid waste can only be done in containers specifically designed for the collection, including containers and litter bins.

5. Deposition in public spaces any other solid waste that can not be domestic or only be made public at the time of their removal or transportation and always using suitable containers.

6. The owner or keeper and the vehicle driver must provide the cleanliness of the wheeled vehicle before entering public roads when comes from land where works are carried out.

Article 13

Removal and transport

1. Are prohibited the release, the abandonment, dumping and treatment of solid waste out of local, approved plants and equipment.

2. Before proceeding with the removal and transport of solid waste, economic agents responsible for these operations must ensure the existing availability at the treatment site, the landfill or incinerator.

3. In setting the various times of placement and containers for collecting and organizing the removal of routes and transportation of solid waste should be considered the specific conditions of each zone in order to minimize both the risk of injury to health or the environment or the nuisance for citizens or for circulation.

Article 14

Liquid pollutants

1. Except in relief operations in a state of need, it is prohibited:

1) Loosen or whiling away wastewater and any liquid pollutants in public spaces;

2) To release waste water into sewage drainage systems contrary to applicable standards and technical regulations;

3) Launch waste water or any liquid not coming from household waste pollutants in storm water drainage system.

2. It is forbidden to build or use sinks, tanks or tanks for release of waste water in areas covered by the general drainage system, unless exceptional authorization and conditions expressly established by the competent public authority.

Article 15

Cleaning

Economic operators who carries on business in the area of public space or adjoining site and communicating with public spaces, should keep clean and free of debris, including fats and oils produced in the course of its business, whether squats or area public spaces contiguous and communicating with these places.

Article 16

Lunar New Year

1. Up to 90 days before the festivities of the Lunar New Year, the bureau must submit to the authority one tender proposal, effective in public spaces under their jurisdiction, which should contain:

1) an indication of public premises and surrounding areas which could take place the burning of firecrackers and firing rockets and fire firework;

2) A description of permitted products;

3) The periods and times that allowed the burning of firecrackers and firing rockets and fire firework.

2. Unless serious grounds, the hours provided for in the notice of proposal should be within the range between 08:00 and 02:00 hours.

3. The tender notice must be accompanied by favorable opinions of the Public Security Police, the Fire Department and the Customs Service.

4. It is forbidden to burn firecrackers, launch rockets and fire fireworks in places, times, schedules or different conditions than is established in the announcement approved by order of guardianship.

Article 17

Principal Commissioner relationship

The person or entity that charges a third party of any commission must ensure that this other person complies strictly in the development of the commission, the duties of the present law.

CHAPTER II OCCUPATION AND EXPLOITATION OF PUBLIC SPACES

Article 18

Object

This chapter sets out the general discipline of some permits and licenses for occupation or exploitation, in particular benefit of public spaces.

Article 19

Mandatory

The whole situation, activity, project or event that depends on authorization or license, in accordance with this chapter may only be maintained and exploited if their student has a valid permit or license to do so.

SECTION I

Construction and urban design

Article 20

License

1. Without prejudice to the authorization imposed by the legal system of urban construction, lacks the leave provided for in this section for the performance of any particular works in public spaces, including:

1) The fixed sealing temporary removal or replacement movable sealing;

2) The temporary removal of traffic signs;

3) The temporary removal of any other piece of urban equipment;

4) The placement and cable repair the technical gallery.

2. The installation of technical infrastructure must be made at an appropriate depth, determined by the competent public authority, and in technical galleries, unless the placement in ditches is more favorable to the public interest.

Article 21

The public interest

1. When it is proposed the existence of temporary difficulties for vehicles or pedestrians on the use of certain street layout or public space as a result of works, the competent authority for licensing communicates the timetable for their implementation, in writing, to potentially interested in carrying out similar works in that place, so that the works to be implemented by various stakeholders will take place in the meantime.

2. If any interested referred to above anything endeavor at that time but then earlier than two years counted from that communication, comes require the execution of works in the same place, a license will involve compensatory payment of an amount corresponding to the amount double the rates in force, even if the person concerned is exempt from these fees, unless the necessity of the works were impressive to the date of such communication or is determined by force majeure.

Article 22

Coordination

The license may provide for the possibility of being amended by the competent authority in the organization and timing of the work to reconcile the various works to be carried at the same time.

Article 23

Bail

1. The license can not be issued without that show made the payment of the fees that are due and paid a deposit, as set out in Table.

2. The security ensures compliance with legal rules or techniques applicable to works to be carried, as well as the observance of sealing duties, signage, cleaning, replenishment area affected by construction and other conditions of the permit.

Article 24

Duty to reconstitution

1. Within the period set in the license for the completion of works and within the area affected by its implementation, the holder must remove all materials and equipment, as well as, inter alia:

1) Repair and restore the pavements, sidewalks, curbs and any other existing things on site;

2) Paint the markings in accordance with the instructions of the competent authority;

3) Replace or replace things removed or damaged by works, in particular the brackets and vertical signposts, the place names boards, railings and metal barriers;

4) Restore the landscaped areas and irrigation systems.

2. If the works have involved the destruction of concrete pavement, executed or repavimentado less than five years, it must be repaved area bounded by the existing expansion joints, without prejudice to compliance with other duties set in the permit.

3. Checking up the failure of all or part of the obligations of the preceding paragraphs, the competent authority sets a deadline the licensee to carry out this provision missing, subject to administrative sanction procedures that may arise.

4. Once the period referred to above, if it persists a situation of non-compliance, the competent public authority shall take the steps referred to in Article 144, paragraph 2 of the Administrative Procedure Code, but the person who is in breach in any case, responsible for all expenses, including compensation and financial penalties.

Article 25

Warranty period

1. The fixed license, depending on the circumstances of the case and the relevant technical rules, the period or vesting periods of the works performed in public spaces under this section.

2. In any case, the minimum guarantee period is 2 years from the date of provisional acceptance.

SECTION II

Pejamento

Article 26

License

1. It has no license under this section, unless the case is applicable another authorization or license, any situation, activity, work or special interest event involving the temporary removal of street furniture or occupying area of space public, namely:

1) The implementation of fences, railings and scaffolding laid down in the legal and regulatory discipline of urban construction;

2) The implementation of structures or frames for circuses, carousels, festivals, shows or other activities in public places;

3) Other pejamentos permanent or temporary.

2. On all matters not think specifically regulated in this section is applicable to pejamento license, mutatis mutandis, the arrangements in the previous section.

Article 27

The public interest

1. pejamento license or its renewal must be rejected if the activity of particular interest mentioned in the previous item can cause serious trouble for vehicle traffic and pedestrians or compromise normal collective use of the site.

2. The fixed license, depending on the circumstances, the specific content of sealing duties, signage, cleaning and reconstruction within the area affected by pejamento.

3. Without prejudice to the other cases provided for in the applicable rules or specified in the permit, the competent authority shall revoke the license if:

1) The activity referred to in the previous article went on to result, in the opinion of the competent authorities, major inconvenience to the health or public health;

2) the holder has been convicted two or more times in less than six months for breach of cleaning duties laid down in the license.

SECTION III

Advertising

Article 28

Licenses

1. Licensing posting advertising messages in a building, vehicle or structure in order to be visible or audible in public areas, shall be governed by the provisions of the advertising law and discipline under this section.

2. The license shall be requested on behalf of any of the following persons or entities:

1) owner, possessor or holder of advertising media;

2) Person or entity responsible for the distribution of the advertising message;

3) Advertiser.

3. If the display requested requires the execution of construction works subject, in legal terms, the work permit, advertising display of the license will not be issued without being issued a work permit by the competent authority.

4. The placement of advertising on media with metal components or stone affixed to the wall or construction of overseas hangers necessarily imply obtaining liability insurance relating to the fixing of propaganda and publicity material.

Article 29

Languages

1. The texts of the advertisements may use several languages, provided that one of them is an official language of the MSAR.

2. To assess the content of advertising messages, as provided in the advertising legislation, the IACM may require the applicant to submit the certified translation into an official language of the texts that are written in other languages, except the names of firms or brands with effective registration in Macao.

Article 30

Bail

1. The applicant for the license shall pay the amount of deposit equivalent to fifteen percent of the amount of the fee for the license, with a minimum value $ 500.00 (five hundred) patacas and a maximum of $ 5 000.00 (five thousand) patacas.

2. The interested party may request the return of the collateral value after cease the effects of the license, provided that the licensee has fulfilled all its obligations and, if applicable, has paid the fines which have been applied.

3. The license applicant may lodge the deposit to the IACM for cash deposit, bank guarantee or certified check.

Article 31

Terms of the licensing procedure

1. The licensing procedure should be completed within 15 days from the date on which the applicant offers all the documents and information required by the IACM.

2. If, under the legislation, the views of another entity is required, the period referred to in the previous paragraph is 50 days.

3. In the situation referred to in the preceding paragraph, the consulted authority shall submit its opinion within 30 days, counting from the receipt of the application the IACM for this purpose.

Article 32

Display of claims and tablets

In addition to meet the criteria set out in Article 20 of Law No. 7/89 / M, of 4 September, the claims and tablets should be placed in conditions that do not harm or affect the circulation on public roads and so not to intercept the street lighting or cover up signposts stuck or police numbering.

Article 33

Obligations

1. The licensee has the following obligations:

1) Remove the advertising materials and support within the period fixed by the IACM in the situations given in the following paragraph;

2) Keep the material or advertising media in good condition cosmetic and cleaning;

3) To clean the place of posting material or advertising media after their removal;

4) Ensure that the materials or advertising media do not constitute danger to persons or property, as well as their maintenance in a safe condition;

5) take appropriate action and if necessary to temporarily remove the material or advertising media in order to prevent situations of greater risk, particularly due to tropical storm.

2. The IACM notifies the licensee and other persons or entities mentioned in paragraph 2 of Article 28, so that any of them remove the media and advertising support, within the period prescribed in the following cases:

1) If not issued the license or advertising posting advertising or advertising medium does not match the contents of the permit;

2) If the license expires, is not renewed or is revoked by the IACM;

3) If the material or advertising media can create or increase risk to persons or property, even for factors beyond the licensee, and the hazard can not be eliminated with conservation of works or other measures.

3. If the material or advertising media are not removed within the prescribed period, the bureau can perform the removal directly or through a third party.

Article 34

Performance unofficial

1. The demolition of advertising media must be automatically determined by the Board of Directors of the IACM and promptly executed without the application of paragraph 2 of the previous article, if the work of posting advertising medium has been held without being issued a license to work legally required.

2. The Board of Directors shall IACM commission, its staff or through a third party, the appropriate action to cover or hide the advertising message, especially during the procedure laid down in paragraphs 2 and 3 of the previous article, where:

1) The display of the advertising message has not been licensed; or

2) The advertising message posted contrary to the provisions of Chapter I of Law No. 7/89 / M, of 4 September, or other mandatory provisions.

3. The costs of the measures carried out are supported by the persons or entities who committed the unlawful acts referred to in paragraphs 1 and 2 or, where that is not determinable, by those that are identifiable through the posted messages, except if they prove that the affixing advertising is not their part.

Article 35

Exceptions

1. Self-license or administrative authorization to display promotional text inside the doors, windows and shop windows of the shops.

2. Self-license or administrative authorization on temporary placement of flower baskets, panels with colorful flowers or banners for less than 48 hours, provided they do not impair the movement of pedestrians or vehicles, or access to buildings.

3. After the 48 hour period referred to above, the person or entity responsible for placing flower baskets, panels with flowers or colorful flags should proceed immediately to their removal.

4. In the case of the placement referred to in paragraph 2 would prejudice the movement of pedestrians or vehicles, or access to buildings, as well as with the obligation in the preceding paragraph not be met, the bureau must remove the objects placed in public spaces considering them as solid waste and is entitled to reimbursement of the costs of removal, the exercise in accordance with paragraph 3 of Article 34

CHAPTER III SUPERVISION AND SANCTIONS

SECTION I

Common provisions

Article 36

Competence

1. Except for the specific cases within the competence of other public services, in accordance with their charters, powers to monitor compliance with this law and apply the sanctions provided for therein are committed to the IACM.

2. If an Administration officer or police officer witness facts punishable under this law should, as appropriate, prepare and submit its official report or document referred to in Article 52 to the competent authority to apply sanctions, unless witnessed the facts is to apply the provisions of the penal laws.

3. The IACM staff with oversight functions enjoys the public authority, under Articles 25 and 26 of the Statute of the IACM, approved by Law No. 17/2001.

4. The power to impose penalties and possible sanctions belongs to the Chairman of the IACM Administration, may be delegated to any member of the Board of Directors, in accordance with the rules of delegation.

Article 37

Administrative offenses

1. In addition to the actions described in paragraphs 2 and 3, an administrative offense any act which, fulfills all the following conditions:

1) contravenes any provision of this Ordinance or law or administrative regulation to send out to pursue the discipline in this Act, and

2) meets one unlawful conduct described and sanctioned in catalog of offenses approved by order of the Chief Executive and published in the Official Bulletin.

2. If the administrative offense is committed by a representative, employee or principal collaborator who breach the duty to ensure that that person fulfills the obligations laid down in this diploma, is also the principal autonomously sanctioned for breach of this duty, with the fine fixed in Article 45, paragraph 2, provided that the unlawful conduct of the Commissioner there has been on the job entrusted to him, even if intentionally or against the principal's instructions.

3. Failure attributable to the offender, even by way of negligence, the program that has been specifically set it under n. ° 2 of Article 51, provides new administrative offense, liable to a fine amount corresponding to double that whose execution was replaced by joining the education system and civil service.

4. The catalog referred to in subparagraph 2) of paragraph 1 autonomously spells out the comminated conduct with the sanctions provided for in this law.

5. If, after the drafting of the police report or accusation, the offender continues or repeats the conduct or the illegal situation it is considered that there is an autonomous administrative offense for each day that the misconduct or unlawful situation is detected again.

6. The administrative violations is subject to the regime established by Decree-Law No. 52/99 / M, of 4 October, and the special rules set forth in this law.

Article 38

Sanction types

The administrative violations the following sanctions may be applied:

1) Fine fixed and predetermined value;

2) variable by a fine of between fixed and predetermined, minimum and maximum limits;

3) Adherence to the provision of civil service system;

4) Additional sanctions not involving deprivation of personal freedom.

Article 39

Neglect

The negligent conduct is sanctioned.

Article 40

Graduation sanction

1. Should there be the application of any of the penalties provided for in paragraphs 2) and 4) of Article 38, the determination of the sanction should consider the offender's guilt, their background and economic standing as well as the damage, danger or risk caused or contributed to the unlawful conduct.

2. Should there be the application of the fine provided for in paragraph 2) of Article 38, if the offender is a recidivist the minimum and maximum limits for the fine shall be doubled.

3. If the agent from the infringement effective economic benefit of higher value than the upper limit of the fine and no other means of eliminating the benefit, can the maximum limit of the fine rise up to the amount of the benefit, and should not, however exceed three times the legally established limit.

4. It is considered a recidivist offender who commits an offense within one year after the date on which became final a decision which sanctioned for abuse identical.

5. Should there be applying any sanction for conduct related to the burning firecracker or rocket fire and fire Fireworks, the penalty decision must especially consider the age of the offender and the concrete situation of danger or verified damage .

Article 41

Sanction the implementation of the suspension

1. In case of serious grounds may enforce the sentence be suspended for a period not less than six months nor more than one year.

2. If during the period of suspension if it may be new offense, the sanction is executed concurrently with the suspension, without prejudice to paragraph 2 of the previous article.

Article 42

Responsibility for administrative offense

1. The offenses covered in this chapter can be committed by natural persons, legal persons, by unincorporated associations or by special committees.

2. If the violation of certain duty proves attributable to certain economic activities or the use of certain building but not able to identify the individuals involved, the offense is considered committed:

1) the owner of the shop, in the case of facts concerning the activity of that establishment;

2) persons or entities engaged in law or in fact, the administration of the building consists in horizontal property regime or, in the absence of management, the owners and other people who are in detention material building or part of it, if it's facts relating to cleaning, use or maintenance of common parts;

3) the owner, co-owners and other people who are in detention material certain fraction or a certain building is not made in regime of horizontal property, in the case of facts relating to cleaning, use or conservation of this fraction or that building.

3. The provisions of the preceding paragraph, subparagraphs 2) and 3) shall not apply to persons who have made contribution to the IACM unlawful situation or justifying its inability to act to prevent or eliminate this illegal situation.

4. Without prejudice to the following paragraph, the unlawful conduct has been committed by minor who has not completed 12 years, the offense is considered committed by those who accompanied and watched the lowest.

5. The smaller pipelines that have not yet completed eight years and conducts guy mental disorder carrier are not sanctioned.

Article 43

Fulfilment of omitted obligations

When the offense results from the omission of a duty to act, the application of sanctions and the payment of the fine does not release the offender's compliance, it is still possible.

Article 44

Competition

The provisions of this Regulation shall not affect:

1) the application of other more serious penalties laid down in statutory or regulatory standards;

2) Criminal liability that the case involved.

SECTION II

Fines and sanctions

Article 45

Common offenses

1. unlawful acts which do not justify special reprehensibility are sanctioned with a fine of $ 300.00 (three hundred patacas).

2. The unlawful acts that justify mild censorship are sanctioned with a fine of $ 600.00 (six hundred patacas).

Article 46

Serious offenses

The unlawful acts contrary to the general interests of creating a healthy and ecologically balanced environment, heritage preservation and gradual improvement of quality of life are sanctioned with a fine which shall be set between:

1) $ 700.00 (seven hundred patacas) and $ 5 000,00 (five thousand patacas), where is a legal person;

2) $ 700.00 (seven hundred patacas) and $ 2 500,00 (two thousand five hundred patacas) when it is not is a legal person.

Article 47

Very serious infringements

Illegal acts that could cause danger or damage to health and the unlawful acts that damage equipment, infrastructure and other existing things in public spaces are sanctioned with a fine to be set between:

1) $ 2 000,00 (two thousand patacas) and $ 10 000.00 (ten thousand patacas), where is a legal person;

2) $ 2 000,00 (two thousand patacas) and $ 5 000,00 (five thousand patacas) when it is not is a legal person.

Article 48

Additional sanctions

1. In the case of serious or very serious may be applied cumulatively with the fine and depending on the degree of the offender's guilt, the following sanctions:

1) Withdrawal of the objects that served or were intended to be used for committing the offense;

2) Deprivation of the right to subsidies or benefits granted by public entities or services;

3) establishment of Closing whose operation is subject to authorization, permit or license the administrative authority;

4) effective suspension of permits, licenses or permits.

2. The additional penalty provided for in point 2) above can only be applied when the offense has been committed in the exercise or because of activity in favor of which the subsidy or benefit, provided that the entity that applies the sanction is the competent authority to assign the benefit or the benefit.

3. The sanctions provided for in paragraphs 3) and 4) of paragraph 1 may only be applied when the offense has been committed in the exercise or because of the activity referred to authorizations, licenses and permits or because of operation the establishment and provided that the entity that applies the sanction is the competent authority to issue the permit, license or permit.

4. The sanctions specified in subparagraphs 2), 3) and 4) of paragraph 1, have a maximum duration of two years, counted from the date of the implementation thereof.

SECTION III

Of provision of civic service

Article 49

Content

The offender who adheres to the provision of civil service system has to fulfill a IACM-defined program that includes attendance at training sessions on individual behavior matters and collective in public areas, as well as the performance of work under the direction and authority of IACM for the benefit of the community.

Article 50

Voluntary and open membership

1. The provision of civil service system based on free and voluntary participation of the offender.

2. Only resident offenders in Macao may adhere to the provision of civic service scheme.

3. To adhere to the provision of civil service system, the offender must submit an application to the expiry of the hearing and defense in which it states assume liability resulting from the offense and requires linking to this scheme.

Article 51

Effects of accession to the provision of civil service system

1. Adherence to civic service provision arrangements replace the fine but does not prevent the application of the sanction that the case can fit.

2. The IACM defines the program and the binding period of the offender to provide alternative service arrangements, taking into account the specific circumstances of the case, but an offense implies cumulatively:

1) The frequency of training sessions up to a total of 6 hours, any infringement; and

2) The provision of out community service as part of the tasks of the competence of the IACM, up to a total of 20, 40 or 70 hours, depending on whether, respectively, of common, serious or very serious offense.

3. The IACM should provide the training sessions and organize the provision of civic service within nine months following the date on which the request provided for in paragraph 3 of the previous article; Elapsed this period of nine months, the sanction prescribes.

4. In the year following the date in which they start the training sessions or the provision of labor, the offender may not apply to accede to the provision of arrangements for community service for another offense, identical or different, however committed.

SECTION IV

Sanctions procedure

Article 52

Education and prosecution

1. If an administration officer with supervisory or police authority powers witness facts punishable by application of this law, the penalty procedure can be immediately learned, deducted and the

prosecution notified the offender through the pre-printed document fill which included the following elements:

1) Location of the competent authority to apply the sanctions and their office hours;

2) Identification of the person who committed the punishable facts and / or the person responsible for an administrative offense pursuant to Article 42;

3) Indication of general volunteer domicile of the perpetrator and also, if you, the business address;

4) Brief description of the tort defendant, indicating the place and time where it occurred;

5) Indication of the rules which provide for and punish the wrongful act charged;

6) Identification of at least one witness who has also witnessed an offense charged;

7) fine indication applicable to the offense;

8) an indication of the sanctions applicable to the offense;

9) An indication of the right to file defense within 10 days from the date it is delivered to the offender the indictment document referred to in this article;

10) the fact that in the same period of 10 days referred to in the previous paragraph, can offer immediate payment of the fine and that in case of immediate payment, the amount payable will be equal to the minimum limit of the fine;

11) An indication of the possibility of paying the fine in installments;

12) Indication of the proceedings that the competent authority may, ex officio, to ascertain the economic situation of the offender;

13) Right indication of the residents in Macao to request, within the period referred to in paragraph 9), the replacement of the fine by providing civil service system;

14) information on the deposit of the regime for non-residents in the MSAR;

15) Signatures of the person who committed the punishable facts or received the indictment, the witness and the agent deducts the charge.

2. The error due to the lack of any of the elements referred to above is remedied by a further notice to the offender to exercise the rights of hearing and defense before the penalty decision.

3. Where responsibility for the administrative offense is attributable to certain economic agent, the notification of the indictment the offender is considered immediately performed without the need of its mailing, with the delivery of pre-printed document to the Commissioner that the economic operator find the location.

Article 53

Hearing and defense

1. Within 10 days from the date of notification of accusation sent by mail or delivery date of the pre-printed document referred to in the previous article, the offender can:

1) Object to the charges;

2) Object to the charges in advance and require payment of the fine in installments in the event of being issued penalty decision;

3) Take responsibility for the infringement and require immediate payment of the fine, pursuant to Article 54;

4) State that assumes responsibility for the infringement and, being resident in Macao, require linking the provision of civic service scheme.

2. If the offender nothing require the relevant authority to apply sanctions promotes its own initiative, the necessary steps to ascertain the economic situation of the offender and may, for this purpose, namely, to contact their employer and the administrative authorities of the place residence.

SECTION V

The payment of fines

Article 54

Immediate payment

1. It is said immediate payment of the fine that is voluntarily offered by the offender to the expiry of the hearing and defense.

2. In case of immediate payment, the amount to be paid corresponds to the minimum limit of the fine.

3. If immediate payment of the fine in installments is required, the amount of the first installment is at least half the amount of the fine or, in the case of serious infringements and very serious in the amount of $ 700.00 (seven hundred patacas), and this benefit is offered to the expiry of the hearing and defense, with the last installment take place within 18 months of the date of the infringement.

4. Non-payment of the provision implies maturity of all others, in which case, if payment of the total amount owed is not made within 30 days of the due date of the first installment missing, proceed to the collection coercive in general terms.

5. In the case of serious or very serious, immediate payment of the fine does not extinguish the sanctioning procedure in the part concerning the possible application of sanctions.

6. If a non-resident offender in Macao offer immediate payment of the fine, you will not be required the security provided for in Decree-Law No. 52/99 / M, of 4 October, although the sanctions procedure is to take part in on the introduction of additional penalty.

Article 55

Payment after the penalty decision

1. The penalty decision can establish payment of the fine in installments, either in the offender's application sequence, or by unofficial initiative of the IACM, since this form of payment proves justified given the economic situation of the offender.

2. Having penalty decision imposing any fine and admit paying in installments, the amount of the first installment is at least half the amount of the fine or, in the case of serious infringements and very serious in the amount of $ 700.00 (seven hundred patacas), and payment must be made within 10 days of the date of notification of the penalty decision, with the last installment take place within the year following the same date.

3. When you pay the fine in installments the provisions in paragraph 4 of the preceding article.

4. Any penalty decision imposing any fine and determine your payment in one installment, this must be done within 30 days of the date of notification of the penalty decision.

Article 56

Liability for payment of fines

1. Liability for payment of fines rests with the person or entity to whom the administrative offense is imputed.

2. Where there are several persons responsible, the payment of the fine total may be required of either being applicable to the right to return of those responsible, Article 490 of the regime Civil Code.

3. Without prejudice to the liability of the offenses which can be directly attributable, the guy who use other people in the development of their business jointly liable to pay the fine in that its directors are convicted, directors, managers, officers, agents, employees or employees, as long as the offense has been committed on the development of economic activity and even intentionally or against the subject's instructions.

4. The officers, directors or legal person managers, although improperly constituted, and associations without legal personality, that may do it, have not objected to the practice of administrative offense by the respective legal entity or partnership, individual account and additionally the payment of fines when they are sentenced, although the fine from the investment date shall have been dissolved or liquidated.

5. If the fine is applied to an unincorporated association, the association is responsible for common heritage and, should that not suffice, the assets of each of the associates jointly and severally.

6. If the offense is committed by a minor who has completed 12 years, but that is not emancipated and has no source of income, the responsibility for the payment of fines rests jointly and severally on their legal representatives.

7. Those responsible for the payment of fines are also responsible in the same way, the reimbursement of costs incurred by the IACM to restoring the situation prior to the offense.

Article 57

Destination of the amounts of fines

The amounts of fines imposed under the sanctioning competence of the IACM are your own recipe.

EMISSION LIMITS OF AIR POLLUTANTS AND MANAGEMENT STANDARDS OF INSTALLATIONS OF INDUSTRIAL ESTABLISHMENTS CEMENT PRODUCTION

Administrative Regulation No. 12/2014

The Chief Executive, after consultation with the Executive Council, decrees, under point 5) of Article 50 of the Macau Basic Law, to stand as independent administrative regulation, the following:

CHAPTER I GENERAL PROVISIONS

Article 1

Object

This administrative regulation lays down the arrangements to be met by industrial plants cement production, determining, in particular, the emission limits of air pollutants and facilities management standards with a view to reducing pollution in the environment for these establishments and ensure the health of the population.

Article 2

Scope of application

This administrative regulation applies to industrial establishments cement production established in the Special Administrative Region of Macau, hereinafter referred to as the MSAR.

Article 3

Definition

For the purposes of this administrative regulation means by industrial establishments cement production of those engaged exclusively or mainly activities relating to the procedures of cement production, including loading and unloading, transport, storage, manufacture and packing their materials.

CHAPTER II EMISSION LIMITS OF AIR POLLUTANTS AND FACILITIES MANAGEMENT

SECTION I

Emission limits of air pollutants

Article 4

Emission limits

1. Industrial establishments cement production shall comply with the emission limits of air pollutants listed in Annex I map the Administrative this Regulation and which is an integral part, from the entry into force of this administrative regulation to the 30 June 2015.

2. The industrial establishments cement production shall comply with the emission limits of air pollutants listed in Annex II map to this administrative regulation and which is an integral part, from 1 July 2015.

Article 5

Inspection report

Industrial plants cement production must submit every six months to the Directorate of Environmental Protection Bureau, hereinafter called DSPA, an inspection report on the compliance with the emission limits of air pollutants mentioned in the previous article, written by an inspection institution recognized by the DSPA and has quality certification.

SECTION II

Facilities management

Article 6

Loading and unloading of raw materials and cement clinker

1. The loading and unloading of raw materials and cement clinker by means of the vehicle, ship or other mode of transportation must be conducted using tools closed for transportation in conjunction with closed systems, avoiding dissipation dust in the air.

2. The industrial establishments cement production shall, at least once a month, inspection and maintenance of the facilities referred to above.

Article 7

Transport and storage of raw materials and cement clinker

1. The transport of raw materials and cement clinker must be carried out through closed equipment, avoiding dissipation dust in the air.

2. The storage of raw materials and cement clinker should be carried out in closed systems, avoiding dissipation dust in the air.

3. The industrial establishments cement production shall, at least once a month, inspection and maintenance of equipment and facilities referred to in the preceding paragraphs.

Article 8

Deposition of other materials that may impact on the air quality

1. The remaining materials other than raw materials and cement clinker and that can impact on air quality, including sand and stone, shall be deposited in areas endowed with sidings and roofs.

2. The areas referred to above shall be provided with automatic water sprinkler systems or subject to appropriate hedging measures, avoiding dust dissipation in the air.

3. The preceding paragraphs does not exclude those contained in other legislation applicable to the materials referred to in paragraph 1, or the instructions, guidelines and legal orders or contractually stipulated by the authority.

Article 9

Manufacturing and packaging

1. The cement manufacture and packaging must take place in closed systems, avoiding dissipation dust in the air.

2. The areas of manufacturing and cement packaging must be provided with equipment for collection and treatment of dust, preventing its dissipation in the air.

3. The industrial establishments cement production shall, at least once a month, inspection and maintenance of facilities and equipment referred to in the preceding paragraphs.

Article 10

Transportation vehicles

1. The inputs and outputs to transport vehicles shall be provided with facilities for automatic washing of vehicles, avoiding dust dissipation in the air.

2. The transport vehicles should be thoroughly washed by high-pressure washing equipment, before leaving the industrial establishments cement production, avoiding dust dissipation in the air.

3. During the transport of materials, vehicle bodies must be fully covered by suitable materials to prevent dust dissipation in the air and spill of materials transported on the ground.

4. industrial establishments cement production shall, at least once a month, inspection and maintenance of the facilities referred to in paragraph 1.

Article 11

Roads within the premises

Should be carried out regular cleaning and rinsing of the channels, including roads, industrial plants within the cement production, avoiding dissipation dust in the air.

CHAPTER III SUPERVISION AND PENALTIES

Article 12

Oversight

1. the enforcement of this administrative regulation lies with DSPA.

2. The DSPA as part of its duties, performs the monitoring of air pollutant emissions by industrial establishments cement production and inspection of their premises and equipment.

3. The heads of industrial establishments cement production shall provide the necessary collaboration whenever the DSPA to ask the exercise of their supervisory functions, in particular presenting samples, technical data on the air pollution control and supporting documents for inspection and maintenance of respective facilities and equipment as well as providing the supervisory staff access to the establishment.

4. The staff of DSPA may request other public bodies, including the Public Security Police and the Macao Economic Services, hereinafter referred to as SDR, collaboration that is deemed necessary for the exercise of their supervisory functions.

Article 13

Administrative offenses

Without prejudice to other legal or contractual penalties, the breach of this administrative regulation constitutes an administrative offense punished with a fine of:

1) 100,000 to 400,000 patacas, in the case of infringement of Article 4;

2) 10000-200000 patacas in the case of breach of any of the articles 6 to 11 and n. The 1 to 3 of Article 23;

3) 10000 to 50,000 patacas in the case of infringement of Article 5, paragraph 3 of Article 12 or paragraph 4 of Article 23

Article 14

Graduate fines

1. Fines are graded taking into account:

1) the seriousness of the administrative offense;

2) the degree of guilt and background of the offender;

3) damage.

2. The gravity of the administrative offense is assessed taking into account the concentration levels of air pollutant emissions exceeding the limits set by this administrative regulation and the frequency of their occurrence or the degree of violation of the provisions on facilities management, as cases.

Article 15

Relapse

1. For the purposes of this administrative regulation, it is considered recurrence practice of administrative offense under this section within one year after the administrative penalty decision has become unimpugnable and provided between the practice of administrative offense and the previous non It has been more than five years.

2. In case of recidivism, the minimum amount of the fine is increased by a quarter and the maximum value remains unchanged.

Article 16

Liability of legal persons

1. Corporate bodies, although improperly constituted, unincorporated associations and special committees are responsible for the practice of administrative offenses referred to in this Chapter when committed by its organs or representatives in its name and in the collective interest.

2. The liability referred to in the previous paragraph shall not apply when the agent acted against the express orders or instructions properly issued.

3. The responsibility of the entities referred to in paragraph 1 does not exclude the liability of the respective agents.

Article 17

Liability for payment of fines

1. If the offender is a legal person, the fine payment account, jointly with that, administrators or who otherwise to represent, when they are judged responsible for the infringement.

2. If the fine is applied to an unincorporated association or a special committee, it accounts for their common heritage and, should that not suffice, the assets of each of the partners or members jointly and severally.

Article 18

Sanctioning competence

Responsibility for the application of sanctions for administrative infringements of this administrative regulation is the Director of DSPA.

Article 19

The payment of fines and compulsory collection

1. Payment of the fine shall be effected within 15 days from the date of receipt of notification of the penalty decision.

2. In the absence of voluntary payment of the fine within the preceding paragraph, the procedure is compulsory collection under tax foreclosure process by the competent authority, serving as enforceable the certificate of the penalty decision.

Article 20

Proceeds of fines

The fines levied by administrative violation of this administrative regulation constitutes the MSAR revenue.

Article 21

Communication

For the purposes of Article 40 of Decree-Law No. 11/99 / M of 22 March, the DSPA notify the SDR information concerning administrative infringement proceedings this administrative regulation, including the nature and gravity of the administrative offense and its penalty decision.

CHAPTER IV FINAL AND TRANSITIONAL PROVISIONS

Article 22

Subsidiary law

In all that is not specifically provided for in this administrative regulation shall apply the subsidiary of the Administrative Procedure Code and the Decree-Law No. 52/99 / M, of 4 October (General rules of administrative procedure and related offenses).

Article 23

Transitional provision

1. During the first 18 months of application of this administrative regulation, the provisions of Article 6 shall not apply to industrial establishments cement production established before its entry into force Comments should adopt effective measures to prevent the dissipation dust in the air.

2. During the first nine months of validity of this administrative regulation, paragraphs. The 1 and 2 of Article 8 does not apply to industrial establishments cement production established before its entry into force, should adopt the same effective measures to prevent dust dissipation in the air.

3. During the first month of validity of this administrative regulation, paragraphs. The 1 and 4 of Article 10 does not apply to industrial establishments cement production established before its entry into force, should adopt the same measures effective to prevent dust dissipation in air.

4. During the first month of validity of this administrative regulation, industrial plants cement production established before its entry into force shall submit to the DSPA a plan of work on the implementation of equipment and facilities referred to in paragraph 1 Article 6, paragraph 1 of Article 8, as well as presenting successively monthly tables clarifying on the status of implementation of the plan.

Article 24

Implementation

This administrative regulation enters into force on 1 June 2014.

Approved on May 16, 2014.

Post up.

The Chief Executive, Mr Chui Sai On.

ATTACHMENT

EMISSION LIMITS OF AIR POLLUTANTS FROM INDUSTRIAL PLANTS CEMENT PRODUCTION

(referred to in paragraph 1 of Article 4)

Air pollutants	Limit values of concentration of emission sources (mg / m 3)	Limit values of concentration of unorganized emissions in the manufacturing area [(1)] (mg / m 3)	Inspection methods
Particles	30	-	GB / T 16157
	-	1.0	GB / T 15432

Note: The limit values indicated refer to the values of the Standard GB 4915-2004 "Air pollutant emission control for the cement industry", the People's Republic of China.

[(1)] The limit of the concentration values of disorganized emissions in the manufacturing area refers to the difference between the values of the concentration of particles in the total suspension (PTS) registered respectively in the emission monitoring point and the reference point in the one hour period. The emission and referral monitoring points should be located 20 meters from the manufacturing area, downwind and upwind, respectively. If there is no visible boundary of the manufacturing area, the points are adjusted to 20 meters off the desktop.

EMISSION LIMITS OF AIR POLLUTANTS FROM INDUSTRIAL PLANTS CEMENT PRODUCTION

(referred to in paragraph 2 of Article 4)

Air pollutants	Limit values of concentration of emission sources (mg / m 3)	Limit values of concentration of unorganized emissions in the manufacturing area [(1)] (mg / m 3)	Inspection methods
Particles	20	-	GB / T 16157
	-	0.5	GB / T 15432

Note: The limit values indicated refer to the values of the Standard GB 4915-2013 "Air pollutant emission control for the cement industry", the People's Republic of China.

[(1)] The limit of the concentration values of disorganized emissions in the manufacturing area refers to the difference between the values of the concentration of particles in the total suspension (PTS) registered respectively in the emission monitoring point and the reference point in the one hour period. The emission and referral monitoring points should be located 20 meters from the manufacturing area, downwind and upwind, respectively. If there is no visible boundary of the manufacturing area, the points are adjusted to 20 meters off the desktop.

FIXING THE EXHAUST GAS EMISSION LIMITS TO BE MET BY NEW CARS ON IMPORTATION

The Chief Executive, after consultation with the Executive Council, decrees, under point 5) of Article 50 of the Macau Basic Law, to stand as independent administrative regulation, the following:

ARTICLE 1 OBJECT

Administrative Regulation No. 1/2012

This administrative regulation lays down the arrangements to be met by new cars with propulsion engine fitted with at least three wheels, when imported, and the new replacement engines, setting the standards for exhaust emissions of greenhouse gases, particularly in the form of hydrocarbons, carbon monoxide and nitrogen oxides, and particulate emissions, to reduce the environmental impact.

ARTICLE 2

APPLICATION

1. This administrative regulation applies to new vehicles with propulsion engine fitted with at least three wheels, whose maximum speed is, by construction, more than 25 km / h and it is intended, by its function, for use on the public roads, not using rails.

2. This administrative regulation applies also mutatis mutandis, to new engines for replacement of vehicle engines.

ARTICLE 3

EXCEPTIONS

Exceptions to the application of this administrative regulation vehicles which are:

1) The temporary admission;

2) In transit to third country or territory.

ARTICLE 4

APPROVAL

1. In the process of approval of makes and models of vehicles, the importing authority shall submit before the start of the inspection phase, the Directorate of Services for Traffic Affairs, hereinafter DSAT, the following documents:

1) Certificates issued by the manufacturer in accordance with any of the standards for exhaust emissions and any of the specifications of the on-board diagnostic, contained respectively in Annexes I and II to this administrative regulation, of which they form part;

2) Statements issued by the importing authority, in accordance with the requirements of Annexes I and II; and

3) Any other documents necessary for the approval process in accordance with required by DSAT.

2. In the absence of certificates of conformity issued by the manufacturer or insufficient information provided in them, they must be issued by laboratory accredited by the DSAT.

3. The new vehicles to be imported, provided with at least three wheels, with drive motor, whose maximum speed is, by construction, more than 25 km / h and it is intended, by its function, for use on the public highway, not using rails, must meet the requirements of the standards contained in exhaust emissions of Annex I.

4. The new vehicles referred to above must be equipped with a diagnostic system on board, the structure must meet any of the specifications in Annex II.

5. If the brands and models of vehicles have been approved before the entry into force of this administrative regulation, the importing authority on importation of such vehicles for the first time after the entry into force of this law, shall also produce the DSAT the documents referred to in paragraph 1 or paragraph 2.

ARTICLE 5 º

EXEMPTIONS

May be exempted by order of the Chief Executive, compliance with the requirements of Annexes I and II, vehicles intended exclusively for police and firefighters, rescue, diplomatic missions and considered within the public interest.

ARTICLE 6 TH

IMPORT BAN

The importation of vehicles which do not meet the requirements of Annexes I and II and the consequent allocation of registration is prohibited.

ARTICLE 7 TH

REQUIREMENTS OF MARKETING AND REGISTRATION OF ASSIGNMENT

They are allowed the marketing and allocation of registration of vehicles imported after the entry into force of this Administrative Regulation, provided that they have been confirmed by DSAT to comply with the types approved by meeting the requirements of Annexes I and II.

ARTICLE 8 TH

IDENTIFICATION

From September 1, 2013, the importing entity shall display, in a visible manner, at points of sale of automobiles a warning, depending on the model to be approved by Transport Bureau, indicating that they have been confirmed for this to be in compliance with the requirements of Annexes I and II to this administrative regulation.

ARTICLE 9 TH

COMPETENCE

1. Monitoring compliance with the provisions of this administrative regulation is up to the DSAT, which may, if necessary, the intervention of the Public Security Police Force.

2. It is for the DSAT verification of the documents referred to in paragraphs 1 and 2 of Article 4

3. The contents of Annexes I and II may be amended by order of the Chief Executive, to be published in the Official Gazette of the Special Administrative Region of Macao, a proposal from the Directorate of Environmental Protection Bureau, hereinafter referred to as DSPA.

4. DSPA must undertake at least once a year, review the contents of Annexes I and II.

ARTICLE 10 º

FINES

1. The infringement of Article 7 or Article 14, paragraph 2, is punished with a fine 30000-100000 patacas per vehicle or per replacement engine.

2. The infringement of Article 8 shall be punished with a 3000 patacas fine.

3. In case of recidivism, the minimum amount of the fine is increased by a quarter and the maximum value remains unchanged.

4. Recidivism is the offense committed before two years after the commission of another offense of the same nature and after the penalty decision becomes final.

ARTICLE 11

PROCEDURE FOR THE APPLICATION OF FINES

1. It is up to the DSAT preparing and initiating the procedure for enforcement of fines imposed in the previous article.

2. The power to determine the opening of the procedure, to appoint trainer and to apply the penalties is up to the director of DSAT.

ARTICLE 12

PAYMENT AND TREATMENT OF FINES

1. Fines must be paid within 20 days from the date of notification of the sanction order.

2. In the absence of voluntary payment of fines within the period prescribed in the preceding paragraph shall be compulsory collection under tax foreclosure process by the competent authority, serving as executive title to sanction order of the certificate.

3. Application of fines may be appealed to the Administrative Court.

4. The fines constitutes a revenue Special Administrative Region of Macao.

ARTICLE 13

PRESCRIPTION

1. The procedure for applying the penalties prescribed after the two-year course on the date of commission of the offense.

2. Fines prescribe after the lapse of four years from the date on which the penalty decision becomes unimpugnable.

ARTICLE 14

TRANSITIONAL PROVISION

1. vehicles which do not meet the requirements of Annexes I and II, whose demand abroad has been made by the date of publication of this administrative regulation shall not apply to n. The 3 to 5 of Article 4 and Articles 6 and 7, provided that the respective importing entity presented in DSAT, within 15 days from the entry into force of this administrative regulation, the following documents:

1) Order Document vehicles issued by the foreign supplier;

2) List of vehicles in stock; and

3) Declaration signed by the respective importing entity, it was made to order vehicles before the date of publication of this administrative regulation, in which the quantity, make and model of vehicles ordered.

2. be prohibited from 1 September 2013, the marketing and the allocation of license plates for vehicles referred to above and imported before the entry into force of this administrative regulation which do not meet the requirements of Annexes I and II.

ARTICLE 15

IMPLEMENTATION

This administrative regulation enters into force 30 days after the date of its publication.

Adopted on 16 December 2011.

Post up.

The Chief Executive, Mr Chui Sai On.

ANNEX I

EMISSION STANDARDS ON EXHAUST

Table I

Application in vehicles with gross weight, by construction, equal to or less than 3 500kgs				
Vehicles passengers	Gasoline	1	Euro 4 in Directive 70/220 / EEC of the European Parliament and the EU Council, as amended by Directive 2003/76 / EC on the approximation of the laws of the Member States on measures to be taken against air pollution by gases from positive-ignition engines of motor vehicles	Table III
		2	Emission standards set in the second phase Bin 5 Road Vehicle Emission Control and Engines, New and Used, in Title 40 Environmental Protection, Part 86 of the Federal Code of Regulations of the United States of America	Table VI
		3	Emission standards set out in the Safety Regulations for Road Vehicles (Decree No. 67 of 28 July 1951, the Ministry of Transport), as amended by Decree No. 49 of April 6, 2005, the Ministry of Land and Japan's Transport	Table IX
		4	Emission standards established in Phase IV of the National PRC GB18352.3-2005 standards (Methods of Measurement and Pollutants Emission Limits for Passenger Vehicles (Phase III and Phase IV China))	Table X
	Diesel oil	1	Euro 4 in Directive 70/220 / EEC of the European Parliament and the EU Council, as amended by Directive 2003/76 / EC on the approximation of the laws of the Member States on measures to be taken against air pollution by gases from positive-ignition engines of motor vehicles	Table III

		2	Emission standards set in the second phase Bin 5 Road Vehicle Emission Control and Engines, New and Used, in Title 40 Environmental Protection, Part 86 of the Federal Code of Regulations of the United States of America	Table VI
		3	Emission standards set out in the Safety Regulations for Road Vehicles (Decree No. 67 of 28 July 1951, the Ministry of Transport), as amended by Decree No. 49 of April 6, 2005, the Ministry of Land and Japan's Transport	Table IX
		4	Emission standards established in Phase IV of the National PRC GB18352.3-2005 standards (Methods of Measurement and Pollutants Emission Limits for Passenger Vehicles (Phase III and Phase IV China))	Table X
Vehicles goods	Gasoline	1	Euro 4 in Directive 70/220 / EEC of the European Parliament and the EU Council, as amended by Directive 2003/76 / EC on the approximation of the laws of the Member States on measures to be taken against air pollution by gases from positive-ignition engines of motor vehicles	Table III
		2	Emission standards set in the second phase Bin 5 Road Vehicle Emission Control and Engines, New and Used, in Title 40 Environmental Protection, Part 86 of the Federal Code of Regulations of the United States of America	Table VI
		3	Emission standards set out in the Safety Regulations for Road Vehicles (Decree No. 67 of 28 July 1951, the Ministry of Transport), as amended by Decree No. 49 of April 6, 2005, the Ministry of Land and Japan's Transport	Table IX
		4	Emission standards established in Phase IV of the National PRC GB18352.3-2005 standards (Methods of Measurement and Pollutants Emission Limits for Passenger Vehicles (Phase III and Phase IV China))	Table X
	Diesel oil	1	Euro 4 in Directive 70/220 / EEC of the European Parliament and the EU Council, as amended by Directive 2003/76 / EC on the approximation of the laws of the Member States on measures to be taken against air pollution by gases from positive-ignition engines of motor vehicles	Table III
		2	Emission standards set in the second phase Bin 5 Road Vehicle Emission Control and Engines, New and Used, in Title 40 Environmental Protection, Part 86 of the Federal Code of Regulations of the United States of America	Table VI
		3	Emission standards set out in the Safety Regulations for Road Vehicles (Decree No. 67 of 28 July 1951, the Ministry of Transport), as amended by Decree No. 49 of April 6, 2005, the Ministry of Land and Japan's Transport	Table IX
		4	Emission standards established in Phase IV of the National PRC GB18352.3-2005 standards (Methods of Measurement and Pollutants Emission Limits for Passenger Vehicles (Phase III and Phase IV China))	Table X

Table II

Application in vehicles with gross weight, by construction, more than 3 500kgs				
Vehicle passengers	Gasoline	1	Emission standards for vehicles and heavy Otto-cycle spark ignition engine of the year engines 2005 and onwards laid down in the Road Vehicle Emission Control and Engines, New and Used, contained in 40 Environmental Protection, parts of 86 of the Code of Federal Regulations of the United States of America	Table VII

		2	Emission standards set out in the Safety Regulations for Road Vehicles (Decree No. 67 of 28 July 1951, the Ministry of Transport), as amended by Decree No. 49 of April 6, 2005, the Ministry of Land and Japan's Transport	Table IX
		3	Emission standards established in Phase III of the National Standards of PRC GB14762-2008 (Methods of Measurement and Limits of Pollutants Vehicle and Engine Emission Gasoline Used in Heavy Vehicles (Phase III and Phase IV China))	Table XIII
	Diesel oil	1	Euro 4 in Directive 2005/55 / EC of the European Parliament and the EU Council on the approximation of the laws of the Member States relating to measures to be taken against the emission of gaseous and particulate pollutants from internal combustion engines by compression used in vehicles and polluting gas emissions from positive-ignition engines fueled with natural gas or liquefied petroleum gas for use in vehicles	Table IV and Table V
		2	Emission standards and additional provisions for heavy-duty engines the ignition diesel by 2007 year compression and following established the Road Vehicle Emission Control and Engines, New and Used, contained in 40 Environmental Protection, parts of 86 Code of Rules federal United States of America	Table VIII
Vehicle passengers	Diesel oil	3	Emission standards set out in the Safety Regulations for Road Vehicles (Decree No. 67 of 28 July 1951, the Ministry of Transport), as amended by Decree No. 49 of April 6, 2005, the Ministry of Land and Japan's Transport	Table IX
		4	Emission standards established in Phase IV of the National Standards of PRC GB17691-2005 (Methods of Measurement and pollutants emission limits for vehicles and ignition engines Compression and Ignition Combustion Gases (Phase III and Phase IV China V phase))	Table XI and Table XII
Vehicles goods	Gasoline	1	Emission standards for vehicles and heavy Otto-cycle spark ignition engine of the year engines 2005 and onwards laid down in the Road Vehicle Emission Control and Engines, New and Used, contained in 40 Environmental Protection, parts of 86 of the Code of Federal Regulations of the United States of America	Table VII
		2	Emission standards set out in the Safety Regulations for Road Vehicles (Decree No. 67 of 28 July 1951, the Ministry of Transport), as amended by Decree No. 49 of April 6, 2005, the Ministry of Land and Japan's Transport	Table IX
		3	Emission standards established in Phase III of the National Standards of PRC GB14762-2008 (Methods of Measurement and Limits of Pollutants Vehicle and Engine Emission Gasoline Used in Heavy Vehicles (Phase III and Phase IV China))	Table XIII
	Diesel oil	1	Euro 4 in Directive 2005/55 / EC of the European Parliament and the EU Council on the approximation of the laws of the Member States relating to measures to be taken against the emission of gaseous and particulate pollutants from compression-ignition engines for use in vehicles and the emission of gaseous pollutants from positive ignition engines fueled with natural gas or liquefied petroleum gas for use in vehicles	Table IV and Table V
		2	Emission standards and additional provisions for heavy-duty engines the ignition diesel by 2007 year compression and following established the Road Vehicle Emission Control and Engines, New and Used, contained in 40 Environmental Protection, parts of 86 Code of Rules federal United States of America	Table VIII

		3	Emission standards set out in the Safety Regulations for Road Vehicles (Decree No. 67 of 28 July 1951, the Ministry of Transport), as amended by Decree No. 49 of April 6, 2005, the Ministry of Land and Japan's Transport	Table IX
		4	Emission standards established in Phase IV of the National Standards of PRC GB17691-2005 (Methods of Measurement and pollutants emission limits for vehicles and ignition engines Compression and Ignition Combustion Gases (Phase III and Phase IV China V phase))	Table XI and Table XII

Table III

Category		Reference mass (RW) (kg)	Emission limits								
			Carbon monoxide (g / km)		Hydrocarbons (g / km)		Nitrogen oxides (g / km)		Hydrocarbons + Oxides of Nitrogen (g / km)		Particulates (g / km)
			Gasoline	Diesel oil	Gasoline	Diesel oil	Gasoline	Diesel oil	Gasoline	Diesel oil	Diesel oil
M (1)	-	Total	1.0	0.50	0.10	-	0.08	0.25	-	0.30	0.025
N1 (2)	I	RW ≦ 1305	1.0	0.50	0.10	-	0.08	0.25	-	0.30	0.025
	II	1305 <RW ≦ 1760	1.81	0.63	0.13	-	0.10	0.33	-	0.39	0.04
	III	1760 <RW	2.27	0.74	0.16	-	0.11	0.39	-	0.46	0.06

Note: The values set correspond to the requirements under the Euro 4 standard laid down in Directive 70/220 / EEC of the European Parliament and the EU Council, as amended by Directive 2003/76 / EC, it is necessary to take the test procedures of this standard.

Category M vehicles: vehicles with at least four wheels, used for the carriage of passengers;

Vehicles of category N: vehicles with at least four wheels, used for the carriage of goods (vehicles of category N with a maximum authorized mass not exceeding 3 500kgs are classified into vehicles of category N1).

(1) Except vehicles of category M with a maximum mass exceeding 2 500kgs;

(2) Including vehicles of category M with a maximum mass exceeding 2 500kgs.

Table IV

Emission limits (ESC and ELR tests)				
Carbon monoxide (g / kWh)	Hydrocarbons (g / kWh)	Nitrogen oxides (g / kWh)	Particles (g / kWh)	Smoke opacity (m -1)
1.5	0.46	3.5	0.02	0.5

Table V

Emission limits (tests ETC)			
Carbon monoxide	Non-methane hydrocarbons	Nitrogen oxides	Particles

(g / kWh)	(g / kWh)	(g / kWh)	(g / kWh)
4.0	0.55	3.5	0.03

Note: The values set out in Table IV and Table V correspond to the requirements under the Euro 4 standard, in Directive 2005/55 / EC of the European Parliament and the EU Council, being necessary to take the test procedures of this standard.

ESC: European Cycle Steady Steady;

ELR: European Cycle Response Load;

ETC: European Transient Cycle Regime.

Table VI

Duration	Non-methane organic gases (g / mi)	Carbon monoxide (g / mi)	Nitrogen oxides (g / mi)	Formaldehyde (g / ml)	Particulates (g / ml)
000mi 50[(1)]	0,075	3.4	0.05	0.015	-
Life [(2)]	0.090	4.2	0.07	0.018	0.01

Note: The values set correspond to those provided in the emission standards set in the second phase Bin 5 Road Vehicle Emission Control and Engines, New and Used, contained in 40 Environmental Protection, parts of 86 of the Federal Code of Regulations of the United States America, being necessary to adopt testing procedures of those standards.

(1) Optional tests in certain cases are consistent with the relevant standards;

(2) The definition conforms to the relevant standards.

Table VII

Category	Non-methane hydrocarbons + Oxides of Nitrogen (g / bhp-hr)	Carbon monoxide (g / bhp-hr)
gross weight ≦14 000lb	1.0	14.4
gross weight> 14 000lb	1.0	37.1

Note: The values set equivalent to the requirements in emission standards for vehicles and heavy-duty engines of the 2005 year of the spark-ignition engine Otto cycle and following, established in Road Vehicle Emission Control and Engines, New and Used, contained in Title 40 Environmental Protection, Part 86 of the Federal Code of Regulations of the United States, it is necessary to adopt testing procedures of those standards.

TABLE VIII

Non-methane hydrocarbons (g / bhp-hr)	Nitrogen oxides (g / bhp-hr)	Carbon monoxide (g / bhp-hr)	Particulates (g / bhp-hr)	Smoke opacity (%)
0.14	0.20	15.5	0.01	20 [(1)] / 15 [(2)] / 50 [(3)]

Note: The values set equivalent to the requirements in emission standards and additional provisions for heavy-duty engines the ignition diesel by 2007 year compression and following established the Road Vehicle Emission Control and Engines, New and Used, in Title 40

Environmental protection, Part 86 of the Federal Code of Regulations of the United States, it is necessary to adopt testing procedures of those standards.
(1) In the acceleration mode;
(2) In charge mode;
(3) In the peak level of one of the above modes.

TABLE IX

Category			The conditionsTests	Carbon monoxide (g / km)	Non-methane hydrocarbons (g / km)	Nitrogen oxides (g / km)	Particulates (g / km)
Gasoline vehicles	Transportation vehicles	-	10 • 15M + 11M	1.15	0.05	0.05	-
Gasoline vehicles	Passenger vehicles and goods	Cars automatic	10 • 15M + 11M	4.02	0.05	0.05	-
		Cars (gross weight ≦ 1,7ton)	10 • 15M + 11M	1.15	0.05	0.05	-
		Medium vehicles (1,7ton <gross weight ≦ 3,5ton)	10 • 15M + 11M	2.55	0.05	0.07	-
		Trucks (gross vehicle weight> 3,5ton)	JE05M	16,0g / kWh	0.23 g / kWh	0.7 g / kWh	-
Diesel vehicles	Transportation vehicles	Cars (gross weight ≦ 1,265ton)	10 • 15M + 11M	0.63	0.024	0.14	0.013
		Medium vehicles (gross vehicle weight> 1,265ton)				0.15	0.014
	Passenger vehicles and goods	Cars (gross weight ≦ 1,7ton)	10 • 15M + 11M	0.63	0.024	0.14	0.013
		Medium vehicles (1,7ton <gross weight ≦ 3,5ton)	10 • 15M + 11M	0.63	0.024	0.25	0.015

		Trucks (gross vehicle weight> 3,5ton)	JE05M	2,22g / kWh	0,17g / kWh	2.0 g / kWh	0,027g / kWh

Note: The values set equivalent to the requirements in emission standards set out in the Safety Regulations for Road Vehicles (Decree No. 67 of 28 July 1951, the Ministry of Transport), as amended by Ordinance No. 49 of 6 April 2005, the Ministry of Land and Transport of Japan, being necessary to adopt testing procedures of those standards.

TABLE X

Category	Level	Reference mass (RM) (kg)	Carbon monoxide (g / km)		Hydrocarbons (g / km)		Nitrogen oxides (g / km)		Hydrocarbons + Oxides of Nitrogen (g / km)		Particulates (g / km)
			Gasoline	Diesel oil	Gasoline	Diesel oil	Gasoline	Diesel oil	Gasoline	Diesel oil	Diesel oil
Category I	-	Total	1.00	0.50	0.10	-	0.08	0.25	-	0.30	0.025
Category II	I	RM ≦ 1305	1.00	0.50	0.10	-	0.08	0.25	-	0.30	0.025
	II	1305 <RM ≦ 1760	1.81	0.63	0.13	-	0.10	0.33	-	0.39	0.040
	III	1760 <RM	2.27	0.74	0.16	-	0.11	0.39	-	0.46	0.060

Note: The values set equivalent to the requirements in emission standards established in Phase IV of the National PRC GB18352.3-2005 Standards (Measurement Methods and Pollutants Emission Limits for Passenger Vehicles (Phase III and Phase IV China)), being necessary to adopt testing procedures of those standards.
Category 1 vehicles: M1 vehicles whose number of seats, including the driver, is not more than six and a maximum mass not exceeding 2 500kgs;
Category 2 vehicles: cars provided for in these emission standards, except in the case of category 1 (Vehicles of categories M1, M2 and N1 with a maximum mass not exceeding 3 500kgs, are classified into cars.
M1 vehicles: passenger vehicles whose number of seats, including the driver, is not more than nine;
M2 vehicles: passenger vehicles whose number of seats, including the driver, is more than nine and a maximum authorized mass, by construction, does not exceed 5 000kgs;
N1 vehicles: Goods vehicles with a maximum authorized mass, by construction, is not more than 3 500kgs).

TABLE XI

Limits of the ESC test and the ELR				
Carbon monoxide (g / kWh)	Hydrocarbons (g / kWh)	Nitrogen oxides (g / kWh)	Particles (g / kWh)	Smoke opacity (m -1)
1.5	0.46	3.5	0.02	0.5

TABLE XII

Limits Test ETC			
Carbon monoxide	Non-methane hydrocarbons	Nitrogen oxides	Particles

(g / kWh)	(g / kWh)	(g / kWh)	(g / kWh)
4.0	0.55	3.5	0.03

Note: The values set out in Table XI and Table XII equivalent to the requirements in emission standards established in Phase IV of the National Standards of PRC GB17691-2005 (Methods of Measurement and pollutants emission limits for vehicles and Ignition Engines Compression and Ignition Combustion Gases (Phase III, Phase IV and Phase V of China)), being necessary to adopt testing procedures of those standards.
ESC: European Cycle Steady Steady;
ELR: European Cycle Response Load;
ETC: European Transient Cycle Regime.

TABLE XIII

Carbon monoxide (g / kWh)	Total hydrocarbons (g / kWh)	Nitrogen oxides (g / kWh)
9.7	0.41	0.98

Note: The values set equivalent to the requirements in emission standards established in Phase III of the National Standards of PRC GB14762-2008 (Methods of Measurement and Pollutants Emission Limits for Vehicles and Gasoline Engines Used in Heavy Vehicles (Phase III and China's Phase IV)), being necessary to adopt testing procedures of those standards.

ANNEX II THE DIAGNOSTIC SYSTEM SPECIFICATIONS ON BOARD

Implementation of the specifications of the on-board diagnostic of new vehicles when imported	
1	The diagnostic system specifications standards on board, in Directive 70/220 / EEC of the European Parliament and the EU Council, as amended by Directive 2003/76 / EC on the approximation of the laws of the Member States relating to measures to taken against air pollution by gases from spark-ignition engines of motor vehicles
2	The diagnostic system specifications standards on board, in Directive 2005/55 / EC of the European Parliament and the EU Council on the approximation of the laws of the Member States relating to measures to be taken against the emission of gaseous and particulate pollutants from compression-ignition engines for use in vehicles and the emission of gaseous pollutants from positive ignition engines fueled with natural gas or liquefied petroleum gas for use in vehicles
3	The diagnostic system specifications on board, the Environmental Protection Bureau of the United States of America
4	The diagnostic system specifications on board, the Ministry of Land and Transport of Japan
5	Specifications diagnostic system on board, established in Phase IV of the National PRC GB18352.3-2005 Standards (Measurement Methods and Pollutants Emission Limits for Passenger Vehicles (Phase III and Phase IV China))
6	Specifications diagnostic system on board, established in Phase IV of the National People's Republic of China GB17691-2005 Standards (Measurement Methods and pollutants emission limits for vehicles and ignition engines Compression and Ignition Combustion Gases (Phase III, Phase IV and Phase V of China))
7	Specifications diagnostic system on board, established in Phase III of the National Standards of PRC GB14762-2008 (Methods of Measurement and pollutants emission limits for vehicles and engines Gasoline Used in Heavy Vehicles (Phase III and Phase IV China))

FUND FOR ENVIRONMENTAL PROTECTION AND ENERGY CONSERVATION

Administrative Regulation No. 21/2011

The Chief Executive, after consultation with the Executive Council, decrees, under point 5) of Article 50 of the Macau Basic Law, to stand as independent administrative regulation, the following:

CHAPTER I GENERAL PROVISIONS

Article 1

Nature and regime

1. The Fund for Environmental Protection and Energy Conservation, hereinafter FPACE is a legal person of public law, with administrative and financial autonomy and its own assets, which works with the Directorate of Environmental Protection Bureau, hereinafter by DSPA.

2. FPACE governed by this administrative regulation and other applicable legislation.

Article 2

Purposes

The FPACE aims to:

1) improve the quality of the environment;

2) To promote energy conservation and emission reduction of pollutants;

3) Monetize water resources;

4) support and promote the development of environmental industry;

5) support and promote the measures taken by convenient for improving the quality of life, when it has been affected by any environmental impact.

Article 3

Guardianship

1. FPACE is subject to the authority of the Chief Executive.

2. In exercising its supervisory powers, the responsibility of the Chief Executive, namely:

1) To approve and promulgate the private budget as well as their revisions and amendments;

2) To approve the annual report and management accounts;

3) accept the plan and the guidelines for financial management;

4) Define guidelines and issue directives with a view to achieving the objectives of FPACE;

5) To authorize expenses falling under FPACE assignments, which exceed the legally defined as jurisdiction of the Administrative Council;

6) To approve the agreements and protocols to be signed with other public or private entities of the MSAR and other acts that require approval;

7) To authorize the acquisition of property and the sale or encumbrance of real property of FPACE heritage;

8) To consider and decide on any questions concerning the powers of FPACE to financially support a particular project or activity.

Article 4

Support

The FPACE is supported technically and administratively by DSPA.

CHAPTER II BOARD OF DIRECTORS

Article 5

Composition

1. FPACE is managed by an Administrative Council.

2. The Administrative Council consists of five members, to be appointed by order of the Chief Executive, fixing the term of office, and are part of it:

1) The Director of the DSPA, chairman;

2) A representative of the Office for Development of the Energy Sector, hereinafter GDSE;

3) A representative of the Finance Services, hereinafter referred to as DSF.

3. When appointing representatives GDSE, the DSF and the remaining members of the Board, Chief Executive also appoints their substitutes.

4. In his absence or incapacity, the president is replaced by his legal substitute and the other members are replaced by their alternate members.

5. The President shall designate from among DSPA officials, the secretary of the Board and its substitute, who attend the meetings without voting rights.

Article 6

Skills

1. The Administrative Council:

1) Collect revenues FPACE;

2) To authorize the expenses necessary to accomplish FPACE assignments;

3) To prepare the proposed private budget FPACE and your changes and submit them for approval by the Chief Executive;

4) Prepare the annual management accounts, submitting to the approval of the Chief Executive;

5) propose to the entity safeguard the measures deemed necessary to the proper financial management of the FPACE that do not fall within the scope of its own powers;

6) To acquire essential furniture and equipment to the development of initiatives that fall within the scope of FPACE assignments;

7) Enter into agreements and protocols with other public or private entities of the MSAR;

8) Decide on all that interest to FPACE and not by law be excluded from its jurisdiction.

2. The Board may delegate to the President the power to authorize expenditures up to the limit of 50,000 patacas, shall, however, acts in the use of this delegation be ratified at the meeting of the Board following the practice.

Article 7

Powers of the President of the Board

The Chairman of the Board:

1) submit to the Board all matters requiring deliberation of this body, proposing to adopt the measures it deems necessary for the proper functioning of FPACE;

2) To represent the FPACE in any relations with public or private entities where there to intervene;

3) To implement the decisions of the supervisory entity and the resolutions of the Board;

4) exercise the powers delegated to him by the Board.

Article 8

Operation

1. The Administrative Council shall meet regularly twice a month and extraordinarily whenever the president convenes on its own initiative or upon proposal of any of its members.

2. The Board may only deliberate when present the majority of its members.

3. Decisions are taken by majority vote of the members present.

4. In the event of a tied vote, the chairman has the casting vote.

5. It is forbidden to abstain all the members present at the meeting and are not prevented from voting.

6. When the matters of discussion so requires, the President, on his own initiative or at the request of the Board, may invite to participate in meetings without the right to vote, persons whose presence becomes necessary manifest interest.

7. Each meeting minute is drawn up, signed by all members present, which should contain the succinct account of what it has occurred, indicating, inter alia, the date and place of the meeting, the agenda, the members present, the subjects appreciated the explanations of vote may be issued and decisions taken.

Article 9

Wages

1. The members and the secretary of the Board are entitled to a monthly remuneration corresponding to 50% of the 100 index table of salaries of civil servants.

2. In the case of replacement, the substitute is entitled, for each meeting they attend, the share corresponding to the amount of the division referred to above by the number of meetings held in the respective month, which is deducted from the salary of the replaced.

CHAPTER III FINANCIAL MANAGEMENT

Article 10

Recipes

The revenues of FPACE:

1) Revenues from budgetary transfers from the MSAR budget;

2) Revenues assigned to it by any public or private entities;

3) The amounts from the repayment of financial support granted in the framework of its powers;

4) interest or other income resulting from the application of own availability carried out in accordance with the law and any property or that has fruition;

5) The product donations, inheritances, gifts and bequests;

6) The product disposals and transfers of assets or rights of their assets;

7) any other revenue assigned to it by law, contract or otherwise.

Article 11

Moving accounts

Changes in FPACE of funds is made by check or money order with the signature of two Board members, one of them being the president or his replacement.

Article 12

Applications

The FPACE revenues are intended to meet the costs arising from their tasks.

Article 13 º

Budgetary and accounting rules

The organization of FPACE budget, accounting for revenues and expenses and other obligations under this administrative regulation, applies the provisions of public financial management system.

CHAPTER IV GRANT OF FINANCIAL AID

Article 14

To grant financial aid plans

The plans of financial support by FPACE consist of administrative regulation.

Article 15

Commission of appreciation

1. Requests under the plans of financial support by FPACE are analyzed by an Evaluation Panel.

2. The Evaluation Commission has to examine requests for financial support and issue reasoned opinion on granting or not support, within 30 days of the complete proceedings of the case date.

3. The Evaluation Committee consists of a president, who has the casting vote, and for a maximum of six members, all appointed by order of the Chief Executive, fixing the term of office.

4. The order of the Chief Executive designating the members of the Evaluation Panel may also designate their substitutes.

5. The Evaluation Committee may only deliberate when presence of the majority of its members.

Article 16

Remuneration of the members of the Evaluation Panel

1. Members of the Evaluation Panel are entitled to a monthly remuneration corresponding to 50% of the 100 index table of salaries of civil servants.

2. In the case of replacement, the substitute is entitled, for each meeting they attend, the share corresponding to the amount of the division referred to above by the number of meetings held in the respective month, which is deducted from the remuneration of a member .

CHAPTER V FINAL AND TRANSITIONAL PROVISIONS

Article 17

Extinction

Upon termination, the assets of FPACE paid to the MSAR.

Article 18

Transitional provision

The budget FPACE for the current financial year is submitted to the Chief Executive within 15 days from the date of publication of this administrative regulation.

Article 19

Implementation

1. This administrative regulation enters into force 30 days after the date of its publication.

2. Except as provided in the preceding paragraph to Article 18, which shall enter into force on the day following the publication of this administrative regulation.

Approved on May 19, 2011.

ADMINISTRATIVE CONDITIONING OF CERTAIN ECONOMIC ACTIVITIES

Decree-Law No. 47/98 / M

26 October

As is generally recognized, the administrative conditioning of certain economic activities is required by the bounden responsibility of public authorities in safeguarding the ways in which such activities may conflict with the interests of the community, especially in terms of security and public health and environmental balance .

Nevertheless, it is equally recognized that conditioning, when needed, should be as light and streamlined as possible in order not to be an unjustified obstacle to the freedom of enterprise.

These concerns simplification and cutting red tape, as well as the teachings however harvested from the application of Decree-Law No. 31/93 / M, of 28 June, now lead the review of constant administrative licensing regime of the said diploma.

In these terms;

After hearing the Consultative Council;

The Governor decrees, pursuant to paragraph 1 of Article 13 of the Macau Organic Statute, be enforced as law in Macau, the following:

CHAPTER I GENERAL PROVISIONS

Article 1

(Purpose and scope)

1. This law establishes the administrative conditioning regimen of activities and events specified in Tables I and II annexed hereto.

2. This law does not apply:

a) In the production and realization of films by public services or bodies;

b) At the news footage intended purposes incurred in the media;

c) At laundries and dry cleaners inserted into plants;

d) To the storage of combustible products;

e) At the storage of dangerous goods carried out within industrial units, to support the establishment of the activity in which they operate;

f) At raffles, sweepstakes or similar devoid of commercial or held under concession contracts nature;

g) At other activities or events that are subject to special legislation.

Article 2

(Conditioning Shape)

The administrative conditioning takes the form of:

a) Authorization of mandatory prior notification, as provided by Table I;

b) Licensing in the cases provided in Table II.

Article 3

(Mandatory notification or license)

The practice or exploitation of any of the activities or events specified in the tables annexed hereto without its sponsor or owner of the establishment dispose of authorization or valid license for this purpose in accordance with this law.

Article 4

(General prohibition)

It is forbidden the placing of bets or any games of chance and to sell any unauthorized services in establishments and places where the activities take place or planned events in Tables I and II.

Article 5

(General Requirements)

1. The general requirements for the authorization and licensing under this Law:

a) Compliance, in legal terms, the tax liabilities inherent to the activities to be performed;

b) The adequacy of facilities or local nature of the activity or event to be held, particularly in terms of floor space, hygiene, safety, location and respect for environmental balance.

2. The authority responsible for granting the authorization or license may set other requirements or operating rules for certain types of activities or events, by order, posture or other appropriate legal instrument, to be published in the Official Gazette.

Article 6

(Not applicable hourly limitations)

1. The hourly operating limits of this law are not applicable to establishments that exploit any of the activities listed in paragraphs 4 and 6 of Table I and in paragraphs 2-7 and 11 of Table II,

provided that such establishments are situated in hotels, apartment hotels, tourist complexes, hostels or exclusively commercial buildings.

2. Unless otherwise specified, the hourly limitations are also inapplicable to the establishments referred to above which are located in commercial podium, with independent access, buildings not exclusively commercial.

Article 7

(Display Requirement for authorization or license)

1. presentation of the license or proof of prior notification, whenever requested by the supervisory bodies is mandatory.

2. Proof of prior notification is done by copying the Model A, attached to this document, or equivalent document bearing the stamp and the 'received' statement, with the date, affixed by the competent authority.

3. In the case of establishment subject to licensing, the license must be posted in a conspicuous place on it.

Article 8

(Information relating to authorizations and licenses)

The competent authorities give knowledge to the Finance Services and the Public Security Police of the following:

a) Notifications received prior specifying cases of express authorization, provided tacit consent and refusal;

b) Approval or rejection of the application license;

c) Endorsement of license;

d) Revocation and license expiry statement.

CHAPTER II SYSTEM OF PRIOR NOTIFICATION

SECTION I

General provisions

Article 9

(Time limit and form)

1. The beginning of the activities or the completion of the events listed in Table I shall be subject to prior notification to the competent authority upon delivery of the Model A, with a least:

a) From 20 days, in the case of the production of motion pictures;

b) From 10 days in all other cases.

2. The applicant may replace the Model A by written document specifying, sufficient and clearly all the mandatory information elements to which it relates that model.

3. In the case of the Model A or the elements that must accompany contain defects or irregularities, the competent authority uses the most expedient way to invite the applicant to rectify the situation, subject to their confirmation in writing.

Article 10

(Raffles, lucky draws or similar - complementary element to the Model A)

In the case of raffles, sweepstakes or similar, the Model A should be accompanied by the regulation, stating obligatorily:

a) The number of awards and corresponding monetary value;

b) The number of tickets to be issued and the price of each;

c) The identification of the persons directly responsible for the sale or collection of tickets and the prize extractive operations;

d) The indication of the date, time and venue of the extraction, which must be present a representative of the competent authority.

Article 11

(Movies - complementary element to the Model A)

With regard to the production and realization of film fiction films, the Model A should be accompanied by full copy of the script.

Article 12

(Addressed Entity)

1. The notice is sent:

a) At the Cultural Institute of Macau, as provided in paragraph 1 of Table I;

b) At the Municipality, as provided for in paragraphs 2 to 5 of Table I;

c) The Institute of Macao Sports, when gyms are concerned bodybuilding or maintenance;

d) The Directorate of Gaming Inspection and Coordination, where such restrictions pursue the realization of raffles, sweepstakes or similar, which is not within the scope of concession contracts.

2. The Macao Cultural Institute sends copy of the notice to the Public Security Police Force whenever there are circumstances set out in paragraph 1.2. Table I.

3. The jurisdiction of local municipality shall send a copy of the notice:

a) When the Public Security Police, as provided for in paragraphs 2 and 3 of Table I;

b) When the Fire Department, as provided in paragraph 2 of Table I.

Article 13

(Tacit authorization)

1. The lack of response to the notice gives the applicant the right to promote the event or start operations, according to the terms and conditions notified to the competent authority, unless that the have asked to correct any failure or irregularity model A or the elements that must be attached.

2. Tacit consent not take place if:

a) It is possible to fix the shortcomings or irregularities referred to in the latter part of the previous paragraph to the fourth business day prior to scheduled start of the activity or the event;

b) The applicant is legally prevented from exercising the activity, notably by interdiction or disqualification sentence has become final or meet is serving a sentence of disqualification from the practice of the intended activity;

c) The competent authority if you have the opposite, less than one year, the substantially identical content notification, formulated by the applicant;

d) The notification contains an indication of nonconforming opening hours with the standards established in this Act or that may be established pursuant to paragraph 2 of Article 5

3. When tacit authorization pursuant to sub-paragraph is not possible a) of the preceding paragraph, and this impossibility is not supplied by express authorization of the competent authority, the correction of shortcomings or irregularities determines the conversion of the notice, since the Interested enter a new date for the commencement of the activity or the event, observing the minimum period of notice referred to in paragraph 1 of Article 9

Article 14

(Refusal of authorization)

1. The competent authorities to appreciate the notice may object to the activity or the event, or set conditions or terms of which must depend on the legality of same on the ground:

a) In any general public interest reasons other than purely economic;

b) The failure or inconsistency of the notified face elements to the general or specific requirements of this law or as may be established under paragraph 2 of Article 5

2. In the cases referred to in paragraph 1.1. Table I, the competent authority may refuse the use of public roads and other public domain goods if the script's content to extract, objectively, the possibility of the image of the Territory to be grossly distorted or misrepresented.

Article 15

(Expiry of Authorization)

1. The authorization expires by express waiver of the holder and by the final judgment of sentence that decrees the bankruptcy of the holder.

2. In the case of authorization to engage in activity that also fallen:

a) By change of place of business;

b) On the death of the natural person or dissolution of the legal person, holder of the authorization, unless the successors require, within 120 days, the change of ownership;

c) If the activity is not initiated within 60 days from the start date indicated in the application;

d) For the assignment of the establishment, since its installation has been authorized under transferable condition;

e) On the final judgment of decision determining the eviction of the establishment of facilities;

f) For the interdiction of the holder involving the impossibility of exploration activity.

Article 16

(Revocation of Authorization)

1. The authorization shall be revoked if it is found:

a) has been obtained by misrepresentation or other unlawful means;

b) That the operation of the business or of the event went to work, on reasonable grounds, notorious disorderly conduct, public security or tranquility or significant inconvenience to public health;

c) The exploitation of the work or making various event that what was said in notice;

d) Failure to comply with the general requirements of Article 5 or limitations imposed in response to the notification.

2. In the case of authorization to engage in activity that is also revoked if it is found:

a) Changing facilities so that impair their physical characterization or intended, when the situation is not capable of settlement with the competent authority;

b) The termination of the establishment's business;

c) Repeated breach of the rules applicable to the activity and noise pollution control standards or other technical standards of environmental protection.

3. It is assumed the cessation of activity whenever the establishment remains doors closed to the public for more than 60 days, consecutive or not, within one calendar year.

4. For the purposes of subparagraph c) of paragraph 2, it is considered breach reiterated the practice of three offenses of the same nature or five offenses, regardless of their nature, in less than two years.

SECTION II

Requirements and prohibitions in special

Article 17

(Barbers, hairdressers and beauty salons)

1. operation of barber shops, hairdressers and beauty salons before 8.00 hours and beyond 22.00 hours is prohibited.

2. The request of interested parties or associations, the competent authority may authorize special hours of operation during festive seasons.

Article 18

(Namely bodybuilding or maintenance)

1. When located in buildings that include fractions for housing, bodybuilding gyms or maintenance can only work between 6.00 hours and 24.00 hours and can only be installed in the basement, on the ground floor or the places referred to in paragraph 2 of Article 6

2. The time limit referred to above is inapplicable if the competent authority attesting the appropriate dynamic and sound insulation property on the building in which it operates.

CHAPTER III LICENSING REGIME

SECTION I

General provisions

Article 19

(License)

The license is titrated by document in accordance with the Model B, attached to this document, enabling the owner of the establishment to carry out the activity specified therein during its period of validity.

Article 20

(Skills)

1. The granting, renewal and replacement of licenses is the responsibility of municipalities, except for the establishments of saunas and massage, such as 'health club' and type 'karaoke', whose competence is committed to Macau Government Tourist Services.

2. The entities referred to in the preceding paragraph may request the applicant clarification they may deem convenient and make the steps they may wish to check the fulfillment of general and special requirements.

Article 21

(Refusal licenses)

Licensing authorities may refuse to leave or grant it by imposing conditions which must depend on the legality of the exercise activity or event to be held on the grounds mentioned in paragraph 1 of Article 14

Article 22

(Validity and renewal of licenses)

1. The license is valid for a maximum period of one year from the date of issue.

2. Notwithstanding the preceding paragraph, the license is considered to be renewed by paying the fixed rate, unless the licensing authority to notify the licensee or its representative to decide otherwise within 60 days before the expiry of his expiration date.

3. A certificate of payment of the fee goes to all legal purposes as proof of license renewal.

4. The non-renewal of a license shall, if the applicant wishes to continue to conduct business, new licensing process.

Article 23

(Forfeiture of licenses)

The license expires:

a) When you experience any of the causes specified in Article 15;

b) At the end of their period of validity, if there is no place to be renewed;

c) For the new license issued following the change or extension of the scope of permitted activities.

Article 24

(Revocation of licenses)

The license is revoked whenever there is any of the grounds provided for in Article 16

Article 25

(Seizure of licenses)

Where the license is declared lapsed or revoked, it is the licensor grasp it, for what may request the cooperation of the Public Security Police Force.

Article 26

(Duplicates of licenses)

1. The applicant, by filling in the Model C attached to this document, and the payment of the fee corresponding to half of the original fee, may require the issuance of duplicate of license lost, destroyed or damaged.

2. The duplicate shall contain such details and in the case of replacement, the original license is collected by the licensor, with the corresponding registration process.

Article 27

(Fees)

1. For the issue of licenses referred to this law is charged according to the schedule approved by the Governor, to be published in the Official Gazette.

2. In case of withdrawal or lapse of the license is not due any reimbursement for fees paid.

SECTION II

Requirements and prohibitions in special

Article 28

(Public Entertainment)

1. For the purposes of this law, shows up any views, starring professionals or amateurs and for the public, excluding those that are performed by groups or musical bands in hotels, apartment hotels, tourist resorts and inns.

2. The license for the performance of any show is necessarily preceded by their age rating, in accordance with their own legislation.

3. Within the urban centers, the shows can not take place in the period between 0.00 hours and 8.00 hours when they perform outdoors or out of purely commercial buildings, theaters and cinemas, or any the establishments referred to in the final part of paragraph 1.

Article 29

(Safety conditions in shows, cinemas and theaters)

1. The public performances and exhibitions in cinemas and theaters can not take place without the presence of 2 or more firefighters, as determined by the commander of the Fire Department.

2. The levy referred to in the preceding paragraph shall not be required for sites or facilities that have undergone prior certification of safety conditions for the purpose in view, without conditions or limitations.

3. The prior certification of safety conditions, taking into account the type of construction, the general state of the electrical installation of the fire protection systems and escape routes, is proved by a security certificate, issued by the Body firefighters, with a shelf life of 1 year.

4. The security certificate may be revoked at any time when you show the degraded conditions that substantiate the issue.

Article 30

(Activities of Table III)

1. In addition to the other requirements applicable under this law are conditions required for the licensing of activities listed in Table III of age and suitability of the applicant.

2. Among other relevant circumstances, it is considered indiciador of lack of suitability that the applicant has been convicted by final judgment for less than three years the date of application, a criminal offense punishable with imprisonment of more than one year unless there has been rehabilitation.

Article 31

(Billiards games and "bowling")

1. In establishments operating billiards games and "bowling" is forbidden entry to children under 16 and students wearing school uniform, unless accompanied by parents or person exercising parental authority.

2. When located in buildings that include fractions for housing, establishments referred to in the preceding paragraph may only work between 8.00 hours and 24.00 hours and can only be installed in the basement, on the ground floor or in the places listed in paragraph 2 of Article 6

3. The time limit referred to above is inapplicable if the competent authority attesting the appropriate soundproofing of the establishment on the building in which it operates.

Article 32

(Machinery fun and video games)

1. It is considered amusement machines and video games those who do not pay premiums in cash or convertible into cash, they develop games whose results depend exclusively or essentially on the player's skill.

2. For licensing purposes, amusement machines and video games are classified according to their nature, in one of the following groups:

a) Intended for children;

b) Intended for over 16 years.

3. In establishments where they exploit the machines and the games referred to in the preceding paragraphs, even in conjunction with other activities, is prohibited:

a) The operating between 0.00 hours and 8.00 hours;

b) The operation, in the same room, machines and games covered by the classification of subparagraphs a) and b) of the preceding paragraph;

c) The change in the number or characteristics of the machines and equipment covered by the license.

4. In engine rooms or games classified in subparagraph b) of paragraph 2 shall be refused entry to children under 16 and the entry of students wearing school uniform, unless accompanied by parents or person exercising parental authority.

Article 32a

(Internet cafes)

1. It is understood by Internet cafes establishments, primarily, available to the public computer terminals for internet access, or to practice internal network games.

2. The establishments referred to in the preceding paragraph, when situated in buildings that include fractions for housing, can only work between 8.00 hours and 24.00 and only in the basement, on the ground floor or in commercial podiums with independent access to the dwellings.

3. When the competent authorities certify the dynamic and acoustic insulation of establishments face the buildings in which they are inserted, cease to apply the time limit referred to above.

4. The time limits provided for in paragraph 2 shall not apply in the case of the Internet cafes are situated in hotels, apartment hotels, tourist complexes, hostels or exclusively commercial buildings.

* Amended - See Also: Law 10/2003

Article 32b

(Entry and residence)

1. Any entry into Internet cafes to children under 12 years.

2. Entry in the major Internet cafes under 12 and under 16 and students wearing school uniform is only allowed after 16.00 hours, Monday through Friday, and from 8.00 hours on Saturdays , Sundays, holidays and during school holidays.

3. Users referred to in the preceding paragraph may stay in cybercafés up to 22.00 hours from Sunday to Friday, and up to 24.00 hours on Saturdays, school holidays and public holidays, when they are not eve the business day.

4. Limitations of constant access and permanence in paragraphs 1, 2 and 3 shall cease in the case of minors and students are accompanied by their parents or who exercises parental power.

5. Access to pornographic, violent games and, without prejudice to Article 4, the interactive games of chance is prohibited to any person during the period in which minors and students are allowed to stay in Internet cafes .

6. The preceding paragraph shall not apply in the separate compartments for adults.

7. It is posted at the entrance of Internet cafes in place and clearly visible way, a notice with the access conditions contained in this article.

* Amended - See Also: Law 10/2003

Article 32-C

(Filtering and registration)

1. Must be installed on computers filtration systems allowing them to block access to content referred to in paragraph 5 of the previous article, during the period in which minors and students are allowed to stay in Internet cafes.

2. In establishments where there are separate compartments for adults, installation of the systems referred to in the preceding paragraph is required only on computers used by minors.

3. For monitoring purposes, computerized records of the contents are made used by minors, which are kept for a period of three months.

* Amended - See Also: Law 10/2003

Article 33

(Saunas and massages)

1. It is only permitted commercial exploitation of saunas and massage establishments in the places referred to in Article 6

2. In saunas and massage establishments is prohibited:

a) The entry under 18;

b) The display of masseurs.

Article 34

(Type establishments "health club")

1. Establishments such as 'health club' include adequate facilities for the practice of sports or physical exercise, with the necessary dependencies of support, and may have provided that in duly separate areas, sauna cabins and own massage service establishments of this type.

2. It is only permitted commercial exploitation of establishments such as 'health club' in the places referred to in Article 6

3. When located in areas referred to in paragraph 2 of Article 6, establishments such as 'health club' can only work between 6.00 hours and 24.00 hours.

4. The time limit referred to above is inapplicable if the competent authority attesting the appropriate dynamic and sound insulation property on the building in which it operates.

Article 35

(Type establishments "karaoke")

1. It is only permitted commercial exploitation of establishments such as 'karaoke' in the places referred to in Article 6

2. In establishments such as 'karaoke' is forbidden entry to children under 16 and students wearing school uniform.

Article 36

(Trade pornographic materials)

1. In establishments engaged, exclusively, the commercial exploitation of pornographic materials is prohibited:

a) The entry under 18;

b) The placement of pornographic material in shop windows or in a place where they can be outside of viewing the establishment;

c) Commercial advertising that exceeds expressions such as 'trade in pornographic' or equivalent;

d) The production of pornographic or obscene material.

2. to establishments engaged in non-exclusive basis, the commercial exploitation of pornographic materials are subject to the prohibitions set out in subparagraphs b) to d) of the preceding paragraph also being forbidden access to pornographic material and its sale to minors 18 years.

3. In the rental establishments or sale of image storage media, discs 'laser' and supplies, is required, in particular, wrapping and display of pornographic material in suitably guarded sites and separated from the remaining material.

Article 37

(Storage of hazardous materials, nuisance or unhealthy)

For the purposes of this law, it is considered:

a) Dangerous products: substances or compound of substances classified as dangerous under the law that governs access to manufacturing activities;

b) Products nuisance or unhealthy: the litter, waste and any other products or substances due to bad odors, noxious fumes or other similar effects can contribute to decrease to an appreciable extent, the quality of life in the surrounding medium.

Article 38

(Repair of Motor Vehicles)

It is forbidden to run repair establishments for motor vehicles between 20.00 hours and 8.00 hours.

SECTION III

Process

Article 39

(Application procedure)

1. The permit is required by delivering the licensor Model C duly completed.

2. In the case of a company whose constitution occurred less than 3 months from the date of application, registration certificate at the Commercial and Automobile Registry can be replaced by copy of the deed or the mere indication of the Official Gazette where the social pact has been published.

3. When the request respects the work provided in Table III, the application is accompanied by a criminal record certificate or equivalent document accepted by the licensor.

4. The licensing authority shall notify the applicant within three working days of receiving the application, for a maximum period of 60 days, subject to rejection, cover any defects or irregularities in the Model C or documentation presented contain.

5. The applicant may submit, with knowledge of the licensor, copy of the initial application to the other entities involved.

6. Where it is concerned the licensing of exploration of different activities in multipurpose facilities for various entities, their initial requirements can be delivered together with the competent authorities to carry out the licensing of operating the core business or to which the issue of necessary license, which automatically makes its referral to other competent bodies.

Article 40

(Opinions of other entities)

Before granting the license, the licensor requests necessarily the opinion:

a) From the Land, Public Works and Transport Bureau and the Fire Department, for any kind of activity specified in Table II;

b) Of the Macau Health Bureau, for the activities provided for in paragraphs 3, 4 and 7 of Table III;

c) From the Public Security Police and the Municipality territorial jurisdiction, when this is not the licensor in the case of the activities specified in Table III;

d) The Institute of Macao Sports, in the case of establishments such as 'health club'.

Article 41

(Application deadlines and issuing opinions)

1. The opinions referred to in the previous article are requested within 3 business days of receipt of the application or, if applicable, after the supply of shortcomings or irregularities.

2. The opinion shall be delivered by the entity requested within 15 working days of the request, understanding their lack after that period, as opposed to lack the granting of the license.

Article 42

(Deadline decision)

The decision on granting, endorsement or replacement license shall be issued within 10 working days of receipt of the application or, if applicable, the date:

a) the receipt of the advice mentioned in the previous article or the time limit for their issue;

b) The correction of defects or irregularities in the application or the elements that must follow.

Article 43

(Local Change and extension to other activity)

The licensee granted pursuant to this statutory instrument to extend the scope of the activity to other activities specified in Table II, or wishing to transfer or extend the facility to another location, you must perform new licensing application.

Article 44

(Other subsequent changes)

1. Following the completion of the Model C and payment of the fee corresponding to half of the original fee, the licensing authority may authorize the registration of license ownership change or modification of the establishment name where the activity is exploited, provided that maintain the general requirements set out in Article 5

2. The physical alteration of the premises in which they develop licensed activities, notably involving restoration, architectural, construction or decoration, shall be applied to the licensor, by filling in the Model C, getting its conditional approval to the opinion in accordance with Article 40

CHAPTER IV SUPERVISION AND SANCTIONS

Article 45

(Oversight)

1. The supervision of the provisions of this law is assigned:

a) To the competent authorities to receive the notice or to decide licensing under the events or activities concerned;

b) To law enforcement authorities in their respective areas of jurisdiction.

2. The records of proceedings raised by the police are sent to the entities referred to in subparagraph a) of the preceding paragraph.

3. The heads of the entities referred to in subparagraph a) of paragraph 1 designate staff the supervisory mission and give you the credentials necessary for this purpose.

Article 46

(Offences)

When more serious offenses should not be considered to constitute administrative offenses punishable with a fine of:

a) 30 000,00 200 000,00 patacas, or 100 000,00 500 000,00 patacas, depending on whether the offender is a natural or legal person, the continuation or resumption of which is operational whose permit or license has been revoked ;

b) 20 000,00 to 100 000,00 patacas, or 50 000,00 300 000,00 patacas, depending on whether the offender is a natural or legal person, the exercise of activity provided in Table III without valid license title;

c) 15 000.00 70 000.00 patacas or of 30 000.00 to 200 000.00 patacas, depending on whether the offender is a natural or legal person, the exercise of the activity subject to prior notification or licensing without the corresponding authorization or without valid license title;

d) 10 000.00 40 000.00 patacas or of 20 000.00 to 100 000.00 patacas, depending on whether the offender is a natural or legal person conducting activities or holding events in violation of the terms and conditions notified to the competent authority or fixed by it, as well as conducting activities in violation of operating rules laid down in Article 5 paragraph 2 and set out in paragraph 1 of article 17, paragraph. 1 of article 18, paragraph 3 of Article 28, paragraph 1 of article 29, paragraphs 1 and 2 of Article 31, paragraphs 3:04 Article 32, paragraph 2 of Article 32a, paragraphs 1, 2, 3 and 5 of Article 32b, Article 32-C, paragraph 2 of Article 33, paragraph 3 of Article 34, Article 35 paragraph 2 and Articles 36 and 38; *

e) 2 000,00 15 000,00 patacas, or 4 000.00 50 000.00 patacas, depending on whether the offender is a natural or legal person, the breach of the obligations set out in Article 4, paragraphs 1 and 3 of Article 7, paragraph 7 of Article 32b and in paragraph 2 of Article 44. *

* Changed - See Also: Law 10/2003

Article 47

(Precautionary measures)

1. In situations that constitute the offenses covered in subparagraphs a) to c) of the preceding article, the Head of the competent authority may decide to close and seal the premises or the immediate cessation of the event in question.

2. The lifting of seals:

a) may be permitted for the time strictly necessary to conservation tasks or maintenance of facilities or machinery and other equipment that are inside;

b) It is determined immediately cease the circumstances justifying such a measure.

Article 48

(Prohibition of the activity exercise)

1. The practice of three offenses of the same kind in less than two years shall, irrespective of the applicable fines, bans on carrying on business for a period of one year.

2. The withdrawal of authorization or license the basis of the circumstances described in subparagraphs a) of paragraph 1 and c) of Article 16 paragraph 2 shall, regardless of the penalty that fits the case, the ban on conduct of business for a period of two years.

Article 49

(Penalty Competence)

The application of penalties under this law is responsible to the head of the entities referred to in subparagraph a) of paragraph 1 of Article 45

Article 50

(Payment and treatment of fines)

1. The fine is payable within 10 days from the date of notification of the penalty decision.

2. In the absence of voluntary payment of the fine within the period prescribed in the preceding paragraph, the procedure is compulsory collection under tax foreclosure process by the competent authority, serving as enforceable the certificate of the penalty decision.

3. The application of the fine can be appealed to the Administrative Court, which has suspensive effect.

4. The fines constitutes recipe:

a) Of the municipalities when they applied for;

b) Territory, in other cases.

Article 51

(Subsidiary law)

The offenses referred to in this Chapter shall subsidiarily apply in all matters not contrary to the provisions of this law, and with the necessary adaptations, the provisions of Section II of Chapter IV of Decree-Law No. 66/95 / M of 18 December.

CHAPTER V TRANSITIONAL AND FINAL PROVISIONS

Article 52

(Licenses issued under previous legislation)

1. A renewal of licenses issued under previous legislation or its unofficial translation in operating permit, as applicable, is subject to the verification of the requirements of this law.

2. Exceptions to the provisions of the preceding paragraph, while the licenses remain in the current beneficiary ownership:

a) The bodybuilding gyms or maintenance, pool games and "bowling", saunas and massage establishments, those of a kind "health club" and "karaoke", with regard to location requirements;

b) The barber shops, hairdressers and beauty salons, as regards the legal suitability of the site for commercial purpose.

3. Establishments whose continuity is permitted under the provisions of subparagraph a) of the preceding paragraph remains subject to the hourly limitations that currently apply to them, even if they are coupled or inserted in establishments otherwise, unless in the situations given in Article 18 to Article 31 paragraph 2 and paragraph 3 of Article 34, the competent authority attesting the appropriate dynamic isolation and / or acoustic property.

4. Failure of the hourly limitations mentioned in the preceding paragraph shall be punished in accordance with subparagraph d) of Article 46

Article 53

(Replacement securities registration)

1. Within one month from the date of entry into force of this law, the Macao Economic Services refers to the territorially competent Municipality, accompanied by the relevant bureaucratic procedures, the Industrial Register of Securities, Industrial Installation Registration Titles or Establishment Registration domesticated bonds issued under Decree-Law No. 95/85 / M of 9 November and that report the activities set out in Table II.

2. The municipalities shall undertake the replacement of the license registration certificates provided for in this law within 6 months from the date of its entry into force, in chronological order, without payment of fee and starting on the title that has been issued later date.

3. The owners of establishments whose title has been replaced by license are notified to undertake the survey, by registered letter with acknowledgment of receipt, addressed to the address of your office or headquarters, as indicated in the title.

4. The lack of response to the notification referred to above, within the prescribed period constitutes cessation of presumption of activity and license revocation foundation.

Article 54

(Specific obligations of the competent authorities)

Competent authorities should:

a) Provide to the interested parties, although it required only verbally, written information about the requirements, general and special conditions and formalities required to obtain a permit or license;

b) Provide free, in care settings to users, Models A and C.

Article 55

(Changing tables and Designs)

Tables and models attached to this law can be changed by order.

Article 56

(Repeals)

It is repealed all legislation contrary to the provisions of this law and, in particular:

a) The Decree-Law No. 31/93 / M, of 28 June;

b) The Decree-Law No. 57/95 / M, of 13 November.

ENVIRONMENT AND NATURE PROTECTION STRATEGY[1]

ENVIRONMENTAL PROTECTION

With the rapid economic development in recent years, several major infrastructure and private projects are being built in Macau, but then also emerging environmental issues; the public is increasingly aware of environmental protection and management, having gradually been concerned with the potential impacts on the environment caused during the stages environment caused during the stages of construction and exercise activities. To this end it has already been mentioned in the Action Lines.

Governance of the Government of the Macao Special Administrative Region, 2010 the need to draw up an environmental impact assessment procedure (hereinafter referred to as AIA). In order to strengthen the protection of the environment and as one of the environmental management measures, the role that AIA plays refers to scientific procedures to define the potential impacts on the environment caused by the project, before his execution, and presented policies and response measures that can prevent or eliminate the impacts that harm the environment. Since its inception, the Directorate the Environmental Protection Bureau (DSPA) has been carrying out actions to the evaluation system of the establishment of the Environmental Impact Assessment (EIA). In 2009, the DSPA prepared the "Instructions for the preparation of the environmental impact assessment report ', in order to standardize and harmonize the contents of the EIA report. In August 2011, the collection of opinions on 'exploratory text to create an evaluation system of environmental impact' was held in order to raise awareness and give basic understanding on EIA, listening and collecting the opinions of community about the EIA regime to be able to establish a scheme of its kind in Macau, which launched its compilation of opinions, giving preliminary response to some key issues for the community to further understand the factors to consider for the regime of establishment of AIA.

To accelerate action towards the establishment of EIA regime and, based on the collection of opinions and the results of related research, DSPA introduced in 2013 for the first time, the 'List Qualifying Construction Projects Need This tying the Environmental Impact Assessment "(experimental), with the hope that, through this pilot list, strengthen the awareness of the services responsible for the construction, the promoters units and sectors related to the concept and operation of the EIA, and continue to promote training and awareness, and exchanges to transmit to society more accurate knowledge of the scheme. In coordination with the management of other schedules or other pollution control measures, the systematization of the AIA will be able to ensure, in more effectively, the environmental quality in order to help promote the sustainable development of Macao.

Environmental protection is crucial in ensuring a quality standard of living. The Environment Council of Macao was restructured in 1998. The responsibilities of the Council include: give opinions toward the strategies for the protection of the environment, nature and ecological balance; introduce measures to go along with the enforcement of environmental laws; and enhance scientific researches in protection of the environment, nature and ecological balance.

ENVIRONMENTAL INFRASTRUCTURES

The Solid Waste Incineration Plant came into operation in 1992. Its processing of solid waste is the most advanced currently in the Asia-Pacific region geared towards environmental protection.

Since the opening of the three hi-tech sewage treatment plants in 1995, Macao's wastewater has been effectively treated to reduce pollution.

A fourth sewage treatment plant will be constructed in the Macao International Airport site.

[1] Environmental Protection Planning of Macao (2010-2020)

The Environmental Protection Bureau was set up by the Macao SAR Government on 29 June 2009. Major duties of the Bureau are to formulate environmental policy, organise environmental publicity and educational programmes, enhance environmental awareness of the general public, expedite the work on environmental impact assessment and environmental planning, promote the formulation and enforcement of legislations in relation to environment threatening acts, foster the implementation of environment management and the development of environmental industries, as well as to assist the Government in the implementation of international environmental conventions, and enhance international and regional communication and co-operation.

Macao is best positioned to develop environmental consultancy services, making use of its close relationship and association with developed nations in the European Union, particularly in areas of information and technology and in trade, and exploiting its unique status of a "meeting point" between the East and the West. Studies or assessment of impact in the environment, subsequent design of environmental protection plans for major development projects, or impact studies or assessment of waste pollution for a factory or business enterprise, option studies for solutions and techniques, and subsequent implementation of such solutions are but some of the areas of an environmental protection consultancy services can offer in Macao.

1.POLITICAL BACKGROUND

LOCAL: CHAPTER I GENERAL PRINCIPLE

Since its return to China, the Macao Special Administrative Region (MSAR) has experienced rapid social and economic development. In the meantime, new pressures and challenges in environmental protection issues have been arising. Environmental quality will be one of the core competitive edges for the sustainable development of Macao and the citizens have also shown greater demands for environmental quality, which urged the MSAR Government for a higher environmental management capability.

1.2 Along with the implementation of the *"Outline of the Plan for the Reform and Development of the Pearl River Delta (2008-2020)"*, and signing of the "*Guangdong-Macao Cooperation Framework Agreement*", Macao will greet a new wave of social and economic development, with the regional positioning as a "Global center of tourism and recreation". In addition, a couple of international conventions on environmental protection have been applicable to Macao; therefore, improving the environmental quality and advancing the effective implementation of international conventions has become one of the important goals in the environmental protection works of Macao.

1.3 In order to promote sustainable development in social and economic spheres and meet the need for the ongoing, fast economic and social development and the regional integration policy, it is necessary for Macao to formulate a people-oriented environmental protection plan, aimed to improve living environment, on the basis of all- round, systematic and scientific evaluation and analysis and of wide-ranging public opinions.

2.Existing Environmental Problems and Challenges

Local : Chapter I General Principle

2.1 Transportation, energy consumption and regional air pollution have been increasing

With the increase of vehicles in Macao, the environmental problems have become worse. Data showed that the greenhouse gas emissions caused by land transport increased by 70% from 2001 to 2009. Meanwhile, the concentrations of pollutants such as nitrogen dioxide (NO2), respirable particulates (PM10) and carbon monoxide (CO) have also been rising continuously along with the increase in land transport capacity. All these indicate that measures targeting land transport play a vital role in improving the air quality of Macao.

In respect of energy consumption, the consumption of heavy oil, which bears relatively more heavily on air pollution, exhibited a downtrend year by year. On the other hand, the greenhouse gas emissions of Macao were also decreasing since 2005, indicating considerable achievements in promoting the use of clean energy. However, in order to reduce the overall carbon emissions in Macao, it is necessary to make efforts to save the types of energy with a relatively higher consumption, including electricity, kerosene and light diesel oil, etc.

Along with rapid industrial development in the Pearl River Delta Region in recent years, the emissions of air pollutants increased accordingly. Since Macao is geographically connected to the Delta, the air quality of Macao is by no means exempted from the impact of the cross-regional transfer of air pollutants within the city cluster in the Pearl River Delta.

2.2Ensure the security of potable water and operation of wastewater treatment system; quality of water environment is to be remediated comprehensively

In respect of potable water, the quality of effluent from local water treatment plant has been affected by the saline tide in recent years. Meanwhile, because the raw water for the potable water of Macao is supplied from mainland, regional cooperation and coordination becomes an important part to ensure the raw water quality and water resources protection in Macao.

At present, Macao Peninsula Wastewater Treatment Plant (WWTP) is under a relatively higher pressure from wastewater treatment, while other WWTPs receive relatively less wastewater. This situation has caused some impact on the stable operation of the entire wastewater treatment system in Macao.

Monitoring data in recent years indicated that the quality of coastal waters in Macao has shown a trend of deterioration year by year. Moreover, cases of dead fish even occurred in some waters in the past few years. Among the coastal waters, the Canal dos Patos, North Patane Bay and Inner Harbor are more seriously polluted. In addition, there are still problems such as mistaken connection of pipelines and illegal discharge of sewage due to the drainage network not yet being renovated and optimized. Meanwhile, the rainwater run-off pollution has also caused some burden on the coastal waters. It can be seen that the pollution of coastal waters is in urgent need of systematic and holistic study and improvement to drive the execution of related treatment measures.

2.3 Strengthening the reduction and resourcing of solid wastes

The recovery rate of domestic solid waste through the existing waste recycling system in Macao was estimated to stand at 18.6% in 2009, which was relatively low compared to the surrounding regions. However, the quantity of solid waste generated was on constant increase.

In the background of fast socioeconomic growth in recent years, the solid waste generated by enterprises increased correspondingly, but the standards and norms governing enterprises' waste generation were relatively insufficient; in combination with the lack of relevant economic control measures, a majority of the small and medium enterprises had a limited input into environmental protection, causing their poor performance in pollution treatment and resources recycling and reuse.

According to the results of the Macao public environmental awareness surveys in 2010 and 2011, although residents have realized that each one has a part to play in environmental protection, a relatively low percentage of them actually take actions in their daily life. There is still a relatively larger room for improvement especially in respect of the separation of domestic solid waste, purchase of products with eco-labels and rejection of over-packaging. These reflect the insufficient policies in reducing and resourcing solid wastes in Macao.

2.4Increased pressure in ecological environment, urging for the improvement in preservation of ecological environment

The results on the status quo analysis of land use in Macao showed that the land used for construction has increased significantly in recent years, but the coastline suitable for ecosystem development has been reducing gradually. Meanwhile, the land use structure has also undergone great changes, resulting that the land used for ecological purpose is squeezed continuously by urban development.

Statistical data of recent years indicated only a limited growth in green area of Macao. Moreover, the fragmentation of landscape and blockade of the passage caused a very high pressure on animals' inhabitation and foraging.

There is not much indigenous vegetation in Macao, however, quite many cases of alien species invasion and the plague of plant diseases and pests have been observed in recent years, affecting the normal growth of indigenous ecosystem.

2.5With the ambient noise pollution worsening, it is necessary to reduce the level of traffic noise pollution and strengthen management of the community noise

Existing monitoring data indicated that traffic noise was one of the major sources of noise pollution in Macao. Because the transportation system is relatively dense in Macao, particularly in the Macao Peninsula, and the buildings are in close proximity to the roads, it is relatively hard to eliminate the effect of traffic noise on overall ambient noise. As the volume of transportation increases further in the future, it is foreseen that the traffic noise pollution will be more salient.

With the booming economy, the prosperity of tourist gambling industries and the increase of population density, various districts in Macao are subject to certain degrees of impact by noises from community, industrial and commercial activities as well as construction works. In fact, the total number of complaints about noise disturbance in Macao was on the increase in recent years, indicating the deterioration of the overall ambient noise environment in Macao.

2.6Strengthening the management and supervision of the environmental radiation is needed

As a highly developed city, the number of electromagnetic radiation sources, such as radio and television towers, telecommunication, radar, navigation equipment, high-voltage power transmission and transformation equipment, transportation system, and industrial, research and facilities will inevitably increase. It is expected to have more and more electromagnetic radiation sources located in close vicinity to residential and office buildings, which might cause a potential threat to the life and health of local residents.

2.7 More attention should be paid on the light pollution problem

As a city taking tourism and gambling as the key industry, the lighting of advertising signs on the streets, decorative lighting on exterior walls of buildings, large-screen displays and landscape lighting, which are everywhere on the street in Macao, indicates the prosperity of the city on one hand, however, on the other hand, these over-bright lighting in the the close vicinity of residents may have not only an adverse effect on human health and ecosystem, but also waste of energy.

VISION AND PLANNING

"Building a Low Carbon Macao, Creating Green Living Together" is the vision of the Environmental Planning. In light of this vision, Macao will continuously strive for a low carbon economic development mode featuring low pollution, low emissions and environmental friendliness, in order to avoid the consumption of enormous environmental resources during economic and social development. The vision above has different connotations on the three levels as follows:

3.1Under the guiding "people-oriented" principle, it means to create a beautiful, leisurely city suitable for living and tourism by building low carbon communities based on the core concept of low energy consumption, low pollution and by optimizing spatial environment;

3.2On the level of the city in general, it means to assimilate resources conservation and environmentally friendly lifestyle, consumption and work modes into all walks of life to build a society, which practices resource-conserving, recycling and environmental friendliness;

3.3On the level of regional coordination, it means to create a quality living area with good environment in the Pearl Revier Delta region through joint prevention and control and the coordination in environmental and ecological development, connecting all the joints on the green network (green roads and spaces) and the blue network (coastal spaces) in the whole region.

4.FOUR PRINCIPAL CONCEPTS OF THE PLANNING

The Environmental Planning is based on four core principal concepts, namely, sustainable development, low carbon development, public participation and regional cooperation, with improving the living environment and ensuring residents' health as the important goal of the Environmental Planning.

4.1 Concept of sustainable development

This planning adheres primarily to the sustainable development concept that the economic and social development should not sacrifice the environment. Taking the improvement and protection of local and regional environmental quality as the starting point, by strengthening environmental protection and ecological construction, it aims to ensure the health and security of local and regional living environment, promote interaction, harmony and synchronized development among environmental protection, society and economics, achieving the coordination among the improvement of environmental quality, optimization of economic growth pattern, promotion of social and economic development, as well as regional resources and environmental carrying capacity.

4.2 Concept of low carbon development

This planning follows the concept of low carbon development to formulate environmental protection strategies and action plans featuring the establishment of low carbon communities. In the area of production and consumption, strategies and action plans regarding the establishment of a low carbon production and consumption system are proposed, in accordance with the regional positioning of Macao as a "Global center of tourism and recreation", in order to promote the development of low carbon city, low carbon region, and achieve a "win-win-win" situation among economic, social development and ecological conservation.

4.3 Concept of public participation

This planning lays emphasis on the concept of public participation during the formulation and implementation of the Environmental Planning, enabling public participation in the entire process of the planning including formulation, implementation and performance assessment. For this purpose, the

Government needs to formulate practicable environmental protection policies, collect and adopt different opinions, experience and capabilities in the process of planning, execution and decision making; the enterprises need to take up the responsibility of reducing pollution and resources consumption; and the general public needs to take part in saving resources, waste reuse and recycling and nature conservation. Through the cooperation of government agencies, enterprises and general public, by taking the responsibility of each party, this makes environmental protection as the social consensus and vogue, to achieve the planning vision of building low carbon Macao.

Concept of regional cooperation

This planning proposed the cooperation with other regions in the Pearl River Delta on multiple dimensions and levels, including joint prevention and control of air pollution, cooperation in the prevention and treatment of water pollution, establishment of a cooperation mechanism for waste recycling and reuse as well as hazardous waste treatment, implementation of environmental information sharing and joint construction of ecosystem. At the meantime, planning on transportation and urban development has also been proposed in Macao. The present Environmental Planning is to be in coordination with those local planning projects, apart from strengthening the coordination with regional planning, promoting the environmental protection works and enhancing jointly the environmental and residential quality of Macao.

5.CONNOTATION OF THE PLANNING

The present Environmental Planning incorporates three principal themes, namely "Optimizing the Environment Suitable for Living and Tourism", "Promoting a Conservation and Recycling-oriented Society" and "Integrating into the Green and Quality Region", with the implementation of district-based and category-based management according to the three environmental functional districts, puts forward action plans for the 15 areas of concern and establishes 11 green indicators for the Environmental Planning. The main contents of this planning include the following respects:

(1) Attaching equal importance to the conservation of ecological environment and pollution prevention and control

•After making scientific survey and studies and sorting out the entire environmental problems in Macao, on the basis of taking public opinions and recommendations into consideration, this planning formulates, in a forward-looking way, the short-term (till 2012), medium-term (till 2015) and long-term (till 2020) action plans which attach equal importance to the conservation of ecological environment and pollution prevention and control.

(2) Putting forward the concept of environmental functional district management

•This planning puts forward the concept of environmental functional district management for the first time. It divides Macao into three environmental functional districts, namely, "District for strict environmental protection", "District for environment oriented development" and "District for environmental optimization and control", and prompt the control of the intensity of development in different areas via various measures, in order to reduce the impact of social and economic development on the environment.

(3) Formulating green indicators for the Environmental Planning

•11 green indicators for the Environmental Planning are formulated to push forward the short, medium and long-term environmental protection work, strive for the implementation of the planning goals stage by stage, and enhance the environmental quality gradually.

(4) Emphasizing mutual participation of the general public

•This planning emphasizes that the environmental protection work relies on participation of the government,enterprises and general public to meet the preset goals of the environmental protection policies and measures.

(5) Rolling approach to the implementation of the planning

•This planning adopts the rolling approach to the implementation of the planning, namely, the "Planning - Implementation - Evaluation - Amendment - Updating", to ensure continuous improvement of the planning in the process of social development.

(6) Guaranteeing the implementation of the planning

•The implementation of the action plans of the Environmental Planning is guaranteed via different execution and supervision mechanisms to achieve the vision of "Building a Low Carbon Macao, Creating Green Living Together".

(7) Coordination with other plannings

•This planning will cope with other planning such as the urban and transportation plannings of Macao, as well as regional plannings such as "Outline of the Plan for the Reform and Development of the Pearl River Delta (2008- 2020)" and the "Regional Cooperation Plan on Building a Quality Living Area", to integrate the low carbon and environmental concepts into all aspects of social development in Macao.

6.GOALS OF THE PLANNING

6.1 Promotion of the objectives in three phases

The present Environmental Planning will be executed in three phases,namely,the short term (2010-2012),medium term (2013-2015) and long term (2016-2020).

•Short-term goals (2010-2012) :

By formulating different measures for prevention and control of air pollution; conducting overall evaluation on the quality of coastal waters; establishing water supply warning, forcast and emergency response mechanisms; upgrading environmental infrastructures; encouraging and promoting conservation of energy and water resources; promoting separation and recycling of domestic solid waste; reducing energy consumption per unit of GDP; enhancing greening development; and promoting energy saving lighting equipment and design, the environmental quality will gradually be improved and the environmental management ability will be enhanced.

In response to some extremely urgent environmental problems,the DSPA has already begun to implement relevant short-term action plans while conducting the environmental planning.

•Medium-term goals (2013-2015) :

Through controlling exhausts from motor vehicles and major industrial air pollution sources; continually promoting energy and water conservation and undertaking comprehensive remediation of coastal waters; establishing the solid waste separation and recycling system; intensifying the construction of solid waste treatment facilities; supervising community noise; improving the environmental monitoring network; preventing deterioration of ecosystems; and strengthening regional cooperation in environmental protection, etc., the environmental pollution will basically be under control and a good security pattern for ecological environment will preliminarily be formed. Moreover, rules, regulations and technical standards for environmental management will gradually be formulated, enhancing the environmental management ability to a more advanced level.

•Long-term goals (2016-2020) :

Through continual promotion of green commuting; establishing water recycling systems; improving the management system for the whole solid waste handling process; carrying out comprehensive measures aimed for reducing, resourcing and detoxification of waste; safely disposing hazardous waste; stepping up prevention and control of noises from transportation, industries, commercial activities and construction; strengthening supervision over prevention and control of light pollution; enhancing greening development; establishing the management system for environmental functional districts; and improving the regional environmental cooperation mechanism, etc., the regional environmental quality will further be improved, a harmonious, healthy and balanced ecosystem will basically be formed, and a relatively complete system of laws, regulations and technical norms for environmental protection will gradually be established.

6.2 Green indicators of the planning

In order to better evaluate the degree to which the goals set in the Environmental Planning are met and keep track of the execution for the Environmental Planning, the present document sets forth 11 quantified green indicators,in respects of the utilization of resources and energy, environmental quality, pollution control and recycling, and ecological conservation. Specifically, they include the following: energy consumption per unit of GDP; utilization rate of clean energy; utilization rate of recycled water; annual compliance rate of ambient air quality; total evaluation index of coastal waters; centralized treatment rate of urban domestic wastewater; average reduction of regional ambient noise; recovery rate of recyclable waste; recycling rate of special and hazardous waste; centralized recovery rate of electronic and electrical equipment waste; and rate of urban green area.

CHAPTER II PROMOTING ENVIRONMENTAL FUNCTIONAL DISTRICT MANAGEMENT

In spite of the small land area of Macao, there are still various kinds of land parcels or districts with different functions or uses. Since the environmental impacts posed by different districts vary, and also their contribution to the entire ecosystem of the city, it is inappropriate to impose same environmental management systems and environmental quality standards on all these different areas. In view of this fact, the present Environmental Planning conducts for the first time the environmental functional district, which divides the entire territory of Macao into three types,namely, "District for strict environmental protection", "District for environment oriented development" and "District for environmental optimization and control", according to their environmental features, in order to implement better environmental strategies step-by-step with well classification in the future. On this basis, this planning puts forward suitable development orientations for different functional districts,and will gradually establish corresponding quality standards for air, noise, water and other environmental elements in the respective districts. It is expected to achieve a final balance between urban construction and ecological conservation by introducing environmental protection measures during urban development.

1.MANAGEMENT OF THREE ENVIRONMENTAL FUNCTIONAL DISTRICTS

In view of the environmental features of single environmental element such as air, water, ecology and noise, etc., the origin of environmental problems and the status quo of the environment in Macao as well as the requirements for future development planning, the present Environmental Planning undertakes environmental functional district based on each environmental element, for the purpose of protecting and improving regional environment. Based on the functional district by environmental elements, it then takes into consideration on natural conditions, social and economic standing, and environmental management needs of Macao, as well as the difference of various areas in service functions, ecological sensitivity and the impact of human activities, so as to formulate the classifying standards for the environmental functional districts.

1.1 District for strict environmental protection

It is referred to areas which are relatively more ecologically sensitive, with the ecological environment extremely susceptible to damage and hard to be recovered once damaged, and which, therefore, must be strictly protected and restricted in respect of construction. The precious natural resources in such areas shall be protected by forestalling any development activities which are by no means related to environmental protection and construction of the ecosystem.

1.2 District for environment oriented development

It is referred to areas with ecological sensitivity in the intermediate range and the ecological environment is relatively vulnerable. For this reason, such areas are suitable to be moderately exploited under the guidance of relevant environmental management guidelines or standards. Considering the fact that the older districts in Macao have almost been fully developed and there is a significant difference between the development of the old and new districts, strategically, the older districts shall be gradually renovated and developed with restrictions, while the newer districts shall be moderately developed under the guidance of urban development planning, in an effort to plan the urban development reasonably. While developing these areas, greening efforts shall also be exerted to protect the urban landscape and various natural landscape elements and cultural elements.

1.3 District for environmental optimization and control

It is referred to areas where development can be moderately optimized and controlled on condition that such development will not result in the deterioration of environmental quality or damage to the ecological functions. Considering the relatively serious pollution caused by facilities in such areas, strict control on pollution should be conducted through optimizing the local industrial layout, adjusting the structure and treating industrial pollution sources. In the meantime, measures should be taken vigorously to improve and elevate the regional ecological functions.

2.GRADUAL OPTIMIZATION AND IMPLEMENTATION OF THE ENVIRONMENTAL FUNCTIONAL DISTRICTS

2.1 Short-term (2010-2012):

Relevant studies for deepened and phase-by-phase implementation of the environmental functional districts are to be conducted. According to the needs and requirements of the environmental functional districts for the protection of ecological environment, and also taking into consideration the socioeconomic development in each environmental functional district, corresponding management guidelines for each district would be formulated and effective environmental protection measures would be promoted in the respective district.

2.2 Medium-term (2013-2015):

Through gradually putting in place the environmental functional district management and optimizing the relevant environmental quality standards and pollutant emission standards, gradually impose the corresponding quality standards and management requirements in each environmental functional district to prevent and control pollution, and to explore the requirements for the implementation of environmental functional district management in the process of socioeconomic development and project construction.

2.3 Long-term (2016-2020):

To incorporate the environmental functional district management into the routine environmental management system for systemic management, implement the environmental functional districts in an all-round way, and apply classified control and guidance over the environmental quality of different districts and different environmental elements according to the environmental quality standards for the environmental functional districts based on single element5 ; to make the environmental quality in each environmental functional district achieve the environmental quality standards by implementing major action plans and projects; and to exercise supervision and provide guidance for social economic activities and projects with the view of improving environmental quality and environmental functional districts management, and provide guidance for and amendment to the long-term major action plans and projects in respect of environmental protection.

5The environmental functional districts based on single elements mainly include the atmospheric environment, water environment and acoustic environment.

CHAPTER III OPTIMIZING THE ENVIRONMENT SUITABLE FOR LIVING AND TOURISM

The main purpose of "Optimizing the Environment Suitable for Living and Tourism" is to provide a beautiful and comfortable environment for citizens and tourists in Macao. It is a crucial factor for driving Macao to be the "Global center of tourism and recreation" and toward sustainable development, in order to turn Macao into a low carbon, environmentally friendly city suitable for living and tourism. For this purpose, efforts are to be carried on in the following seven areas of concern, including improvement of air quality, enhancement of water environment quality, treatment and disposal of solid waste, control of noise pollution, conservation of ecological environment, prevention and control of light pollution, and protection of environmental radiation. Effective actions would be taken in respect of the prevention and control of environmental pollution, conservation of the ecological environment, and strengthening of the environmental management, etc., so as to improve the overall environmental quality of the region, foster an atmosphere for green living, and achieve the goal of optimizing the environment suitable for living and tourism.

1.IMPROVEMENT OF AIR QUALITY

.1 To alleviate air pollution in the transportation sector

To advocate public transport priority and green commuting, curb the increasing trend of motor vehicles,and promote environmentally friendly vehicles gradually by means of changing the structure of vehicle fuels, promoting tax preferences for environmentally friendly vehicles, imposing stricter exhaust emission standards for motor vehicles, gradually eliminating vehicles with serious pollution, and promoting development of emission control technologies, etc.

1.2 To strengthen supervision over the management of atmospheric environment

To formulate emission standards for major air pollutants, strengthen networking and automation of various online monitoring data on air pollution sources, undertake surveys on stationary air pollution sources and figure out the inventory of pollution sources, and gradually carry out district-based management of atmospheric environmental functional districts.

1.3 To control major air pollution sources

To control emissions from scattered pollution sources such as cooking fume from restaurants and gasoline vapor from gas stations by formulating technical guidelines and emission standards and strengthening supervision, and to control emissions from major air pollution sources by engineering, technical and managerial measures.

2.ENHANCEMENT OF WATER ENVIRONMENT QUALITY

2.1 To ensure security of potable water supply

To improve the liaison and coordination mechanism between Guangdong Province and Macao, protect the environment of potable water sources and ensure security of the water supply.

2.2 To construct and renovate wastewater treatment facilities

To accomplish the capacity expansion and upgrading of the wastewater treatment plants (WWTPs), renovate the wastewater piping in the old districts of the city, and strengthen the wastewater treatment planning for the new town reclamation zone.

2.3 To strengthen the protection for coastal water environment

To gradually undertake prevention and control projects for point source and non-point source pollution of the coastal waters on the basis of relevant study results, conducting remediation projects on major polluted waters.

2.4 To gradually improve the water environment monitoring network

To construct the water environment monitoring and supervision system, including monitoring network for potable water sources protection and coastal waters, and actively promote cross-regional automated online monitoring of water quality.

3.TREATMENT AND DISPOSAL OF SOLID WASTE

3.1 To optimize the end-of-pipe treatment facilities

To promote environmentally sound treatment and resource recovery for the sludge generated from WWTPs, plan and construct new fly ash landfill with due criteria, and upgrade the treatment processes of the old refuse incineration plant.

3.2 To strengthen the whole-process supervision and management of solid waste

To manage solid waste separation according to the quantity, type and nature of the solid waste generated,strengthen supervision on hazardous wastes, formulate pollution prevention and control guidelines for the solid waste, and gradually introduce the "Polluter pays principle" and the "Producer responsibility scheme", and establish a complete solid waste information management system.

3.3 To establish a special and hazardous waste recycling and innocuous treatment management system

To establish a relatively complete management system for the special and hazardous waste by establishing an electronic and electrical equipment waste recycling system and a mechanism promoting reutilization of special wastes such as scrapped tires, and strengthening the innocuous treatment of poisonous or harmful domestic waste, etc.

4.CONTROL OF NOISE POLLUTION

4.1 To optimize the monitoring system for acoustic environmental quality

To establish a monitoring system for acoustic environment which will help the management department understand better the state of noise pollution, provide bases for decision making concerning the acoustic environment protection and feed data for different factor analyses related to noise, etc.

4.2 To control noise sources

To put noise under control from the following perspectives, namely, the control of noise sources, the control of noise transmission channels, and the protection of noise-sensitive receivers; formulate the Regulation on the "Prevention and Control of Ambient Noise", strengthen the control of noise from piling works and community activities, increase publicity and education targeting all social sectors to reduce noise disturbances, and take various measures to control noise from industry, commerce, traffic and construction.

4.3 To reduce noise at the stage of urban planning

To reduce noise at source during the stage of urban planning, and manage the acoustic environment by preventive means such as environmental impact assessment and green design.

5.CONSERVATION OF ECOLOGICAL ENVIRONEM

5.1 To plan and deploy the green areas reasonably

To establish an urban ecosystem network consisting of green points (greening nodes), lines (linear greening and corridors), areas (parks and leisure zones), spaces (vertical greening) and rings (coastal greening corridor around the islands).

5.2 To strengthen the maintenance of ecological and environmental resources and cultural heritage districts

To make holistic investigation into local ecosystems, to implement district-based protection by dividing them into different environmental functional districts according to their nature and the protected targets, and to apply protective measures for the sensitive ecosystem, together with continual monitoring.

5.3 To strengthen protection of animals and plants

To preserve the sites of inhabitation, foraging and propagation for animals, maintain and enhance the diversity of plants, and to retain or open up passages for animals to migrate during urban planning and construction according to the characteristics of different species.

6.PREVENTION AND CONTROL OF LIGHT POLLUTION

6.1 To formulate light pollution control measures and relevant regulations

To provide regulations for the brightness of large-area decorative lighting and the protective distance between them and the residential areas, hospitals and parks, and to formulate control measures and other regulations for large-scale lighting, decorative lighting, advertising signs and outdoor electronic displays, etc.

6.2 To promote application of green lighting products and devices

To encourage the use of green lighting products and modes via incentive systems and economic tools, and to promote the application of green lighting products and devices.

6.3 To prevent and control light pollution through architectural design

To prevent and control the light pollution from glass curtain walls; and specifically, to control and manage the quantity of such walls in view of the environment, climate, function and planning requirements, and also to strengthen the environmental design, and utilize green building materials.

7.PROTECTION OF ENVIRONMENTAL RADIATION

The main purpose of "Optimizing the Environment Suitable for Living and Tourism" is to provide a beautiful and comfortable environment for citizens and tourists in Macao. It is a crucial factor for driving Macao to be the "Global center of tourism and recreation" and toward sustainable development, in order to turn Macao into a low carbon, environmentally friendly city suitable for living and tourism. For this purpose, efforts are to be carried on in the following seven areas of concern, including improvement of air quality, enhancement of water environment quality, treatment and disposal of solid waste, control of noise pollution, conservation of ecological environment, prevention and control of light pollution, and protection of environmental radiation. Effective actions would be taken in respect of the prevention and control of environmental pollution, conservation of the ecological environment, and strengthening of the environmental management, etc., so as to improve the overall environmental quality of the region, foster an atmosphere for green living, and achieve the goal of optimizing the environment suitable for living and tourism.

MAJOR ACTION PLANS FOR OPTIMIZING THE ENVIRONMENT SUITABLE FOR LIVING AND TOURISM

MAJOR ACTION PLAN 1 EFFECTIVE PREVENTION AND CONTROL OF ENVIRONMENTAL POLLUTION

(1) Strengthen the control and management of air pollution

Short-term : to introduce and promote the use of environmentally friendly vehicles; provide tax subsidies for new vehicles in compliance with environmentally friendly emission standards; promote the application of more environmentally friendly buses for public transportation; promote the application of exhaust particulate filter devices for heavy duty vehicles and carry out studies on policies aimed to eliminate vehicles with heavy pollution; to study the formulation of gas exhaust emission standards for newly-imported and in-use vehicles, improve laws and regulations governing gas exhaust emissions of vehicles; to study and formulate standards for lead-free gasoline and light diesel used for vehicles, and review and optimize relevant regulations constantly; to control the cooking fume from restaurants and conduct studies on cooking fume emission standards and supervision strategies; to conduct studies on the formulation of indoor air quality management guideline for general public places; and to conduct the preliminary works for the survey of stationary air pollution sources.

Medium-term : to establish the air quality environmental functional district system and formulate relevant environmental quality standards; to optimize the public transportation system and to effectively integrate the light rail transit, bus, taxi and pedestrian systems; to install rapid exhaust testing devices for vehicles at traffic hotspots to monitor continually the gas exhaust emission of vehicles in motion; to formulate indoor air quality standards and encourage schools, hotels, government agencies and enterprises to carry out indoor air quality monitoring and improvement plans; to conduct all-round investigation into and study on the air pollutant emissions from industrial and commercial venues; to establish archives of major air pollution sources, databases of pollution sources and platforms for environmental statistics; to carry out studies on air pollutant emission standards for industrial and commercial venues with relatively serious pollution and corresponding pollution control strategies; to conduct studies on carbon emission reduction and low carbon development for Macao to help realize the low carbon development vision; to constantly promote and improve the exhaust emission control measures for heavy oil power generation units to reduce the air pollution caused by power generation; and to gradually optimize the online monitoring data gridding and automation for various air pollution sources on the basis of the existing online monitoring system.

Long-term : to control the number of motor vehicles properly and continue to eliminate the high-pollutant emitting vehicles; to optimize the transportation network and structure to reduce the air pollutant emissions from the transportation sector; to introduce and promote environmentally friendly vehicles more vigorously; to formulate air pollutant emission standards for industrial and commercial venues with relatively serious air pollution and the corresponding control measures; and to gradually push forward and improve the atmospheric environmental functional district system.

(2) To protect water resources and improve water environment

Short-term : to establish water supply (saline tide and emergency) forecast alerting, and emergency response mechanisms; to carry out study on pollution control of the Canal Dos Patos, undertake survey on the status quo of its water environment, and formulate a comprehensive remediation plan for the canal; to expand the capacity and upgrade the technologies of the Macao Peninsula WWTP, and complete the effluent quality improvement and relevant projects for the Taipa WWTP; and to conduct holistic water quality evaluation and improvement strategies for coastal waters, make investigation and overall evaluation on the coastal aquatic environment; and to plan for the coastal water environment monitoring network.

Medium-term : to improve the potable water sources management system, ensure the security of potable water supply in Macao, and undertake pollution prevention and control projects for local water sources protection zones (ponds and reservoirs); to formulate and implement gradually the pollution remediation plan for the Canal Dos Patos and carry out the pollution remediation project orderly; to carry out study on coastal water pollution simulation and push forward projects for the prevention and control of coastal waters pollution and the protection of coastal ecosystems; to conduct study on the sewage interception projects; to control the surface runoff pollution in Macao, and adopt optimized management measures which are suitable for Macao, according to the district-based control of surface runoff pollution; to undertake the sewage piping reconstruction project and the rainwater/sewage separation mechanism for the old districts of the city; to amend the "*Regulation of Water and Wastewater Drainage of Macao (RADARM)*" and improve the water environment standards of Macao SAR gradually; to establish technical norms for surface water and wastewater monitoring and formulate evaluation and screening methods for priority pollutants; to conduct survey on water pollution sources and establish water pollution sources databases; to carry out study on water pollutant discharge reporting system as well as the online monitoring of pollution sources and the risk response plans, strengthen the supervision over the industrial and commercial point source pollution.

Long-term : to strengthen continually the protection of potable water sources, including undertaking prevention and control projects for pollutions in the protected zones, ecological recovery and establishment projects, and environmental emergency, alerting and management capacity building projects; and to reinforce the pollution emergency response plans.

(3) To establish the management system and safe treatment and disposal of solid waste

Short-term : to optimize the refuse incineration plant constantly, undertake technological upgrading for the old plant and raise the emission standards; to formulate long-term monitoring mechanisms and relevant measures for the fly ash landfill to improve the environmental quality within and surrounding the landfill; to conduct studies and demonstration projects on devices for recycling of typical electronic waste and explore the efficiency of those devices as the pre-treatment for electronic waste recycling; to carry out preliminary studies on the solid waste billing system, promoting the reduction and recycling of solid wastes; and to conduct study and investigation on restricting the production and use of plastic bags in Macao.

Medium-term : to plan and construct new fly ash landfill in compliance with due criteria on the basis of technical evaluation and reasonable siting; to establish a safe treatment system for the hazardous waste; to strengthen the environmentally sound treatment process and disposal of toxic and harmful domestic wastes and construct the environmentally sound treatment facilities for scrapped light tubes and storage batteries, etc; to strengthen the management of electronic and electrical equipment waste and design plans for the electronic and electrical equipment waste recycling and treatment which are suitable for Macao; to explore the establishment of a management mechanism for the reutilization of scrapped tires; to optimize and update continually various types of solid waste treatment technologies and introduce more effective and advanced waste treatment technologies and facilities, which can help promoting the development of environmental protection industries.

Long-term : to conduct study on gradually introducing the “Polluter pays principle” and “Producer responsibility scheme” policies through management standards, billing systems and guidelines for solid waste recycling and treatment; to formulate technical norms for the hazardous waste treatment and establish a safe collection, treatment and disposal system for hazardous wastes; to establish a management system for the closed hazardous waste treatment facilities (e.g. the fly ash landfill); to establish an electronic and electrical equipment waste recycling network, and based on the existing waste recycling system, establish gradually a recycling and treatment system for the electronic and electrical equipment waste and to establish a whole process solid waste information management system.

(4) To control the noise pollution

Short-term : to formulate the Regulation on the “*Prevention and Control of Ambient Noise*” for strengthening the regulation of noise from piling works and community activities; to enhance the environmental awareness of the society by strengthening publicity and popularization of laws on noise prevention in order to reduce the noise disturbances at source; to make investigation on the main low-frequency noise sources or frequency variant facilities, such as air conditioning and ventilation devices, and conduct studies on the control strategies, monitoring methods and standards.

Medium-term : to intensify noise prevention publicity targeting the decorative works and construction industries, establish partnerships with the industries for joint noise control; integrating with the eco-building guideline, to promote and implement on a trial basis the noise prevention measures for constructions, including putting up temporary noise barriers at the construction site and setting independent temporary noise barriers at the site of noisy construction equipments; to establish and improve the noise control guidelines for the industrial and commercial venues to strengthen the supervision over industrial and commercial noise; to carry out studies on strengthening supervision over the industrial and commercial noise sources, requiring them to utilize low-noise fans and cooling units, together with low-noise or speed-control cooling towers, etc.

Long-term : to properly set noise barriers on flyovers and the above-ground section of the future light rail transit system; to carry out studies on the utilization of noise reducing surfaces for appropriate road sections, and particularly, for the roads in the new districts of the city and those renovated in the old districts; to continue noise supervision after the enactment of the Regulation on the "*Prevention and Control of Ambient Noise*" ; to take districts into consideration in the planning and development of the new districts, preventing projects with a relatively high level of noise from being constructed in the noise sensitive areas, and plan the road system in the new districts reasonably; and conduct studies on the criteria for establishing traffic-calmed areas, and evaluate and select communities in the old and new districts and the world heritage core site which are suitable for establishing traffic-calmed areas.

(5) To prevent and control light pollution

Short-term : to formulate and implement on a trial basis the light pollution control guidelines for advertising signs, decorative lighting of buildings and outdoor electronic displays; and to promote energy-saving green lighting equipment and design, and encourage the application of energy-saving and environmentally friendly lighting equipment, in order to reduce the light pollution while saving energy.

Medium-term : to conduct studies in formulating technical standards for the prevention of light pollution; and to gradually establish the light pollution database and formulate relevant control policies.

Long-term : to formulate technical criteria and standards for light pollution prevention and control in the lighting and construction industries; and to carry out studies in the establishment of light pollution prevention and control supervision system and management procedures.

(6) To protect from the environmental radiatio

Short-term : to provide training on nuclear radiation for technicians; and to start the preliminary preparations for the nuclear radiation survey for conducting baseline survey on radiation sources.

Medium-term : to establish the nuclear emergency response plans in collaboration with the public emergency alerting and alarming system; to enhance the understanding of people from different sectors on electromagnetic radiation and radioactive pollution through publicity; and to strengthen the radiation supervision capacity, conduct supervision and management of radiation, increase investment into the environmental radiation management, and improve the relevant management mechanism.

Long-term : to incorporate the users of radiation sources into the scope of radiation supervision and establish a responsibility system and a responsibility-transfer system for the radiation sources management; and to construct safe storage facilities for low radioactivity waste and realize the goal of putting under surveillance and storing the low radioactivity waste safely in the entire territory of Macao.

MAJOR ACTION PLAN 2 CONSERVATION OF ECOLOGICAL ENVIRONMENT

(1) To optimize ecological security

Short-term : to strengthen road greening, develop vertical greening and roof greening to raise the ratio of green area in Macao, in particular on the Macao Peninsula.

Medium-term : to take full advantage of the important construction projects such as construction of the Cotai new districts, renovation of the old districts on Macao Peninsula, construction of the light rail transit system, and development of the new town reclamation zone to optimize the spatial layout of green areas and create green area networks.

Long-term : to organically connect spots of isolated green areas, such as parks, green areas on the street, courtyard gardens and nurseries, etc. through ramp greening, pavement trees, roadside greenbelts and isolation strip greening, etc.; to promote development of the green areas system and green corridors on Macao Peninsula in collaboration with the urban planning, in order to create the "green lung" of Macao; to construct the peninsular and island green belts comprising the coastal, inland lake and water pond greening in the new town reclamation zone; to cooperate with neighboring regions in ecological conservation in order to preserve the regional ecological and environmental resources jointly; as well as to conduct feasibility studies of introducing the ecological compensation system.

(2) To protect biodiversity

Short-term : to construct bird-watching houses in the Ecological Zones I and II, facilitating the visit and learning of citizens and students; to construct footpaths, with some rare protected plants on both sides of the paths, for studying the nature, exhibiting their roles in ecological conservation and education.

Medium-term : to undertake ecosystem recovery projects; to construct near-shore ecological screens by planting *Mangrove*, in order to maintain ecological balance in the coastal areas and recover the marine ecological environment; to investigate and straighten out rare animal and plant resources in Macao and neighboring regions; to strengthen the management and protection measures for ecological zones; to keep the water exchange between the Ecological Zone I and the outside areas, maintaining the passages for planktons to enter the external waters; and to improve distribution of *Mangrove* in the Ecological Zone II favorable for the inhabitation and propagation of fish, benthos and for the foraging of birds.

Long-term : to properly arrange building layout on the migration route of birds to avoid obstructing the birds from migrating to the wetland; for the lighting planning, to place restrictions on excessively bright lighting in order to avoid dizziness of birds and impacts on their inhabitation; to moderately monitor the impact of land reclamation on the aquatic animals; and to develop the existing green areas into green ecological corridors with rich habitats to ensure the passage of birds within the city.

CHAPTER IV PROMOTING A CONSERVATION AND RECYCLING-ORIENTED SOCIETY

Saving energy, reducing emissions and low carbon development is one of the priority policies of the Macao SAR Government. It is also an inevitable choice for the sustainable development of Macao. Under the theme of "Promoting a Conservation and Recycling-oriented Society", actions will be taken in the following five areas of concern: promotion of energy conservation and renewable energy; recycling of solid waste; recycling of water resources; emission reduction of enterprises; and construction of low carbon production and consumption system, with the aim of building Macao into an environmentally friendly, conservation-oriented and low carbon city through actions in respect of saving energy and resources, realization of material recycling and establishment of a low carbon socioeconomic system. For this purpose, based on the major action plans set forth in the consultation document and taking the public opinions solicited into consideration, the present Environmental Planning puts forward the short, medium and long-term action plans for promoting a conservation and recycling-oriented society.

1.PROMOTION OF ENERGY CONSERVATION

1.1 To increase the proportion of clean energy

To optimize the energy structure, raise the proportion of renewable energy used, promote application of the solar energy, and establish demonstration projects for solar energy.

1.2 To improve the environmental management system of enterprises

To popularize the environmental management system in enterprises, implement clean production processes, and establish more comprehensive environmental management systems, and tighten supervision over the pollutant discharge of enterprises.

1.3 To promote energy-saving in buildings

To promote energy-saving in buildings, enhance the energy utilization efficiency and increase the application of renewable energy by implementing the guidelines for environmentally friendly constructions.

2.RECYCLING OF RECOVERABLE WASTE

2.1 To enhance waste reduction at source

To promote separation and recycling of domestic, industrial and commercial waste and issue corresponding waste separation guidelines and provisions; and to establish an urban waste treatment system based on the principles of "Reduction at the sources, separated collection, classified transportation, recycling and comprehensive treatment".

2.2 To promote recycling and diversified utilization of waste

To introduce technologies and strategies for reutilizing different forms of waste in a diversified way, for example, establishing the food waste recycling management system and promoting recycling of the construction waste and the bottom ash generated from domestic waste incineration, and to promote cross-border cooperation among Macao, Guangdong and Hong Kong in the recycling of waste resources.

3.IMPLEMENTATION OF WATER RESOURCES RECYCLING

3.1 To popularize water conservation devices and facilities

To adopt and popularize water conservation devices, to reduce the leakage rate of the water piping, and to undertake actions for water conservation in industrial, domestic,commercial and public facilities.

3.2 To utilize the non-regular water resources

To construct water reclamation plants, formulate guidelines on the utilization of recycled water, gradually expand the scale of water reclamation and the rainwater collection system in the mountain areas and the new districts of the city.

4.EMISSION REDUCTION OF ENTERPRISES

4.1 To popularize environmental management and clean production

To enhance the technology level of industrial and commercial sectors in Macao, popularize environmental management systems, implement clean production processes, reduce the energy consumption per unit output value and pollutant emission of industrial enterprises, and strictly implement the pollutant emission guidelines and regulations for enterprises.

4.2 To improve and promote subsidizing systems for the environmental protection works of commercial enterprises

To improve the "Environmental Protection and Energy Conservation Fund" mechanism in order to en-hance its role in driving commercial enterprises to save energy and water and reduce air pollutant emis-sion, etc.

5.CONSTRUCTION OF THE LOW CARBON PRODUCTION AND CONSUMPTION SYSTEM

5.1 To advocate green living

To advocate green living styles and enhance the awareness on environmental protection of the citizens;to strengthen water conservation education by formulating and implementing environmental protection education and publicity plans targeting primary and secondary schools and different social sectors;and to drive environmental protection works such as energy conservation and emissions reduction,emphasizing waste separation and treatment, and advocate green products, etc., in order to enhance citizens' sense of responsibility in environmental protection.

5.2 To develop environmental protection industries

To develop the environmental protection industries by keeping track of the dynamics of international environmental protection industries, and to introduce the newest environmental protection technologies and concepts through holding various international exhibitions and conferences about environmental protection, in order to enhance the environmental management level of local industries.

MAJOR ACTION PLANS FOR PROMOTING A CONSERVATION AND RECYCLING-ORIENTED SOCIETY

Major Action Plan 1

Conservation of Resources and Energy

(1) To optimize the energy structure and strengthen the energy management

•Short-term : to optimize continually the pollution control technologies in the power generation process,together with the efficiency of natural gas power generation. In addition, increase moderately the proportion of outsourced electricity.

•Medium-term : to increase the rate of clean energy utilization by optimizing the energy structure.

•Long-term : to promote and encourage the development and application of renewable energies, making them the effective supplementary energy; to undertake demonstration projects for solar energy in public buildings; and to promote the energy audit and assessment system, as well as establish corresponding institutional systems.

(2) To promote energy-saving in constructions

•Short-term : to conduct studies on the guidelines for environmentally friendly constructions of Macao and gradually implement those guidelines in public projects on a trial basis.

•Medium-term : to apply gradually the environmentally friendly construction technologies in all the public constructions, and promote the application of those technologies to private constructions with potentially more serious environmental impacts; and to disseminate knowledge of energy conservation and resource recycling for green buildings to enterprises and general public through various education and publicity activities, in order to enhance gradually the environmental protection awareness of the construction industry.

•Long-term : to apply the relevant guidelines for environmentally friendly constructions to all the private construction projects, and review and update the guidelines in due course, in order to reduce the environmental impact of the buildings themselves and the construction of them through relatively advanced environmental protection measures; and in respect of the planning of the new districts and renovation of the old districts of the city, to enhance the energy utilization efficiency and increase application of the renewable energies through implementing the guidelines for environmentally friendly constructions.

(3) To guide the entire society to save energy

•Short-term : to formulate and implement gradually the "Guideline for Environmental Management in Public Administrations" in order to push the public administrations to commit to environmental protection behaviors; and to promote eco-purchasing and formulate the "Guideline for Green Procurement in Public Administrations" and the "Suggestions on Environmentally Friendly Product Specifications", in order to help the government agencies purchase energy-conserving, water-saving and low-pollution products preferentially and enhance the market of environmentally friendly products.

•Medium-term : to constantly optimize and enrich the environmental management guidelines; and to promote the implementation of environmentally friendly behaviors in enterprises.

•Long-term : to introduce a market-oriented energy conservation mechanism and promote systematic energy management models, in order to further enhance energy conservation during the operation of the enterprises.

Major Action Plan 2

Realization of Resources Recycling

(1) To recycle the recoverable waste

•Short-term : to encourage continually citizens to reduce the quantity of waste produced by incentive means; to separate recyclable waste resources according to the types and publicize the application of recyclable products;to enhance the willingness of the public to recycle waste by incentive means through cooperation with social associations, and to push the public to choose products made of recyclable materials of their own accord; to promote recycling of the food waste and introduce small-scale food waste treatment systems for preliminary experiments on their application; and to conduct studies on the diversified utilization of construction waste and investigate the recycling of construction wastes.

•Medium-term : to enhance the recycling rate of construction waste; to explore billing plans for construction or special waste treatment; to evaluate and formulate the food waste treatment plans most suitable for the reality of Macao; to conduct studies on the feasibility of recycling the bottom ash from incineration; to promote research and development, together with the application of technologies on the transformation and recycling of recoverable materials; to establish gradually a relatively comprehensive waste separation and recycling system; and to carry out studies on the technical standards, cross-border cooperation procedures and supervision measures for recycling of recoverable wastes.

•Long-term : to encourage recycling industries and gradually improve the environmentally sound pretreatment technologies for the recovery of recoverable meterials, which are suitable for Macao; and on the basis of complying with national laws and relevant standards, to explore new cooperation models for cross-border recycling of recoverable materials, establishing a cyclic industry system in the greater Pearl River Delta region.

(2) To recycle the water resource

•Short-term : to implement tiered pricing system for potable water and formulate preferential policies to encourage enterprises to save water, and enhance the recycling rate of water; to utilize water-conserving devices in public facilities in the first place, and apply them gradually to industrial, commercial and domestic facilities; and to reduce the leakage rate in the water piping system.

•Medium-term : to formulate standard for utilization of recycled water and incorporate the standard into the "Regulation of Water and Wastewater Drainage of Macao (RADARM)"; to enhance the utilization rate of recycled water in domestic, industrial and commercial sector and reduce the consumption of potable water; and to enhance the re-utilization of recycled water in wastewater treatment plants and implement the production and utilization of recycled water.

•Long-term : to further increase the scale of the utilization of recycled water in Macao and construct water reclamation facilities in appropriate WWTPs to enhance the water reclamation production of Macao.

Major Action Plans 3

Construction of the Low Carbon Economic and Social Systems

(1) Emission reduction and low carbon production system of enterprises

•Short-term : to establish the "Environmental Protection and Energy Conservation Fund" in order to support the low carbon oriented transformation of commercial enterprises, and particularly, in the projects aimed to improve air quality, save energy and water, etc.; to continue the "Macao Green Hotel Award" activity, and constantly improve the evaluation standards for the award.

•Medium-term : to popularize the environmental management system in enterprises and promote implementation of clean production processes; and to form a comprehensive environmental management system for enterprises by gradually formulating the pollutant emission standard system and technical guidelines for pollution treatment,in order to strengthen the supervision over the pollutant emission of enterprises.

•Long-term : to strengthen cooperation among Guangdong, Hong Kong and Macao in respect of the clean production of enterprises, circular economy, environmental protection industries, research and development of new and renewable energies,clean energy infrastructure construction, as well as research, development,production and application of new energy vehicles, etc.

(2) To construct a low carbon consumption system

•Short-term : to publicize the concept of conservation, low carbon and green consumption, making the low carbon consumption modes and living style deeply rooted in the mind of the public and become a conscious action of them.

•Medium-term : to formulate the list of recommended energy-saving products and encourage the government agencies to give such products priority in their purchasing, in order to promote energy conservation actions to the public.

•Long-term : to promote the development of environmental protection industries in Macao through international conferences such as the "Macao International Environmental Co-operation Forum & Exhibition (MIECF)", with the participation of industries and associations, gradually introduce the latest international environmental protection technologies, and enhance the environmental protection management capability of local enterprises to help form a distinctive ecological industry cluster with relatively sharp competitive edge.

CHAPTER V INTEGRATING INTO THE GREEN AND QUALITY REGION

In order to achieve the objective of building a quality living area, according to requirements in the "Outline of the Plan for the Reform and Development of the Pearl River Delta (2008-2020)" and under the "Guangdong-Macao Cooperation Framework Agreement", the cooperation with the greater Pearl River Delta region and Hong Kong should be strengthened in the next decade. Availing the opportunity of cooperating with the greater Pearl River Delta region, focus should be laid on joint prevention and control of regional pollutions and the formulation of corresponding regional development coordination mechanisms, in order to ensure the coordination and complementarity of regional development.

Actions would be taken in the areas such as optimizing the environmental functional district management, strengthening the coordination mechanism for reigional environmental security, realization of joint prevention and control of regional pollution, exploring joint treatment and disposal channels of solid and hazardous waste, protecting jointly the ecosystem in the Pearl River Delta region, and establishing collaboratively a low carbon region, etc.

Through actions like enhancing the regional coordination on environmental protection and building low carbon cities and region collaboratively, promote the integration of Macao into the green and quality-living region and realize the goal of building a quality-living community. For these purposes, based on the major action plans set forth in the consultation document, the present Environmental Planning will be amended according to the public opinions solicited, and put forward the short, medium and long-term action plans in respect to integrating Macao into the green and quality region.

1.OPTIMIZATION OF THE ENVIRONMENTAL FUNCTIONAL DISTRICTS

1.1 To implement the environmental functional district management

To incorporate the local environmental functional districts into the routine environmental management system; and to supervise and guide the socioeconomic activities and construction projects, in view of improving the environmental quality and the district-based environmental management, in order to enhance the overall environmental quality in the region.

1.2 To establish quality standards of single environmental element for the functional districts

To implement the district-based management and control by gradually adopting corresponding quality standards for the functional districts by single environmental element (mainly the atmospheric environment, aquatic environment and acoustic environment).

2.ENVIRONMENTAL PROTECTION COOPERATION IN THE PEARL RIVER DELTA REGION

2.1 To jointly prevent and control regional pollution

Through joint prevention and control of air pollution, to protect the water resource collaboratively and establish a cooperation mechanism for the recycling of recoverable waste and the treatment of hazardous waste, etc., to enhance the cooperation in environmental protection issues and circular economy in the greater Pearl River Delta region.

2.2 To proactively participate in the establishment of eco-systems in the greater Pearl River Delta region

To proactively participate in the establishment of eco-systems in the greater Pearl River Delta region, in order to construct ecosystems in good status and optimize the ecological pattern.

3.JOINT BUILDING OF A LOW CARBON CITY AND REGION

3.1 To strengthen the publicity and education on environmental protection and low carbon development

To strengthen the publicity and education on environmental protection and low carbon development, and create an atmosphere of green communities by establishing green schools as a starting point.

3.2 To promote the low carbon concept in urban planning

To follow the low carbon concept in urban planning and layout, and to build low carbon demonstration areas in collaboration with urban planning, and to build a low carbon region integrating with the construction of the quality-living community in the Pearl River Delta region.

MAJOR ACTION PLANS FOR INTEGRATING INTO THE GREEN AND QUALITY REGION

Major Action Plan 1

Strengthening Regional Cooperation in Environmental Protection

To optimize and implement the environmental functional management

•Short-term : to conduct studies on the formulation of the emergency response plans for environmental incidents in Macao.

•Medium-term : to formulate environmental functional districts according to single environmental element,in order to support the district-based and category-based management, and formulate environmental quality standards and management guidelines for different functional districts, gradually carry out the district-based environmental management; to optimize the layout of pollutant discharge outlets in Macao for enhancing the environmental capacity, in collaboration with the near-shore environmental functional districts and requirements for seawater of Zhuhai; and to strengthen the environmental monitoring and management for important coastal waters.

•Long-term : to construct regional ecological corridors and integrate into the "Green network" in the Pearl River Delta region.

(2) To promote environmental protection cooperation in the Pearl River Delta region

•Short-term : to conduct joint studies on hydrology and water quality, analysing and investigating basic data for the hydrology, topography, geology and water quality of local waters and coastal waters of Macao, in order to provide support for the protection of water resources and remediation of water pollution.

•Medium-term : to join the Guangdong-Hong Kong-Pearl River Delta region air quality monitoring network,achieving the connection and sharing of data preliminarily; to establish a cross-border framework and mechanism for the treatment of recoverable hazardous and electronic waste; to protect the regional ecological tourism resources by constructing cross-border nature reserves and a comprehensive regional eco-system.

•Long-term : to provide supports for the material recycling and resourcing in Guangdong-Hong Kong-Macao by promoting the development and construction of regional circular economy industrial parks, enhancing the development and studies on the reutilization of renewable resources.

Major Action Plan 2

Joint Building of a Low Carbon City and Region

•Short-term : to keep track on the environmental awareness and behavior of the Macao citizens by conducting the studies on public environmental awareness survey continuously; to conduct diversified publicity and interaction activities for popularizing the low carbon concept, fostering a highly favorable environment for building low carbon communities and integrating the communities' resources in various aspects; to conduct diversified publicity and education activities on low carbon consumption in communities and schools, etc.; to encourage more schools to participate in the "Green School Partnership Program", enhancing the education on low carbon knowledge in schools; to encourage the teachers and students to take an active part in the environmental supervision and low carbon publicity and education activities in the society, and also adopt the more environmentally friendly teaching modes and equipment; and to constantly conduct the "Environmental Education Design Project" to further promote the environmental education.

•Medium-term : to promote environmentally friendly education modes and equipment in schools; and to create a good walking environment and construct energy-saving building blocks in respect of the urban spatial arrangement.

•Long-term : to promote the all-round development of low carbon cities and communities by creating demonstrative areas for low carbon city.

CHAPTER VI IMPLEMENTATION, SUPERVISION AND GUARANTEE

The purpose of establishing the implementation and supervision system is to ensure the effectiveness and quality of the execution of the Environmental Planning. Through formulating the implementation mechanism of the planning, policies and systems for environmental protection, and the guarantee and supervision mechanisms of the execution of the Environmental Planning, the Government and citizens can share the content of the planning and review its implementation in a more objective view. Meanwhile, extensive public participation, institutionalized arrangement for supervision and highly transparent information releasing mechanism will also help perfecting the planning, realizing the vision of low carbon city and green living environment and providing solid supports for the execution of the planning.

1.IMPLEMENTATION MECHANISM

(1) Establishment of the planning implementation system

In order to ensure the implementation of the Environmental Planning, economic and technical policies and measures in favor of environmental protection would be adopted, harmonizing the Environmental Planning and the economic and social development, together with other plannings. Also, an implementation system which is led by the Government and supported by the society would be established.

(2) Coordination of government agencies

The implementation of the action plans of the Environmental Planning involves works in various aspects. While the DSPA plays a leading role, other government agencies also have a part to play in mutual cooperation, in order to promote and implement the measures jointly. During the implementation of the planning, a cross-departmental group communication mechanism will be established, coordinating various government agencies to carry out the various action plans under this planning in an orderly manner.

(3) Public participation and responsibility

Everyone shares the responsibility in environmental protection. In order to achieve the planning vision of "Building a Low Carcon Macao, Creating Green Living Together", all communities in the society, including the government, enterprises and general public, shall interact and communicate with each other well.

•The primary responsibility of the Macao SAR Government is to lead and promote the implementation of the planning, to formulate regulations and operation modes for achieving the objectives, and to set necessary policy measures and facilities. Meanwhile, the Government also plays a supervisory and managerial role in this process, and through exercising the legal competences and duties in environmental protection, each government agency shall coorperate with each other and participate jointly in supervising the implementation of the Environmental Planning.

•Enterprises are important stockholders in the environmental protection, especially at the moment when Macao is right in the rapid social and economic development. Therefore, multiple measures would be taken to promote the voluntary environmental management in enterprises, and pushing enterprises to resolve their own pollution problems properly and to fulfill their social responsibility, and promoting the low carbon economic development.

•The public is the principal participant in the environmental management. The level of environmental pollution and resource consumption is directly affected by the public behaviors. Therefore, each citizen would have the obligation to practice an environmentally friendly consumption style, so as to gradually establish a paradigm of ecological ethics and creation of low carbon green lives.

(4) To improve the establishment of legislation and standards

Given the fact that there is imperfection and a lack of provision in the existing legal system with the weak norms of legal liability, in order to optimize the environmental management of Macao, legislative work should be planned on the basis of the existing environmental laws, to gradually improve the development of environmental legal system and structure.

•To formulate specific laws and regulations for environmental protection, such as the "Prevention and Control of Ambient Noise", "Standards for Gas Exhaust Emission from Newly Imported Vehicles", "Standards for Lead-free Gasoline and Light Diesel Used for Vehicles", "Environmental Protection and Energy Conservation Fund", and the "Environmentally Friendly, Energy-efficient Product and Equipment Funding Plan", etc., and to strengthen the laws and regulations in respect of air, water and acoustic environment protection;

•To formulate environmental protection standards, such as the emission standards for major air pollution sources, the environmental quality standards and the acoustics norm, etc.;

•To review the table of gaseous pollutant emission parameters to be met by the newly imported heavy and light duty motorcycles on a regular basis, and put forward amendment proposals in response to the actual needs and technological development trend;

•To conduct studies on and promote legislation about environmental management, such as the legislation of environmental licensing and environmental impact assessment;

•To conduct studies on legislation related to the implementation of international environmental agreements and conventions in Macao.

TABLE OF THE STANDARD AND LEGISLATION RESEARCH PROJECTS PROPOSED UNDER THE *ENVIRONMENTAL PLANNING* (2010-2020)

Environmental field	Standard and legislation research projects proposed under this planning
Basic	Review of the Law of Environmental framework
Acoustic Environment	Formulation of the Regulation on the "Prevention and Control of Ambient Noise",[Amendment to Noise Law (Decree-law No.54/94/M)] and Amendment to Acoustics Norm (Order No.241/94/M)
	Standards of Ambient Noise
Atmospheric Environment	Legislation related to the Protection of Atmospheric Environment
	Standards for Gas Exhaust Emission from Newly Imported Vehicles
	Emission Standards for Major Air Pollution Source
	Standards for Lead-free Gasoline and Light Diesel Used for Vehicles
	Exhaust Emission Standards for In-use Vehicles
	Standards of Environmental Air Quality
Aquatic Environment	Regulation of Water and Wastewater Drainage of Macao (Amendment)
	Standards of Surface Water Environment
Solid Waste	Legislation related to the Prevention and Control of Solid Waste Pollution
	Standards for Management,Disposal and Treatment of Solid Wastes
Light Environment	Technical Criteria and Standards for Light Pollution
Natural Ecosystem	Regulation for Managing the Nature Reserve
Environmental Management	Environmental Protection and Energy Conservation Fund
	Environmental Impact Assessment System
	Guidelines for Managing the Environmental Planning
International Conventions	Import and Export Control on Persistent Organic Pollutants(POPs)
	Import Control Of Hazardous Wastes

To enhance the environmental management ability of the government

In order to carry out the environmental policies and measures proposed in the present *Environmental Planning*, we will progressively build up any required environmental management system, including environmental publicity and education, release of environmental information, environmental monitoring, environmental impact assessment system and environmental licensing system, etc., in order to have laws and norms to be followed in the implementation of environmental management, gradually improving the design and implementation of the environmental management system and environmental policies of the government. In addition, through strengthening the team of qualified personnel and the construction of infrastructures, the capability in decision making of the Government and the execution of environmental legislations would be strengthened, gradually enhancing the environmental emergency response capability of the Macao SAR Government.

2.Supervision Mechanism

(1) Supervision system

In an effort to supervise and implement the *Environmental Planning*, a cross-departmental environmental planning group should be established to monitor the execution of the action plans and major projects under the present planning according to the principle of Plan-Do-Check-Action cycle (PDCA cycle), in order to resolve the errors and problems in the planning. The supervision system mainly includes the following aspects:

To formulate annual work plans: to formulate annual work plans according to the short, medium and long-term planning tasks.

To evaluate and assess the implementation of the planning in various phases: to conduct evaluation and assessment on the effectiveness of the planning, assessing the status of implementation of the objectives and action plans in the present *Environmental Planning* in the end of 2012 and 2015, in order to summarize the execution status of the plananing and analyze the experience and problems in the implementation of the planning, serving as references for the implementation of the planning in later phases and for amending the planning. Also, evaluation reports will be publicized to the public in a timely manner, making known to the public the status of implementation of the planning. In the year of 2020, which is the end of the present planning, a comprehensive review about the implementation of the planning would be carried out to evaluate the level of compliance of the planning objectives and indicators, as well as the implementation status and effectiveness of the action plans and major projects of the planning. At the meantime, on the basis of summarizing the experience of the first *Environmental Planning*, the DSPA will prepare the environmental protection planning of the next phase, as the continual, enduring, foreseeing and targeted strategies for the environmental protection work of Macao.

(2) Publicizing the environmental information of the government

In order to enhance the depth and width of the environmental information released, ensuring the public to have the right to know, participate and supervise, information about the status of the environment will timely be publicized through the media easily reached by the general public such as the government website, reports, newspapers, magazines, radio and television. On the other hand, through promoting the publication of the environmental information of enterprises by establishing the publication system of enterprise environmental information, encouraging the enterprises to publicize the environmental information of their own in a voluntary and initiative manner, enhancing the effectiveness of public supervision on the environmental protection behavior of the enterprises.

(3) Evaluation of the implementation of the *Environmental Planning*

The implementation of the *Environmental Planning* is a long-term and dynamic process, and it is required that the intent of the planning be imparted to different government agencies and relevant organizations. Meanwhile, the implementation of the planning may be affected by various factors. It is, therefore, necessary to establish a mechanism to evaluate the effectiveness of the inplementation of the planning, in order to ensure the achievement of the anticipated planning goals. In reference to the national and international evaluation indicator systems for similar planning, and in consideration of the operability, possibility for evaluation and representativeness of the indicators, an evaluation indicator system for the implementation of the action plans and major projects under this planning would be established. Through assessing the overall objectives, goals of different phases and the indicator system formulated in this planning, the extent of accomplishment of the objectives and the main problems can be analyzed. Also, the difficulties in achieving the goals of later phase planning can be predicted. The purpose of the assessment is to gradually make the implementation of the *Environmental Planning* to be the starting point for leading the quantitative environmental management, systematic management and regular management. By evaluating the implementation of the planning, the execution of the planning can be promoted and the planning can be improved. The evaluation will primarily be based on quantitative methods, supported by qualitative methods, and will also cover the input-output transformation status.

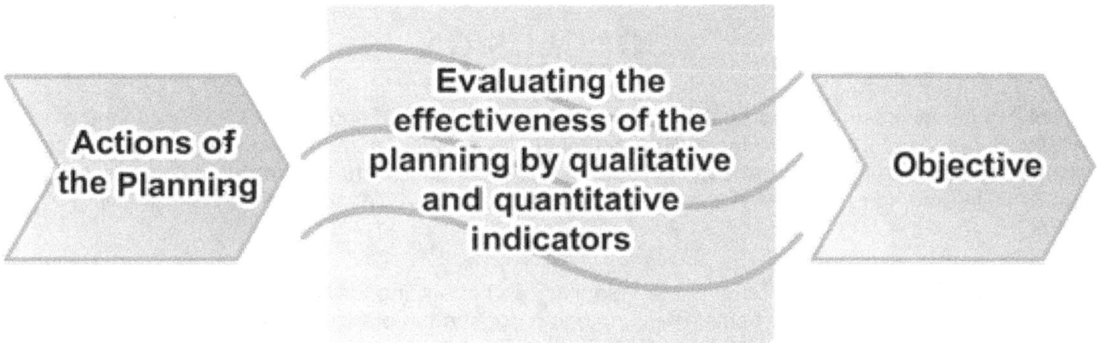

3.Guarantee Mechanism

The "Environmental Protection Planning of Macao (2010-2020)" is the first forward-looking and programmatic planning document of Macao in the field of environmental protection. In order to ensure that the entire action plans contemplated in the planning is executed in an orderly manner, there is the need to establish a comprehensive system to guarantee the input of resources and the coordination among various government agencies concerned.

(1) To focus on resource input

In an effort to achieve the goals set in the present planning, the Macao SAR Government will invest corresponding human and material resources required to carry out the action plans under the planning, and particularly, reserve sufficient fiscal budget as support. Meanwhile, in order to ensure effective implementation of and continual amendment to the planning, corresponding scientific and technical support would be issued in due course, for example, training local scientific and technological personnel in respect of environmental protection and introducing advanced technologies and equipment, for the purpose of enabling science and technology to play a role in environmental protection in the future.

(2) To establish cross-departmental coordination and cooperation mechanisms

Environmental protection involves multifaceted efforts. The DSPA will inevitably take up the main and major duties of the environmental protection work; even so, the implementation of the environmental planning still requires the cooperation and coordination of other government agencies. In fact, the present planning has got strong support from other government agencies from the beginning. In the future, upholding the concept of coordination, a cross-departmental communication mechanism would be established to put in place and evaluate the action plans under the planning, achieving the vision of "Building a Low Carbon Macao, Creating Green Living Together" through joint efforts.

(3) To have the general public participate

To have the action plans in the planning to be implemented effectively, the Macao Government will play a leading role as a leader and promoter, but the realization of various planning goals also relies on the participation and cooperation of all the social communities. The government, enterprises and general public shall do their own part respectively, cooperating and interacting with each other to ensure implementation of all the work under the planning.

(4) To implement the planning in a roll-on way

Environmental protection is complicated, ever-changing and wide-reaching; therefore, the formulation and implementation of the Environmental Planning is a long and dynamic process. There is the need to review, optimize and improve the planning based on the development reality and in a roll-on approach featuring a chain of “Planning – Implementation – Evaluation – Amendment – Updating” actions, in order to ensure advancement of the action plans and achievement of the goals set forth in the planning.

CONCLUSION

For resolving the increasing stress on the environment and resources, and also responding to the ever-increasing demands of the citizens for environmental quality protection and improvement in ecological environment, the Environmental Protection Bureau (DSPA) conducted the environmental master planning of Macao SAR, in order to realize the vision of "Building a Low Carbon Macao, Creating Green Living Together".

On the basis of coordinating with other related planning and analyzing the current challenges in the environment, the present Environmental Planning has proposed the planning vision and objectives, together with a preliminary scheme for environmental functional districts and environmental functional district management.

Under the three principal themes of "Optimizing the Environment Suitable for Living and Tourism", "Promoting a Conservation and Recycling-oriented Society" and "Integrating into the Green and Quality Region", this planning has also established 11 green indicators for the Environmental Planning, proposed 15 areas of concern and their strategic direction, formulated various major actions, and established the implementation and supervision mechanisms, in order to enhace the environmental management capability of the Macao SAR Government and guarantee the execution of the planning. In the meantime, this planning, based on the requirements in the vision of "Building a Low Carbon Macao, Creating Green Living Together" has also proposed a demand for coordinating the regional environment, taking into consideration of the integrated development in the environment, building jointly a quality-living area.

The "Environmental Protection Planning of Macao (2010-2020)", as the first environmental planning of Macao, has systematically depicted the roadmap of future environmental management works in Macao. The Environmental Planning, on the one hand, has proposed objectives in improving environmental quality and guidance in actions to be taken for Macao up to year 2020.On the other hand, it has also acted as the foundation of the environmental management works in Macao, in the view of harmonizing the environment, society and economy, leading for the sustainable social and economic development.

This planning aims to establish the planning objectives and indicators in a forward-looking way, and execute and implement the actions for improving the environment according to their priority. We have to point out that formulation and implementation of this planning is a dynamic process, which relies on the participation of general public, and should be reviewed, amended and improved in accordance with the actual status of the social and economic development, supported by the input of corresponding resources, in order to facilitate and ensure the implementation of this planning.

In fact, the Environmental Planning is a starting point for the environmental protection works. It is hoped that in the coming decade, by formulating the implementation mechanism for the execution of the present planning document in view of different environmental elements and by the coordination of different government agencies and sectors of the society, action plans in the atmospheric, acoustic, ecological and aquatic environments would be carried out. By implementing effective control measures for pollution, we hope to reduce the pollutants produced at source and maintain achievements in nature conservation and greening in the city. More importantly, by educating the citizens for good awareness in environmental protection, consumption motives and commuting habit, it is hoped that while the Macao citizens are enjoying the abundant material lives, they can also have breaths of fresh air, tastes of clean drinking water and experiences of a comfortable natural environment.

However, since the environment is a complex, variable and extensive system, protecting the environment is a hard and enduring task. It is impossible that all the existing pollution problems in the environmental can completely be resolved in the next decade. A wonderful and quality environment must be achieved by continuous planning, governmental policies, efforts of the enterprises and public participation.

It is the responsibility of everyone to protect our environment. Let us fulfill our responsibilities in environmental protection , creating a quality ecological environment and sharing wonderful green living together.

TRAVELING TO MACAO

US STATE DEPARTMENT SUGGESTIONS

COUNTRY DESCRIPTION: Macau, formerly a Chinese territory under Portuguese administration, became a Special Administrative Region (SAR) of the People's Republic of China on December 20, 1999, with a high degree of autonomy, except in the areas of defense and foreign policy. Macau retains its own currency, laws, and border controls. Facilities for tourism are well developed. Gambling, tourism, textile and apparel manufacturing are the major factors in Macau's economy. Macau's revenue from tourism exceeds exports. Macau, population 437,000, covers a thirteen-square-mile area on the mainland of China bordering the South China Sea and the small, adjacent islands of Taipa and Coloane.

ENTRY/EXIT REQUIREMENTS: Passports are required. A visa is not required for tourist visits of up to 30 days. For further information on entry requirements contact the Embassy of the People's Republic of China, 2300 Connecticut Avenue, N.W., Washington D.C. 20008, Tel: (202) 328-2500 through 2502, or the Consulates General of the PRC in Chicago, Houston, Los Angeles, New York City, and San Francisco. For more information regarding PRC visas, travelers to Macau may contact the visa section of the Embassy of the People's Republic of China at (202) 265-9809 or (202) 338-6688. Travelers may also consult the Macau Tourist Office,(operated as Integrated Travel Resources Inc.), 5757 West Century Boulevard, Suite 660, Los Angeles, CA 90045-6407, Tel: (310) 670-2234 or Fax: (310) 338-0708. See also the Macau Government home page at http://www.macau.gov.mo.

The pataca (US$1.00 to approximately 7.78 patacas) is the official currency in Macau. Included in the cost of ferry tickets from Macau to Hong Kong is a departure tax of 19 patacas. The airport departure tax for flights from Macau to China is 80 patacas, and 130 patacas for flights to other destinations.

In an effort to prevent international child abduction, many governments have initiated procedures at entry/exit points. These often include requiring documentary evidence of relationship and permission for the child's travel from the parent(s) or legal guardian not present. Having such documentation on hand, even if not required, may facilitate entry/departure.

DUAL NATIONALITY: Under Chinese nationality law, persons who are of Chinese descent and who were born in mainland China, including Macau, are Chinese citizens. However, under an agreement between the United States and the People's Republic of China, all U.S. citizens entering Macau on their U.S. passports, including such persons who may be considered Chinese nationals by the Chinese authorities, are considered U.S. citizens by the Macau SAR authorities for purposes of ensuring consular access and protection during their legal stay in Macau.

However, dual national residents or former residents of Macau who wish to ensure U.S. consular access and protection after the initial 30-day period of visa-free admission into Macau, should declare their U.S. nationality to the Macau Immigration Department upon arrival. Dual national residents of Macau who enter Macau on travel documents other than their U.S. passports, and who desire to guarantee U.S. consular protection, should declare their U.S. nationality as soon as possible after entry. This declaration of change of nationality will ensure U.S. consular protection and will also result in loss of one's Chinese nationality (but not necessarily one's right of abode). Whereas failure to declare U.S. nationality may jeopardize U.S. consular protection, such failure will not jeopardize U.S. citizenship itself.

Dual nationals contemplating onward travel into mainland China should be attentive to use of their U.S. passports. Dual nationals who enter or depart China using a U.S. passport and a valid PRC visa retain the right of U.S. consular access and protection under the U.S.-PRC Consular Convention. The ability of the U.S. Embassy or Consulates General to provide normal consular services would be extremely limited should a dual national enter the PRC on a Chinese or other non-U.S. passport.

In addition to being subject to all Macau SAR laws affecting U.S. citizens, dual nationals may also be subject to laws of Macau that impose special obligations on Macau citizens. For additional information, see the Consular Affairs home page on the Internet at http://travel.state.gov for our dual nationality flyer.

SAFETY AND SECURITY: A fall in violent crime in the Macau SAR occurred after the return of Macau to Chinese sovereignty on December 20, 1999. According to the Macau Security Bureau, there were eleven cases of murder in the first ten months of 2000 in Macau as opposed to thirty-five cases in the same period in 1999. Kidnappings also fell from twenty to seven cases in the same period. These criminal acts were not aimed at Americans or other foreign tourists.

CRIME: Petty street crime occasionally occurs in tourist areas in Macau, including in and around casinos. The loss or theft abroad of a U.S. passport should be reported immediately to the local police and to the U.S. Consulate General in Hong Kong. The Macau Immigration Department, in normal circumstances, will facilitate the person's travel to Hong Kong to apply for a replacement passport at the American Consulate General. U.S. citizens may refer to the Department of State's pamphlet *A Safe Trip Abroad* for information on safeguarding valuables, protecting personal safety, and other suggestions for promoting a more trouble-free journey. The pamphlet is available by mail from the Superintendent of Documents, U.S. Government Printing Office, Washington, D.C. 20402, via the Internet at http://www.access.gpo.gov/su_docs, or via the Bureau of Consular Affairs home page at http://travel.state.gov.

MEDICAL FACILITIES: Several major hospitals in Macau have adequate medical facilities and are able to provide emergency medical care. Highly developed medical facilities and trained personnel are available in Hong Kong, which is about an hour by jetfoil and ten minutes by helicopter from Macau.

MEDICAL INSURANCE: The Department of State strongly urges Americans to consult with their medical insurance companies prior to traveling abroad to confirm whether their policy applies overseas and whether it will cover emergency expenses such as a medical evacuation. U.S. medical insurance plans seldom cover health costs incurred outside the United States unless supplemental coverage is purchased. Further, U.S. Medicare and Medicaid programs do not provide payment for medical services outside the United States. However, many travel agents and private companies offer insurance plans that will cover health care expenses incurred overseas including emergency services such as medical evacuations.

When making a decision regarding health insurance, Americans should consider that many foreign doctors and hospitals require payment in cash prior to providing service and that a medical evacuation to the U.S. may cost well in excess of $50,000. Uninsured travelers who require medical care overseas often face extreme difficulties, whereas travelers who have purchased overseas medical insurance have, when a medical emergency occurs, found it life-saving. When consulting with your insurer prior to your trip, ascertain whether payment will be made to the overseas healthcare provider or whether you will be reimbursed later for expenses you incur. Some insurance policies also include coverage for psychiatric treatment and for disposition of remains in the event of death.

Useful information on medical emergencies abroad, including overseas insurance programs, is provided in the Department of State's, Bureau of Consular Affairs brochure, *Medical Information for Americans Traveling Abroad*, available via the Internet at http://travel.state.gov/medical.html and through the Bureau's autofax service at (202) 647-3000.

OTHER HEALTH INFORMATION: Information on vaccinations and other health precautions may be obtained from the Centers for Disease Control and Prevention's hotline for international travelers at 1-877-FYI-TRIP (1-877-394-8747), via the CDC autofax service at 1-888-CDC-FAXX (1-888-232-3299) or via the CDC's Internet site at http://www.cdc.gov.

TRAFFIC SAFETY AND ROAD CONDITIONS: While in a foreign country, U.S. citizens may encounter road conditions that differ significantly from those in the United States. The information below concerning Macau is provided for general reference only, and may not be totally accurate in a particular location or circumstance.

Safety of Public Transportation: Good
Urban Road Conditions/Maintenance: Good
Rural Road Conditions/Maintenance: Good
Availability of Roadside Assistance: Good

Traffic moves on the left in Macau, and roads are narrow and winding. Traffic is generally congested throughout the day. Taxis are plentiful and inexpensive, as are public buses.

For additional general information about road safety, including links to foreign government sites, see the Department of State, Bureau of Consular Affairs home page at http://travel.state.gov/road_safety.html. For specific information concerning Macau driving permits, vehicle inspection, road tax and mandatory insurance, contact the Macau Tourist Office (operated as Integrated Travel Resources, Inc.), 5757 W. Century Boulevard, Suite 660, Los Angeles, California 90045-6407 (Tel: (310) 670-2234, Fax: (310) 338-0708), or the Macau Transport Department (Comissariado de Transito de Macau, Ave Sidonio Pais, Macau (Tel: (853) 374-214, Fax: (853) 522-966).

AVIATION SAFETY OVERSIGHT: As there is no direct commercial air service by Macau carriers at present between the U.S. and Macau, the U.S. Federal Aviation Administration (FAA) has not assessed Macau's Civil Aviation Authority for compliance with international aviation safety standards. For further information, travelers may contact the Department of Transportation within the U.S. at 1-800-322-7873, or visit the FAA's Internet website at http://www.faa.gov/avr/iasa.

The U.S. Department of Defense (DOD) separately assesses some foreign air carriers for suitability as official providers of air services. For information regarding the DOD policy on specific carriers, travelers may contact DOD at (618) 229-4801.

At present, Eva Air, a Taiwan-based company, is the only passenger air service flying to the United States (with stopover in Taipei) from Macau International Airport. See the Macau International Airport home page at http://www.macau-airport.gov.mo/.

CUSTOMS REGULATIONS: Macau customs authorities enforce strict regulations concerning temporary importation into or export from Macau of items such as firearms, ivory, certain categories of medications, and other goods. It is advisable to contact the Embassy of the People's Republic of China in Washington or one of China's consulates in the United States, or the Macau Marine and Customs Police, Calcada da Barra, N 47, Capitania Dos Portos, Macau (Tel: (853) 559-944, Fax: (853) 371-136), for specific information regarding customs requirements.

CRIMINAL PENALTIES: While in a foreign country, a U.S. citizen is subject to that country's laws and regulations, which sometimes differ significantly from those in the United States and may not afford the protections available to the individual under U.S. law. Penalties for breaking the law can be more severe than in the United States for similar offenses. Persons violating Macau laws, even unknowingly, may be expelled, arrested, or imprisoned. Penalties for possession, use, or trafficking in illegal drugs in Macau are strict and convicted offenders can expect jail sentences and heavy fines.

SPECIAL CIRCUMSTANCES: The official languages in the Macau SAR are Chinese and Portuguese. English, however, is spoken in tourist areas. There are no currency restrictions for tourists in Macau. Although the pataca is the official currency in Macau, Hong Kong currency is commonly used in transactions, especially in tourist areas. Pegged to the value of the Hong Kong dollar, a pataca is worth slightly less than one Hong Kong dollar. Travelers visiting Macau from Hong Kong may wish to bring sufficient Hong Kong dollars to cover their expenses. Credit cards and ATM network debit cards are widely accepted in Macau. Banks and major hotels accept travelers' checks.

CHILDREN'S ISSUES: For information on international adoption of children and international parental child abduction, please refer to our Internet site at http://travel.state.gov/children's issues.html or telephone (202) 736-7000.

REGISTRATION/U.S. CONSULATE GENERAL LOCATION: There is no U.S. diplomatic or consular presence in Macau. Consular assistance for U.S. citizens is provided by the U.S. Consulate General in Hong Kong. U.S. citizens living in or visiting Macau are encouraged to register at the Consular Section of the U.S. Consulate General in Hong Kong and obtain updated information on travel and security within Macau. The address is 26 Garden Road, Central, Hong Kong. The telephone number in Hong Kong is (852) 2523-9011 or (852) 2841-2211; fax (852) 2845-4845. The e-mail address of the American Citizen Services Section of the Consulate General is: acshnk@netvigator.com. The mailing address (from the U.S.) of the Consulate General is PSC 461, Box 5, FPO AP 96521-0006; the Internet home page is http://www.usconsulate.org.hk.

ENTRY REGULATIONS

Passport:
All travellers entering or leaving Macau must be holders of valid passports or some other valid travel documents.

Visas:
If travel arrangements are made through an agent, the visa processing is handled by Macau operator.

b) Hong Kong SAR residents with Hong Kong SAR Identity Card can stay in Macau for a period of up to 1 year.
Holders of Children passport without photo should provide another travel document with photo for reference
c) Holders of Travel Documents issued by the authorities of the People's Republic of China
Visa are available on arrival in Macau
There are three types:

INDIVIDUAL -	MOP$100 for an individual traveller for a single stay of up to 30 days in Macau, children under 12 years of age pay MOP$50
FAMILY -	MOP$200 for couples, husband travelling with wife and/or children (under 12 years of age) of same surname or on proof of their relationship within the same passport.
GROUP -	MOP$50 per person for bona fide groups of 10 or more.

TRANSPORTATION SYSTEM

BUS NETWORK

Route No.	Start	End
1	Fai Chi Kei	Barra/Terminal
10	Portas do Cerco	Barra/Terminal
10a	Jetfoil Terminal	Barra/Terminal
11	Barra/Terminal	Largo Ouvidor Arriaga
12	P. Serenidade/Terminal	Jetfoil Terminal
15	Terraço Panorâmico	Povoaçõa K?H

16	Canal Hortas	Mercado S. Lourenço
17	P. Luís Camões	Jetfoil Terminal
18	Portas do Cerco	Barra/Terminal
19	P. Serenidade/Terminal	Macau Palace Casino
1a	R. Coimbra	Barra/Terminal
2	P. Serenidade/Terminal	Barra/Terminal
21	Barra/Terminal	Vila de Coloane
21a	Barra/Terminal	Praia Hac Sa
22	R. 1 Iao Hon	Jockey Club
23	Est. Ilha Verde/Terminal	NAPE/Alm. C. Assumpção
25	Portas do Cerco	Praia Hac Sa
26	Fai Chi Kei	Vila de Coloane
26a	Fai Chi Kei	Praia Hac Sa
28A	Jetfoil Terminal	Jockey Club
28B	Est. Ilha Verde/Terminal	Meia Laranja
28BX	Est. Ilha Verde/Terminal	Hotel Lisboa
28C	Portas do Cerco	Serviços Migração
3	Portas do Cerco	Jetfoil Terminal
30	R. Lei Pou Chon	Jockey Club
32	Fai Chi Kei	Hotel Lisboa
33	Fai Chi Kei	Jockey Club
34	Barra/Terminal	Terraço Panorâmico
35	Terraço Panorâmico	Av. Padre T. Pereira
3a	P. Ponte Horta	Jetfoil Terminal
4	Fai Chi Kei	Av. Almeida Ribeiro

5	Portas do Cerco	Barra/Terminal
6	P. Serenidade/Terminal	Hospital S. Januário
7	R. 1 Iao Hon	Barra/Terminal
8	Est. Ilha Verde/Terminal	Meia Laranja
8a	Est. Ilha Verde/Terminal	Hotel Lisboa
9	Portas do Cerco	Barra/Terminal
9a	Portas do Cerco	Palácio
AP1	Portas do Cerco	Aeroporto Internacional de Macau

TAXI

FARES

First 1,500 meters	$ 10.00
For each 220 meters afterwards	$ 1.00
Every minute during waiting time which the taxi is hired but not in motion at passenger's request	$ 1.00
Each piece of baggage transported in the baggage compartment at passenger's request	$ 3.00
Additional Fee	
Taipa to Coloane	$ 2.00
Macau to Coloane	$ 5.00
When boarding taxi at the Macau Airport	$ 5.00
Note : No additional fee will be charged when the taxi is hired from Taipa and Coloane to Macau or from Coloane to Taipa.	
Calling Service : 519519 / 939939	

For any Complaints

IACM -- Tel : 337676

Police Force -- Tel : 573333
Judiciary Force -- Tel : 557777

TRANSPORTATION TO HONG KONG

MACAU HONG KONG

Day Service						
0700*	0845#	1030*	1215#	1400*	1545*	1730*
0715	0900*	1045*	1230*	1415*	1600*	1745*
0730*	0915*#	1100*	1245#	1430*	1615*	1800*
0745*	0930*	1115*	1300*	1445*	1630*	
0800*	0945*	1130*	1315*	1500*	1645	
0815*	1000*	1145	1330*	1515	1700*	
0830*	1015	1200*	1345	1530*	1715*	
Night Service						
1815	1930*	2100*	2230*	2359*	0115*#	0400*
1830*	1945	2130*	2245	0015#	0130	0600*
1845	2000*	2145*	2300	0030*	0145*#	0630
1900*	2015	2200*	2330*	0045#	0230*	
1915*	2030*	2215	2345*	0100*	0300	
* VIP Cabin (6 Seats or 4 Seats) & Super class available.						
# Optional Sailing						

HONG KONG MACAU

Day Service						
0700*	0845	1030*	1215#	1400*	1545*	1730*
0715#	0900*	1045*	1230*	1415*	1600*	1745*
0730*	0915*	1100*	1245#	1430*	1615*	1800*
0745*#	0930*	1115*	1300*	1445*	1630*	
0800*	0945*	1130*	1315*	1500*	1645	
0815*	1000*	1145	1330*	1515	1700*	
0830*	1015	1200*	1345	1530*	1715*	
Night Service						
1815	1930*	2100*	2230*	2359*	0115	0445
1830*	1945	2130*	2245	0015*#	0130*	0600

1845*	2000*	2145*	2300*	0030	0145*#	
1900*	2015#	2200*	2330*	0045#	0230*	
1915*	2030	2215	2345*	0100*	0400*	

PRICES

Hong Kong➡Macau				
	VIP Cabin (6 seats)	VIP Cabin (4 seats)	Super Class	Econ. Class
Weekdays	$1,392	$928	$232	$130
Weekends & Holidays	$1,482	$988	$247	$141
Night Service	$1,560	$1,040	$260	$161
Macau➡Hong Kong				
	VIP Cabin (6 seats)	VIP Cabin (4 seats)	Super Class	Econ. Class
Weekdays	$1,398	$932	$233	$131
Weekends & Holidays	$1,488	$992	$248	$142
Night Service	$1,566	$1,044	$261	$162
Macau Kowloon				
	Toruist Class			
Weekdays, Weekends & Holidays	$93			

MACAO CONSULATES

BANGLADESH
Consulate General of the People's Republci of Bangladesh
Room 3807, China Resources Building 26, Harbour Road - Wan Chai Hong Kong
Tel : (852) 2827 4278
Fax: (852) 2827 1916
E-mail : bangladt@netvigator.com

BHUTAN
Honorary Consulate of Bhutan
Unit B, 1st Floor, Kowloon Centre 29-43, Ashley Road Kowloon - Hong Kong
Tel : (852) 2376 2112
Fax: (852) 2376 3331

MYANMAR
Consulate General of the Union of Myanmar
Rooms 2401-2405, Sun Hung Kai Centre 30 Harbour Road - Wan Chai Hong Kong
Tel : (852) 2827 7929
Fax: (852) 2827 6597
E-mail : myancghk@netvigator.com

INDIA
Consulate General of India
Unit D, 16th Floor, United Centre 95 Queensway Hong Kong
Tel : (852) 2529 1289
Fax: (852) 2865 4617
E-mail : cgiinfo@pacific.net.hk

ISRAEL
Consulate General of Israel
Admiralty Centre Tower II Room 701, 18 Harcourt Road, Hong Kong
Tel : (852) 2529 6091
Fax: (852) 2865 0220
Hompepage : http://www.cgis.com.hk
E-mail : isrcons@asiaonline.net

JAPAN
Consulate General of Japan
46-47th Floor, One Exchange Square 8, Connaught Place Central Hong Kong
Tel : (852) 2522 1184
Fax: (852) 2868 0156
Homepage : http://www.japan.org.hk

KOREA
Consulate General of Korea
5-6 Floors, Far East Finance Centre 16, Harcourt Road Hong Kong
Tel : (852) 2529 4141
Fax: (852) 2861 3699
E-mail : korcon@netvigator.com

LAO PEOPLE'S DEMOCRATIC REPUBLIC
Consulate General of Lao People's Democratic Republic
1002 Arion Commercial Centre 2-12 Queen's Road West Hong Kong
Tel : (852) 2544 1186
Fax: (852) 2544 1187

MALAYSIA
Consulate General of Malaysia
24th Floor, Malaysia Building 50 Gloucester Road - Wan Chai Hong Kong
Tel : (852) 2527 0921
Fax: (852) 2865 1628
E-mail : mwhkong@netvigator.com

NEPAL
Consulate General of Nepal
Unit 1206, Greenfield Tower concordia Plaza 1 Science Museum Road Tsim Sha Tsui East - Hong Kong
Tel : (852) 2369 7813
Fax: (852) 2824 2970
E-mail : mwhkong@netvigator.com

PAKISTAN
Consulate General of Islamic Republic of Pakistan
Room 3706, 37th Floor China Resources Building 26, Harbour Road - Wan Chai Hong Kong
Tel : (852) 2827 1966
Fax: (852) 2827 2189
E-mail : parephk@netvigator.com

PHILIPPINES
Consulate General of the Republic of Philippines
Room 602, 6th Floor United Centre, 95 Queensway Hong Kong
Tel : (852) 2823 8500

Fax: (852) 2866 9885
E-mail : prhk@aisaonline.net

SINGAPORE
Consulate General of Singapore
9th Floor, Unit 901, Tower I - Admiralty Centre 18, Harcourt Road Hong Kong
Tel : (852) 2527 2212
Fax: (852) 2861 3595
E-mail : sporecon@hk.super.net

THAILAND
The Royal Thai Consulate General
8th Floor, Fairmont House 8, Cotton Tree Drive Central - Hong Kong
Tel : (852) 2532 5121
Fax: (852) 2521 8629
E-mail : thaihkcg@hk.super.net

SUPPLEMENTS

ENVIRONMENTAL ORGANIZATIONS AND ENVIRONMENTAL GOVERNMENT AGENCIES IN CHINA

THE PEOPLE'S REPUBLIC OF CHINA

ALL-CHINA ENVIRONMENT FEDERATION (ACEF) - www.acef.com.cn

BEIJING FORESTRY SOCIETY (BFS) - www.bjfs.org.cn

CENTER FOR BIODIVERSITY AND INDIGENOUS KNOWLEDGE (CBIK) [southwest China] - www.cbik.org

CENTER FOR LEGAL ASSISTANCE TO POLLUTION VICTIMS (CLAPV) - www.clapv.org

CHINA ASSOCIATION OF ENVIRONMENTAL PROTECTION INDUSTRY (CAEPI) - www.caepi.org.cn

CHINA DIALOGUE - www.chinadialogue.net

CHINA ENVIRONMENT FORUM, WOODROW WILSON INTERNATIONAL CENTER FOR SCHOLARS - http://www.wilsoncenter.org/program/china-environment-forum

CHINA ENVIRONMENTAL AWARENESS PROGRAM - www.chinaceap.org

CHINA ENVIRONMENTAL INDUSTRY NETWORK (CEIN) - www.cein.net/en/Default.htm

CHINA ENVIRONMENTAL NEWS ALERT, NATURAL RESOURCES DEFENSE COUNCIL (NRDC) - www.nrdc.cn/eblog/greenlawchina

CHINA ENVIRONMENTAL PROTECTION FOUNDATION (CEPT) - www.cepf.org.cn

CHINA FORUM OF ENVIRONMENTAL JOURNALISTS (CFEJ) - www.cfej.net

CHINA GREEN BUILDINGS [blog] - http://chinagreenbuildings.blogspot.com

CHINA GREEN NEWS - http://eng.greensos.cn

CHINA GREEN TIMES [newspaper] - www.greentimes.com

CHINA GREENSPACE [blog] - http://chinagreenspace.blogspot.com

CHINA, INTERNATIONAL RIVERS - http://internationalrivers.org/en/china

CHINA NEW ENERGY - www.newenergy.org.cn

CHINA RENEWABLE ENERGY INFORMATION - www.frankhaugwitz.info

CHINA RENEWABLE ENERGY INFORMATION PLATFORM - http://eninfo.cresp.org.cn

CHINA SUSTAINABLE ENERGY PROGRAM - www.efchina.org

CHINA SUSTAINABLE INDUSTRIAL DEVELOPMENT NETWORK (CSID) - www.csid.com.cn/index1.asp

CHINA–US CENTER FOR SUSTAINABLE DEVELOPMENT - www.chinauscenter.org

CHINA WILD PLANT CONSERVATION ASSOCIATION - http://plant.cwca.org.cn

CHINA WILDLIFE CONSERVATION ASSOCIATION (CWCA) - www.cwca.org.cn/index.htm

CHINADIALOGUE - www.chinadialogue.net

CHINA'S GREEN BEAT - www.chinasgreenbeat.com

CHINESE RENEWABLE ENERGY INDUSTRIES ASSOCIATION (CREIA) - www.creia.net

CHINESE SOCIETY OF ENVIRONMENTAL SCIENCES (CSES) - www.chinacses.org

CHINESE SOCIETY OF FORESTRY (CSF) - www.csf.org.cn

CHINESE SOCIETY OF LANDSCAPE ARCHITECTURE (CHSLA) - www.chsla.org.cn

CHINESE WIND ENERGY ASSOCIATION - www.cwea.org.cn

CLEAN AIR ASIA – CHINA OFFICE - http://cleanairinitiative.org/portal/countrynetworks/china

CONSERVATION INTERNATIONAL – CHINA PROGRAM - www.conservation.org.cn and www.conservation.org/where/asia-pacific/china/Pages/overview.aspx

ECOLINX FOUNDATION - www.ecolinx.org

ECOLOGIA - www.ecologia.org

ECOLOGICAL SOCIETY OF CHINA (ESC) - www.esc.org.cn

ENVIRONMENTAL DEFENSE FUND, BEIJING OFFICE - www.edf.org/offices/beijing-china

ENVIRONMENTAL LAW INSTITUTE, CHINA PROGRAM - www.eli.org/Program_Areas/china.cfm

EPA–CHINA ENVIRONMENTAL LAW INITIATIVE - www.epa.gov/ogc/china/initiative_home.htm

FRIENDS OF NATURE (FON) - www.fon.org.cn

FUTURE GENERATIONS CHINA - http://china.future.org

GLOBAL ENVIRONMENT INSTITUTE (GEI) - www.geichina.org

GLOBAL FOOD SAFETY FORUM (GFSF) - www.gfsf.org.cn

GLOBAL VILLAGE OF BEJING (GVB) - www.gvbchina.org.cn and www.gvbchina.org

GLOBAL WATER PARTNERSHIP CHINA - www.gwp.org/gwp-in-action/China/ and www.gwpchina.org/ChinaGWP.aspx

GREEN ANHUI - www.green-anhui.org

GREEN CAMEL BELL - www.gcbcn.org

GREEN EARTH VOLUNTEERS (GEV) - www.greensos.cn and www.virtualfoundation.org/about/consortium/greenearth.html

GREEN WATERSHED - www.greenwatershed.org

GREENPEACE EAST ASIA [has an office in Beijing] - www.greenpeace.org/eastasia/

INNOVATION CENTER FOR ENERGY & TRANSPORTATION (iCET) - www.icet.org.cn

INSTITUTE FOR ENVIRONMENT AND DEVELOPMENT (IED) - www.ied.org.cn

INSTITUTE OF PUBLIC & ENVIRONMENTAL AFFAIRS - www.ipe.org.cn

INTERNATIONAL FUND FOR CHINA'S ENVIRONMENT (IFCE) - www.ifce.org

INTERNATIONAL INSTITUTE FOR SUSTAINABLE DEVELOPMENT – CHINA - www.iisd.org/china/

INTERNATIONAL RIVERS NETWORK – CHINA - www.internationalrivers.org/programs/china

IUCN CHINA - www.iucn.org/about/union/secretariat/offices/asia/asia_where_work/china

JANE GOODALL INSTITUTE CHINA (JGI CHINA) - www.jgichina.org

JOINT U.S.-CHINA COLLABORATION ON CLEAN ENERGY (JUCCCE) - www.juccce.org

LEAD CHINA - www.lead.org.cn

NATURAL RESOURCES DEFENSE COUNCIL (NRDC), CHINA OFFICE - www.nrdc.cn

NATURE CONSERVANCY – CHINA - www.nature.org/china

PACIFIC ENVIRONMENT, CHINA - http://pacificenvironment.org/section.php?id=183

PANDA MOUNTAIN, US-CHINA ENVIRONMENTAL FUND - www.uscef.org

POPULATION COUNCIL, CHINA - www.popcouncil.org/countries/china.asp

SAVE CHINA'S TIGERS - www.savechinastigers.org

SHANGAI ROOTS & SHOOTS, THE JANE GOODALL INSTITUTE SHANGHAI - www.jgi-shanghai.org

SHANGRI-LA INSTITUTE FOR SUSTAINABLE COMMUNITIES - http://waterschool.cn

SINO-ECOLOGISTS ASSOCIATION OVERSEAS (SINO-ECO) - www.sino-eco.org

SINO-ITALIAN COOPERATION PROGRAM FOR ENVIRONMENTAL PROTECTION - www.sinoitaenvironment.org/indexe02.asp

SHANGHAI ENVIRONMENT ONLINE - www.envir.online.sh.cn/eng/

SHAN SHUI CONSERVATION CENTER - www.shanshui.org

SNOW LEOPARD TRUST - CHINA - http://www.snowleopard.org/learn/program-countries/china

THE THIRD POLE.NET, UNDERSTANDING ASIA'S WATER CRISIS - www.thethirdpole.net

THREE GORGES PROBE, PROBE INTERNATIONAL - http://journal.probeinternational.org/three-gorges-probe/

TIBET ENVIRONMENTAL WATCH (TEW) - www.tew.org

TEBETAN PLATEAU PROJECT (TPP), EARTH ISLAND INSTITUTE - www.earthisland.org/tpp/

TIBET'S ENVIRONMENT AND DEVELOPMENT ISSUES, ENVIRONMENT AND DEVELOPMENT DESK (EDD), DEPARTMENT OF INFORMATION AND INTERNATIONAL RELATIONS (DIIR), CENTRAL TIBETAN ADMINISTRATION (CTA) - http://tibet.net/important-issues/tibets-environment-and-development-issues/

UNITED NATIONS DEVELOPMENT PROGRAM CHINA (UNDP China) - www.undp.org.cn

US-CHINA PARTNERSHIP FOR ENVIRONMENTAL LAW, ENVIRONMENTAL LAW CENTER, VERMONT LAW SCHOOL - www.vermontlaw.edu/x1463.xml

WILD AID, CHINA - www.wildaidchina.org

WILD CHINA FILM - www.wildchina.cn

WILDLIFE CONSERVATION SOCIETY – CHINA - www.chinabiodiversity.com/index.php

WORLD RESOURCES INSTITUTE, CHINA - http://projects.wri.org/sd-pams-database/china

WORLDWATCH INSTITUTE, CHINA PROGRAM - www.worldwatch.org/chinawatch

WWF–CHINA - www.wwfchina.org

GOVERNMENT ENVIRONMENTAL & CONSERVATION AGENCIES OF THE PEOPLE'S REPUBLIC OF CHINA

English Language Home Page of Primary Environmental Agency:
MINISTRY OF ENVIRONMENTAL PROTECTION - http://english.mep.gov.cn

AGRO-ENVIRONMENTAL PROTECTION INSTITUTE (AEPI, MOA), CHINESE ACADEMY OF AGRICULTURAL SCIENCES (CAAS) - http://www.caas.cn/en/administration/research_institutes/research_institutes_out_beijing/77864.shtml

BEIJING CLIMATE CENTER (BCC) - http://bcc.cma.gov.cn

BIODIVERSITY COMMITTEE OF THE CHINESE ACADEMY OF SCIENCES - www.brim.ac.cn

CHINA CLIMATE CHANGE INFO-NET, DEPARTMENT OF CLIMATE CHANGE, NATIONAL DEVELOPMENT AND REFORM COMMISSION - www.ccchina.gov.cn

CHINA COUNCIL FOR INTERNATIONAL COOPERATION ON ENVIRONMENT AND DEVELOPMENT (CCICED) - www.cciced.net/encciced

CHINA ENVIRONMENTAL CULTURE PROMOTION ASSOCIATION (CECPA) - http://www.tt65.net

CHINA INSTITUTE OF WATER RESOURCES AND HYDROPOWER RESEARCH (IWHR) - www.iwhr.com/english.asp

CHINA METEOROLOGICAL ADMINISTRATION (CMA) - www.cma.gov.cn

CHINA NATIONAL ENVIRONMENTAL MONITORING CENTER (CNEMC) - www.cnemc.cn

CHINA NATIONAL URBAN AIR QUALITY REAL-TIME PUBLISHING PLATFORM, CHINA NATIONAL ENVIRONMENTAL MONITORING CENTER (CNEMC) - http://113.108.142.147:20035/emcpublish/

CHINA OCEANIC INFORMATION NETWORK, STATE OCEANIC ADMINISTRATION - www.coi.gov.cn

CHINA POPULATION AND DEVELOPMENT RESEARCH CENTER (CPDRC) - www.cpdrc.org.cn

CHINESE ACADEMY OF AGRICULTURAL SCIENCES (CAAS) - www.caas.net.cn

CHINESE ACADEMY FOR ENVIRONMENTAL PLANNING (CAEP) - www.caep.org.cn

CHINESE ARCTIC AND ANTARCTIC ADMINISTRATION (CAA) - www.chinare.cn/en

CHINESE NATIONAL ARCTIC AND ANTARCTIC DATA CENTER (NADC) - www.chinare.org.cn

CHINESE RESEARCH ACADEMY OF ENVIRONMENTAL SCIENCES (CRAES) - www.craes.cn

CLEANER PRODUCTION IN CHINA, NATIONAL DEVELOPMENT AND REFORM COMMISSION (NDRC) - www.chinacp.com

GATE TO THE POLES, POLAR RESEARCH INSTITUTE OF CHINA - www.polar.gov.cn/en/index or www.polar.org.cn/en/index

INSTITUTE OF BOTANY, CHINESE ACADEMY OF SCIENCES - www.ibcas.ac.cn

INSTITUTE OF ENVIRONMENT AND SUSTAINABLE DEVELOPMENT IN AGRICULTURE (IEDA), CHINESE ACADEMY OF AGRICULTURAL SCIENCE (CAAS) - http://www.caas.cn/en/administration/research_institutes/research_institutes_beijing/77801.shtml

KUNMING INSTITUTE OF BOTANY (KIB), ACADEMY OF SCIENCES - www.kib.ac.cn

MINISTRY OF AGRICULTURE (MOA) - www.agri.gov.cn and English version: http://english.agri.gov.cn

MINISTRY OF LAND AND RESOURCES (MLR) - www.mlr.gov.cn

MINISTRY OF WATER RESOURCES (MWR) - www.mwr.gov.cn

MINISTRY OF ENVIRONMENTAL PROTECTION - www.mep.gov.cn or www.zhb.gov.cn

NATIONAL HEALTH AND FAMILY PLANNING COMMISSION (NHFPC) - www.nhfpc.gov.cn

POLAR RESEARCH INSTITUTE OF CHINA (PRIC) - www.pric.gov.cn

SHENYANG ACADEMY OF ENVIRONMENTAL SCIENCES - www.syhky.com

STATE FORESTRY ADMINISTRATION - www.forestry.gov.cn

STATE OCEANIC ADMINISTRATION - www.soa.gov.cn

YELLOW RIVER CONSERVANCY COMMISSION (YRCC) - www.yellowriver.gov.cn

HONG KONG

(Special Administrative Region of The People's Republic of China)

Environmental & Conservation Organizations in Hong Kong

ANIMALS ASIA - www.animalsasia.org

ARK EDEN - www.arkedenonlantau.com

ASSOCIATION FOR GEOCONSERVATION (AGHK) - www.rocks.org.hk

BUSINESS ENVIRONMENT COUNCIL (BEC) - www.bec.org.hk

CHINA EXPLORATION AND RESEARCH SOCIETY (CERS) - www.cers.org.hk

CIVIC EXCHANGE - www.civic-exchange.org

CLEAR THE AIR (CTA) - www.cleartheair.org.hk

THE CONSERVANCY ASSOCIATION - www.conservancy.org.hk

DESIGNING HONG KONG - www.designinghongkong.com

EARTH CARE - www.earth.org.hk

ECO EXPO ASIA - http://ecoexpoasia.hktdc.com

ENVIRONMENTAL CAMPAIGN COMMITTEE (ECC) - www.ecc.org.hk

ENVIRONMENTAL CONTRACTORS MANAGEMENT ASSOCIATION (ECMA) - www.ecma.org.hk

FRIENDS OF THE EARTH HONG KONG - www.foe.org.hk

FRIENDS OF THE HARBOUR - www.friendsoftheharbour.org

GREEN COUNCIL - www.greencouncil.org

GREEN LANTAU ASSOCIATION - www.greenlantau.com

GREEN PENG CHAU ASSOCIATION - www.greenpengchau.org.hk

GREEN PARTY HONG KONG - www.greenparty.hk

GREEN POWER - www.greenpower.org.hk

GREEN SENSE - http://greensense.org.hk

GREENPEACE EAST ASIA [has an office in Hong Kong] - www.greenpeace.org/eastasia/

HKNATURE.NET - www.hknature.net

HONG KONG ALTERNATIVES - www.hkalternatives.com

HONG KONG BIRD WATCHING SOCIETY (HKBWS) - www.hkbws.org.hk

HONG KONG DOLPHIN WATCH - www.hkdolphinwatch.com

HONG KONG ENVIRONMENTAL INDUSTRY ASSOCIATION (HKENVIA) - www.hkenvia.org

HONG KONG FLORA AND VEGETATION - www.hkflora.com

HONG KONG GEOGRAPHICAL ASSOCIATION (HKGA) - www.hkga.org

HONG KONG GREEN BUILDING COUNCIL (HKGBC) - www.hkgbc.org.hk

HONG KONG GREEN MANUFACTURING ALLIANCE (HKGMA) - www.gma.org.hk

HONG KONG LEPIDOPTERIST'S SOCIETY (HKLS) - www.hkls.org

HONG KONG OUTDOORS - www.hkoutdoors.com

HONG KONG SUSTAINABLE DEVELOPMENT FORUM (HKSDF) - http://hksdf.org.hk

HONG KONG WASTE MANAGEMENT ASSOCIATION (HKWMA) - www.hongkongwma.org.hk

HONG KONG WEEE RECYCLING ASSOCIATION (HKWRA) - www.hkwra.org.hk

THE JANE GOODALL INSTITUTE HONG KONG - www.janegoodall.org.hk

KADOORIE FARM & BOTANIC GARDEN - www.kfbg.org

THE KADOORIE INSTITUTE, UNIVERSITY OF HONG KONG - www.hku.hk/kadinst/

LIVING ISLANDS MOVEMENT (LIM) - www.livingislands.org.hk

OCEAN PARK CONSERVATION FOUNDATION - www.scuba.net.hk/oceanpark/

SAVE OUR SHORELINES (SOS) - www.saveourshorelines.bizland.com

SOCIETY FOR THE PREVENTION OF CRUELTY TO ANIMALS (Hong Kong SPCA) - www.spca.org.hk

SOCIETY FOR THE PROTECTION OF THE HARBOUR - www.harbourprotection.org

WWF HONG KONG - http://wwf.org.hk

Hong Kong Government Environmental & Conservation Agencies

English Language Homepage of Primary Environmental Agency:
ENVIRONMENTAL PROTECTION DEPARTMENT (EPD) - www.epd.gov.hk/epd/eindex.html

AGRICULTURE, FISHERIES AND CONSERVATION DEPARTMENT (AFCD) - www.afcd.gov.hk

CENSUS AND STATISTICS DEPARTMENT - www.censtatd.gov.hk

CENTRE FOR FOOD SAFETY (CFS), FOOD AND ENVIRONMENTAL HYGIENE DEPARTMENT (FEHD) - www.cfs.gov.hk

ENVIRONMENT BUREAU - www.enb.gov.hk

ENVIRONMENTAL CAMPAIGN COMMITTEE (ECC) - www.ecc.org.hk

ENVIRONMENT & CONSERVATION FUND (ECF) - www.ecf.gov.hk

ENVIRONMENTAL PROTECTION DEPARTMENT (EPD) - www.epd.gov.hk

FOOD AND ENVIRONMENTAL HYGIENE DEPARTMENT (FEHD) - www.fehd.gov.hk

HONG KONG AWARDS FOR ENVIRONMENTAL EXCELLENCE (HKAEE) - www.hkaee.org.hk

HONG KONG COUNCIL ON SMOKING AND HEALTH (COSH) - www.smokefree.hk

HONG KONG OBSERVATORY [weather service] - www.weather.gov.hk/contente.htm

HONG KONG WASTE REDUCTION WEBSITE - www.wastereduction.gov.hk

HONG KONG ZOOLOGICAL AND BOTANICAL GARDENS (HKZBG) - www.lcsd.gov.hk/en/parks/hkzbg

MARINE DEPARTMENT - www.mardep.gov.hk

OCCUPATIONAL SAFETY & HEALTH COUNCIL (OSHC) - www.oshc.org.hk

SUSTAINABLE DEVELOPMENT - www.susdev.gov.hk

WATER SUPPLIES DEPARTMENT (WSD) - www.wsd.gov.hk

MACAO

(Special Administrative Region of The People's Republic of China)

Environmental & Conservation Organizations in Macao
ENVIRONMENT PROTECTION ASSOCIATIONS [Directory], GOVERNMENT PRINTING BUREAU - http://en.io.gov.mo/Priv/categories/26.aspx

ENVIRONMENTAL ENGINEERING LABORATORY, UNIVERSITY OF MACAU - www.fst.umac.mo/en/lab/environ/index.html

Macao Government Environmental & Conservation Agencies and Related Agencies

Primary Environmental Agency:

DIRECTORATE OF ENVIRONMENTAL PROTECTION SERVICES - www.ambiente.gov.mo or www.dspa.gov.mo

CONSUMER COUNCIL - http://cc.informac.gov.mo

DIRECTORATE OF METEOROLOGICAL AND GEOPHYSICAL SERVICES (SMG) - www.smg.gov.mo/www/c_index.php

MACAO CARTOGRAPHY AND CADASTRE BUREAU - www.dscc.gov.mo

MACAO HERITAGE NET [historic preservation], CULTURAL AFFAIRS BUREAU - www.macauheritage.net/en/default.aspx

MARINE AND WATER BUREAU - www.marine.gov.mo

STATISTICS AND CENSUS SERVICE (DSEC) - www.dsec.gov.mo/e_index.html

TAIWAN – REPUBLIC OF CHINA

Environmental & Conservation Organizations in Taiwan

BAT ASSOCIATION OF TAIWAN - http://www.bats.org.tw/

CHINESE WILD BIRD FEDERATION - www.bird.org.tw

GLOBAL CHANGE RESEARCH CENTER, NATIONAL TAIWAN UNIVERSITY - www.gcc.ntu.edu.tw

DEPARTMENT OF WATER RESOURCES AND ENVIRONMENTAL ENGINEERING, TAMKANG UNIVERSITY - http://www2.tku.edu.tw/~tewx/english.htm

GREEN CITIZENS' ACTION ALLIANCE - www.gcaa.org.tw

GREEN PARTY TAIWAN - www.greenparty.org.tw

THE JANE GOODALL INSTITUTE TAIWAN - www.goodall.org.tw

KUROSHIO OCEAN EDUCATION FOUNDATION - www.kuroshio.org.tw

SOCIETY FOR WILDLIFE AND NATURE (SWAN) - www.swan.org.tw

TAIWAN ACADEMY OF ECOLOGY - http://ecology.org.tw

TAIWAN ENVIRONMENTAL ENGINEERING ASSOCIATION (TEEA) - www.teea.org.tw

TAIWAN ENVIRONMENTAL INFORMATION ASSOCIATION (TEIA) - www.e-info.org.tw

TAIWAN ENVIRONMENT PROTECTION UNION (TEPU) - http://tepu.yam.org.tw

TAIWAN NATURE TRAIL SOCIETY - http://naturet.ngo.org.tw

TAIWAN WATCH INSTITUTE - www.taiwanwatch.org.tw

WETLANDS TAIWAN - www.wetland.org.tw

WILD AT HEART LEGAL DEFENSE ASSOCIATION - http://en.wildatheart.org.tw

Taiwan Government Environmental & Conservation Agencies

English Language Home Page of Primary Environmental Agency:

ENVIRONMENTAL PROTECTION ADMINISTRATION (EPA) - www.epa.gov.tw/en/

AVIATION SAFETY COUNCIL (ASC) - www.asc.gov.tw

CENTRAL WEATHER BUREAU (CWB) - www.cwb.gov.tw

COUNCIL OF AGRICULTURE (COA) - http://eng.coa.gov.tw

COUNCIL OF INDIGENOUS PEOPLES (CIP) - www.apc.gov.tw

ENVIRONMENTAL PROTECTION ADMINISTRATION (EPA) - www.epa.gov.tw

NATIONAL PARKS OF TAIWAN, MINISTRY OF THE INTERIOR - http://np.cpami.gov.tw

TAIWAN FORESTRY RESEARCH INSTITUTE (TFRI) - www.tfri.gov.tw

TAIWAN OCEAN RESEARCH INSTITUTE (TORI) - www.tori.narl.org.tw

TAIWAN WATER CORPORATION (TWC) - www.water.gov.tw

WATER RESOURCES AGENCY (WRA), MINISTRY OF ECONOMIC AFFAIRS - www.wra.gov.tw

CHINESE CITY GOVERNMENT ENVIRONMENTAL BUREAUS

Beijing Municipal Environmental Protection Bureau (BJEPB)
www.bjepb.gov.cn and www.ebeijing.gov.cn/Government/Departments/t929914.htm

Guangzhou Environmental Protection Bureau (GZEPB)
www.gzepb.gov.cn/english/default.htm

Hong Kong Environment Bureau
www.enb.gov.hk/en/index.html

Hong Kong Environmental Protection Department (EPD)
www.epd.gov.hk/epd/eindex.html

Macao Directorate of Environmental Protection Services (DSPA)
www.dspa.gov.mo

Shanghai Environmental Protection Bureau (SEPB)
www.sepb.gov.cn/fa/cms/shhj/YWB/index.htm

Habitat Environment of Shenzhen City
www.szhec.gov.cn

Taipei City Government – Department of Environmental Protection (DEP)
http://english.dep.taipei.gov.tw

Air Quality Index for Beijing, Shanghai, Guangzhou, Chengdu, Shenyang, Hong Kong, Macao, Taiwan and Many More Locations

Most Recent Air Quality, U. S. Embassy Beijing Air Quality Monitor
www.stateair.net/web/post/1/1.html

Most Recent Air Quality, U. S Consulate Shanghai Air Quality Monitor
www.stateair.net/web/post/1/4.html

—

Most Recent Air Quality, U. S. Consulate Guangzhou Air Quality Monitor
www.stateair.net/web/post/1/3.html

—

Most Recent Air Quality, U. S. Consulate Chengdu Air Quality Monitor www.stateair.net/web/post/1/2.html

Most Recent Air Quality, U. S. Consulate Shenyang Air Quality Monitor
www.stateair.net/web/post/1/5.html

Hong Kong Air Pollution: Real-time Air Quality Index (AQI)
http://aqicn.org/city/hongkong/

Air Quality Index Bulletin
Macao Directorate of Meteorological and Geophysical Services (SMG)
www.smg.gov.mo/www/ccaa/iqa/daily/fe_iqa_index_latest.htm

Taiwan Air Quality Monitoring Network
Environmental Protection Administration Taiwan (EPA)
http://taqm.epa.gov.tw/taqm/en/Default.aspx

Air Pollution in China: Real-time Air Quality Index Visual Map – AQI
http://aqicn.org/map/china

IMPORTANT LEGAL CONTACTS

LAWYERS IN MACAO

Antonio Ribeiro Baguinho - Lawyers and Private Notary
Antonio Ribeiro Baguinho
Avenida da Amizade, 555,
Landmark Building, 13th Floor, Suite 1308,
Macau
Tel: (853)2878-8128
Fax: (853)2870-5351
E-mail: info@arblegal.com
Website: António Ribeiro Baguinho - ARB Legal
Specialties - banking and finance, civil law, commercial law, contraction, corporate, criminal law, family law, general, immigration, insurance, labor law, real estate, taxes

C & C Advogados
Rui Jose da Cunha
Avenida da Praia Grande, No. 759,
3 Floor
Macau
Tel: (853)2837-2642
Fax: (853)2855-3098
E-mail: ccadvog@ccadvog.com
Website: C&C Macau Lawyers
Specialties - banking and finance, civil law, commercial law, corporate, criminal law, family law, general, immigration, labor law, real estate, taxes

DSL Lawyers
Av. da Praia Grande 409,
China Law Building 16/F,
Macau
Tel: (853) 2822 3355
Fax: (853) 2872 5588
Email: mail@dsl-lawyers.com
Website: DSL Lawyers Macau
Specialties - aeronautical/maritime, banking/financial, civil law, collections, commercial law, contracts, corporations, foreign claims, foreign investments, government relations, insurance, commercial/business law, labor relations, marketing agreements, patents/trademarks/copyrights, taxes

Manuela Antonio - Lawyers and Notaries
Manuela Antonio
Alameda Dr. Carlos D'Assumpção nos. 411-417,
Edificio Dysnasty Plaza, 15th Floor D-H,
Macau
Tel: (853)2859-1128
Fax: (853)2834-5678
E-mail: info@mantonio.net
Website: Manuela Antonio Lawyers and Notaries
Specialties – aviation, banking & finance, capital markets, corporate / M&A, criminal, data protection, employment and immigration, family, gaming, insurance, intellectual and industrial property, leisure and hospitality, litigation, dispute resolution and arbitration, project finance, real estate and construction, public and administrative law, public procurement, notary services, regulatory and compliance, tax, transportation and shipping.

Mario Paz - Barristers and Solicitors
Mario Paz (Mario Anisio Da Assuncao Paz)
Av. Marciano Baptista, nos. 26-54,
Centro Comercial "Chong Fok", 8 andar "H",
Macau
Tel: (853)2878-5716
Fax: (853)2878-5718
E-mails: mario.paz@macaubarristers.com
Specialties - civil law, commercial law, criminal law, real estates, family law, general, immigration, labor law

MdME - Lawyers and Private Notary
Avenida da Praia Grande, 409, China Law Building, 21/F and 23/F A-B, Macau
Tel: (853) 2833 3332
Fax: (853) 2833 3331
Email: anabg@mdme.com.mo
Website: MdME Lawyers | Macau
Specialties - aeronautical/maritime, banking/financial, civil law, commercial law, contracts, corporations, criminal law, family law, foreign investments, government relations, insurance, commercial/business law, labor relations, patents/trademarks/copyrights, taxes, transportation law

Porfirio Azevedo Gomes Notary & Law Firm
Porfirio Azevedo Gomes
Monica Tavira Neves
Avenida da Praia Grande, n. 265,
"Kam Lai Kok" Building, 3 Floor, "A-B",
Macau
Tel: (853)2832-2459, (853)2832-2513
Fax: (853)2832-9192
E-mail: ccibcm@macau.ctm.net
Website: Porfirio Azevedo Gomes Law Firm
Specialties - banking and financial, civil Law, commercial law, corporate, criminal law, family law, general, immigration, insurance, labor law, real estate, taxes law

EMERGENCY CONTACTS

Emergency Call 999	Fire Station 572222
Hospital Conde S. Januário 313731	Hospital Kiang Wu 378311

The Police 573333	Macao Customs Services 559944
Judiciary 557777	Electricity Problem 339922
Water Supply Problem 2990992	Telephone Fault Report 121
Directory Enquiries (Chinese / English) 181	Directory Enquiries (Portuguese) 185
International Telephone Enquiries 101	International Calls to Overseas 191
International Calls to PRC 155	Electricity Info. Line 339911
Telecom mobile service - CTM 1000	Telecom mobile service - SMARTONE 1628
Telecom mobile service - HUTCHISON 1118	

HOSPITALS

Macau Oriental Health Center(Tap Seac) Av.Cons Ferreira Alm. Fax 568872 522232	North Health Center(Fai Chi Kei) Fax 260630 562922
Patane Health Center Av. Demétrio Cinatti Pto. 31A Fax 952872 514036	T. Barbosa Health Center(Toi San) Av. A Tamag Barbosa, Peng Man bl. A cv Fax 400517 400011
Areia Preta Health Center Mercado Iao Hon Veng Tim San Chun bl 2 r/c Fax 415193 413178	Porto Interior Health Center Const?Brito Ed Misto 4? Fax 923196 920024
S. Lourenço Health Center Tv Inácio Bapto. 2 r/c Fax 972198 313418	Taipa Health Center Largo Gov. Tamag Barb? Fax 827640 827096
Hospital Conde S. Januário 577199	Hospital Kiang Wu 378311
Coloane Health Center Largo Pres A Ram?Eanes,Coloane 882030	

OTHER USEFUL CONTACTS

Macau Parking Company Ltd. Av. Da Praia Grande, no. 93, Edf. Tai Wah, 14-andar Tel : 323232	Centre of Productivity and Technological Transference of Macau Rua de Xangai, no. 75, Edf. ACM, 6-7 andar Tel : 781313
Macao Polytechnic Institute Rua Luís Gonzaga Gomes, Macau Tel : 702588 Fax :308801	Portuguese Institute of Orient Av. Conselheiro Ferreira de Almeida, no. 5-G Tel : 530227
Macau Collective Transportation Co. Ltd. Aterro do Pac On, Avenida Son On, Lote I, Taipa Tel : 850060	Macau Urban Transportation Co. Ltd. Estrada Marginal da Ilha Verde, no. 2, r/c Tel : 233232

CONTACT LIST OF GOVERNMENT INSTITUTES AND PUBLIC SERVICES OF MSAR

OFFICE OF THE CHIEF EXECUTIVE

Chief-of-Cabinet : Mr. Ho Veng On
Address : Central Office of the Government of Macau SAR, Avenida da Praia Grande, Macau
Tel: (853) 726 886
Fax: (853) 726 168
Homepage:http://www.macau.gov.mo/
E-mail:info@macau.gov.mo

GOVERNMENT INFORMATION BUREAU

Director : Mr. Chan Chi Ping
Vice-Director : Ms. Ho Wai Heong
Address : Rua de S. Domingos, n.º;1, A-B
Tel: (853) 332886
Fax: (853) 376372
Homepage:http://www.gcs.gov.mo/
E-mail:gcspress@macau.ctm.net

MACAU FOUNDATION

President : Mr. Wu Zhilang
Address : Avenida da República nº6, r/c
Tel: (853) 966777
Fax: (853) 968658
Homepage:http://dawning.iist.unu.edu/Macau/Macau_Foundation/index.html

FOUNDATION FOR COOPERATION AND DEVELOPMENT OF MACAU

Acting President : Ms. Elias Farinha Soares
Address : Av. da Amizade, nº918, Edf. World Trade Centre, 16ºC
Tel: (853) 725188
Fax: (853) 725688
Homepage:http://www.fcdm.org.mo/
E-mail:info@fcdm.org.net

MACAU ECONOMIC AND TRADE DELEGATION IN BRUSSELS (IN EUROPEAN UNION)

Co-ordinator : Ms. Tereza Sanches
Address : Avenue LOUISE, 375 - 1050 BRUXELAS
Tel: (00322) 6471265
Fax: (00322) 6401552
E-mail:deleg.macao@skynet.be

MACAU-CHINA ECONOMIC AND TRADE DELEGATION IN PORTUGAL

Permanent representant & Co-ordinator : Mr. Raimundo Arrais do Rosário
Address : Av. 5 de Outubro, nº115, 5º andar, Lisboa
Tel: (0035121) 7979334
Fax: (0035121) 7936644

2. IN THE SCOPE OF THE SECRETARY FOR ADMINISTRATION AND JUSTICE

OFFICE OF THE SECRETARY FOR ADMINISTRATION AND JUSTICE

Chief-of-Cabinet : Grace Cheong
Address : Central Office of the Government of Macau SAR, Avenida da Praia Grande, Macau
Tel: (853) 726886
Fax: (853) 726880

PUBLIC ADMINISTRATION AND CIVIL SERVICES

Director : Ms. Lídia da Luz
Vice-Director : Mr. José Chu
Vice-Director : Mr. Tou Chi Man
Address : Rua do Campo, nº162, Edf. Administração Pública, 21.º- 27.º andares
Tel: (853) 323623
Fax: (853) 594000
Homepage:http://www.informac.gov.mo/
E-mail:helpdesk@informac.gov.mo

JUSTICE AFFAIRS SERVICES

Director : Mr. Cheong Weng Chon
Vice-Director : Ms. Diana Maria Loureiro
Acting Vice-Director : Ms. Leong Pou Ieng
Address : Rua do Campo no. 162, Edifício Administração Pública, 19.ºandar
Tel : 564225, 595298
Fax : 318052, 710432
Homepage:http://www.dsaj.gov.mo/
E-mail : info@dsaj.gov.mo

IDENTIFICATION SERVICES

Director : Mr. Lai Ieng Kit
Vice-Director : Ms. Chan Hoi Fan
Address : Largo do Senado, n.º18-20, Edf. Comercial China, 2.º- 5.ºandares
Tel: (853) 356960/370777
Fax: (853) 374300
Homepage:http://www.dsi.gov.mo/
E-mail:dsi@macau.ctm.net

OFFICIAL PRINTING SERVICES

Administrator : Mr. António Martins
Address : Rua da Imprensa Nacional
Tel: (853) 573822
Fax: (853) 596802

Homepage:http://www.imprensa.macau.gov.mo/
E-mail:iom@macau.ctm.net

LEGISLATIVE AFFAIRS OFFICE

Co-ordinator : Mr. Jorge Costa Oliveira
Vice-Co-ordinator : Ms. Patrícia Ferreira

Vice-Co-ordinator : Mr. Amílcar Feio
Address : Av. da Praia Grande, n.º619, Edif. Si Toi, 11.ºandar
Tel: (853) 337209-10 / 374302-3
Fax: (853) 337224

PROVISIONAL MUNICIPALITY OF MACAU

President : Mr. José Sales Marques
Vice-President : Mr. Lau Sio Io
Address : Av. Almeida Ribeiro
Tel: (853) 387333
Fax: (853) 341890
Homepage:http://www.cmmp.gov.mo/
E-mail:webmaster@cmmp.gov.mo

PROVISIONAL MUNICIPALITY OF THE ISLANDS

President : Mr. Joaquim Madeira de Carvalho
Vice-President : Ms. Cheung So Mui
Address : Rua Correia da Silva, Edf. Câmara das Ilhas, Taipa
Tel: (853) 827012
Fax: (853) 825363 / 827931
Homepage:http://www.cmip.gov.mo/
E-mail:cmip@macau.ctm.net

3. SECRETARY FOR ECONOMY AND FINANCE

OFFICE OF THE SECRETARY FOR ECONOMY AND FINANCE

Chief-of-Cabinet : Mr. Lei Song Fan
Address : Central Office of the Government of Macau SAR, Avenida da Praia Grande, Macau
Tel: (853) 726886
Fax: (853) 726665

ECONOMIC SERVICES

Acting Director : Mr. Sou Tim Peng
Vice-Director : Mr. Lo Ioi Weng
Address : Rua do Dr. Pedro José Lobo, n.º 1-3, Edif. Banco Luso Internacional, 6.º- 7.ºandares
Tel: (853) 562622
Fax: (853) 590310
Homepage:http://www.economia.gov.mo/
E-mail:info@economia.gov.mo

FINANCE SERVICES

Director : Mr. Carlos Ávila
Vice-Director : Mr. Eric Ho Hou Yin
Vice-Director : Ms. Ieong Pou Yee
Address : Av. da Praia Grande, n.º575-579, Edf. Finanças
Tel: (853) 571600
Fax: (853) 300133
Homepage:http://www.dsf.gov.mo/

STATISTICS AND CENSUS SERVICES

Acting Director : Ms. Lok Kit Sim
Acting Vice-Director : Mr. João Carlos Yeong
Address : Alameda Dr. Carlos d'Assumpção, n.º 411-417, Edf. Dynasty Plaza, 16.º- 17.ºandares
Tel: (853) 728188
Fax: (853) 561884
Homepage:http://www.dsec.gov.mo/
E-mail:info@dsec.gov.mo

LABOUR AND EMPLOYMENT SERVICES

Director : Mr. Shuen Ka Hung
Vice-Director : Ms. Noúmia M. Lameiras
Acting Vice-Director : Mr. Wong Chi Hong
Address : Rotunda de Carlos da Maia
Tel: (853) 564109
Fax: (853) 550477
Homepage:http://www.dste.gov.mo/
E-mail:dsteinfo@dste.gov.mo

GAMBLING INSPECTION AND COORDINATION SERVICES

Director : Mr. Manuel Joaquim das Neves
Vice-Director : Mr. António Pedro Paiva
Address : Av. da Praia Grande, n.º762-804, Edf."CHINA PLAZA", 21º andar
Tel: (853) 569262
Fax: (853) 370296

SOCIAL SECURITY FUND

President : Mr. Fung Ping Kuen
Vice-President : Mr. Chi Kin Chan
Address : Rua de Eduardo Marques, n.º 2-8
Tel: (853) 532850
Fax: (853) 552561

MACAU PENSION FUND

President : Ms. Winnie Lau
Vice-President : Ms. Ermelinda Mª da Conceição Xavier
Address : Av. da Praia Grande, n.º575-579, Edf. Finanças 16.º 17.ºandares
Tel: (853) 594733 / 592620
Fax: (853) 594391
Homepage:http://www.fp.gov.mo/
E-mail:fp@fp.gov.mo

CONSUMER COUNCIL

President : Mr. Alexandre Ho
Address : Rua Central, n.º77-79, r/c
Tel: (853) 972983 / 307820
Fax: (853) 307816
Homepage:http://www.consumer.gov.mo/
E-mail:ccm@informac.gov.mo

MACAU TRADE AND INVESTMENT PROMOTION INSTITUTE

President : Mr. Lee Peng Hong
Address : Av. da Amizade, n.º918, Edf. World Trade Center, 4º 5.ºandares
Tel: (853) 710300
Fax: (853) 590309

Homepage:http://www.ipim.gov.mo/
E-mail:ipim@ipim.gov.mo

MACAU MONETARY AUTHORITY

President : Mr. Anselmo Teng
Address : Calçada do Gaio, nos. 24 e 26
Tel: (853) 568288
Fax: (853) 325432
Homepage:http://amcm.macau.gov.mo/
E-mail:amcmmgee@macau.ctm.net

4. IN THE SCOPE OF THE SECRETARY FOR SECURITY

OFFICE OF THE SECRETARY FOR SECURITY

Chief-of-Cabinet : Mr. Vong Chun Fat
Address : Calçada dos Quartéis, Quartel de S. Francisco
Tel: (853) 7997510
Fax: (853) 580702

PUBLIC SECURITY FORCES SERVICES

Acting Director : Mr. Chan Peng Sam
Acting Vice-Director : Ms. Kok Fong Mei
Address : Calçada dos Quartéis, Quartel de S. Francisco
Homepage:http://www.fsm.gov.mo/
E-mail:info@fsm.gov.mo / crime@fsm.gov.mo
Tel: (853) 559999
Fax: (853) 315543

PUBLIC SECURITY POLICE

Commander : Mr. José Proença Branco
Vice-Commander : Mr. Lei Siu Peng
Address : Av. do Dr. Rodrigo Rodrigues, Edf. Comforseg
Tel: (853) 573333
Fax: (853) 780826

JUDICIARY POLICE

Director : Mr. Wong Sio Chak
Vice-director : Mr. João Manhão
Address : Rua Central, Macau
Tel: (853) 557777
Fax: (853) 594275

MARINE AND CUSTOMS POLICE

Commander : Mr. Choi Lai Hang
Vice-Commander : Ms. Lai Man Wa
Address : Calçada da Barra, n.º47, Capitania dos Portos
Tel: (853) 559944
Fax: (853) 371136

MACAU PRISON

Director : Mr. Lee Kam Cheong
Vice-Director : Ms. Loi Kam Wan
Address : Estrada de Cheoc Van, COLOANE
Tel: (853) 881211
Fax: (853) 882659

MUNICIPAL POLICE

Commander : Mr. Lau Chong Ha
Address : Estrada do Repouso, n.º19, r/c
Tel: (853) 361837
Fax: (853) 365199

FIRE-BRIGADE

Commander : Mr. Ma Io Weng
Vice-Commander : Mr. Eurico Lopes Fazenda
Address : Estrada Coelho do Amaral, n.º 2-6
Tel: (853) 572222
Fax: (853) 361128

MACAU SECURITY FORCES HIGHER SCHOOL

Director : Mr. Hoi Sio Iong
Acting Vice-Director : Mr. Cheong Iok Kuan
Address : Calçada do Quartel, Coloane
Tel: (853) 871112
Fax: (853) 871117

THE SECRETARY FOR SOCIAL AFFAIRS AND CULTURE

OFFICE OF THE SECRETARY FOR SOCIAL AFFAIRS AND CULTURE

Chief-of-Cabinet : Mr. Alexis Tam Chon Weng
Address : Central Office of the Government of Macau SAR, Avendia da Praia Grande, Macau
Tel: (853)726886
Fax: (853) 727594

HEALTH SERVICES

Director : Mr. Rogério A. dos Santos
Vice-Director : Ms. Chan I Wa
Vice-Director : Mr. Koi Kuok Ieng
Vice-Director : Mr. Kun Sai Hoi
Address : Estrada do Visconde de S. Januário
Tel: (853) 313731 / 3907120
Fax: (853) 713105
Homepage:http://www.ssm.gov.mo/

EDUCATION AND YOUTH AFFAIRS SERVICES

Director : Mr. Luís Amado de Viseu
Vice-Director : Mr. Sou Chio Fai
Acting Vice-Director : Ms. Leong Lai
Address : Av. da Praia Grande, n.º926, Edf. Jardim S. Francisco
Tel: (853) 555533
Fax: (853) 317307
Homepage:http://www.dsej.gov.mo/
E-mail:webmaster@dsej.gov.mo

CULTURAL INSTITUTE

President : Ms. Ho Lai Chun da Luz, Heidi
Vice-President : Ms. Kit Kuan Mac
Vice-President : Ms. Lam Wan Nei
Address : Praceta de Miramar, Edf. San On, loja 87-U
Tel: (853) 700391
Fax: (853) 700404-5
Homepage:http://www.icm.gov.mo/
E-mail:postoffice@icm.gov.mo

GOVERNMENT TOURIST OFFICE

Director : Mr. João M. Costa Antunes
Vice-Director : Ms. Maria Helena de Senna Fernandes
Acting Vice-Director : Mr. Manel Gonçalves Pires Junior
Address : Largo do Senado, n.º9, Edf. Ritz
Tel: (853) 315566 / 513355
Fax: (853) 510104
Homepage:http://www.macautourism.gov.mo/defaultie.asp
E-mail:mgto@macautourism.gov.mo

SOCIAL WELFARE INSTITUTE

President : Mr. Ip Peng Kin
Vice-President : Mr. Iong Kong Io
Address : Estrada do Cemitério, n.º6
Tel: (853) 512512
Fax: (853) 559529

MACAU SPORTS DEVELOPMENT BOARD

President : Mr. Manuel Silvério
Vice-President : Mr. Vong Iao Lek, Alex
Address : Av. do Dr. Rodrigo Rodrigues, Forum de Macau, Bloco I, 4.ºandar
Tel: (853) 580762 / 588202/ 590015-6
Fax: (853) 343708 / 337332
Homepage:http://www.sport.gov.mo/
E-mail:sport@macau.ctm.net

TERTIARY EDUCATION OFFICE

Co-ordinator : Mr. Chan Pak Fai
Address : Calçada de Stº Agostinho, nº9, Edif. Nam Yue, 14ºe 15ºandares
Tel: (853) 345403-4 / 811434
Fax: (853) 318401
Homepage:http://www.gaes.gov.mo/
E-mail:webadmin@gaes.gov.mo

UNIVERSITY OF MACAU

Rector : Prof. Iu Vai Pan
Vice-Rector : Prof. Rui Martins
Address : Av. do Padre Tomás Pereira SJ, Taipa
Tel: (853) 831622
Fax: (853) 831694
Homepage:http://www.umac.mo/
E-mail:webmaster@umac.mo

MACAU POLYTECHNIC INSTITUTE

Rector : Prof. Lei Heong Iok
Vice-Rector : Mr. Chao Keng Kuai
Address : Rua de Luíz Gonzaga Gomes, Edf. do Antigo Liceu de Macau
Homepage:http://www.ipm.edu.mo/
E-mail:helpdesk@ipm.edu.mo
Tel: (853) 578722
Fax: (853) 530766

INSTITUTE FOR TOURISM STUDIES

President : Ms. Virgínia Maria Trigo
Acting Vice-President : Ms. Ian Mei Kun
Address : Rampa do Forte de Mong Há

Tel: (853) 598339 / 561251
Fax: (853) 521694
Homepage:http://www.ift.edu.mo/
E-mail:iftcsb@ift.edu.mo

SECRETARY FOR TRANSPORTS AND PUBLIC WORKS

OFFICE OF THE SECRETARY FOR TRANSPORTS AND PUBLIC WORKS

Chief-of-Cabinet : Mr. Francis Wong
Address : Central Office of the Government of Macau SAR, Avendia da Praia Grande, Macau
Tel: (853) 726886
Fax: (853) 727566

LANDS, PUBLIC WORKS AND TRANSPORT SERVICES

Director : Mr. Jaime Carion
Vice-Director : Mr. Li Canfeng
Vice-Director : Mr. Chan Hon Kit
Address : Estrada de D. Maria II, n.º 32-36, Edif. CEM
Tel: (853) 722488
Fax: (853) 313047
Homepage:http://www.dssopt.gov.mo/
E-mail:mailto:dssopt2@macau.ctm.net

CARTOGRAPHY AND REGISTRY SERVICES

Acting Director : Mr. Cheong Sio Kei
Address : Estrada de D. Maria II, n.º 32-36, Edif. CEM, 5.º- 6.ºandar
Tel: (853) 340040-2
Fax: (853) 340046
Homepage:http://www.dscc.gov.mo/
E-mail:dscc@macau.ctm.net

PORT AUTHORITY

Director : Ms. Wong Soi Man
Vice-Director : Mr. Vong Kam Fai
Address : Calçada da Barra, n.º47, Capitania dos Portos

Tel: (853) 559922
Fax: (853) 511986
Homepage:http://www.cpm.gov.mo/
E-mail:cpm@macau.ctm.net

NAVAL DOCKYARD

Director : Mr. Chao Chon
Address : Rua de S. Tiago da Barra, Doca D. Carlos I
Tel: (853) 9880825 / 335895
Fax: (853) 317030

POSTAL SERVICES

Director : Mr. Carlos Roldão Lopes
Vice-Director : Ms. Au Vai Vá
Vice-Director : Ms. Lau Wai Meng; Address : Largo do Senado
Tel: (853) 574497
Fax: (853) 336603
E-mail:cttmacau@macau.ctm.net

METEOROLOGICAL AND GEOPHYSICAL SERVICES

Director : Mr. Fong Soi Kun
Vice-Director : Mr. António Viseu
Address : Rampa do Observatârio, Taipa
Tel: (853) 850522 / 8986213
Fax: (853) 850557
Homepage:http://www.smg.gov.mo/
E-mail:smg@macau.ctm.net

HOUSING INSTITUTE

Director : Mr. Chiang Coc Meng
Address : Rua do Campo, n.º162, Edf. Administração Pública,12.º- 14.º andares
Tel: (853) 594875 / 9875303
Fax: (853) 305909
Homepage:http://www.ihm.gov.mo/
E-mail:info@ihm.gov.mo

OFFICE FOR DEVELOPMENT OF TELECOMUNICATIONS AND INFORMATION TECHNOLOGY

Co-ordinator : Mr. Tou Veng Keong
Address : Av. da Praia Grande nº 789 2º andar
Tel: (853) 356328
Fax: (853) 3969182
Homepage:http://www.gdtti.gov.mo/
E-mail:ifx@gdtti.gov.mo

OFFICE FOR DEVELOPMENT OF INFRASTRUCTURE

Co-ordinator : Mr. A. José Castanheira Lourenço
Vice-co-ordinator : Mr. Leung Henry Yee Hang
Address : Av. do Dr. Rodrigo Rodrigues, Edf. Nam Kwong, 10.ºandar F
Tel: (853) 713724-6
Fax: (853) 713728

ENVIRONMENTAL PROTECTION COMMITTEE

President : Mr. Ng Pak Meng
Address : Rua de Sanches de Miranda, nº3
Tel: (853) 725134
Fax: (853) 725129

CIVIL AVIATION AUTHORITY

President : Mr. Rui Balacó
Vice-President : Mr. Chan Weng Hung
Address : Rua do Dr. Pedro José Lobo, n.º 1-3, Edf. Banco Luso Internacional, 26.º- 27.º andares
Tel: (853) 511213
Fax: (853) 338089
Homepage:http://www.macau-airport.gov.mo/
E-mail:accm@macau.ctm.net

COMMISSION AGAINST CORRUPTION

Commissioner : Mr. Cheong Iu
Address : Alameda Dr. Carlos d'Assumpção, n.º 411- 417, Edf. Dynasty Plaza, 14.º andar.
Tel: (853) 326300/361212
Fax: (853) 373824
Homepage:http://www.ccac.org.mo/
E-mail:ccac@informac.gov.mo

COMMISSION OF AUDIT

Commissioner : Ms. Fátima Choi Mei Lei
Address : Rua do Dr. Pedro Josú Lobo, n.º 1-3, Edif. Banco Luso Internacional,28.º andar
Tel: (853) 711211
Fax: (853) 711218

EXECUTIVE COUNCIL

Address : Central Office of the Government of Macau SAR, Avenida da Praia Grande, Macau

Tel: (853) 7978120
Fax: (853) 725468

LEGISLATIVE ASSEMBLY

ASSISTANT OFFICE FOR THE LEGISLATIVE ASSEMBLY

Address : Alameda Dr. Carlos d'Assumpção, n.º 411-417, Edf.Dynasty Plaza, 8.ºandar
Tel: (853) 728377 / 728379 / 728397
Fax: (853) 727857
Homepage:http://www.al.gov.mo/
E-mail:info@al.gov.mo

COURTS

COURT OF FINAL APPEAL

President : Mr. Sam Hou Fai
Address : Praceta 25 de Abril, Edf. dos Tribunais de Segunda e Última Instâncias, Macau
Tel: (853) 3984 100
Fax: (853) 326 747

COURT OF SECOND INSTANCE

President : Mr. Lai Kin Hong
Address : Praceta 25 de Abril, Edf. dos Tribunais de Segunda e Última Instâncias, Macau
Tel: (853) 3984 116
Fax: (853) 326 747

COURT OF FIRST INSTANCE

President : Ms. Tam Hio Wa
Address : Avenida da Praia Grande, Edf. do Tribunal Judicial de Base, Macau
Tel: (853) 590 9171
Fax: (853) 336 506

EXAMINING MAGISTRACY

Alameda Dr. Carlos d'Assumpção, n.º 411-417, Edf.Dynasty Plaza, 4º andar
Tel: (853) 7966 513
Fax: (853) 728 275

ADMINISTRATIVE COURT

Av. da Praia Grande, Edf. BCM, 10ºandar, Macau
Fax: (853) 355 593

PROCURATORATE

Procurator-General of Procuratorate : Mr. Ho Chio Meng
Alameda Dr. Carlos D' Assumpção, NAPE, Edf. Comercial Tai Fung Macau
Tel: (853) 7978271

Fax: (853) 727621

STRATEGIC BUSINESS CONTACTS IN MACAO

OFFICIAL DEPARTMENTS

ECONOMIC AFFAIRS
Direcção dos Serviços de Economia
Rua Dr. Pedro José Lobo, 1-3
Edif. Luso-Internacional, 25th Floor,
Macau
Tel : (853) 562622
Fax : (853) 590310

FINANCE
Direcção dos Serviços de Finanças
Av. Praia Grande, 575,
Macau
Tel : (853) 571600
Fax : (853) 300133

MONETARY AUTHORITY
Autoridade Monetária e Cambial de Macau
Rua Pedro Nolasco da Silva, Nº 45,
Macau
Tel : (853) 325416
Fax : (853) 325433
Telex : 88480 AMCM OM

PUBLIC WORKS AND TRANSPORT
Direcção dos Serviços de Solos,
Obras Públicas e Transportes
Estrada de D. Maria
Edif. CEM 1-5 Ground Floor
Macau
Tel : (853) 722488
Fax : (853) 340019

STATISTICS
Direcção dos Serviços de Estatística
Alameda Dr. Carlos
Assumpção, 411-417,
Edf. Dynasty, 17° andar
Macau
Tel : (853) 728188
Fax : (853) 972705

TOURISM
Direcção dos Serviços de Turismo
Largo do Senado, Nº 9 Edif. Ritz,
Macau
Tel : (853) 315566
Fax : (853) 510104

OFFICE OF THE FUTURE MACAU SPECIAL ADMINISTRATION REGION OF P.R. CHINA
Office of the Chief Executive of Macau S.A.R. of P.R.China
Edif. Tai Fung,

418, Alameda Dr. Carlos d' Assumpção,
Macau
Tel : (853) 377935
Fax : (853) 345851

TRADE / INVESTMENT PROMOTION ORGANISATIONS

EURO-INFO CENTRE, MACAU
Av. da Amizade 918, Edf. World Trade Centre,
17° andar, Macau
Tel : (853) 713338
Fax : (853) 713339

I.C.E.P.
Av. da Amizade, No. 918,
Edif. World Trade Centre, 16° " D",
Macau
Tel : (853) 728300
Fax : (853) 728303

MACAU TRADE AND INVESTMENT PROMOTION INSTITUTE
Av. da Amizade 918,
Edf. World Trade Centre, 4° & 5° andares,
Macau
Tel: (853) 710528
Fax: (853) 590309

WORLD TRADE CENTER MACAU
Av. da Amizade, N° 918
Edif. World Trade Centre, 17° Andar,
Macau
Tel : (853) 727666
Fax : (853) 727633

INDUSTRIAL PARK & PRODUCTIVITY CENTER

SPIC - CONCORDIA INDUSTRIAL PARK LTD.
Av. da Amizade, 918 14/F Apartment
A & B Edf. World Trade Center,
Macau
Tel : (853) 786636
Fax : (853) 785374

MACAU PRODUCTIVITY AND TECHNOLOGY TRANSFER CENTER
Rua de Xangai, 175,
Edf. ACM, 6 andar,
Macau
Tel: (853) 781313
Fax: (853) 788233

BUSINESS ASSOCIATIONS

ASSOCIAÇÃO DE BANCOS DE MACAU
Av. da Praia Grande, N° 575
Edif. Financas, 15th Floor, Macau
Tel: (853) 511921, 511922
Fax: (853) 346049

BUILDING CONTRACTORS & REAL ESTATES
Associação dos Construtores Civis e Empresas de Fomento Predial de Macau
Rua do Campo, 103, 6th Floor A, Macau
Tel : (853) 573226
Fax : (853) 345710

MACAU REAL ESTATE AGENTS ASSOCIATION
Rua Luis Gonzaga Gomes,
Ed. Lei Kai 3B,
Macau
Tel: (853) 316600/706204
Fax: (853) 701686

ASSOCIAÇÃO DOS MEDIADORES DO FOMENTO PREDIAL DE MACAU
Avenida do Dr. Rodrigo Rodrigues,
First International Commercial Center,
1st Floor, Rm P109-110,
Macau
Tel : (853) 707171
Fax : (853) 705527

CHAMBER OF COMMERCE
Associação Comercial de Macau
Rua de Xangai, N° 175,
Edif. ACM, 5/F,
Macau
Tel : (853) 576833
Fax : (853) 594513
Telex : 88229 TWHMA OM

CHINESE ENTERPRISES ASSOCIATION
Associação das Empresas Chinesas de Macau
Av. do Dr. Rodrigues, 223-225,
Edf. Nam Kwong, 8 andar, Macau
Tel : (853) 576833
Fax : (853) 594513
Telex : 88229 TWHMA OM

EXPORTERS AND IMPORTERS
Associação dos Exportadores e Importadores de Macau
Av. Infante D. Henrique N° 60-62,
3rd Floor Centro Comercial " Central",
Macau
Tel: (853) 375859, 553187
Fax: (853) 512174

INDUSTRY
Associação Industrial de Macau
Rua Dr. Pedro José Lobo, 34-36
Edif. AIM, 17th Floor,
Macau
Tel : (853) 574125
Fax : (853) 578305

Associação dos Industriais de Tecelagem e Fiação de Lã de Macau
Av. da Amizade 57-67B,
Edif. Kam Wa Kok, 6th Floor A,
Macau

Tel : (853) 553378
Fax : (853) 511105

LAWYER'S ASSOCIATION
Associação de Advogados de Macau
Av. de Amizade, No. 918,
Edif. World Trade Centre, 12° A-B,
Macau
Tel: (853) 728121, 728122
Fax: (853) 728127

SHIPPING
Macau Shipper's Association
Rua do Comandante Mata e Oliveira, No.32,
Edf. A.I.M., 17° Andar,
Macau
Tel : (853) 574125
Fax : (853) 578305

Macau Air Freight Forwarding Association
Av. Cons. Ferreira de Almeida, No. 36A-B,
Multigroup Comm. Bldg.,
Macau
Tel: (853) 312312
Fax: (853) 335563

Macau Shipping Agencies Association
Av. Horta e Costa, N° 7, D-E, Macau
Tel : (853) 528207
Fax : (853) 302667

SME ASSOCIATION
Associação de Pequenas e Médias Empresas de Macau
Avenida Doutor Mario Soares,
Yang Cheng Commercial Centre,
9° andar F, Macau
Tel : (853) 750507
Fax : (853) 750508

TRAVEL AGENTS

Associação de Agências de Turismo de Macau
Rua de Nagasaki ZAPE,
Edif. Xin Hua, 10° Andar,
Macau
Tel : (853) 7998811
Fax : (853) 706611

PUBLIC UTILITY COMPANIES

ELECTRICITY
CEM-Companhia de Electricidade de Macau, S.A.R.L.
Est. D. Maria II, Ed. CEM, r/c,
Macau
Tel : (853) 339933
Fax : (853) 308361

TELECOMMUNICATION
CTM-Companhia de Telecomunicações
Rua de Lagos, Telecentro, Taipa
Tel : (853) 8913822
Fax : (853) 8913813

WATER
SAAM - Sociedade de Abastecimento de Águas de Macau, S.A.R.L.
Avenida do Conselheiro Borja N° 718, Macau
Tel : (853) 233332
Fax : (853) 234657

MACAU REPRESENTATIVE OFFICES ABROAD

MISSÃO DE MACAU EM LISBOA
Av. 5 de Outubro, 115, 5° 1050, Lisboa
Portugal
Tel : (351-1) 7979334
Fax : (351-1) 7979328

DELEGAÇÃO DE MACAU EM BRUXELAS
Av. Louise, 375-BTE 9, B-1050, Brussels
Belgium
Tel : (32-2) 6471265
Fax : (32-2) 6401552

AIRLINES

AIR KORYO
Rua da Praia Grande, No. 55,
Edif. Cen. Com. Hoi Wong, 20° Andar, "C",
MACAU
Tel : 356635
Fax : 356631

AIR MACAU
Av. da Praia Grande,
Edif. Tai Wah, 9/F,
MACAU
Tel : 3966888
Fax : 3966866

CNAC-CHINA NATIONAL AVIATION CORP.
Av. Dr. Mário Soares,
Edif. Bank of China, 28/F, Bloco C,
MACAU
Tel : 788034
Fax : 788036

EAST ASIA AIRLINES (HELICOPTER)
Ground Floor, Macau Maritime Terminal,
Av. de Amizade,
MACAU
Tel : 725939
Fax : 725942

EVA AIRWAYS
Novos Aterros do Porto Exterior,
Edif. Dynasty Plaza, Lote 8, 21/F,
MACAU
Tel : 726866
Fax : 726840

SINGAPORE AIRLINES
Rua Dr. Pedro Jose Lobo, No. 1-3,
Edif. Banco Luso Internacional, 10° Andar,
MACAU
Tel : 711728/9
Fax : 711732

TRANS ASIA AIRWAYS
Rua de Pequim, 244-246,
Edif. Macau Finance, 11° Andar, B-C,
MACAU
Tel : 701777/556
Fax : 701565

BANKS

BANK OF AMERICA (MACAU LTD.)
Av. de Alm. Ribeiro, 70-76, Macau
Tel : (853) 568821
Fax : (853) 570386

BANK OF CHINA
Av. Dr. Mário Soares, Edif. Banco China, Macau
Tel : (853) 781828
Fax : (853) 781833

CITIBANK NA
Av. da Praia Grande, 251-253, Macau
Tel : (853) 378188
Fax : (853) 578451

BANCO COMERCIAL DE MACAU
Av. da Praia Grande, 572, Macau
Tel : (853) 7910000
Fax : (853) 580967

BANCO COMERCIAL PORTUGUÊS
Av. Dr. Mário Soares, Edif. Banco China,
21° Andar "F", Macau
Tel : (853)786769
Fax : (853) 786772

BANCO DELTA ASIA S.A.R.L.
Avenida do Conselheiro Ferreira de Almeida No. 79, Macau
Tel : (853) 559898
Fax : (853) 570068

DEUTSCHE BANK
90, Ave. Alm. Ribeiro, 7° Andar,
Nam Wah Comm. Edif. Macau

Tel : (853) 378440
Fax : (853) 304939

BANCO ESPÍRITO SANTO DO ORIENTE
Av. Dr. Mário Soares BOC Bldg., 28, E&F, Macau
Tel : (853) 785222
Fax : (853) 785228

FINIBANCO (MACAU)
Av. da Praia Grande No. 811, r/c, P.O. Box 3110, Macau
Tel : (853) 322678
Fax : (853) 322680

GUANGDONG DEVELOPMENT BANK, MACAU
Av. da Praia Grande, No. 269, Macau
Tel : (853) 323628
Fax : (853) 323668

HONG KONG & SHANGHAI BANKING CORP.
Av. da Praia Grande, 639, Macau
Tel : (853) 553669
Fax : (853) 322831

LIU CHONG HING BANK LIMITED
Avenida da Praia Grande, No. 693,
Edif. Tai Wah, r/c, Macau
Tel : (853) 339982
Fax : (853) 339990

BANCO LUSO INTERNACIONAL LTD
Av. Dr. Mário Soares, 47, Macau
Tel : (853) 378977
Fax : (853) 578517

BANCO NACIONAL ULTRAMARINO
Av. de Alm. Ribeiro, No. 22-38, Macau
Tel : (853) 355111
Fax : (853) 355653

BANQUE NATIONALE PARIS
Av. Alm. Ribeiro No.61, Central Plaza,
10° Andar C & D, Macau
Tel : (853) 562777
Fax : (853) 560626

OVERSEAS TRUST BANK
Rua da Santa Clara, No. 5-7,
Edif. Ribeiro R/C C-D, Macau
Tel : (853) 329338
Fax : (853) 323711

SENG HENG BANK LTD.
18/F, Seng Heng Bank Tower, Macau Landmark
Avenida da Amizade
Tel : (853) 555222
Fax : (853) 338064

STANDARD CHARTERED BANK
Av. de Amizade, Z. A. P. E., 8/F,
Office Tower Macau Landmark, Macau
Tel : (853) 786111
Fax : (853) 786222

TAI FUNG BANK LTD.
418, Alameda Dr. Carlos Assumpção, Macau
Tel : (853) 322323
Fax : (853) 570737

TAIPEI BUSINESS BANK
Nos. 52-58, Av. Infante D. Henrique, Macau
Tel : (853) 715175
Fax : (853) 715035

BANCO TOTTA & AÇORES
Av. da Praia Grande, 429, 21° andar, Macau
Tel : (853) 573299
Fax : (853) 563852

BANCO WENG HANG
Av. Almeida Ribeiro, 241, Macau
Tel : (853) 335678
Fax : (853) 576527

HOTELS

HOTEL BEVERLY PLAZA
Av. do Dr. Rodrigo Rodrigues, Macau
Tel: 782288
Fax: 780684

HOTEL FORTUNA
63, Rua de Cantão, Macau
Tel: 786333
Fax:786363

HOTEL FU HUA LDA.
98, 102, R. Francisco Xavier Pereira, Macau
Tel: 553838
Fax:527575

GRAND VIEW HOTEL
142, Est. Governador Albano de Oliveira, Taipa, Macau
Tel: 837788
Fax:837777

HOTEL GRANDEUR
Rua de Pequim, Outer Harbour, Macau
Tel: 781233
Fax: 781211

HOTEL GUIA
1-5, Estrada do Engenheiro Trigo, Macau

Tel: 513888
Fax: 559822

HOLIDAY INN MACAU
Rua de Pequim, Macau
Tel: 781707
Fax: 782321

HYATT REGENCY MACAU
Estrada Almirante Marques Esparteiro No.2, Taipa Island, Macau
Tel: 831234
Fax: 830195

HOTEL KINGSWAY
Rua de Luis Gonzaga Gomes No. 230, Macau
Tel: 702888
Fax: 702828

HOTEL LISBOA
Avenida de Amizade, Macau
Tel: 577666
Fax: 710574

MANDARIN ORIENTAL
Avenida de Amizade, Outer Harbour, Macau
Tel: 567888
Fax: 594589

HOTEL METRÓPOLE
No. 493-501, Rua da Praia Grande, Macau
Tel: 388166
Fax: 388553

HOTEL MONDIAL
No. 8-10, Rua de António Basto, Macau
Tel: 566866
Fax: 514083

HOTEL NAM YUE
International Center Avenida do Dr. Rodrigo Rodrigues , Macau
Tel: 726288
Fax: 726726

HOTEL NEW CENTURY
Av. Padre Tomás Pereira No. 889, Taipa Island, Macau
Tel: 831111
Fax: 832222

HOTEL NEW WORLD EMPEROR
Rua de Xangai, Macau
Tel: 781888
Fax: 782287

HOTEL PRESIDENTE
355, Av. de Amizade, Macau
Tel: 553888
Fax: 552735

HOTEL RITZ MACAU, LTD.
Rua Comendador Kou Ho Weng, Macau
Tel: 339955
Fax: 317826

HOTEL ROYAL
Estrada da Vitoria No. 2-4, Macau
Tel: 552222
Fax: 563008

HOTEL SINTRA
Avenida D. João IV, Macau
Tel: 710111
Fax: 715057

POUSADA DE S. TIAGO
Fortaleza de S. Tiago da Barra, Av. da República, Macau
Tel: 378111
Fax:552170

POUSADA DE COLOANE
Praia de Cheoc Van, Coloane Island, Macau
Tel: 882144
Fax: 882251

THE WESTIN RESORT
Estrada de Hac Sa Coloane Island, Macau
Tel: 871111
Fax: 871122

MACAU OVERSEAS REPRESENTATIVE OFFICES

The Macau Overseas Representative Offices of the Macau Government Tourist Office carry out various activities for tourist promotion, including providing travel information, distribution of news, organization of seminars, incentives or special interest programmes, and handling arrangements for special educational trips to Macau for trade and media people.

MGTO Marketing Representative
Suite 1303, Shun Tak Centre
200 Connaught Road, Central
Hong Kong
Tel: (852) 2549-8884
Fax: (852) 2559-6513
e-mail: dnetwork@netvigator.com

Contact: Ms. Winnie Pau

JAPAN

Mile Post Consultants, Inc.
Sanden Building, 3rd Floor
5-5, Kojimachi 3-chome
Chiyoda-ku, Tokyo 102-0083,
Japan
Tel: (81) 3-5275-2537
Fax: (81) 3-5275-2535
e-mail: macau@milepost.co.jp
Contact: Ms. Fumihiro Sakakibara

TAIWAN

Compass Public Relations Ltd.
3rd Floor, 150 Tun Hwa North Road
Taipei, Taiwan
Tel: (886) 2-2546-6086
Fax: (886) 2-2546-6087

email: mgtottwn@ms27.hinet.net
Contact: Ms. Pauline Leung

SOUTH KOREA

Glocom Korea Co. LTD.
Suite 1105, Paiknam Building (President Hotel)
188-3, Eulchiro 1-Ka, Chung-Ku,
Seoul, Korea
Tel: (82) 2-778-4402
Fax: (82) 2-778-4404
e-mail: glocomco@chollian.net
Contact: Mr. Lew Hwa-Kyu
Cti Network Pte Ltd.
321, Orchard Road
#09-01 Orchard Shopping Center
Singapore 238866
Tel: (65) 7323239
Fax: (65) 7323205

e-mail: cti-network@pacific.net.sg
Contact: Ms. Grace Tong

MALAYSIA

Pacific World Travel Sdn Bhd
2.5 & 2.6, Bangunan Angkasa Raya Jalan Ampang,
50450 Kuala Lumpur
Malaysia
Tel: (60-3) 241-2899
Fax: (60-3) 248-1357
e-mail: pwt@melewar.com

Contact: Ms. Cherry Lee

PHILIPPINES

Asia Pacific Projects, Inc
9th Floor PDCP Bank Centre
Herrera corner Leviste Streets
Salcedo Village, Makati City, Philippines
Tel: (63-2) 817-2644
Fax: (63-2) 813-4781
e-mail: mgtophil@info.com.ph
Contact: Ms. Narzalina Z. Lim

THAILAND

Pacific Leisure (Thailand) Ltd.
8th Floor, Maneeya Center Building
518/5 Ploenchit Road, Patumwan Bangkok 10330
Thailand
Tel: (66) 2-2555989
Fax: (66) 2-6520509
e-mail: destinations@plt.co.th

Contact: Ms. Jarunee Tantinukul

AUSTRALIA

ICON Services Pty.Ltd.
Level 5, 17 Bridge Street
Sydney, NSW 2000,
Australia
Tel: (61) 2-8272-7878 (or 1300 300 236 in Australia only)
Fax: (61) 2-9241-6510
e-mail: macau@icongsa.com.au

Contact: Ms. Nicki Keegan

NEW ZEALAND

Aviation & Tourism International / ICON Aviation
P.O.Box 99230 Newmarket
Auckland
New Zealand
Tel: (64) 9 522 5948
Fax: (64) 9 522 2429
e-mail: chrisj@iconaviation.co.nz
Contact: Mr. Chris Jones

MEMBERS OF THE CONSULAR CORPS ACCREDITED TO MACAU SAR

HONORARY CONSULS ACCREDITED TO MACAU SAR

BHUTAN
Unit B, 1st Floor, Kowloon Centre
29-43, Ashley Road
Kowloon - Hong Kong
Tel : 23762112
Fax: 23763331

ESTONIA
13/F A-B, World Trade Centre
918, Avenida da Amizade
Macau
Tel : (853) 332266
Fax: (853) 727768

GUINEA-BISSAU
Avenida da Amizade, R/C
Edf. Chong Yu, Loja N
Macau
Tel : (853) 703333
Fax: (853) 702663

GUINEA-CONACRY
Macau Finance Centre, 9K
Rua de Pequim
Macau
Tel : (853) 703233
Fax: (853) 703214

MALI
Rua de Foshan, 51
Centro Comercial San Kin Yip, 19?A
Macau
Tel : (853) 786638
Fax: (853) 780383

MOZAMBIQUE
Suite G, 6th Floor, Shun Kit Bld.
Rua Inacio Baptista, 1
Macau
Tel : (853) 970003
Fax:(853) 970481

NAMIBIA
Room 509, Manning House
38-48, Queen's Road
Central
Hong Kong
Tel : 25861339
Fax: 28771264
E-mail : henry@spider.net.hk

PERU
Av. Almeida Ribeiro, 54-60 R/C
Macau
Tel : (853) 574344
Fax:(853) 593199

UNITED KINGDOM
Hong Kong & Shanghai Banking Corp. Ltd.
Macau Managemnet Office

73-75, Av. da Praia Grande
Macau SAR
Tel : (853) 553670
Fax: (853) 315421

SURINAME
Shun Tak Holdings Ltd.

OFFICIALLY RECOGNISED REPRESENTATIVES OF INTERNATIONAL ORGANIZATIONS

EUROPEAN UNION OFFICE OF THE EUROPEAN COMMISSION
19th Floor, St. John's Bld.
33, Garden Road
Central - Hong Kong
Tel : 25376083
Fax: 25221302

UNITED NATIONS HIGH COMMISSIONER FOR REFUGEES SUB-OFFICE
9th Floor, Yau Ma Tei Carpark Bld.
250, Shanghai Street
Kowloon
Hong Kong
Tel : 27809271
Fax: 27705504
E-mail : chiho@unhcr.ch

COUNTRY REPRESENTATIONSARGENTINA
Suite 1210-1212, Jardine House
1, Connaught Place
Hong Kong
Tel : 2523 3208
Fax: 2877 0906
E-mail : consarhk@netvigator.com

AUSTRALIA
Harbour Centre, 21st-24th Floors
25 Harbour Road
Hong Kong
Tel : 2827 8881
Fax: 2585 4457
E-mail : Webmaster@australia.org.hk

AUSTRIA
Room 2201, Chinachem Tower
34-37 Connaught Road
Central - Hong Kong
Tel : 25228086
Fax: 25218773
E-mail : autconhk@pacific.net.hk

BANGLADESH
Room 3807, China Resources Building
26, Harbour Road - Wan Chai
Hong Kong
Tel : 28274278/9

Penthouse 39/F West Tower
Shun Tak Centre
200, Connaught Road
Central - Hong Kong
Tel : 28594855
Fax: 28574377

Fax: 28271916
E-mail : bangladt@netvigator.com

BELGIUM
9th Floor, St. John's Building
33, Garden Road
Hong Kong
Tel : 25243111
Fax: 28685997
E-mail : consulhk@netvigator.com

BRASIL
Room 2014-21, Sun Hung Kai Centre
30 Harbour Road
Hong Kong
Tel : 25257002
Fax: 28772813
E-mail : cgbrahkg@netvigator.com

CANADA
One Exchange Square, 14th Floor
8, Connaught Place
Hong Kong
Tel : 28104321
Fax: 28106736
Homepage : http://www.canada.org.hk

CHILE
Suite 1408, Great Eagle Centre
23, Harbour Road - Wan Chai
Hong Kong
Tel : 28271826
Fax: 28272060
E-mail : cghonghk@netvigator.com

COLOMBIA
Unit A, 6th Floor - C.M.A. Building
64-66 Connaught Road - Central
Hong Kong
Tel : 25458547
Fax: 25448347
E-mail : concolhk@hutchcity.com

CZECH REPUBLIC
Room 1204-05, Great Eagle Centre
23 Harbour Road - Wan Chai
Hong Kong
Tel : 28022212
Fax: 28022911
E-mail : gkcrhk@netvigator.com

DENMARK
Room 2402 B, Great Eagle Centre
23 Harbour Road - Wan Chai
Hong Kong
Tel : 28278101
Fax: 28274555
E-mail : danconhk@netvigator.com

EGYPT
Suite No. 1, 22 Floor, Sino Plaza
255-257 Gloucester Road,
Causeway Bay Hong Kong
Tel : 2827 0668
Fax: 2827 2100
E-mail : egyptcg@netvigator.com

FINLAND
1818, Hutchison House
10, Harcourt Road
Hong Kong
Tel : 25255385
Fax: 28101232
E-mail : sanomat.hng@formin.fi

FRANCE
26th Floor, Admiralty Centre, Tower II
18 Harcourt Road
Hong Kong
Tel : 25294351
Fax: 28669693
E-mail : consinfo@france.com.hk

GERMANY
21st Floor, United Centre
95 Queensway
Hong Kong
Tel : 25298855
Fax: 28652033
E-mail : germancg@netvigator.com

GREECE
Suites 2503/2504, Two Pacific Place
88, Queensway
Hong Kong
Tel : 27741682
Fax: 27059796

HUNGARY
Suite 3202, Citibank Tower
3, Garden Road
Central
Hong Kong
Tel : 28787555
Fax: 28787010
E-mail : consulhu@netvigator.com

INDIA
Unit D, 16th Floor, United Centre
95 Queensway
Hong Kong
Tel : 25291289
Fax: 28654617
E-mail : cgiinfo@pacific.net.hk

ISRAEL
Room 701 - Admiralty Centre, Tower II
18, Harcourt Road
Hong Kong
Tel : 25296091
Fax: 28650220
Hompepage : http://www.cgis.com.hk
E-mail : isrcons@asiaonline.net

ITALY
Room 805, Hutchison House
10, Harcourt Road
Hong Kong
Tel : 25220033/6
Fax: 28459678
Homepage :
http://home.netvigator.com/~itconshk
E-mail : itconshk@netvigator.com

JAPAN
47th Floor, One Exchange Square
8, Connaught Place
Central - Hong Kong
Tel : 25221184
Fax: 28680156
Homepage : http://www.japan.org.hk

KOREA
5-6 Floors, Far East Finance Centre
16, Harcourt Road
Hong Kong
Tel : 25294141
Fax: 28613699
E-mail : korcon@netvigator.com

MALAYSIA
24th Floor, Malaysia Building
50, Gloucester Road - Wan Chai
Hong Kong
Tel : 25270921
Fax: 28651628
E-mail : mwhkong@netvigator.com

MEXICO
Room 1304, Great Eagle Centre
23, Harbour Road - Wan Chai
Hong Kong
Tel : 25113305
Fax: 28453404
E-mail : mexicohk@netvigator.com

MYANMAR
Rooms 2401-24/F Sun Hung Kai Centre
30 Harbour Road - Wan Chai

Hong Kong
Tel : 28277929
Fax: 28276597
E-mail : myancghk@netvigator.com

NETHERLANDS
Suite 5702, 57/F, Cheung Kong Center
2, Queens Road - Central
Hong Kong
Tel : 25225127
Fax: 28685388
Homepage : http://www.neth-consulate-hk.org
E-mail : nlgovhon@netvigator.com

NEW ZEALAND
Room 6501, Central Plaza
18, Harbour Road - Wan Chai
Hong Kong
Tel : 25255044
Fax: 28452915
E-mail : nzcghk@netvigator.com

NIGERIA
Rooms 3309-10, 33rd Floor
China Resources Building
26, Harbour Road - Wan Chai
Hong Kong
Tel : 28278813
Fax: 28278892
E-mail : ngrconhk@netvigator.com

NORWAY
Room 1502, Great Eagle Centre
23, Harbour Road - Wan Chai
Hong Kong
Tel : 25879953
Fax: 25871786
E-mail : generalkonsulat-hong-kong@ud.dep.telemax.no

PAKISTAN
Room 3706, 37th Floor China Resources Building
26, Harbour Road - Wan Chai
Hong Kong
Tel : 28271966
Fax: 28272189
E-mail : parephk@netvigator.com

PERU
10th Floor, Wong Chung Ming Commercial House
16, Wyndham Street
Central - Hong Kong
Tel : 28682622
Fax: 28400733
E-mail : Conperhk@netvigator.com

PHILIPPINES
Room 602, 6th Floor
United Centre, 95 Queensway
Hong Kong
Tel : 28238503
Fax: 28669885
E-mail : prhk@asiaonline.net

POLAND
Suite 1006, One Pacific Place
88, Queensway
Hong Kong
Tel : 28400779
Fax: 25960062

PORTUGAL
Consulate General of Portugal
Rua Pedro Nolasco da Silva, 45
Macau SAR
Tel : (853) 356660
Fax :(853) 356658

RUSSIA
Rooms 2932-2940
29th Floor, Sun Hung Kai Centre
30, Harbour Road
Hong Kong
Tel : 28777188
Fax: 28777166
E-mail :cgrushk@hknet.com

SAMOA
Unit A, 30th Floor, Morrison Plaza
5-9A Morrison Hill Road Wan Chai
Hong Kong
Tel : 25722777
Fax: 25752666

SINGAPORE
9th Floor, Unit 901, Tower I
Admiralty Centre
18, Harcourt Road
Hong Kong
Tel : 25272212
Fax: 28613595
E-mail :sporecon@hk.super.net

SOUTH AFRICA
27/F, Great Eagle Centre
Rooms 2706-2710
23 Harbour Road - Wan Chai
Hong Kong
Tel : 25773279
Fax: 28901975
E-mail :sacghgk@netvigator.com

SPAIN
8th Floor, Printing House
18, Ice House Street

Hong Kong
Tel : 25253041
Fax: 28772407

Sweden
8th Floor, The Hong Kong Club Bld.
3A, Chater Road
Hong Kong
Tel : 25211212
Fax: 25960308
E-mail
:generalkonsulat.hongkong@foreign.ministry.se

SWITZERLAND
3703, Gloucester Tower
The Landmark - 11, Pedder Street
Hong Kong
Tel : 25227147/8
Fax: 28452619
E-mail :Swisscg@hon.rep.admin.ch

THAILAND
8th Floor, Fairmont House
8, Cotton Tree Drive
Central - Hong Kong
Tel : 25216481/5
Fax: 25218629
E-mail :thaihkcg@hk.super.net

TURKEY
3rd Floor, Sino Plaza, Room 301
255-257, Gloucester Road
Causeway Bay - Hong Kong
Tel : 25721331
Fax: 28931771
E-mail :turkcons@netvigator.com

UNITED KINGDOM
1, Supreme Court Road
Hong Kong
Tel : 29013020/1
Fax: 29013066
E-mail :information@britishconsulate.org.hk

USA
26, Garden Road
Hong Kong
Tel : 25239011
Fax: 28451598
Homepage : http://www.usconsulate.org.hk

URUGUAY
Room 1701, Dina House
11, Duddell Street
Central - Hong Kong
Tel : 28680330
Fax: 25301287
E-mail :urukong@hk.super.net

VENEZUELA
Suite 3902, Central Plaza
18 Harbour Road - Wan Chai
Hong Kong
Tel : 27308099
Fax: 27366519
E-mail :consulve@hk.net

BASIC TITLES ON MACAO

IMPORTANT!
All publications are updated annually!
Please contact IBP, Inc. at ibpusa3@gmail.com for the latest ISBNs and additional information

TITLE
Macao A "Spy" Guide - Strategic Information and Developments
Macao A Spy" Guide"
Macao Business and Investment Opportunities Yearbook
Macao Business and Investment Opportunities Yearbook
Macao Business and Investment Opportunities Yearbook Volume 1 Strategic Information and Opportunities
Macao Business and Investment Opportunities Yearbook Volume 2 Leading Export-Import, Business, Investment Opportunities and Projects
Macao Business Intelligence Report - Practical Information, Opportunities, Contacts
Macao Business Intelligence Report - Practical Information, Opportunities, Contacts
Macao Business Law Handbook - Strategic Information and Basic Laws
Macao Business Law Handbook - Strategic Information and Basic Laws
Macao Business Law Handbook - Strategic Information and Basic Laws
Macao Business Law Handbook - Strategic Information and Basic Laws
Macao Business Law Handbook Volume 1 Srategic Information and Basic Laws

TITLE
Macao Business Law Handbook Volume 2 Investment and Trade Laws Volume 2 Investment and Trade Laws
Macao Business Success Guide - Basic Practical Information and Contacts
Macao Company Laws and Regulations Handbook
Macao Country Study Guide - Strategic Information and Developments
Macao Country Study Guide - Strategic Information and Developments
Macao Country Study Guide - Strategic Information and Developments Volume 1 Strategic Information and Developments
Macao Country Study Guide Volume 1 Strategic Information and Developments - Everything you need to know about the country - Geography, history, politics, economy, business, etc.
Macao Criminal Laws, Regulations and Procedures Handbook - Strategic Information, Regulations, Procedures
Macao Customs, Export-Import Regulations, Incentives and Procedures Handbook - Strategic, Practical Information, Regulations
Macao Customs, Trade Regulations and Procedures Handbook
Macao Customs, Trade Regulations and Procedures Handbook
Macao Diplomatic Handbook - Strategic Information and Developments
Macao Diplomatic Handbook - Strategic Information and Developments
Macao Ecology & Nature Protection Handbook
Macao Ecology & Nature Protection Handbook
Macao Ecology & Nature Protection Laws and Regulation Handbook
Macao Economic & Development Strategy Handbook
Macao Economic & Development Strategy Handbook
Macao Electoral, Political Parties Laws and Regulations Handbook - Strategic Information, Regulations, Procedures
Macao Energy Policy, Laws and Regulation Handbook
Macao Export-Import Trade and Business Directory
Macao Export-Import Trade and Business Directory
Macao Foreign Policy and Government Guide
Macao Foreign Policy and Government Guide
Macao Gaming Industry Business Law Handbook
Macao Government and Business Contacts Handbook
Macao Government and Business Contacts Handbook
Macao Government and Policy Guide
Macao Government and Policy Guide
Macao Industrial and Business Directory
Macao Industrial and Business Directory
Macao Information Strategy, Internet and E-Commerce Development Handbook - Strategic Information, Programs, Regulations
Macao Internet and E-Commerce Investment and Business Guide - Strategic and Practical Information: Regulations and Opportunities
Macao Internet and E-Commerce Investment and Business Guide - Strategic and Practical Information: Regulations and Opportunities
Macao Investment and Business Guide - Strategic and Practical Information
Macao Investment and Business Guide - Strategic and Practical Information
Macao Investment and Business Guide - Strategic and Practical Information
Macao Investment and Business Guide - Strategic and Practical Information
Macao Investment and Business Guide Volume 2 Business, Investment Opportunities and Incentives
Macao Investment and Business Profile - Basic Information and Contacts for Succesful investment and Business Activity
Macao Investment and Trade Laws and Regulations Handbook

TITLE
Macao Offshore Investment and Business Guide
Macao Offshore Tax Guide
Macao Recent Economic and Political Developments Yearbook
Macao Recent Economic and Political Developments Yearbook
Macao Recent Economic and Political Developments Yearbook
Macao Starting Business (Incorporating) in Macao Guide
Macao Starting Business (Incorporating) in....Guide
Macao Tax Guide Volume 1 Strategic Information and Basic Regulations
Macao Taxation Laws and Regulations Handbook
Macao Telecom Laws and Regulations Handbook
Macao Telecommunication Industry Business Opportunities Handbook
Macao Telecommunication Industry Business Opportunities Handbook
Macao Transportation Policy and Regulations Handbook
Macao, China SAR Investment, Trade Strategy and Agreements Handbook - Strategic Information and Basic Agreements
Macao: Business in Macao for Everyone: Practical Information and Contacts for Success
Macao: Doing Business and Investing in ... Guide Volume 1 Strategic, Practical Information, Regulations, Contacts
Macao: Doing Business and Investing in Macao Guide
Macao: Doing Business and Investing in Macao Guide
Macao: How to Invest, Start and Run Profitable Business in Macao Guide - Practical Information, Opportunities, Contacts
Macao: Starting Business (Incorporating) in Macao Guide

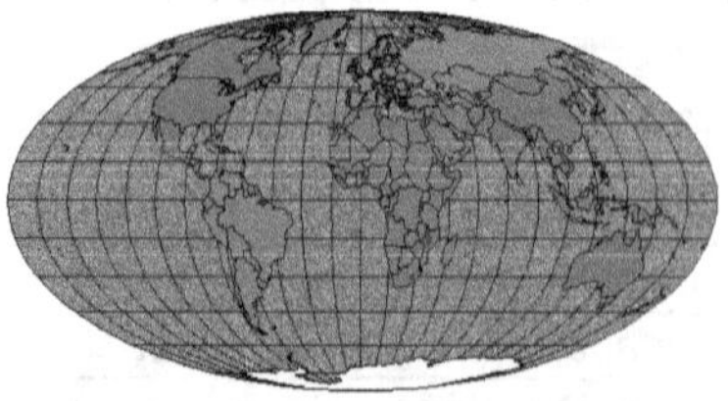

WORLD ECOLOGY LAWS AND REGULATIONS HANDBOOK LIBRARY

Web Address http://www.ibpus.com

Price: $149.95 each

1. Afghanistan Ecology Laws and Regulations Handbook
2. Aland Ecology Laws and Regulations Handbook
3. Albania Ecology Laws and Regulations Handbook
4. Algeria Ecology Laws and Regulations Handbook
5. Andorra Ecology Laws and Regulations Handbook
6. Angola Ecology Laws and Regulations Handbook
7. Anguilla Ecology Laws and Regulations Handbook
8. Antigua and Barbuda Ecology Laws and Regulations Handbook
9. Antilles (Netherlands) Ecology Laws and Regulations Handbook
10. Argentina Ecology Laws and Regulations Handbook
11. Armenia Ecology Laws and Regulations Handbook
12. Aruba Ecology Laws and Regulations Handbook
13. Australia Ecology Laws and Regulations Handbook
14. Austria Ecology Laws and Regulations Handbook
15. Azerbaijan Ecology Laws and Regulations Handbook
16. Bahamas Ecology Laws and Regulations Handbook
17. Bahrain Ecology Laws and Regulations Handbook
18. Bangladesh Ecology Laws and Regulations Handbook
19. Barbados Ecology Laws and Regulations Handbook
20. Belarus Ecology Laws and Regulations Handbook
21. Belgium Ecology Laws and Regulations Handbook
22. Belize Ecology Laws and Regulations Handbook
23. Benin Ecology Laws and Regulations Handbook
24. Bermuda Ecology Laws and Regulations Handbook
25. Bhutan Ecology Laws and Regulations Handbook
26. Bolivia Ecology Laws and Regulations Handbook
27. Bosnia and Herzegovina Ecology Laws and Regulations Handbook
28. Botswana Ecology Laws and Regulations Handbook
29. Brazil Ecology Laws and Regulations Handbook
30. Brunei Ecology Laws and Regulations Handbook
31. Bulgaria Ecology Laws and Regulations Handbook
32. Burkina Faso Ecology Laws and Regulations Handbook
33. Burundi Ecology Laws and Regulations Handbook
34. Cambodia Ecology Laws and Regulations Handbook
35. Cameroon Ecology Laws and Regulations Handbook

36. Canada Ecology Laws and Regulations Handbook
37. Cape Verde Ecology Laws and Regulations Handbook
38. Cayman Islands Ecology Laws and Regulations Handbook
39. Central African Republic Ecology Laws and Regulations Handbook
40. Chad Ecology Laws and Regulations Handbook
41. Chile Ecology Laws and Regulations Handbook
42. China Ecology Laws and Regulations Handbook
43. Colombia Ecology Laws and Regulations Handbook
44. Comoros Ecology Laws and Regulations Handbook
45. Congo Ecology Laws and Regulations Handbook
46. Congo, Democratic Republic Ecology Laws and Regulations Handbook
47. Cook Islands Ecology Laws and Regulations Handbook
48. Costa Rica Ecology Laws and Regulations Handbook
49. Cote d'Ivoire Ecology Laws and Regulations Handbook
50. Croatia Ecology Laws and Regulations Handbook
51. Cuba Ecology Laws and Regulations Handbook
52. Cyprus Ecology Laws and Regulations Handbook
53. Czech Republic Ecology Laws and Regulations Handbook
54. Denmark Ecology Laws and Regulations Handbook
55. Djibouti Ecology Laws and Regulations Handbook
56. Dominica Ecology Laws and Regulations Handbook
57. Dominican Republic Ecology Laws and Regulations Handbook
58. Ecuador Ecology Laws and Regulations Handbook
59. Egypt Ecology Laws and Regulations Handbook
60. El Salvador Ecology Laws and Regulations Handbook
61. Equatorial Guinea Ecology Laws and Regulations Handbook
62. Eritrea Ecology Laws and Regulations Handbook
63. Estonia Ecology Laws and Regulations Handbook
64. Ethiopia Ecology Laws and Regulations Handbook
65. Falkland Islands Ecology Laws and Regulations Handbook
66. Faroes Ecology Laws and Regulations Handbook
67. Fiji Ecology Laws and Regulations Handbook
68. Finland Ecology Laws and Regulations Handbook
69. France Ecology Laws and Regulations Handbook
70. Gabon Ecology Laws and Regulations Handbook
71. Gambia Ecology Laws and Regulations Handbook
72. Georgia Ecology Laws and Regulations Handbook
73. Germany Ecology Laws and Regulations Handbook
74. Ghana Ecology Laws and Regulations Handbook
75. Gibraltar Ecology Laws and Regulations Handbook
76. Greece Ecology Laws and Regulations Handbook
77. Greenland Ecology Laws and Regulations Handbook
78. Grenada Ecology Laws and Regulations Handbook
79. Guam Ecology Laws and Regulations Handbook
80. Guatemala Ecology Laws and Regulations Handbook
81. Guernsey Ecology Laws and Regulations Handbook
82. Guinea Ecology Laws and Regulations Handbook
83. Guinea-Bissau Ecology Laws and Regulations Handbook
84. Guyana Ecology Laws and Regulations Handbook
85. Haiti Ecology Laws and Regulations Handbook

86. Honduras Ecology Laws and Regulations Handbook
87. Hungary Ecology Laws and Regulations Handbook
88. Iceland Ecology Laws and Regulations Handbook
89. India Ecology Laws and Regulations Handbook
90. Indonesia Ecology Laws and Regulations Handbook
91. InternationalEcology Laws and Regulations Handbook
92. Iran Ecology Laws and Regulations Handbook
93. Iraq Ecology Laws and Regulations Handbook
94. Ireland Ecology Laws and Regulations Handbook
95. Israel Ecology Laws and Regulations Handbook
96. Italy Ecology Laws and Regulations Handbook
97. Jamaica Ecology Laws and Regulations Handbook
98. Japan Ecology Laws and Regulations Handbook
99. Jersey Ecology Laws and Regulations Handbook
100.Jordan Ecology Laws and Regulations Handbook
101.Kazakhstan Ecology Laws and Regulations Handbook
102.Kenya Ecology Laws and Regulations Handbook
103.Kiribati Ecology Laws and Regulations Handbook
104.Korea, North Ecology Laws and Regulations Handbook
105.Korea, South Ecology Laws and Regulations Handbook
106.Kosovo Ecology Laws and Regulations Handbook
107.Kuwait Ecology Laws and Regulations Handbook
108.Kyrgyzstan Ecology Laws and Regulations Handbook
109.Laos Ecology Laws and Regulations Handbook
110.Latvia Ecology Laws and Regulations Handbook
111.Lebanon Ecology Laws and Regulations Handbook
112.Lesotho Ecology Laws and Regulations Handbook
113.Liberia Ecology Laws and Regulations Handbook
114.Libya Ecology Laws and Regulations Handbook
115.Liechtenstein Ecology Laws and Regulations Handbook
116.Lithuania Ecology Laws and Regulations Handbook
117.Luxembourg Ecology Laws and Regulations Handbook
118.Macao Ecology Laws and Regulations Handbook
119.Macedonia,Ecology Laws and Regulations Handbook
120.Madagascar Ecology Laws and Regulations Handbook
121.MadeiraEcology Laws and Regulations Handbook
122.Malawi Ecology Laws and Regulations Handbook
123.Malaysia Ecology Laws and Regulations Handbook
124.Maldives Ecology Laws and Regulations Handbook
125.Mali Ecology Laws and Regulations Handbook
126.Malta Ecology Laws and Regulations Handbook
127.Man Ecology Laws and Regulations Handbook
128.Marshall Islands Ecology Laws and Regulations Handbook
129.Mauritania Ecology Laws and Regulations Handbook
130.Mauritius Ecology Laws and Regulations Handbook
131.Mayotte Ecology Laws and Regulations Handbook
132.Mexico Ecology Laws and Regulations Handbook
133.Micronesia Ecology Laws and Regulations Handbook
134.Moldova Ecology Laws and Regulations Handbook
135.Monaco Ecology Laws and Regulations Handbook

136. Mongolia Ecology Laws and Regulations Handbook
137. Monserrat Ecology Laws and Regulations Handbook
138. Morocco Ecology Laws and Regulations Handbook
139. Mozambique Ecology Laws and Regulations Handbook
140. Myanmar Ecology Laws and Regulations Handbook
141. Namibia Ecology Laws and Regulations Handbook
142. Nauru Ecology Laws and Regulations Handbook
143. Nepal Ecology Laws and Regulations Handbook
144. Netherlands Ecology Laws and Regulations Handbook
145. New Caledonia Ecology Laws and Regulations Handbook
146. New Zealand Ecology Laws and Regulations Handbook
147. Nicaragua Ecology Laws and Regulations Handbook
148. Niger Ecology Laws and Regulations Handbook
149. Nigeria Ecology Laws and Regulations Handbook
150. Niue Ecology Laws and Regulations Handbook
151. Northern Mariana Islands Ecology Laws and Regulations Handbook
152. Norway Ecology Laws and Regulations Handbook
153. Oman Ecology Laws and Regulations Handbook
154. Pakistan Ecology Laws and Regulations Handbook
155. Palau Ecology Laws and Regulations Handbook
156. Palestine Ecology Laws and Regulations Handbook
157. Panama Ecology Laws and Regulations Handbook
158. Papua New Guinea Ecology Laws and Regulations Handbook
159. Paraguay Ecology Laws and Regulations Handbook
160. Peru Ecology Laws and Regulations Handbook
161. Philippines Ecology Laws and Regulations Handbook
162. Pitcairn Islands Ecology Laws and Regulations Handbook
163. Poland Ecology Laws and Regulations Handbook
164. Polynesia French Ecology Laws and Regulations Handbook
165. Portugal Ecology Laws and Regulations Handbook
166. Qatar Ecology Laws and Regulations Handbook
167. Romania Ecology Laws and Regulations Handbook
168. Russia Ecology Laws and Regulations Handbook
169. Rwanda Ecology Laws and Regulations Handbook
170. Saint Kitts and Nevis Ecology Laws and Regulations Handbook
171. Saint Lucia Ecology Laws and Regulations Handbook
172. Saint Vincent and The Grenadines Ecology Laws and Regulations Handbook
173. Samoa (American) Ecology Laws and Regulations Handbook
174. Samoa (Western) Ecology Laws and Regulations Handbook
175. San Marino Ecology Laws and Regulations Handbook
176. Sao Tome and Principe Ecology Laws and Regulations Handbook
177. Saudi Arabia Ecology Laws and Regulations Handbook
178. Scotland Ecology Laws and Regulations Handbook
179. Senegal Ecology Laws and Regulations Handbook
180. Seychelles Ecology Laws and Regulations Handbook
181. Sierra Leone Ecology Laws and Regulations Handbook
182. Singapore Ecology Laws and Regulations Handbook
183. Slovakia Ecology Laws and Regulations Handbook
184. Slovenia Ecology Laws and Regulations Handbook
185. Solomon Islands Ecology Laws and Regulations Handbook

186.Somalia Ecology Laws and Regulations Handbook
187.South Africa Ecology Laws and Regulations Handbook
188.Spain Ecology Laws and Regulations Handbook
189.Sri Lanka Ecology Laws and Regulations Handbook
190.St. Helena Ecology Laws and Regulations Handbook
191.St. Pierre & Miquelon Ecology Laws and Regulations Handbook
192.Sudan Ecology Laws and Regulations Handbook
193.Suriname Ecology Laws and Regulations Handbook
194.Swaziland Ecology Laws and Regulations Handbook
195.Sweden Ecology Laws and Regulations Handbook
196.Switzerland Ecology Laws and Regulations Handbook
197.Syria Ecology Laws and Regulations Handbook
198.Taiwan Ecology Laws and Regulations Handbook
199.Tajikistan Ecology Laws and Regulations Handbook
200.Tanzania Ecology Laws and Regulations Handbook
201.Thailand Ecology Laws and Regulations Handbook
202.Togo Ecology Laws and Regulations Handbook
203.Tonga Ecology Laws and Regulations Handbook
204.Trinidad and Tobago Ecology Laws and Regulations Handbook
205.Tunisia Ecology Laws and Regulations Handbook
206.Turkey Ecology Laws and Regulations Handbook
207.Turkmenistan Ecology Laws and Regulations Handbook
208.Turks & Caicos Ecology Laws and Regulations Handbook
209.Tuvalu Ecology Laws and Regulations Handbook
210.Uganda Ecology Laws and Regulations Handbook
211.Ukraine Ecology Laws and Regulations Handbook
212.United Arab Emirates Ecology Laws and Regulations Handbook
213.United Kingdom Ecology Laws and Regulations Handbook
214.United States Ecology Laws and Regulations Handbook
215.Uruguay Ecology Laws and Regulations Handbook
216.Uzbekistan Ecology Laws and Regulations Handbook
217.Vanuatu Ecology Laws and Regulations Handbook
218.Vatican City Ecology Laws and Regulations Handbook
219.Venezuela Ecology Laws and Regulations Handbook
220.Vietnam Ecology Laws and Regulations Handbook
221.Virgin Islands, British Ecology Laws and Regulations Handbook
222.Wake Atoll Ecology Laws and Regulations Handbook
223.Wallis & Futuna Ecology Laws and Regulations Handbook
224.Yemen Ecology Laws and Regulations Handbook
225.Yugoslavia Ecology Laws and Regulations Handbook
226.Zambia Ecology Laws and Regulations Handbook
227.Zimbabwe Ecology Laws and Regulations Handbook

www.ingramcontent.com/pod-product-compliance
Lightning Source LLC
LaVergne TN
LVHW080026210926
848481LV00011B/3117